8/99

St. Louis Community College

Forest Park
Florissant Valley
Meramec

Instructional Resources
St. Louis, Missouri

MAKING A NEW NATION:
THE FORMATION OF SLOVENIA

Dedication

In memory of Professor Adolf Bibič (1933-1996), a good friend
and an esteemed colleague, who had much to do with the
inception of this book.

Acknowledgment

The preparation of this book was assisted financially by the
Rector's Fund of the University of Ljubljana and the Ministry
of Information, Republic of Slovenia

Making a New Nation: The Formation of Slovenia

Edited by

DANICA FINK-HAFNER
University of Ljubljana

and

JOHN R. ROBBINS
University of Adelaide

Dartmouth

Aldershot • Brookfield USA • Singapore • Sydney

Published by
Dartmouth Publishing Company Limited
Gower House
Croft Road
Aldershot
Hants GU11 3HR
England

Dartmouth Publishing Company
Old Post Road
Brookfield
Vermont 05036
USA

British Library Cataloguing in Publication Data
Fink-Hafner, Danica
  Making a new nation : the formation of Slovenia
  1.State succession 2.Slovenia - Politics and government -
  1990-
  I.Title II.Robbins, John R.
  320.9'4973

Library of Congress Cataloging-in-Publication Data
Making a new nation : the formation of Slovenia / edited by Danica
  Fink-Hafner and John R. Robbins.
      p.   cm.
  Includes bibliographical references.
  ISBN 1-85521-656-6
  1. Slovenia–History–1990- 2. Slovenia–Politics and
  government–1990- 3. Post-communism–Slovenia. I. Fink-Hafner,
  Danica, 1959-   . II. Robbins, John R., 1935-
  DR1453.M35   1996
  949.7'3–dc20   96-43128
                                                            CIP

ISBN 1 85521 656 6

Printed and bound by Athenaeum Press, Ltd.,
Gateshead, Tyne & Wear.

Contents

1 Setting the Scene: Problems of Transition

JOHN R. ROBBINS

Directions

The prime aim of this book is to explain and examine the processes by which Slovenia transformed itself from a constituent part of a socialist federation dominated by a single party to an independent state with a liberal democratic political system and a free enterprise economy.

It is also hoped that the experiences recounted here will provide useful material for the revision of theoretical analyses. The equal unpreparedness of both political scientists and political practitioners for the events in Eastern Europe and the Soviet Union at the end of the 1980s indicates the inadequacy of existing theories and the need for such a revision.

It is not intended to deal explicitly and at length with the reasons for the break-up of Yugoslavia.[1] The Slovenian dimension of that event is, in many respects, pivotal (Simić, 1992, p. 87; Cohen, 1993, pp. 59-65) and many aspects of it are necessarily invoked here, but the major concern of this book is the process of state formation in the newly independent country.

The sudden and wholesale conversion of socialist states to aspiring liberal democracies with market economies has presented them with a formidable practical challenge. In the case of Slovenia and the eighteen other secessionist countries which emerged from the collapse of Soviet and East European socialism the problems of transition are exacerbated by the prior necessity of constructing a new state. The rump countries of Russia, Yugoslavia and the Czech Republic, with a reduced compass, also confronted a more complex process of transition, though at least with a ready formed state apparatus in place.

In their turn academics are faced with the daunting task of reading the runes of the existing wisdom for guidance on how the desired transition might best be achieved. There is no shortage of advice but, as yet, the success rate of the transitional countries is, at best, modest, and often verges on the catastrophic.

What is intended in this introduction is neither a comprehensive theoretical digest nor a preview of the expository material to come, and still less a prescription for a successful transition. It is rather a scene-setting exercise, literally laying out the basic terrain which the subsequent authors will traverse.

Back to fundamentals

With the revival of interest in the theory of the state from the 1970s onwards there were many who came merely to write its epitaph or, at least, to signal its terminal decline. Though the state might have been 'brought back in' (Evans, Rueschemeyer & Skocpol, 1985) it was frequently diagnosed as being in an enfeebled condition, weakened by the globalization of the economy and a movement towards supra-national political arrangements (Horsham & Marshall, 1994; Dyson, 1980, pp. 282-7).

There were others who recognized a more robust condition and pointed out that the modern state had an array of functions and powers massively greater than its predecessors (Gurr, 1989; Rose & Miller; 1992; McEachern, 1990). It was also unclear when the supposed golden age of ultimate state sovereignty had occurred, since economic dependency and political subordination have been a persistent historical reality.

A major weakness in this analysis, of whatever persuasion, was that it derived from the condition of established states where many of the fundamentals were taken for granted. The outward aspect of any structure often conceals the crucial underpinnings which maintain it. Indeed, there are instances when the expected underpinning is not even present, as in those medieval cathedrals which turn out to have virtually no foundations to support their massive bulk.

The spate of state creation after the Second World War presented extensive opportunities for the observation and analysis of the political processes involved. The fact that most of these states have floundered from crisis to crisis has confirmed that the construction of a state is not merely a mechanistic process requiring the establishment of an appropriate set of political institutions - parties, parliament, a governmental apparatus and a public bureaucracy. The form of these institutions might be present but, in substance, their operations produced a distortion of the expected outcomes. It was soon realized that an appropriate social base was a necessity for the successful implantation of any political system.

There was a rapid adjustment of perspective. The internal operators of the systems identified their post-colonial inheritance as defective and set about the radical reformation of their political arrangements, almost always in the direction of an intolerant authoritarianism. External observers would usually concur on the unsuitability of the starting position which had confronted these new states, but few thought the prescribed cures were likely to ameliorate the complaint.

One difficulty was in satisfying the high level of expectations which accompanied independence. These had placed great emphasis on economic improvement, but most of the new states failed to produce the desired economic outcomes. The universal measure of a country's well-being and its government's competence was its Gross Domestic Product, most tellingly reduced to GDP per capita. It proved difficult to achieve levels of economic growth which stayed ahead of the increments in a fast-growing population. Again, questions were raised about the pre-colonial inheritance and the continued post-colonial exploitation. Equally, there were accusations of rampant corruption and mismanagement by an elite devoid of any motive other than self-aggrandizement.

A few states, such as Kenya and Ivory Coast for a time, proved an exception to the rule in their ability to achieve high rates of growth. This was ascribed to their willing embrace of free market economics and contrasted with the poor performance of state-controlled systems such as Guinea and Tanzania. Even they ultimately succumbed and seemingly proved the inherent incapacity of the new states to break out of the cycle of poor economic performance, political instability and corrupt, authoritarian government.

The argument about the capacity of new states to carve out a satisfactory economic niche in a global system manipulated by capitalist interests was suddenly skewed by the emergence of the Asian-Pacific economies. Taiwan, South Korea, Singapore, Malaysia and Hong Kong produced high rates of economic growth which disproved the 'closed shop' argument. Their enthusiastic espousal of free enterprise was taken to indicate this as a necessary ingredient of success. Their political arrangements did not, however, produce a palatable accompaniment, since none of them measured up to even the minimum requirements of a functional liberal democracy.

The end of the Cold War and the dismantling of European socialism not only produced another spate of new states and new regimes but also presented the continuing dilemma of reconciling liberal democracy and free market capitalism in a starker light. Their simultaneous achievement was the norm in the western countries which now held the field, but over thirty years of endeavour had failed to present a formula for their application in new states.

The post-socialist states are thus presented with a model, and applauded for willingly adopting it as a goal, but they are given no clear indication of how it might be achieved and no certainty that it is even achievable. The democratization process is difficult enough in itself, though the 'Mediterranean' and Latin American transitions offer some guidance and greater hope. The economic transformation is a much more difficult matter and treads what is essentially new ground. The Asian-Pacific success stories involved making an existing system grow rather than converting it from the ground up. They also purvey the message that a measure of political authoritarianism helps.   Most post-socialists have a commitment to simultaneous political and economic reform and are unwilling to trade off democratic principles against enhanced productivity advances.

Those post-socialist states resulting from secession have the additional complication of legitimizing their new circumstances.   In the more extreme cases this has meant a continuing military engagement which has asserted its own priorities over the processes of democratization and economic reform.   Even in the more favourable instances, the severing of existing ties brought about by secession and the business of forming a new state apparatus have diverted resources from the tasks of political and economic renovation.

Bearing in mind the essential interlocking of these major elements of transition they will each be explored more fully in the following pages.

Democratization

Dahrendorf's much-quoted axiom that a democratic constitution may be implemented in six months (Dahrendorf, 1990, pp. 92-3) appears to be greatly optimistic.   Certainly, a constitution may be written and party organizations formed within six months.   The buildings to house them suitably will take longer to build but conversions will serve in the meantime.   Getting the system to work in a satisfactory way may prove much more difficult. Constitutions often prove inadequate to the purpose set them and the party system may not provide stable government.   Some political leaders may tire of the attempt and seek reversion to authoritarianism.

It is significant that much attention has now been turned to the question of democratic consolidation.   Schmitter (1995, pp. 538-9) defines it as, 'transforming these *ad hoc* patterns into stable structures in such a way that the ensuing forms/channels of access, inclusion/exclusion of actors, resources/strategies for actions and rules/norms about decision making conform to a specific standard: "The guiding principle of democracy is that of citizenship".'

Obviously, Dahrendorf (1990, p. 93) canvasses the same ground in extending to 60 years the period necessary for, 'transforming the constitution and the economy from fair-weather into all-weather institutions which can withstand the storms generated from within and without'.

The experience of the last batch of new states is not rewarding.[2] It is only a minority of the post-colonial regimes established after the second world war which has contrived to establish a recognizable form of democracy and few have done so permanently.

Southern Europe and Latin America provided the last wave of democratizations in the 1970s and 1980s (O'Donnell, Schmitter and Whitehead, 1986).   While the progress of the latter cases is still very much under question and invigilation, the former are regarded as successfully accomplished, with membership of the European Union as their seal of success and guarantee against recidivism.   But the prolonged experience of freely contested elections provides only one side of the equation.   If those elections fail to provide stable government either by working majorities or sustained coalitions the entire system is under threat. Undoubtedly, the ultimate test of democracy is its capacity to withstand a period of governmental instability and unpalatable economic circumstances, but the spectre of Weimar is always present and it is a test best avoided.

Spain provides a useful demonstration and timetable of a successful democratic transition (Preston, 1986; Maravall, 1982). Franco's death in November 1975 permitted the commencement of political reform. The monopoly of his Movement was abandoned in 1976 and parties and trade unions legalized, with some stickiness in extending this to the Communist party and its industrial wing. There was a general election in June 1977, the first competitive election for 41 years. A new constitution was produced and confirmed by referendum in December 1978 and another general election under its aegis was held in March 1979. It took, in this case, over three years to produce a working democratic parliament and government.

Even then it remained under threat from the military 'bunker', still nostalgic for the Franco regime, and from the Basque separatist insurgents of ETA who doubted the democratic credentials of the new regime and denied the validity of the Spanish state. The military finally made its move on 23 February 1981, symbolically occupying parliament. It is significant that it was the king, invoking his monarchical authority, who quelled the incipient revolt. What the outcome might have been had its suppression rested on asserting the legitimacy of a democratically elected government is a matter for conjecture.

The election of the previously banned Socialist party to government in 1982 may be taken as the culminating proof that democracy was firmly established. Its victory, however, was accompanied by the disintegration of its former rival and the previous party of government, the UCD. It was not until the elections of 1993 that the Popular Party was fully established as a viable opposition and alternative government. The time-frame for democratic consolidation in Spain could thus be extended to eighteen years.

Despite its current status as the international norm, democracy has, for most of recent history, been the minority condition and under considerable threat. Even now, the list of adherents is as often diminished as augmented and the number whose attachment is unproblematic and unassailable is relatively small.

Lijphart (1984, pp. 37-45) enumerates only 22 countries which have adhered to his stated democratic standards over the period since 1945. He relaxes his measure in a later work (Lijphart, 1994, p. 1) to include a further two, India and Costa Rica, though one might question the inclusion of Israel in his initial list, not on the grounds of his elastic time-frame, but its treatment of the occupied territories. To take his time-frame any further back would immediately disqualify Japan, Germany, Italy and Austria. Democracy is clearly a fragile plant.

A constant and major problem is in defining democracy and determining its necessary structural components. A universal franchise to be exercised in periodic elections during which parties may freely campaign for votes constitutes an agreed common core to which further refinements may be added. Beyond that, the structural form that it takes, including the constitutional provisions for its operation, are myriad.

The assessment of democratic attainment is even less certain. Is it to be measured by the levels of popular participation in the process, by an acceptance of its outcomes, by general declarations of support for the system, or merely by observing the appropriate operation of its component parts?[3]

It is in this respect that the experience of the long-established democracies is of limited use. Their political systems have generally evolved over time with a measured and gradual infusion of democracy in order to reach their present condition. In some cases, as in France, there has been a more erratic process with occasional reversals, but the overall process has been one of progressive consolidation.

The hub of the matter is the right to participate freely in the political process, since this possibility is denied by authoritarian regimes. The realities of democratic practice indicate that this right is a generalized value which is subject to considerable restriction in operation.

Some theorists emphasize that the realities of everyday life do not permit wholesale participation. Dahl (1990) has pointed out the criteria which limit the propensity to participate; we do not have the time, the expertise or the interest to engage in every public decision.

Others have made a virtue of the limitation and sung the praises of elite democracy (Schumpeter 1954; Berelson 1954). Government is thought best left to a few experts and the requirements of democracy are sufficiently met if the electorate has the ability to change those teams of experts at periodic elections. High levels of participation are in fact likely to cause instability.

A more refined and reserved version of this view was offered by Almond and Verba in the conclusion to their Civic Culture study, seeking to identify the cultural components of a democratic political system. They considered the relatively high propensity of Americans to demand participation in policy making as a flaw rather than a virtue, since it impeded the governmental process (Almond & Verba, 1963, pp. 313-15).

The ready acceptance of this limited form of democratic operation brought an adverse response by the late 1960s both from political theorists (Pateman, 1970) and from political activists, typified by the events of 1968 in Paris, but echoed around the world. A more virulent reaction came from radical left-wing groups such as the Italian Red Brigades and the German Baader-Meinhof Group who regarded the democratic claims of western regimes to be a deceit and a cover for economic exploitation and practical authoritarianism.

In attempting to understand the shifting evaluations of democratic systems it is helpful to regard authoritarianism and democracy as occupying two ends of a participatory spectrum rather than as incompatible opposites. Neither condition is likely to be achieved in any absolute sense and the practical arrangements of any regime will lie somewhere between. Most authoritarian regimes of any longevity make provision for some kind of participation, however token. All democratic regimes ultimately rest on the assertion of authority, accompanied by violence if deemed necessary, and the degree of participation allowed to citizens is always limited.

One might take it that the natural propensity of governing elites is to limit, if not to minimize, the participation of the masses. They will concede only sufficient 'power to the people' to obtain their consent. Those constitutional provisions which offer an increase in citizens' political influence over the policy process, such as the citizen initiated referendum, the recall, and electoral terms of short duration, are infrequently encountered. Constitutional provisions of these kinds may provide the opportunities for participation but whether they are invoked will depend on those propensities and predispositions usually invoked as the chief elements of political culture.

Political culture

The ultimate attainment of democracy rests on the adoption of an appropriate political culture by the population at large. Political culture is nebulous, both in concept and operation, but the political predispositions of the population will permit or impede any of the policy initiatives presented to it. The martial traditions of Chechens or the Islamic fundamentalism of Tajiks produce very different conditions from those in Estonia or Lithuania.

Culture is in a constant reciprocal interaction with social structure, shaping it as well as being shaped by it. A population with no living experience of democratic operation cannot merely assume appropriate habits and attitudes when a democratic structure is implanted. It can, however, rapidly adopt them if the outcomes of its operation are seen as beneficial, and, if the circumstances are maintained, they will become entrenched.

A good deal will depend on the behaviour of the political elite which orchestrates most of the activity. Even though the emergence of a democratic elite is conditional on obtaining substantial public support in the first instance, once established, its pivotal position allows it to direct political interest and activity in one direction rather than another. It may also quite deliberately manipulate public opinion, a possibility which is enhanced if it has media support.

A crucial matter is whether the elite, once it is established, encourages continued political participation, seeking to represent the views and interests of its constituents or merely conscripts their votes on the occasion of elections. The presumed tendency is towards the latter stance, though at times of heightened awareness and political re-alignment there will be an impulsion towards the former.

Communist regimes did foster participation within prescribed limits (Berglund & Dellenbrat, 1991) so that there is not the same problem of mobilization in the post-socialist states as in post-colonial situations or in the aftermath of the right-wing authoritarianism as in Spain and Portugal. Indeed, Yugoslavia's system of self-management produced levels of participation that were cited by theorists such as Pateman (1970, pp. 85-102) and Dahl (1970 pp. 130-2) as models for the achievement of participatory democracy elsewhere.

The major problem is the direction of political activity into appropriate channels and pitching it at sustainable levels. It is here that the 'intermediate associations' of a pluralist society have a key role. Equally important is the receptiveness of the state apparatus and its delivery of positive outcomes in sufficient quantity to encourage the continuance of the activity.

The experience of established democracies indicates that the system can exist tolerably well with low levels of participation. We have earlier encountered the argument (and its rebuttal) that too high a degree of participation is injurious to the overall workings of government. What is preferred by the advocates of limited participation is citizens who nurture an expectation that, when circumstances require it, political activity may be freely engaged in and that it has some prospect of being successful. They are not expected to seek more than a very occasional demonstration of the reality of their expectation. Whatever the acceptability of this argument it would be difficult to gainsay the desirability of such an expectation as a residual requirement.

The heightened expectations which accompany the onset of any new regime make this 'subdued' level of anticipatory participation difficult to achieve, and when citizens are disappointed apathy results, or more damagingly, alienation and ultimately opposition. It is necessary to identify that intermediate point between hyperactivity and sullen withdrawal which marks an appropriate level of participation.

Party systems

The main intermediate body between citizens and the state is the party system. It is responsible for political recruitment, mobilization and education. There is a necessary minimum level of activity which recruits the personnel for parliamentary representation and government and mobilizes the electorate to provide support at election time. How far beyond this basic minimum a party proceeds will vary considerably. Those which approximate to the traditional 'parties of notables' will have a low level of activism. New parties seeking a rapid augmentation of their support and parties such as the Greens with an ideological commitment to popular participation will produce high levels.

The commitment of parties to the continuity of the state is particularly important in the case of transitional countries. Parties which refuse to take up seats, such as Sinn Fein in the British House of Commons or Herri Batasuna in the Spanish Cortes, undermine the legitimacy of those parliaments. Parties which take part in proceedings but lack any commitment to the democratic process are also destabilizing. West European Communist parties before the advent of Euro-Communism, and the Italian neo-fascist MSI before its reformation, had little interest in producing acceptable policy outcomes for a system which they rejected.

The rather finely-balanced requirement is that parties should contain their antagonisms within an overall commitment to the political system (Huntington, 1991, pp. 600-609). Contestation is a necessary part of the system but not to the point of destabilizing or even destroying it, as occurred in a number of European countries in the inter-war period, most notably Italy, Germany, Spain and Portugal.

The ability of the political system to establish an alternating pattern of government and opposition is determined to a large degree by the party system which develops. The two party system recommended by Duverger as a recipe for strong and stable government is, as his many critics pointed out, difficult of achievement. Neither, as current events in the United States demonstrate, does it necessarily produce an uncomplicated and dynamic policy process.

At the other end of the scale the excessive multi-partyism of Italy, the French Third and Fourth Republics and the Weimar Republic creates continual political instability. The Weimar example is considered the ultimate warning because of its ominous consequences and there is great concern lest the proliferation of parties in the transitional regimes, together with continuing economic problems, produce similar results.

The shape of the party system is to a large extent determined by the character of the society which produces it. Any substantial interests not adequately covered by existing parties will soon produce a party of their own. Parties will tend to extend their reach in order to maximize their vote but too far a stretch may offend some existing supporters.

The electoral system exerts an influence on party numbers though not so simplistically as Duverger (1964, p. 217) claimed. While the simple plurality voting system for single member constituencies tends to eliminate minor parties whose support is widely, but relatively thinly, spread, it still permits, the election of minority party representatives from constituencies where they are concentrated. In the United Kingdom this produces the multiple parties of the 'Celtic Fringe' while heavily penalizing the numerically larger but dispersed vote for the Liberal Democratic Party. A good demonstration of the impact of the electoral system is in New Zealand where the adoption of the Mixed Member Proportional system in place of the simple plurality has produced a proliferation of parties.

Party elites also exercise an important influence on the party system. Typologies of parties recognize that they may be formed by notables recruiting electoral support as well as by a popular constituency looking for political representation.

It should also be remembered that the 'iron law of oligarchy', the propensity of organizations to fall under the dominance of their leading officers, was framed in the context of political parties (Michels, 1959). Even those parties committed to mass participation and democratic control are prone to elite domination.

The political ambitions of party elites or even sole leaders may have a significant impact, not only on policy platforms, but on the willingness of parties to collaborate or combine with others. While there may be some distortion due to the preference of journalists for the personalization of their newslines, and there is no doubt that Milošević in Serbia and Mečiar in Slovakia have had a profound influence on events, few will reach the stature of a de Gaulle, though many aspire to it.

The important requirement is, of course, that the party system produces responsible and reliable government, and there is ample evidence that this can be achieved even with numerous parties. The governments of the Netherlands and the Scandinavian countries are considered quite sound despite their multiplicity of parties. It is the willingness of the parties to collaborate and form coalitions that reconciles the number of parties with the need for stable government.

In the transitional regimes a good deal depends on the status of the previously dominant communist party. If it has not lost all credibility or even legality, it will have the advantage of an existing organizational framework and experienced personnel. Other parties must carve out for themselves not only an ideological position and policy programme but the necessary support mechanisms.

Reformed communist parties have maintained or regained power in many of the transitional countries (Ishiyama, 1995, pp. 147-66) partly because of their residual organizational advantages, but also because they can recruit the support of those disadvantaged or disappointed by the process of transition. Only the demonstration of time and circumstances will convince the sceptics that they are committed to normal democratic processes. Just as the confirmation of Spanish democracy came with the replacement of the centre-right government created largely by ex-Francoists, in the post-socialist countries it will require a reformed communist party to concede defeat and relinquish government. By the same token, the acceptance of reformed communists in government is a test of the democratic credentials of those regimes which have initially rejected them.

The acceptance of the role of opposition is a key element in the exercise of democracy (Dahl, 1966). As Przeworski (1991, p. 10) so pithily puts it, 'Democracy is a system in which parties lose elections'. The current government must tolerate the existence of opposing voices together with the prospect of losing power, and those in opposition must accept their exclusion from political power until such time as they can win it democratically.

The post-colonial regimes of Africa quickly demonstrated an unwillingness to accept the possibility of being relegated to opposition and moved to one party rule. In the ex-Soviet Union and Eastern Europe, there is an obvious nostalgia in some quarters for the simplicity of a single party and a reluctance to concede full political access to all contenders for power. The consequence is, of course, to encourage non-democratic challenges.

The role of opposition is often exaggerated by those whose major experience is of confrontational politics within systems and cultures which can tolerate conflict. There are other approaches to democracy such as the consociational form proposed by Lijphart (1977) and its elaboration in a consensus model (Lijphart, 1984, pp. 21-36), identified as a viable and possibly preferable alternative to the Westminster-derived majoritarian model. Differences still occur but they are resolved at a different point of the political process and in a different manner. It is also unusual even for a consensus form of government to be completely inclusive since, except in the grave circumstances which produce 'governments of national unity', there will always be parties which are excluded and therefore opposed to the government.

Either model will face difficulties if it does not ultimately provide for the inclusion of all significant parties in the policy process. The majoritarian model achieves this by alternation, the consensual model by 'grand coalitions' of shifting composition. In either case regional and local government may provide opportunities for involvement in government which are not accessible at national level. The Italian Communist Party has had the compensation of power at these lower levels while being excluded from national government coalitions.

The main requirement of any form of democracy is that it should provide for the accommodation of political differences, and the appropriate mechanisms to achieve that accommodation need to fit the circumstances of the individual society. A further requirement is that, whatever the mechanism, the state should be limited to providing an arena for the resolution of differences, and does not itself become a vehicle for sectional interests.

Pluralism and civil society

The architects of democracy in the transitional regimes see the development of pluralist associations as a major vehicle for achieving their goal. The actions of totalitarian regimes in quickly suppressing or incorporating autonomous associations demonstrates the importance of their role.

The definition of pluralism has changed considerably as a political concept (Erlich, 1982). The older Anglo-European normative interpretation involved a segmented political system parallel to, and possibly a rival of, the state, rather than being a supplicant of it. In some versions, such as Proudhon's, it even supplanted the state. The more recent and empirically-derived interpretation arose in the context of political experience in the United States and principally viewed pluralism as taking the form of pressure group activity to influence governmental policies.

No sooner had pluralism been acknowledged as the main vehicle for the operation of a democratic political system when it was attacked as a fraudulent cover for securing the further advantage of the already privileged.[4]

Another debate branched off from the pluralist mainstream to explore the claims of a new corporatism which joined the major economic groups with the state in an integrated policy process (Lehmbruch and Schmitter, 1982; Williams, 1989). To whose benefit this worked in practice became a matter of contention, but it is a dilution of democracy in the full sense of that concept, and potentially a gross distortion.

Group activity is a necessary part of democratic participation. The individual political actor of classical theory is too atomized to make a realistic impact, even when aggregated with others. But groups rapidly fall victim to the 'iron law of oligarchy' and some groups gain privileged access to the corridors of power while others are excluded. Only a constant re-adjustment of the balance to counter these distortions will maintain any semblance of democratic process and an acceptable distribution of benefits.

What is ideally required is an array of groups, representing all major interests and independent of the state, whose activities they invigilate. They will press for policy concessions which suit their interest and if they are appropriately and equitably accommodated this will produce an acceptance of the regime and an integration of the groups with the political system. No existing system has attained such virtue and the best that can be expected is a close enough approximation to maintain the necessary degree of acceptance.

What is clear from these experiences and the debates surrounding them is that there is no obvious panacea which will resolve the several dilemmas surrounding the operations of democracy and the production of useful policy outcomes. Certainly the restoration of a 'civil society' is not that panacea, though it is probably a pre-condition for a viable solution.

Civil society is an old concept which has been resurrected in recent years and has been a particular point of focus in the socialist countries (Miller, 1992; Bibič & Graziano, 1994). The long and unresolved philosophical debate about the original emergence of the state (Hall, 1986), whether from some form of social contract or by imposition is reflected in conflicting interpretations of the current situation.

A major problem is in disentangling the strands of society and state (Diamond, 1944; Keane, 1988). The original 'minimalist' state, committed only to the defence of the realm from external and internal threats and to the maintenance of law and order within it, left ample scope for the operations of 'civil society'. Today's supposed minimalists merely wish to modify the direction of intervention by the state, not to abandon it. As the state retreats from some areas, it advances in others. It withdraws from some of its economic operations but regulates more forcibly relationships in the last and main bastion of civil society, the family.

What is basically in question is not so much the scale of civil society but its scope. While it may provide an autonomous springboard for forays into the state sphere, the main purpose of these forays is to extract concessions from the state and not to fend it off.[5]

The socialist states were obviously high on the register of formal interventionism but generally tolerated a considerable degree of 'freelance' activity. The notorious and sizeable 'black economy' and official operations 'off the plan' constituted a civil society of sorts in the form of unregulated activity.

A basic dilemma confronting these states is that the relaxation of controls permitting the operation of civil associations may also give licence to criminal elements. The rise of organized crime and violence in many of the transitional regimes is indicative of the complexity of social control. If the state withdraws from some of its control functions there is no guarantee that civil constraints will spontaneously replace them. Some elements of civil society will seek to test the new bounds of tolerable behaviour in ways which are anti-social, but in the absence of authoritative controls there will be little to curb them. Police forces discredited as part of the former oppressive state will find it difficult to adapt to 'community policing'.

The expansion of the role of civil society will also open the door to other, less spectacular but more pervasive, abuses. The exploitation of labour, the oppression of women, poor access to health care and social security and the despoliation of the environment were all issues which prompted liberal democratic states to adopt interventionist policies in the first place. It would be unfortunate if, in the anxiety to retreat from the more oppressive features of state intrusion, private excesses were to be tolerated. It should be remembered that the chief element of a civil society in a liberal democracy is its free enterprise economy and that this is also its chief source of exploitation. What is really in question is the relationship between state and society and, whatever the basis of the original 'social contract', the determination of the state as the vehicle for achieving society's goals rather than the reverse.

Economic performance

The chief factor in the undermining of communism was its failure to match capitalism in productive capacity. The acquisitive urge seemed to leap easily over otherwise impregnable boundaries and to overcome official ideological objections to consumerism. The success of transitional states will ultimately be tested by their ability to meet the economic expectations placed upon them.

They are hindered in this not merely by the problem of finding and applying the appropriate formula, but by the disruption of their existing economic circumstances by political changes. These are exacerbated in the case of the new secessionist states by being exposed to a whole new set of international relationships. The price of secession may be the loss of markets, the disruption of supplies and the cessation of subsidy arrangements. If the secession is challenged by military action there is a further economic cost in the diversion of resources to military purposes and the costs of damage to both property and personnel.

Even without such traumas, the attainment of a new economic order is not an easy one. The impact of market operations on command economies is likely to be disastrous at both micro and macro levels. The collapse of uneconomic undertakings and the reduction in the staff of overmanned industries produce levels of unemployment not previously experienced. This in its turn places burdens upon the state's social security budget (Ellman, 1994, pp. 13-14).

The abandonment of price controls, particularly on accommodation, transport and staple foods, changes the nature of wage determination in terms of the total social wage. Social benefits will also need to be adjusted if those who rely on them are to be kept above the poverty line.

The immediate result of the transition is invariably rampant inflation with its destabilizing consequences. Bringing this under control is usually a first charge on a new government's economic policy, although the conventional treatments will impede other desirable policies. As a consequence, some transitional economies have not achieved the desired results, which inhibits their integration in the international economy, and their access to international capital.

Entrepreneurship is claimed to be the most readily accessed of the capitalist factors of production (Åslund, 1994, pp. 28-9). Most of it is in small scale business operations which may evolve to occupy the space left by the decline of the larger organizations but which cannot immediately do so. The other major source of entrepreneurship identified is from among the ranks of socialist managers, but often with the intention of extracting personal benefit rather than creating a new economy.

The early results of transition bring an axiomatic depression of the gross national product, though its scale is distorted by several factors. Comparisons with the previous socialist economy are made difficult by a different compilation of national accounts and by the possibility that output is understated to avoid taxation. This is principally a question of degree and undoubtedly there is a sharp decline which the more fortunate, or adroit, governments are able to convert into sustained growth within a reasonable space of time.

A major quandary surrounds the matter of government involvement. The anxiety to abandon the extreme interventionism of socialist governments may bring a degree of abdication from economic policy-making that brings injurious consequences. Even if a government opts for substantial intervention, there is no guarantee that it will achieve the desired results. Western governments with long experience of 'tuning' their economies are constantly confronted by discordant results.

A similar dilemma faces governments in respect of budget strategies. The demands of fiscal rectitude from international agencies will indicate the need for a balanced budget, even where that is not a self-generated aim. Increased social dislocation and economic depression will place greater demands on social security payments and produce a lower yield from taxation. Now faced with a periodic electoral reckoning the government must measure the cost in votes of unpopular budgetary measures.

Legitimization

While the authority of any state ultimately rests on its capacity to enforce its will, ultimately by the use of violence within its territorial jurisdiction, it is generally acknowledged that authority is most effective when proceeding from legitimacy rather than force.

Legitimacy, the acknowledgment by the mass of the people that the state which governs it is appropriately constituted, may be generated from a number of sources. An authoritarian regime may base its acceptability on the traditional claims of a monarch, the charismatic appeal of a dictator or the incontestability of an ideological stance. This acceptance may be in the passive form of compliance rather than by active support, but in either event, the regime is not subject to serious challenge.

A democratic state encounters a more complex situation since it is presumed to have the consent of its citizens. It is significant that they are citizens rather than merely subjects and as such are expected to be actively involved in the political process by which they are governed. As we have seen earlier, the achievability, and even the desirability, of high levels of political participation is in question. Certainly the actuality in most countries is of low levels of political activity.

This 'democratic deficit' in the generation of support can be compensated for in a number of ways. Prime among them is the process of political socialization whereby young members of a society are inculcated with the belief that theirs is the best of all political systems, continuously reinforced through their adult experience.

Sceptical observers regard this as an ideological fabrication rather than deriving from a genuine involvement in the political process. Miliband's term 'the engineering of consent' (Miliband, 1972, p. 183) and Herman and Chomsky's (1988) 'the manufacture of consent' indicates their belief that the process is a political contrivance.

Another major device for maintaining regime legitimacy in a democracy is the capacity to change the government by popular will. Defects in current performance can be attributed to the failings of the incumbent government and improvements anticipated when it is replaced. Sceptics may still claim that the choice is an artificially restricted one but at least the appearance of choice and change is present.

If it is the structure of the regime itself that is under question, democratic systems also allow for constitutional change, occasionally by citizen initiated referendum, though usually filtered through the gatekeepers of the political system.

An alternative source of regime support is by the delivery of desired policy outcomes. Citizens may place less emphasis on involvement in policy decisions if the results are to their liking and they are assured of a positive response from the system in seeking access to benefits. This 'subject competence' of Almond and Verba's 'Civic Culture' study (1965, pp. 168-85) is more readily achieved and less destabilizing than the 'citizen competence' which would seem more appropriate to a democracy.

The generation of subject competence rests not only on the policies put forward by politicians but also on the ability of the bureaucracy to make them effective. Officials will supplement and even supplant elected representatives as the principal authors of a democratic culture. This is yet another dilution of the orthodox version of representative democracy but again it reflects the realities of the operations of modern governments.

The success of the bureaucracy in achieving this goal still depends basically on the direction of its political masters and the resources with which they equip it, but a favourable overall result will depend substantially on the quality of the personnel involved.

Transitional regimes which purge their bureaucracies will experience a dislocation in the delivery of services which will take some time to rectify. Those which proceed with the existing staff may find that they are reluctant to shed past working practices. The uncertainty about which of these approaches provides the best path to effective administration means that there should be continuous attention to performance and regular adjustments if the desired levels of delivery are to be achieved.

A newly formed state has a disability in tapping both 'citizen' and 'subject' sources of support. It has no residual legitimacy and has come into being by destroying that of the previous regime. The problems which it faces on establishment will make it difficult to avoid a depression in living standards and other measures of government performance, let alone to demonstrate its ability to produce improvements.

Providing the establishment of the new state has the overwhelming support of its people, it will have a 'honeymoon' period during which there will be some suspension of citizens' critical faculties. The demonstration of intractable difficulties which are not the fault of the government and are preferably ascribable to external forces may prolong this period. Ultimately, however, the capacity of the state to deliver benefits must be demonstrated. The demise of the East European communist regimes is attributable to their failure in this respect. The ability of their successors to secure legitimacy will rest on a better performance.

There are indications that access to a democratic process might offset, to some extent, a failure to deliver economic improvement (Evans & Whitefield, 1995, pp. 485-514). If the former is the more greatly valued, this may prolong the period during which a degree of austerity or even deprivation is tolerated. Failure on both counts would remove the dilemma of choice and totally discredit the regime in question.

State and nation

The ultimate foundation of the legitimacy of the state is its acknowledgment as a 'nation'. While governments may alternate and regimes be modified and even overturned, the state will persist if it has the bedrock of a 'nation' to rest on. A state merely exercises authority over the population of a defined territory. A nation is the political expression of a 'people' whose commonality requires that they are autonomously governed. It assumes an identification between the state and the society which it controls - the recognition that the state is the political embodiment of the people.

The generation and maintenance of an identity which conforms to the bounds of the state is one of the prime tasks of government. It is made easier if there is a pre-existing commonality of religion, language or ethnicity, though this may be counter-productive if there are substantial exclusions.

The conventional expectation is that the 'nation' exists prior to the state. Assertions of German and Italian nationhood in the 19th century prefaced and propelled their movement towards a unified state. Kurds and Catalonians, among many others, protest that they are nations denied the dignity of statehood. The Wilson Doctrine (rather haphazardly) gave substance to such claims in the aftermath of the first world war.

In fact, there is a good deal of reciprocity between state and nation. The concept of 'nation-building' presumes that the required commonality can be contrived if it does not previously exist. The arbitrariness of colonial boundaries has meant that the successor states have had to engage intensively in the creation of a sense of nationhood, though with very limited success. While the prolonged experience of a common government provides the basis for commonality, that experience has to be favourably received if it is to be consolidated into an identification with the state.

Ethnicity and nationalism

While the notion of commonality may be based on a shared political interest which ignores ethnicity, as in the case of Switzerland and, more precariously, in Belgium, it is ethnicity which has become the prime determinant of a 'nation'.

Ethnicity has a great attraction to 'nation-builders' in that it provides the basis for legitimacy without the necessity of any operational justification. A population's acceptance of the appropriateness of a state is based on the premise that this is the natural political outcome of the affinity of its people. It rests on ascription rather than achievement.

The state as an essentially territorial entity begs the question of what constitutes an appropriate territory. The adoption of secure boundaries or prominent landforms or even some supposed geographic symmetry as a determinant usually ignores human distribution. Since the boundaries of most states were established before the rise of democracy and were largely the result of international political settlements and dynastic ambition, little heed was paid to the wishes of their inhabitants. When they are transformed into participating citizens they may well wish to place high on the political agenda the conformation of the state to which they are attached.

The resurgence of ethnic nationalism as a prime determinant of state bounds has surprised and alarmed many academic observers. The persistence of ethnicity as a major political factor had only been acknowledged with some reluctance by social scientists. It was largely regarded as an out-dated, somewhat atavistic, form of political expression and is still presented by many as an artificial construct, prefixed by such terms as 'imagined' (Smith, 1993). Marxists in particular regarded its continued existence as evidence of a capitalist strategy to construct allegiances which would diminish class solidarity. In the socialist world ethnic nationalism was often tolerated, or even encouraged, as a cultural phenomenon but its political consequences were carefully contained.

The rise of active and often violent 'sub-nationalism' in the 1970s, particularly in Western Europe, ultimately alerted political science to the fact that supranational arrangements were not the only reaction to the 'globalizing' tendencies which were occurring. Basques and Bretons, Corsicans, Catalans and the 'Celtic Fringe' of the British Isles produced a euphonious chorus of separatist claims. Even the ostensibly placid Swiss generated a cantonal separatist movement in the Jura, and the demonstrably volatile though ostensibly quite homogeneous Italians were able to construct a fundamental division between north and south.

The last example gives some weight to the proposition that 'ethnicity' is largely a political construct invoked by activists lacking a more substantial base. This evades the question of why they had not done so before and why it proved such an effective rallying cry.

The major problem arising from the resort to ethnic nationalism is not so much the problem of defining ethnicity perceived by disapproving observers but the indiscriminate distribution of most ethnic populations. It is rare that a line can be drawn which comfortably includes all affines but conveniently excludes all those considered alien. A state based on ethnic nationalism then faces the dilemma of having either to accommodate the minority group and thus undermine its own national base or to suppress it and face the hostility of a portion of its population. The third, draconian, possibility is to produce the necessary congruence by the newly-labelled but long extant practice of 'ethnic cleansing'.

The problem becomes exacerbated if the minority concerned is a 'spill-over' from an adjacent state which takes an active interest in its welfare and thus creates an international dimension to the issue. Questions of recognition, trade and even military intervention may ensue. Estonia, Latvia and particularly Moldova were to encounter all of these difficulties in their dealings with their substantial Russian populations.

A diversity of ethnic groups does not preclude a political accommodation. Lijphart's model of consociational democracy, with its stress on elite agreement and a high degree of autonomy for constituent groups, presents one possibility. Ostensibly, both the Soviet Union and Yugoslavia had attained some variant of this, though the main vehicle for elite agreement was the communist party, and the end of its ascendancy dismantled the accommodation which depended upon it.

The best cement of a diversified society is the demonstration of benefits; political, economic or even psychological. The Swiss sense of nation overrides linguistic and religious divisions because it derives from circumstances which give it a participatory political structure, economic prosperity, stability, an avoidance of war and a high international reputation. High levels of local autonomy and guarantees of political inclusiveness mean that none of the constituent groups is disaffected.

International recognition

Externally, a state's legitimacy depends on its recognition by other states and the consequential ability to enter into relationships, including membership of international organizations such as the United Nations and the International Monetary Fund.

External recognition has an important internal dimension. Lack of recognition is an open invitation to dissident groups to challenge the regime. This is particularly the case with secessionist regimes since, without recognition, they are denied easy supplies of arms and other essential materials and hostile action by the state from which they seek to secede will merely be regarded as an exercise in internal control.

The failure of Biafra's attempt at secession from Nigeria and of Rhodesia's unilateral declaration of independence are clear demonstrations of the consequences of non-recognition. The Turkish Republic of North Cyprus survives because of the protection of its mentor, Turkey, but fails to prosper because of its non-recognition. Taiwan proves something of an exception to the rule, though it is effectively a protectorate of the USA and its future status remains in question. Certainly the support, if not the actual intervention, of powerful neighbours can make a crucial difference to the outcome.

Even where recognition is granted, the continuance of good relations with neighbouring states and trading partners is an important element in the maintenance of political stability and the achievement of economic success. A hostile neighbour can act as a sanctuary for dissidents and become a springboard for attacks. A closed border inhibits trade and discourages tourism.

It is difficult enough for a transitional regime to re-position itself diplomatically and to develop new patterns of trade, even in the most favourable of external circumstances. It will be greatly impeded in all its endeavours if it faces obstruction from outside.

Point of departure

The chapters which follow will amplify this rough charting of the ground to be covered. What has been apparent in this preliminary exploration and becomes even more patent in the substantive material is that the process of transition, especially when experienced during the construction of a new state, is a complex one whose multiple strands are intertwined and interdependent.

Continuing the geographical analogy, the difficulty of the exercise arises from the fact that it is not a select band of scientific explorers making the journey, but an entire people. The success of the enterprise will stand or fall by its ability to transform the conditions of all its members and to sustain the conviction that the journey and its hardships were worthwhile.

The chapters which follow will document and analyse the experience of Slovenia in negotiating its passage through the hazardous terrain of state-building.

Notes

1. This is done extensively and effectively elsewhere both academically (van den Heuvel & Siccama, 1992; Cohen, 1993) and in a more documentary form (Silber & Little, 1995).
2. The most extensive and consolidated account of new states (as well as democratic renewal in established states) is in Diamond *et al* (four vols., 1989-91). In an analysis of three waves of democratization Dix (1994, pp. 91-106) identifies only one African country, Botswana, as having fully achieved the necessary standards.
3. Bollen provides six indicators covering his two major definitional strands of political liberalism and political rights and thus produces an index for over a hundred countries. Interestingly Yugoslavia has the highest score among the East European countries as measured in 1965, with 50.8. Poland rates 22.1 and Czechoslovakia 20.5. Spain scores only 10.4 which is below the lowest of the communist countries, Hungary, on 11.6. (Bollen, 1991, pp. 1-20).
4. The most cited adverse comment, probably because of its colourful metaphor is Schnattschneider's (1960, p. 31) claim that 'the flaw in the pluralist heaven is that the heavenly chorus sings with a strong upper-class accent!'
5. Keane, a promoter as well as major analyst of civil society, significantly cites the case of a child-care centre soliciting funding from the state but remaining under autonomous direction (Keane, 1988a p. 20). Such arrangements blur the division between state and civil society, particularly when the 'autonomous' direction is required to account for its financial management and to conform to the state's close regulation of child-minding activities. Nevertheless, elsewhere, Keane (1988, p. 6) dismisses as 'at best half-truths' claims that the division between civil society and the state is 'overlapping and hybrid'.

2 The Origins of an Independent Slovenia

JANKO PRUNK

Introduction

Anyone attempting to describe the origins of the independent Republic of Slovenia today is exposed to the danger of looking at certain questions and problems too much under the influence of recent events whose final outcomes are, as yet, unknown.

However, the methods and ethics of historical science can protect us so that we can avoid these dangers. The first basic statement is that the multitude of objectively evaluated elements of historical development already allows us a general framework for a cautious historical analysis, open to further partial research discoveries.

The most common analysis runs as follows: for the Slovenes, greater autonomy within Yugoslavia's illusory federation was of vital importance. However, because certain decisive forces in the Yugoslav state (the Serbs in particular) were totally opposed to this course, the Slovenes were forced to pursue the realization of their independence outside the Yugoslav framework in the form of an independent state, the Republic of Slovenia.

To begin, a brief description of the development of Slovenes within the Yugoslav state which lasted for nearly three quarters of a century is necessary.

Slovenia under the Hapsburgs

As a small ethnic group on the margin of the Eastern Alps and the Northern Adriatic and at the junction of the Slavic, Germanic, and Romanic worlds, the Slovenes with their entirely Western European cultural identity (with their own literature as early as the 16th century) were shaped in the framework of Central European civilization processes into a mature European nation in the 19th century. This nation, living in an ethnically uniform region in the south of the Hapsburg Monarchy, lacked only administrative and political unity and national political autonomy. By the end of the 19th century, a quite clear awareness prevailed regarding the necessity of administratively uniting all Slovene provinces in a United Slovenia which would acquire national autonomy. This would guarantee further national development and protection against the Germanization trends clearly evident in German nationalist and imperialist circles.

At the end of the 19th century, the impossibility of reaching a national agreement with the ruling German elite in Vienna and with German nationalist circles in general and the threat posed by strong German nationalist pressure from the north and Italian nationalist pressure from the west moved Slovene political leaders, aware of their limited power, to seek an ally in their national struggle in the neighbouring, linguistically-related Croat nation, counting on its greater numbers and stronger national and political position within the Hapsburg Monarchy. They thus hoped to resolve the Slovene national question through some type of joint autonomous Slovene-Croat state formation within the Hapsburg Monarchy.

Before the first world war, this political programme was generally followed by all Slovene political groupings, while some smaller, distinctly anti-Hapsburg and Pan-Slavic circles also looked towards a union with Serbia.

During the first world war, German nationalist pressure on the Slovenes increased and in the event of victory by the Central Powers threatened the programmed Germanization of the Slovenes, who blocked the Germans access to the Adriatic.

Attempts at a South Slav union 1917-1979

Such was the situation on 30 May 1917, when Slovene and Croat representatives in the Vienna Parliament demanded the immediate union of all Southern Slav territories of the Hapsburg Monarchy (i.e. the Slovene and Croat provinces, and Bosnia and Herzegovina) into one independent state body within the Hapsburg Monarchy. Being very important as a reservoir of the troops so badly needed by the Monarchy, they hoped they would succeed. However, the ruling elite in Vienna and Budapest rejected such a compromise even at such a fatal moment. This incited nationalist radicalism among Slovenes and Croats, and at the end of World War I the independent State of Slovenes, Croats, and Serbs in all territories of the former Monarchy was proclaimed in Ljubljana and Zagreb on 19 October

1918. It was administered by the National Parliament of Slovenes, Croats and Serbs in Zagreb which appointed relatively independent national governments for particular regions, for example, Slovenia, Bosnia and Herzegovina, and Dalmatia.

This state was not internationally recognized and as such could not withstand the onslaught of Italian imperialism. The Italian army occupied the whole of Slovene Primorska and a great part of Notranjska, Istria, and Rijeka and even threatened to occupy Dalmatia.

On 24 November 1918, hoping to find in the Serbian army the necessary means for the defence of their national territories, Slovene and Croat politicians voted, although reluctantly, to unite the State of Slovenes, Croats, and Serbs with the Kingdom of Serbia in one state. The Serbs living in Croatia and Bosnia and Herzegovina along with those in the independent Kingdom of Serbia were a second important factor which forced the politicians of the State of Slovenes, Croats, and Serbs to unite unconditionally and immediately with the Kingdom of Serbia. They demanded the realization of their long-held nationalist dream: the union of all Serbs in one state regardless of whether they lived as a minority among other nations such as the Croats, Bosnians, or Hungarians.

In the autumn of 1918 the Slovenes were not in a position to form an independent Slovene state and on 1 December 1918, together with the Croats, with whom they had jointly liberated themselves from German and Hungarian authority, they became part of a larger Yugoslav state, in its first decade called the Kingdom of Serbs, Croats, and Slovenes and later the Kingdom of Yugoslavia. Following this union with Serbia which the Slovene people accepted quite passively - with the exception of a handful of liberal politicians - the Slovenes lost more than a quarter of their national territory and population in Primorska and Carinthia to Italy and Austria. Hopes that the Serbian army and state would help the Slovenes proved to be utopian.

After 1 December 1918, the Slovene nation developed within the framework of the Kingdom of Serbs, Croats, and Slovenes, which had a distinctly centralist organization to ensure its domination by the more numerous Serb nation (which, however, comprised less than half of the population of the whole state). In national politics, the Serb nation and parts of the ruling elite (especially the liberals) among the Slovenes, Croats, and Bosnians propagated a 'national Yugoslav unitarism' according to which all Yugoslav nations were a single nation and which was soon reflected in 'correct' national and educational policies. The Kingdom of Serbs, Croats, and Slovenes placed great stress on its Slavic, Eastern, Balkan, and Orthodox orientation.

All this was foreign to Slovenes and their heritage. As a completely formed, mature, and unique nation with a Western European cultural orientation similar, for example, to the Czechs, Slovenes were no longer in a position nor willing to be assimilated in some new Yugoslav nation that would accept the Serbo-Croat language and a Balkan, predominantly Orthodox, culture. Therefore, from their very incorporation in the

Yugoslav state, the majority of the Slovene intelligentsia and the Slovene people demanded the preservation and the guarantee of Slovene national individuality and a wide national autonomy for Slovenes within the Kingdom of Yugoslavia. This was the essence of Slovene national politics from the existence of the first Yugoslav state until its collapse during the second world war.

In everyday life, the centralism and unitarism were neither particularly conspicuous nor effective in Slovenia. The Slovenes, who ethnically were quite compactly settled, continued to live their unique national life. Their language of communication and official language was Slovene. All the highest administrative posts were held by Slovenes, from the president of the provincial government and the King's provincial regent to the highest mayors and later 'bans' (civil governors). Belgrade, which never included Slovenia in the Greater Serbia concept since no Serbs lived there, quietly tolerated the situation in Slovenia; however, it did not want to legally sanction this Slovene self-administration for fear it would be an example to other provinces where Serbs did live, such as Croatia and Bosnia and Herzegovina.

The Slovenes made swift economic progress within the Kingdom of Yugoslavia. They succeeded in exploiting their better starting position in respect of their more developed industry compared with other parts of Yugoslavia. They continued to expand their industry rapidly, and their goods found a wide and undemanding market in the rest of Yugoslavia. As a result, the demographic structure of Slovenia changed very quickly, and in the twenty years between 1921 and 1940, the farming population in Slovenia fell from 66 per cent to 53 per cent. On the eve of the second world war, Slovenia was quite industrialized but, in spite of this, had still not solved the problem of surplus farm labourers who were leading a miserable existence in rural areas. Slovene agriculture was threatened by a latent crisis due firstly to the lack of farm land, taxes, and other liabilities and secondly to the low price of farm produce in the predominantly agrarian Yugoslavia.

Slovene cultural and scientific life experienced its apex in the Kingdom of Yugoslavia. Ljubljana University, founded in 1919, was the forge for increasing the number of educated and nationally-conscious Slovenes.

In domestic politics, the Slovene nation in the Kingdom of Yugoslavia was divided into three conflicting political camps:

1. The majority conservative camp or 'clericals', represented by the Slovene People's Party which united all Slovene social classes with the majority of the farming population on the basis of Christian social doctrine. The party kept its unity and power until the first half of the 1930s when, due to social and national issues, its leftist labour wing broke off as the Christian Socialist Party and orientated itself toward reformist socialism;
2. The liberal camp, divided into at least three parts: the Liberal Bourgeois Party which frequently changed its name and included a

considerable proportion of the Slovene intelligentsia in its ranks, the Liberal Independent Farmers' Party, and a National Workers' Party;

3. The Marxist camp which was divided into the majority Socialists who belonged to the Second International and followed its policies and the minority Communists, supporters of the Communist International or Comintern. The Socialists held in their hands workers' protection institutions such as the Workers' Assembly, trade unions, and the Labour Exchange and in numerous regions had strong local representation. However, due to the majority electoral system they rarely succeeded in getting into the national parliament.

In 1921, the Communist Party was declared illegal and its members driven to the very margin of political life from where they returned to the scene only in the policies of the Popular Front in the second half of the 1930s.

During the existence of the Kingdom of Yugoslavia, all Slovene political parties and political life had an exceptionally strong ideological tinge, much stronger than in other democratic European countries of the period. Slovene politicians mainly took delight in the clerical-liberal conflicts which marked all politics and thereby created a negative picture of politics itself.

Another sphere of political conflict was the national question. Here the conservative Slovene People's Party fought for a much broader autonomy for the Slovenes, while the liberal and the Marxist parties were largely in favour of the principles of Yugoslav unitarism and centralism. The door was therefore closed to their greater acceptance among nationally conscious Slovenes. The Slovene People's Party, however, was neither principled enough nor consistent enough in its policies. In its relations with Belgrade it was very pragmatic, opportunistic, and ready for tactical compromises which brought it success.

After 1923, the Communist Party in Slovenia favoured Slovene autonomy and self-determination as did the Christian Socialist movement from its very beginning.

For the Slovenes, the Kingdom of Yugoslavia period can be characterized as a period of development and progress in all spheres of life and by the strengthening of their national existence and national consciousness. In spite of the progress made within the Kingdom of Yugoslavia, however, the Slovenes did not succeed in winning their autonomy, due to the intransigence of the dominant Serbs.

Yugoslavia succeeded in maintaining its neutrality for a year and a half after the beginning of the second world war. Only in March 1941, when he realized that the political mood in Yugoslavia was turning against the Axis powers, did Hitler order that Yugoslavia be attacked and crushed. With Yugoslavia broken in pieces, Slovenia found itself in a fatal new situation, occupied and divided among three occupying powers: Germany, Italy, and Hungary. All three occupiers annexed to their states the parts of Slovenia allotted to them, planning and carrying out policies of denationalization, a truly systematic genocide against the Slovenes. This action immediately created a strong resistance movement among the Slovenes, and very early, in the summer of 1941, they took up arms against the occupier. This relatively successful struggle was led by the Liberation Front, a political union of various left-wing political organizations and groups, liberals, Marxists, and Christians who before the war had opposed the policies of both Slovene bourgeois parties. The Liberation Front had a double goal: liberation from the occupier and the establishment of an independent United Slovenia in a restored, federatively reorganized Yugoslavia. Slovene Communists played a decisive role in the leadership of the Liberation Front, and from the very beginning their additional goal was social revolution and the introduction of the Soviet system.

This caused opposition to the Liberation Front among those Slovenes who were anti-Communist. In 1943 and 1944, the Slovene Communists together with other Yugoslav Communist partisans succeeded in gaining international recognition and the help of the anti-Fascist coalition, and at the end of the war they liberated those parts of Slovene national territory in Primorska which had been under Italian occupation between the wars. Although the Western Allies denied Slovenia Trieste, which the Yugoslav partisan army had liberated, Slovenia did succeed in guaranteeing its access to the sea on the Istrian Peninsula at Koper. Thus, after the war, the old Slovene dream of a United Slovenia was, except for Trieste and Carinthia, largely realized.

It was equally important for the Slovenes that within the restored federative Yugoslavia they had gained an autonomous national republic which became the basis for further Slovene national development.

It is true that this Slovene republic within the framework of a federative Yugoslav state was built around the Communist conception of the national question. According to this concept, the realization of national self-determination was in principle only of secondary importance and provisional compared to the basic Communist aim, the transformation of society. In practice, however, the Communist Party dealt with the nations of Yugoslavia very carefully and tactfully because it was aware of the explosiveness of this problem in the Yugoslav situation. In point of fact, in the national policies of the federative Communist Yugoslavia there was a constant struggle between the somewhat illusory self-declared and constitutionally legalized federation and the real federation.

Within the federation, individual nations independently developed only their own cultural policies while all other important spheres of life such as the economy, social development, the political system, foreign policy, and defence were controlled by the central government headed by the League of Communists. In retrospect, it appears that the problem of how to transform the illusory federation into a real one was ever-present. Under the leadership of Tito, Kardelj, and Bakarić, the League of Communists attempted to realize this goal at the end of the 1960s and in the first half of the 1970s with the 1974 constitution which the Serbs even then opposed. These three politicians succeeded in breaking Serb opposition, using instruments of Communist Party policy, but this was already the Party's swan song. By the middle of the 1970s, the Communist Party of Yugoslavia had essentially changed internally from a united, Pan-Yugoslav force into a sort of conglomerate of bureaucratic elites from individual nations and republics.

The disintegration of Yugoslavia and the emergence of an independent Slovenia

Immediately following the deaths of these historic leaders between 1979 and 1982, a national crisis erupted in Yugoslavia: the Albanians in the autonomous region of Kosovo demanded their own republic. This so shocked the Serbs that they reacted frenetically. The old Greater Serbia concept contained in the memorandum of the Serbian Academy of Sciences quickly became manifest. The Serbs demanded the immediate revision of the 1974 constitution, renewed centralization, the abolition of federative state bodies and principles of decision-making, and the abolition of both autonomous regions (Kosovo and Vojvodina) within the Republic of Serbia. In addition, the most radical Serb nationalists even demanded a fundamental transformation of the federation that would leave only four republics: Slovenia, Croatia, Macedonia, and Serbia. The latter would incorporate all of Bosnia and Herzegovina as well as Montenegro. The Serb nationalists were joined by the majority of Serb Communists under the leadership of Slobodan Milošević, who became an even more effective proponent of the Greater Serbia plan.

These Greater Serbia plans met vigorous opposition from the Slovenes and Croats. Owing to their economic power they felt sufficiently strong and self-confident that they would no longer allow themselves to be intimidated by the central government and the Serbs.

Let us take a close look at the situation of Slovenia in the middle of the 1980s, which can only be spoken of (*pars pro toto*) as a developed republic. We have already mentioned that until the end of the 1960s economic decision-making was centralized and the whole economic system and the legislation were essentially arranged to the advantage of the most numerous Serb nation. In spite of this, Slovenia succeeded in achieving a level of productivity and national income two and a half times greater than the Yugoslav average. This very fact already demonstrates the creative capability of Slovenes and their completely Western European life style. In the mid-1970s, with the new 1974 constitution, central economic pressure was loosened and the republics became more autonomous in this sphere. During this period until the collapse of Yugoslavia, Slovenia with only 8.2 per cent of the population produced between 17 per cent and 18 per cent of Yugoslavia's GDP, 25 per cent of Yugoslavia's total exports, and 33 per cent of Yugoslavia's exports to hard currency markets. With their developed manufacturing industry, Slovenes profited from other Yugoslav markets; and because they adapted most quickly to the Western style of management and marketing, they also profited from the joint Yugoslav trade with foreign countries. In the already quite industrialized Slovenia this inspired great self-confidence compared with other republics and the central government. This self-confidence was sometimes exaggerated and unrealistic, especially when we compare the state of development in Slovenia with the state of development in neighbouring Western countries. Slovene industry was mainly engaged in small serial production, much of its industry polluted the environment, Slovenia lacked energy resources, and its agriculture, with the exception of state owned properties, was small and only in rare cases export orientated. Slovenia's transportation infrastructure lagged behind that of Western Europe, although its social infrastructure including education, health services, and cultural activities was relatively well established, and those employed in these fields were the bearers of national consciousness. In the mid-1980s, Slovenia increasingly began to look toward and compare itself with the West. In Slovenia the conviction also prevailed that the Slovene economy must develop as rapidly and as autonomously as possible without waiting for the other republics. Slovenia, therefore, saw the centralizing pressure from Serbia, the central government, and the under-developed republics on its GDP as an obstacle and as a threat to the normal and necessary prospective national development measured against European standards. With only 8.2 per cent of Yugoslavia's population, Slovenia directly or indirectly contributed 20 per cent of the total income of the federation through various taxes, special funds for the underdeveloped regions, etc. It felt especially that the large budget for the army and the military industry was a far too heavy and completely useless burden. The two republics which profited most from the army and the military-industrial complex were Serbia and Bosnia and Herzegovina.

In the middle of the 1980s, the central (Serbian-dominated) government attempted to centralize and somehow unify the previously autonomous national school systems of the republics. Among Slovene teachers and cultural workers this inspired a genuine revolt and a determination to protect Slovene education, literature, and language. From their ranks came most of the contributors to the *Nova revija (New Review)* journal, which in the spring of 1987 published articles on a new Slovene nationalist platform which largely supported an independent Slovene state within a Yugoslav confederation.

From 1988 on, the central government, which was mainly identified only with the Yugoslav army and the League of Communists of Yugoslavia, began open political chicanery and pressure against Slovenia in an attempt to intimidate it.

In these circumstances, the Slovene Communists sided with the Slovene national patriotic option and at a critical moment at the end of September 1989 contributed to the passing of amendments to Slovenia's constitution through which the Republic of Slovenia took back from the Yugoslav Federation some of its original sovereign rights: in particular, the right to manage its own national income and the right to command the armed forces in the Republic of Slovenia (at that moment, the Communists had a large majority in the Republic Assembly). The Slovene government banned a Greater Serbia rally scheduled for 1 December 1989, in Ljubljana, which signalled the end to the Greater Serbia demonstrations. At the same time, the ruling League of Communists of Slovenia decided to free the way for a multiparty political democracy and to introduce a private and free market economy. With these moves, Slovenia far outstripped other Yugoslav republics regarding the issues of political democratization and economic reform and modernization, and its political life became quite incompatible with that in the rest of Yugoslavia. Only Croatia followed Slovenia's example to a limited extent.

In January 1990, the Slovene Communists withdrew from the League of Communists of Yugoslavia and thus another of the links tying Slovenia to Yugoslavia fell away. Slovenia's first democratic elections since the second world war were held in April 1990 and brought a 55 per cent victory for the anti-Communist Demos coalition composed of the Slovene Democratic Union, the Christian Democrats, the Farmers' Union, the Social Democratic Union of Slovenia, and the Green Party of Slovenia. The remaining votes went to the three parties considered the heirs of the former socialist regime: the Communist Union of Slovenia (17 per cent), the Union of Socialist Youth renamed the Liberal Democratic Party (14 per cent), and the Socialist Party of Slovenia (five per cent).

A government was put together by Demos which proclaimed as its most important goal the development of pluralistic democracy and the achievement of Slovene state independence. Further political development ran smoothly without revenge on former Communist officials.

Slovenia offered a confederation agreement to the other Yugoslav republics. Because all except Croatia refused it and because the central federal government rejected it as well, in the autumn of 1990 the Slovene government decided to hold a plebiscite of all the residents of Slovenia, Slovenes and others alike, on the status of Slovenia. The plebiscite was held on 23 December 1990, under international supervision, and of the 92 per cent of the electorate who voted, 88 per cent voted for a free and independent Slovenia.

Throughout the spring of 1991, Slovenia's parliament and government tried unsuccessfully to win over the other Yugoslav republics to a confederation agreement. All the Slovene endeavours fell on deaf ears in all the republics except Croatia since they were without democratic political systems. Therefore, in concert with Croatia, Slovenia decided that the Slovene and Croat parliaments would proclaim the independence of their republics on 25 June 1991. Encouraged by the assured support of the European Community and the United States, the Yugoslav federal government attempted to occupy Slovene borders, using the Yugoslav army to isolate Slovenia from the rest of the world and thus nullify the political decision of the Slovene parliament. Slovenes responded spontaneously to this move by blocking the roads and organizing armed resistance by the Slovene police and Slovene Territorial Defence forces. By the third day of the war, almost all the units of the Yugoslav army, which had not expected such resistance, were immobilized. Soldiers of non-Serb nationalities deserted en masse from the Yugoslav army, and many defected to the Slovene Territorial Defence units. On the fifth day of the war, Yugoslav army headquarters in Belgrade threatened Slovenia with drastic retaliatory measures. At that point the European Community intervened and sent three negotiators to Zagreb to mediate between the fighting parties. Ten days after the start of military operations, a cease-fire was established and soon afterwards a peace agreement was achieved. Quite unexpectedly, the Yugoslav government and army decided to withdraw all its soldiers and equipment from Slovenia within three months. This enabled the Slovene government to establish complete, effective, and sovereign control over all Slovene territory, the basic condition for international recognition of national sovereignty. International recognition was finally granted in December 1991 and January 1992, and in June 1992 the Republic of Slovenia was admitted to the United Nations as a full member.

3   The International Recognition of Slovenia

BOJKO BUČAR

International recognition of Slovenia

The recognition of states is usually regarded as a legal act by which one state, or a group of states, formally recognizes the existence of another state. It would seem, though, that in reality it is a political act based on political considerations which are expressed also in a legal form and certainly have legal consequences. The doctrine of Sir Hersch Lauterpacht, pleading for a duty to recognize entities which satisfy the legal criteria for statehood, was in practice never widely accepted. States rather persisted in their discretionary power to grant or withhold recognition.

Since it is generally accepted that the existence of the state is a matter of fact and not of law, the question might be raised, why then was it so important for Slovenia to achieve international recognition? Sometimes it is claimed that there seem to be certain rights a state is entitled to at the time of its creation, and to certain rights at the time of its recognition; e.g. at the time of its creation a state might claim the right of existence and of non-intervention, but these rights give poor protection in cases of secession from central authorities. Such a state will most probably not be able to make use of the inherent right of states to collective self-defence. But even if we neglect these security questions vital for a new state, it is only the recognition itself, and the subsequent establishment of diplomatic relations, which guarantee certain rights in the international community vital for the existence and development of a state.[1] In contrast to the Germanic legal system, in the common law legal system courts are bound by certificates of the executive branch, which means that non-recognized states may not sue even in fraudulent matters, and English conflict of laws rules frequently direct courts to apply foreign law, but clearly only of recognized states (Akehurst, 1984, pp. 66-67). All of this may seem unimportant in view of the fact that non-recognition may imply suspension of all trade and economic co-operation agreements, as well as of all agreements concerning scientific, technological, cultural and other relations. Postal services and telecommunications may be interrupted and all international air, maritime, road and railway traffic may become blocked. The central or national bank of the old state may recommend to foreign national banks that all accounts of commercial banks having domicile in the new state should be closed, the currency of the new state may not be recognized, citizens may not travel etc. In such circumstances a state may well emerge, but surely may not exist for a long time, since any development is made almost impossible. The nature of developed national economies, especially in small states, seems to be such that they cannot easily survive without international recognition of the state.[2]   Small wonder then that Slovenia, as soon as she declared independence, called upon all states in the international community to recognize the newly established state.

The causes of the disintegration of the Socialist Federative Republic of Yugoslavia were numerous (Bučar, 1991a). Yet from the international relations and foreign policy point of view, the European orientation of some federal units of the federal state seems to have been decisive. The widening economic gap between Yugoslavia and the countries of developed western Europe was in part considered as the unwillingness of some federal units to make both economic and political changes. The goals of establishing genuine democracy, the rule of law and respect for human rights seemed to be drifting into the distant future. The debate on the future of the country intensified after June 1990 when Slovenia declared sovereignty (Bučar, 1990), based on the federal constitution's provisions regarding the constituent states. Since the political debates on a revised form of a federation or confederation seemed to be leading nowhere, on 23 December 1990 Slovenia held a referendum on independence[3] and Croatia promulgated a new constitution. It indicated a clear determination of both federal units to become independent states (Bučar, 1991b).

By the beginning of 1991 all six federal units seem to have agreed that a new form of the state was inevitable. There was opposition from the federal government and the army, both because of their constitutional obligations, but also because of their own vital economic and political interests. The federal government had a good reputation in the international community, partly because of the non-aligned history of Yugoslavia and partly because of the seemingly successful economic reforms it had introduced. On the other hand, partly because economic reforms caused negative social effects for which the federal units were responsible and not the federal government, and partly because of political and nationalistic antagonisms between the federal units, the federal government had little support internally. Departing from the concept of the sovereignty of nations, the federal units started to negotiate on the future of the state without the presence of the army and the federal government.[4] A decision was reached to test the will of the people by way of a referendum in each of the federal units in the year 1991.[5] The escalation of the Yugoslav conflict made the implementation of this decision impossible (Bučar, 1993) and the negotiations broke down.[6]

The debate between the federal units was to a considerable degree based on constitutional issues. According to the *Basic principles of the (federal) Constitution of 1974* the bearers of sovereignty were 'the working people and the nations and nationalities'[7] who were entitled to 'exercise their sovereign rights' in the federal units and in the federal state only 'when in their common interest it is so specified' by the constitution. Furthermore, it was written that 'the nations of Yugoslavia, proceeding from the right of every nation to self determination, including the right to secession' have united in a federal state. The concept of the right of peoples to self-determination became a key issue (Kristan, 1992).

To implement the right of peoples to self-determination seemed to come at a perfect timing also from the standpoint of the international community. The Berlin wall had just fallen and in the *Charter of Paris for a New Europe* of 1990, the international community had *inter alia* recognized the right of the German nation to self-determination, i.e. the re-unification of East and West Germany. It was certainly an important milestone in the implementation of the right of peoples to self-determination. This collective human right had evolved from the political principle after the first world war into a legal principle enshrined in the *Charter of the UN*. From the very beginning it challenged the much older yet equally important right of states to territorial integrity. In the colonial situation, this dilemma was solved by a series of political and legal instruments of which at least two should be mentioned: the *UN Declaration on Granting the Independence to Colonial Countries and Peoples*[8] and the *Declaration of 7 Principles*.[9] The first declaration on the elimination of all forms of colonialism still contains a strong anti-secessionist clause, but which was *nota bene* inserted as a safeguard against the breaking up of colonial territories and not of colonial empires. The Declaration of 7 Principles, while distinguishing the status of the territory of a colony and the territory of the state administering it, still retains the anti-secessionist clause, but limits it to those states which conduct 'themselves in compliance with the principle of equal rights and self determination of peoples ... and thus possessed of a government representing the whole people belonging to the territory without distinction as to race, creed or colour'.

After all major issues of decolonization had been solved there was a general belief that 'the establishment of a sovereign and independent state' was no longer relevant as a mode 'of implementing the right of self determination'. Only a few saw a new wave of decolonization coming (Petrič, 1984, Ginther and Isak, 1991). In view of the integration processes world wide, and especially in Europe, a more relevant process seemed to be 'the free association or integration with an independent State or the emergence into any other political status freely determined by a people'. The focus had moved to the issue encompassed in the statement that 'all peoples have the right freely to determine, without external interference, their political status and to pursue their economic, social and cultural development'. This was the tool, then, together with other international legal and political human rights instruments, which was to be invoked in achieving the desired changes in Eastern Europe. It is small wonder then that in the specific historical context of the CSCE in 1975 a lot of attention was focused on the principle of the inviolability of frontiers and on the human rights basket. The eighth principle in the *Final Act of Helsinki on Equal rights and self-determination of peoples* passed virtually unnoticed, despite the fact that it stated that 'all peoples always have the right, in full freedom, to determine, when and as they wish, their internal and external political status, without external interference, and to pursue as they wish their political, economic, social and cultural development'.

For Slovenia, the notion of the right of peoples to self-determination in the constitutional system of Yugoslavia, as well as in the international community, was of utmost importance. In domestic politics, Slovenia started to argue that if the federal state of Yugoslavia was established by the free will of all the constituent nations the departure of one or more nations from the state would not constitute secession, but dissolution of the state. The difference in legal and material terms, in national as well as in international politics, is, of course, significant. In international politics and law the existence of the right to self-determination would, on the other hand, impose a duty on states to respect this right, which would not only facilitate recognition of a newborn state but would also call for assistance to be given to peoples claiming this right. Slovenia tried to convince foreign governments and international public opinion of its right and refused to recognize that in history the right of peoples to self-determination was mostly achieved in wars and bloodshed, precisely because it challenged the *equivalent* right of states to territorial integrity. Slovenia also failed to acknowledge other limitations on the right to self-determination arising from reasons of security, which are always important political considerations among the international community.[10]

To achieve independence Slovenia had only three options. The first was to reach an agreement of all the parties to the dispute. This was favoured by the international community. The second option was to reach independence by way of a unilateral declaration, hopefully not following the unsuccessful example of Lithuania. The third option was to start a successful secessionist armed conflict. The first option could not be achieved for at least two reasons: first, the federal government and the army, though interested parties, were not involved in the negotiations between the federal units. In respect of the second, negotiations between the federal units failed, and subsequently the federal government was not interested in negotiations with only one federal unit. The third option seemed possible but not probable and was regarded as unnecessary, especially in view of contemporary European developments. The second option, then, was the only viable solution and Slovenian authorities had to proceed with it since they were bound by the special law on the plebiscite to declare independence within six months. The Slovenian Parliament decided, against some better advice from within and outside the country, to declare independence on 25 June 1991 and immediately sought international recognition.[11]

The international community was well aware of the growing crisis in Yugoslavia. It had been informed by its own diplomatic agents,[12] special envoys and media reports, by the Yugoslav federal government and by the governments of the federal units of the state. The message which foreign governments, especially the governments of European states and the USA were sending, was clear enough. They were not ready to recognize a secessionist state and even less a dissolution of a state, excepting as a result of a consensus within the old state. The reasons were numerous and could be summarized as follows: in economic terms there was a fear of who would pay the debts once the debtor state ceased to exist[13] and it would also cause a considerable shrinkage of the common national market.[14] Security reasons were perhaps even more important. A disintegration of a state could end up in armed conflict that would maybe be hard to confine, and in particular would have been a bad example for the then still existing Soviet Union. The latter also provided a political reason which could be added to a general discomfort in view of the possible future international influence of a re-united Germany and the influence the Yugoslav case might have had on all countries with substantial ethnic or other minorities. Also, the integration processes, especially in Europe, made at a first glance all disintegration processes look anachronistic and inappropriate. Last but not least, international legal principles had to be respected, primarily the obligation to respect the territorial integrity of states and the principle of non-intervention in internal affairs.

Since no consensus could be reached within the state of Yugoslavia the international community decided to support the federal government. By the end of May 1991 at the latest it terminated all contacts with federal units and once again the federal government became the sole representative for Yugoslavia. Since Slovenia declared independence from Yugoslavia as Lithuania did from the Soviet Union, the federal government of Yugoslavia reacted like the federal government of the Soviet Union. On the same day that Slovenia declared independence, the federal parliament declared the act illegal and called upon the federal government to protect the borders of the federal state. The next day the army and some detachments of the federal police force tried to close the borders by force, federal authorities closed the air space by decree and the national bank took all necessary measures to discipline the unloyal federal unit in monetary matters (by imposing limited access to hard currency and stopping all credit transactions). But in contrast to Lithuania, Slovenia had its own territorial army and police force. The 'ten days war' of June 1991 started.[15]

The criteria for statehood generally recognized in customary international law are surely a defined territory and a population under the control of a government.[16] Although in theory the concepts of territory and population might create some problems, this was not the case in Slovenia and Lithuania. The problem was rather in the criterion 'government in control of...' or 'effective authorities'. In essence, it is a question of sovereignty, which in international relations means that there is supposedly no higher authority of another state above the law-prescribing and law-enforcing agencies,[17] which enables the state to exercise a treaty making power, the right to representation and the right to wage wars. In cases of secession 'effective authorities' become a crucial issue and as the recent cases of Slovenia and Lithuania show, it was this criterion which was used when central authorities tried to halt the aspirations of peoples for a new state and the recognition of these states by foreign governments. Yet at that time it seemed that the focus had shifted from the issue of 'the control of government' to 'how the control is exercised'.[18] It was becoming an issue of human rights invading the stronghold of the principle of non-interference in internal affairs.

The armed conflict of June 1991 shocked the international community. It was happening in the midst of Europe and the outcome was hard to predict (Bučar, 1991c). The European Union (EC at that time) offered its good offices in the conflict and threatened economic and political sanctions, i.e. unfriendly but legal actions, if the conflict were not to be solved by peaceful means. Yugoslavia accepted the offer and in practice the 'European troika' turned its services into mediation. Its basic aim was to stop all hostilities and influence all the parties to conduct peaceful negotiations in good faith towards a peaceful settlement of the conflict. If the parties could agree the EU would continue co-operation with all the parties concerned, otherwise the EU threatened to break off all relations. In addition, the federal government was put under pressure that if it continued with the armed intervention the EU would recognize Slovenia and Croatia as independent states, while the federal units had to restore their representatives to federal bodies from which they had previously withdrawn. The mediation resulted in the signing of the *Declaration of Brioni* of 7 July 1991 where all parties basically agreed to a three month cooling off period during which no unilateral actions which could worsen the situation would be taken and during which they would try to reach in good faith a peaceful solution for the future of the state. Therefore, Slovenia had to suspend its Declaration of Independence for at least three months. Thus, the conflict in Yugoslavia again became internationalized, ceasing to be an internal affair and acknowledging Slovenia as a party to the dispute. The solution suggested by the EU clearly demonstrated a will to preserve the territorial integrity of the state; it caused the termination of hostilities, yet it did not push for a specific political solution of the crises.[19] This was left to the parties in the conflict.

The three months suspension brought no progress. The parties failed to reach any significant compromise or agreement on the issue of borders and on the question of who should be recognized as the successor to the old state. Federal bodies were not able to resume their work due to the unwillingness of the federal units to participate in good faith. The federal army agreed to withdraw from Slovenia, only to get engaged in another armed conflict, in Croatia, which could already be identified as a prelude to the war in Bosnia. The Hague Conference on Yugoslavia presided over by the EU was unable to change the course of events on the ground. It became obvious that the old state did not exist any more and some political forces thought that maps of new states could be drawn at will. At the same time significant developments occurred in the international community. It became clear that the Soviet Union was falling apart, that new states were emerging and that the era of 'perestroika' and 'glasnost' had come to an end.[20]

The armed conflict in Croatia allowed Slovenia and Croatia to become *de facto* independent states, although they still lacked international legal recognition. The armed conflict required foreign governments and international organizations to acknowledge the existence of *de facto* states and allowed for co-operation, which in cases of non-recognized states would normally not be possible. In any case, Slovenia finally fulfilled the criterion of possessing 'effective authority'. Within the requirements of international law for recognizing an entity as a state, the recognizing state is required to make a determination, reasonably based upon fact, that the entity claiming statehood shows reasonable indications that the international legal requirements will continue to be satisfied. In case of secession or dissolution of a state this is the case when the old government renounces its pretensions or if it is obviously no longer in a position to assert authority within the entity.[21] Also, the economic, political and security reasons which a few months before were in favour of the integrity of the state as a whole, suddenly became either irrelevant or were even used to support the opposing view.

Because of her co-operative policy at The Hague Conference on Yugoslavia which started 5 September 1991, Slovenia was able to proceed towards independence on 7 October 1991, after the three months period stipulated by the *Declaration of Brioni* had passed. The situation in Yugoslavia worsened rapidly and on 29 November 1991 a special Arbitration Committee of the Conference on Yugoslavia found that Yugoslavia was in a process of disintegration.[22] Faced with a situation with which it could not contend any longer, the EC on 16 December 1991 adopted a declaration on the *Guidelines on the Recognition of New States in Eastern Europe and in the Soviet Union*(1991), as well as a *Declaration on Yugoslavia*(1991), whereby it decided to recognize, subject to certain conditions, the ex-Yugoslav federal units as sovereign states, effective as of 15 January 1992.[23] On the basis of this decision, Slovenia was recognized as a sovereign state by Iceland, Sweden and Germany on 19 December 1991, by Belorussia on 27 December 1991, by the Holy See on 13 January 1992 and by San Marino on 14 January 1992. The rest followed on 15 January 1992 and later.[24]

Before recognizing an entity as a state, many states tend to consider the opinion of other states, especially neighbouring states[25] and those which politically demand respect.[26] Nevertheless, historically there have been few instances of collective recognition.[27] But since there is no duty of recognition, states have always been at liberty to request from other states that they showed specific requirements in addition to those demanded by international law. Of such nature are the above-mentioned declarations of the EC, although, since the demands are 'codified', they might very well become international law. In the *Guidelines* strong emphasis is placed on respect for the protection of human rights, whereby EC states affirmed their readiness to recognize those states that have constituted themselves on a democratic basis. *Inter alia* the document demands respect for the provisions of the *Charter of the UN* and the commitments subscribed to in the *Final Act of Helsinki* and in the *Charter of Paris*, especially with regard to the rule of law, democracy and human rights, guarantees for the rights of ethnic and national groups and minorities in accordance with the commitments subscribed to in the framework of the CSCE.[28] In addition, special reference is made to acceptance of all relevant commitments with regard to disarmament and nuclear non-proliferation as well as to security and regional stability and to agreement or arbitration concerning state succession and regional disputes. In the EC Council of Ministers *Declaration on Yugoslavia* strong emphasis is also placed on the respect of human rights. Special reference is made to Chapter II of the draft Convention of 4 November 1991 on human rights and rights of national or ethnic groups.[29] This chapter provides for the guarantees of specific individual rights, respect for most universal international legal and other documents as well as many European documents, including proposals of declarations and conventions. It enumerates specific minority rights including political participation, it provides for special territorial autonomies, international monitoring and a Court of Human Rights. In addition, the Declaration set a deadline of 23 December 1991 for an application for recognition and *inter alia* it demands support for the continuation of the Conference on Yugoslavia, a commitment for adopting constitutional and political guarantees ensuring that there are no territorial claims towards a neighbouring Community State and that no hostile propaganda activities will be conducted against a neighbouring Community State, including the use of nomenclature which implies territorial claims.

How the EC special requirements for recognition were met by ex-Yugoslav federal units was judged by an arbitration committee, which also had to respect international law. This body declared that two federal units (Slovenia and Macedonia) satisfy the requirements of the EC, one federal unit (Croatia) not entirely, and the fourth (Bosnia) had at that time not been fully established (Arbitration Committee, 1992).[30] Regardless of this legal opinion requested by the EC itself, Slovenia and Croatia were recognized immediately, Bosnia after a short time and Macedonia much later. This certainly supports the opinion that political interests and decisions determine the recognition of a state and that political decisions determine whether an issue is a legal issue at all.

After Slovenia had been recognized by member states of the EC, it was only a question of time before she would be recognized by international organizations. Slovenia became a member of the CSCE on 24 March 1992, a member of the UN on 22 May 1992 and subsequently a member of various specialized agencies and other international organizations. Somewhat more complicated was the accession to international financial organizations (Mrak, 1994), since the question of succession is a dragging issue. First it joined EBRD on 23 December 1992. Following decisions of the UN,[31] Slovenia became a member of IMF on 15 January 1993, of the World Bank (IBRD and IDA) and of IFC on 25 February 1993, whereby it was important that she was considered as one of the successor states of Yugoslavia. In this way Slovenia accomplished most of the goals of its foreign relations strategy which had been designed before independence.

However, some strategic goals in its foreign economic and security policy have been poorly met. Problems also emerged in relations with neighbouring countries. Unfavourable conditions within the international community, where *inter alia* the crisis on the Balkans and the succession issue of the former Yugoslavia are dragging on, had to be met by the diplomacy of a small state. It also faces similar problems to those other Central and East European Countries (CEEC) who are in transition from a one party state and a socialist self-management economy to genuine democracy and market economy. Furthermore, Slovenia had to transform its economy from a regional one to that of a nation-state.

The economy of a small state always depends heavily on exports. The independence war of 1991 and the subsequent wars in Croatia and in Bosnia-Herzegovina led to the destruction of the traditional Yugoslav market which represented some 25 per cent of exports from Slovenia.[32] However, since Slovenia has a fairly open economy,[33] trade flows were quickly redirected. Less than ten per cent of exports goes to less developed countries (LDC), less than 20 per cent to central eastern Europe and the rest are exports to developed countries, out of which some 70 per cent are directed to the EU area (Kumar, 1993, pp. 84-88). Over 90 per cent of total exports are manufactured goods and Slovenia is the world's 21st country in export per inhabitant, well ahead of Spain, Portugal or Greece (Svetličič 1993, p. 27). Small wonder then that Slovenia had a vital interest in the institutional and legal-international framework of foreign trade. After Slovenia had achieved independence and before she became recognized as a state, GATT in fact tolerated the unusual situation. After recognition, Slovenia immediately applied for membership but due to the possible precedent for other potential members (e.g. Ukraine, Russia and China) the negotiations dragged on till 30 October 1994 when Slovenia became a full member of GATT 47 and subsequently of the World Trade Organization (WTO).

In view of its new pattern of exports, relations with the EU are even more important. Soon after independence in April 1993 a Co-operation Agreement was signed.[34] In essence, it prolongs the preferential trade agreement which had been concluded with Yugoslavia in 1980, except for the free movement of labour. Since EU economic policies might change after the achievement of a lasting peace in the Balkans and because some other countries[35] had already become associate members of the EU, in Spring 1994 Slovenia initiated negotiations for a European Agreement. Although some questions on the economic effects of such an agreement may be raised (Bučar and Brinar, 1994) it is generally considered that associate membership is a first step towards full membership of the EU.

Slovenia seems determined to become a member of the EU not only for economic reasons but also for security reasons.

The situation in the Balkans still appears far from a lasting peace despite the Paris and Dayton Agreements. Security structures such as the collective security of the UN or mechanisms within the Organization for Security and Co-operation in Europe (OSCE) have proved so far to be somewhat unreliable. Slovenia as a small state could easily become a victim of aggression, especially since the UN Security Council has imposed an arms embargo on all former Yugoslav republics. Therefore, many security concepts have been under consideration (Grizold, 1994) yet for various internal and external reasons no viable solution could be found. The concept of demilitarization which was current before independence proved to be directed only at the federal army. The concept of neutrality vanished after the ten day war in Slovenia and especially since the crisis in the Balkans persisted. There were no candidates for a new special collective self-defence arrangement available. The Western European Union (WEU) is still poorly developed and proved to be inaccessible to Slovenia, therefore a policy of joining NATO naturally developed. However, for various reasons of its own, NATO was (and is) reluctant to expand its membership. Slovenia never joined the North Atlantic Co-operation Council (NACC) - devised for the ex-Warsaw pact members - yet in the beginning of 1994 it managed to sign the Partnership for Peace agreement. Sporadic parliamentary and governmental contacts both with NATO and WEU resulted in its inclusion in the parliamentary assembly of NATO in 1995. None of these activities seem to guarantee adequate safety for a small country bordering the crisis areas of the Balkans and therefore full membership in the EU is still considered a strategic goal of the present government.

Although Slovenia does show better economic results than the rest of CEEC and already meets most of the economic criteria stipulated in Maastricht for full membership of the EU, and even though the text of the association agreement has already been approved by the Commission of the EU as well as by all the member states, the agreement cannot yet be signed, much less ratified. The main reason is the policy of Italy whose demands are not always very clear but seem to require that land ownership in Slovenia should be available to foreigners. This has not been demanded from other countries that have already signed the association agreement and formally it is a criterion that has to be met only after a country becomes a full member of the EU. In consequence of the political stalemate Slovenia pursues certain alternative strategies. It concluded a special agreement with EFTA and became a member of CEFTA in 1996.[36] At present this cannot be an adequate substitute for the EU market, and ideas for an off-shore economy are not considered serious.

Slovenian attempts to join in European integration processes are, of course, not facilitated by the difficulties it encounters in relations with neighbouring states. Most complicated are relations with Italy, a founding member of the EU. Italy has been very helpful in the process of Slovenia's recognition as a state by the EU and it also immediately recognized Slovenia as a successor state to all relevant treaties that had been concluded with Yugoslavia. But, soon afterwards, Italy proposed a trilateral treaty with Croatia and Slovenia on the protection of the Italian minority without any reciprocity for the protection of the Slovenian minority in Italy. After this attempt had been turned down by the Slovenian parliament,[37] Italy demanded a revision of one of the existing treaties between the two countries. It is the treaty on compensation for expropriated Italian property in territories that had been ceded to Yugoslavia after the second world war.[38] Italy invoked the principle of changed circumstances and demanded instead of material compensation the restitution of real property in kind (*in natura*). After prolonged and unsuccessful negotiations, Italy started claiming the right of pre-emption for what had once been Italian property and gradually increased its demands for Slovenia to liberalize transactions in real estate property even before signing the association agreement with the EU. Since there is still a long way to go towards full membership of the EU and no guarantee that Italy will not raise its expectations further and because of a lower purchasing power in Slovenia and an adverse public opinion, the Slovenian government faces serious problems. Despite these ongoing conflicts of interest, Italy is the second largest economic partner of Slovenia after Germany.

Relations with the southern neighbour, Croatia, are also complicated because it was once part of the same state. Succession issues cannot be resolved because of the overall situation in the Balkans; the privatization process coupled with divided state sovereignty triggers issues of property rights; in economic relations balance of payment difficulties are emerging; and certain border disputes have arisen since the administrative borders within Yugoslavia had never been clearly defined. These problems are aggravated by a psychological shock to the population of both states because of the loss of some rights in the neighbouring country, and the situation is made worse by radical political statements and media reports.

Relations with Austria and Hungary seem to be less difficult, although some tensions should not be completely disregarded. Austria's official policies have always been favourable towards Slovenia. It is the fourth largest economic partner of Slovenia, with an Austrian surplus in the balance of payments between the two countries. Politically speaking, a certain fear of a 'German influence' is occasionally felt and in addition there is the constant issue of the Slovenian minority in Austria which opposes the succession of Slovenia to the Austrian State Treaty where *inter alia* the protection of the Slovenian minority is guaranteed. Also, Austria is closely watching Slovenian relations with Italy which show similarities to those between Germany and the Czech Republic and Poland and which might have repercussions for its policy towards Slovenia. On the eastern border relations with Hungary seem to be the least complicated as witnessed by the bilateral treaty on the protection of minorities on both sides of the border. As a result of the cold war there are, however, only poor traffic and communication links between the two countries, which partly explains the absence of tensions between the two countries. Moreover, their economies are not complementary, but rather competitive. Once relations intensify, problems may well arise.

All of the above problems have to be dealt with at the same time as problems of privatization, denationalization and the transition of society and politics in general. As a small state, Slovenia has a modest foreign affairs administration[39] and Slovenian foreign policy remains pragmatic and mostly responds to challenges from the external environment. It is a new state and after an initial success in the process of recognition it has encountered difficulties in the international community which are partly due to historical conficts and complicated legal situations and partly to political problems caused by a newly acquired sovereignty. As time is needed for internal political and economic transformation, so time is needed for the new state to settle its foreign relations. It is much easier to accord juridical equality to a new state and much harder to recognize its political equality. With a small state the process is closely connected to its economic respectability and to the political accountability of its stronger and larger neighbours.

Notes

1.   The non-recognition of states implies at least the non-recognition of governments. This causes problems of: decreased prestige and stability at home, access to state funds on deposit in other states, access to private and government loans because of the legal ability to pledge the state's credit, diplomatic and consular status for its agents, access to foreign courts and immunity from foreign processes, establishment of normal trade relations, capacity to request assistance from recognizing governments (financial, supplies, military aid), respect in other states for its laws and decrees, and the benefit of existing treaty arrangements. The absence of recognition suspends these rights in whole or in part or may be accorded to other claimants (Kaplan and Katzenbach, 1961, p. 121).

2.   Nevertheless the international law doctrine seems to persist that the existence or disappearance of a state is a question of fact and that the effects of recognition by other states are purely declaratory (Report of the Arbitration Committee of the Conference on Yugoslavia, 10 December 1991, pt. 1a).

3.   Of the 93.5 per cent turnout 88.5 per cent of the votes were in favour of independence.

4.   Negotiations between the federal units started on 28 March 1991 and lasted for five weeks. No agreement on a new form of the state could be reached. Slovenia and Croatia favoured a confederation, Serbia and Montenegro a federation. Bosnia pushed for a compromise, a federation of sovereign states. Macedonia would opt for a federation only if all the federal units would stay together, otherwise a confederation model would seem preferable.

5.   Except for Slovenia where the referendum had already been organized.

6.   Croatia was the first of the federal units which could not organize a referendum on the whole of its territory. In certain parts there was a strong, even armed, resistance of the (predominantly Serb) population which was supported by units of the federal army. Serbia supported the idea of determining the will of the people by way of a referendum but would not have it confined to borders of the federal units.

7.   The term 'nations' designated Yugoslavia as a multinational state, while the term 'nationalities' meant minorities.

8. GA Res. 1514 (XV) adopted (89:0:9) on the occasion of the XVth anniversary of the UNO on 14 December 1960.

9. Declaration on Principles of International Law concerning Friendly Relations and Co-operation among States in accordance with the Charter of the United Nations, Annex to GA Res. 2625 (XXV) adopted by consensus on the occasion of the XXVth anniversary of the UNO on 24 October 1970.

10. For example, Austria, was in the State Treaty of 1955, denied the right of integration with Germany, Cyprus in 1960 the right to a union with Greece etc., and the FR of Germany had to exercise considerable diplomatic efforts to be allowed to unite with the German Democratic Republic.

11. Croatia was the only state that recognized Slovenia immediately on 26 June 1991. It had declared independence a day before Slovenia, but at the time it was rather declaratory. Slovenia had not been forwarding custom duties into the federal budget for some time and had taken other measures to secure sovereign authority.

12. It seems that the states have been poorly and ill-informed by their own diplomatic agents. This was probably due to the fact that members of the diplomatic corps rarely left the capital, neglected regional news and newspapers etc.

13. Data on the whole amount of the Yugoslav debt vary somewhat. But it was a developing country heavily indebted and estimates are around $18.2 billion (Mrak, 1994, p. 31). International legal rules in case of secession are somewhat general and the difference between the rather wealthy north of the country and the poorer south of the country represented additional risks.

14. The Yugoslav market was a market of some 21 million people and the disintegration into several markets was neither in the interest of importers to the country, nor of investors.

15. According to some media reports the White House might have known of the planned armed intervention by federal authorities, but did not foresee the armed resistance.

16. Point 1b of the Report of the Arbitration Committee of the Conference on Yugoslavia of 10 December 1991 states 'that the State is commonly defined as a community which consists of a territory and a population subject to an organized political authority; that such a state is characterized by sovereignty'.

17. All other facts, e.g. monetary independence, the presence of foreign troops etc., seem to carry less importance.

18. Point 1c of the Report of the Arbitration Committee of the Conference on Yugoslavia reads: 'for the purpose of applying these criteria (for the recognition of states) the form of internal political organization and the constitutional provisions are mere facts, although it is necessary to take them into consideration in order to determine the Government's sway over the population and the territory'.

19. Austria, which had been showing sound sympathy and recognition towards Slovenia, had been warned by the federal Yugoslav authorities and other governments of European states to stay neutral. Its stand has also been an issue in domestic politics.

20. In August 1991 the unsuccessful coup attempt in the Soviet Union led to the recognition of Baltic states and ended the Gorbachev era.

21. Otherwise a recognition might be considered premature and in violation of international law. It would constitute interference in the internal affairs of a state and could be considered a violation of its territorial integrity. However, there were cases, especially in the colonial situation, where states used to recognize entities which did not entirely meet the required criteria. It was a political sign of support for the new state and states use political and not legal arguments to justify such actions (Mossner, 1977, pp. 64-65). This seems also to be the case of Slovenia's recognition by Lithuania on 30 July 1991, by Georgia on 14 August 1991, by Latvia on 29 August 1991, by Estonia on 25 September 1991 and by Ukraine on 12 December 1991.

22. Opinion No. 1. Relevant are also opinions 2-3 (1991), 8-10 (1992) and 11-15 (1993).

23. The author has been told by the Slovenian Minister of Foreign Affairs at the time, Prof. Dr. Dimitrij Rupel, that this formula was the idea of the Italian Minister of Foreign Affairs, Mr. Gianni De Michelis, an unorthodox diplomat of the time.

24. By the end of 1992 some 100 states had recognized Slovenia and with most of them diplomatic relations have been established (Chronologic List, 1994).

25. Compare also the penultimate paragraph of the *Guidelines* and the last paragraph of the *Declaration on Yugoslavia*.

26. Many states were reluctant to recognize a state before the decision of the EC.

27. At the Berlin Congress in 1878 the Concert of European Great Powers recognized Bulgaria, Montenegro, Serbia and Rumania as states subject to the respect of certain religious freedoms. At The Hague Conference in 1991 the member states of the EC recognized Slovenia and Croatia (EC Presidency, 1991).

28. What seems to be meant are the Document of the Copenhagen and the Moscow meeting of the Conference on the Human Dimension of the CSCE and the Report of the CSCE meeting of experts on national minorities held in Geneva. This is *inter alia* expressly required in the draft Convention under consideration by the Conference on Yugoslavia (Treaty, 1991).

29. These rights were considered as one of the key principles underlying the search for a political settlement of the Yugoslav crises at the EC Conference (US/EC, 1992).

30. Two federal units (Serbia and Montenegro) never applied for recognition since they never recognized the dissolution of the state and claim to continue its existence.

31. The decision of the Arbitration Committee of the Conference on Yugoslavia and the UNSC in Res. 7 (1992) and 821 (1993) *inter alia* decided that the FR Yugoslavia (Serbia and Montenegro) has to apply for membership in the UN as one of the successor states. This has been repeated in GA Res. 47/1 and 47/229. It would be beyond the scope of this paper to analyse the evidence which shows that Yugoslavia is still a member of the UN, although all her rights are suspended.

32. Also, almost all the property of Slovenian enterprises in other parts of former Yugoslavia was expropriated or destroyed.

33. On average 94 per cent of exports and imports are liberalized and the rest is subject to quantitative restrictions (licences and quotas). Tariffs are applied on an *ad valorem* basis, ranging from 0-25 per cent, and are gradually being reduced.

34. It is supplemented by a Joint Declaration on Political Dialogue, a Financial Protocol and a Transport Agreement (Official Journal of the Republic of Slovenia No. 47, 1993, pp. 473-803). The Agreement on the establishment, privileges and immunities of the EC mission in Slovenia was ratified in June 1993.

35. Most notably the Višegrad group, i.e. Poland, the Czech Republic, Slovakia and Hungary. At present there are some ten countries having a European (Association) Agreement with the EU.

36. Since Austria, Finland and Sweden joined the EU in 1995, the European Free Trade Agreement (EFTA) consists only of Switzerland, Norway and Iceland. Yet this small group of countries remains cautious towards future enlargement. Through EFTA a country could have access to the benefits of the European Economic Area (EEA) which allows for certain economic benefits of the EU market. The Central European Free Trade Area (CEFTA) is designed to liberalize trade between countries of the Višegrad group and Slovenia and to harmonize its standards with those of the EU.

37. The Slovenian parliament demanded reciprocity on the issue of minorities since it believes that Italy does not respect its international obligations towards the Slovenian minority while the protection of the Italian minority in Slovenia is well above international standards. Italian allegations of the violation of human rights in respect of the Italian minority in Slovenia were rejected by numerous reports from international organizations which have sent missions to Slovenia (Krmelj, 1994).

38. The treaty had been concluded between Italy and Yugoslavia in 1983 in Rome. Not all of the instalments had been due by the time Italy recognized Slovenia as a successor state to the treaty.

39. In 1995 Slovenia had embassies in 28 countries, four permanent missions to international organizations and six consulates general. Seven new embassies are planned to be open in 1996. Average staff ranges from three to five people. In addition some 250 people work at the foreign ministry. For more detail see Bučar 1995.

4   The Defence of Slovenia

ANTON GRIZOLD

Defending national territory

The declaration of Slovenian independence on 25 June 1991 meant that the new government had to take on all the functions of the state within its territory. It was hoped that this would be a gradual and peaceful process, proceeding by agreement with the federal government and the other constituent republics.

In respect of the armed forces it was proposed that the federal Yugoslav People's Army (YPA) would remain in Slovenia until 31 December 1991, during which period it would be paid for by the Slovenian government.

On 27 June 1991 the YPA intervened militarily in Slovenia, requiring the government to put in train the necessary measures to defend the security, integrity and sovereignty of the new parliamentary state.[1]

The federal government formally covered its military intervention in Slovenia by invoking the federal 1974 Constitution.[2] The single most important strategic cause for the intervention was the attempt by the 'supreme command' to save the existing authoritarian Yugoslav political system on which the YPA was crucially dependent. The 'supreme command' had been, since 1989, a part of the Federal Secretariat for National Defence but it had no constitutional validity. The operative political-military goals of this military intervention were as follows:

1. To reach and take over the Slovenian borders and airports by military force;

2. To cut off Slovenia and Croatia from the international community and;

3. To preserve the existing regime with Serbian domination of the federation and the YPA.

Contrary to expectations, Slovenian forces from the territorial army units and the police supported by the whole population effectively resisted the YPA units.

The outbreak of a war in the heart of Central Europe encouraged the European Union to intervene and to try to achieve a cease-fire as well as to reach an agreement by which the Yugoslav crisis might be resolved in a peaceful way. A conference of representatives of the European Union, the Yugoslav federal government, Slovenia, Serbia and Croatia, adopted a declaration on 7 July 1991. Called the Brioni Declaration (after the Brioni islands, where the meeting was held), it was confirmed by the Slovene Parliament on 10 July 1991 as well as by the Yugoslav federal presidency on 12 July 1991. Slovenia was required to freeze the processes towards independence for three months. After the expiry date of the Brioni Declaration on 7 October 1991, Slovenia continued its progress towards independence. Internally, it consolidated its legal, political, security and other sub-systems, while externally it sought the legal international recognition of the Slovene state.

The refusal of the federal authorities to accept Slovenian independence brought a military confrontation between the YPA and the Slovenian Territorial Defence units and police. Subsequently, the Slovene Armed Forces emerged.

The military confrontation between the YPA and Slovene forces

Since the final outcome of the YPA's military intervention in Slovenia was primarily defined by the nature of Yugoslav federal state authority, which determined the form, social status and functions of the state armed forces as well as defence policy, this issue requires a detailed discussion.

The nature of the Yugoslav defence system and the role of the military

The defence system was an integral part of the Yugoslav socio-political system, where the lines between the armed forces, other constituents of defence system and the political structure were not clearly drawn. The main reason for this can be found in the model of self-management as a Yugoslav variant of democracy, embracing the idea of the withering away of the traditional state apparatus, to be achieved by socialization of the state functions. This practically meant that, apart from the state, all subjects of civil society were, at least formally, included in the direction of social life. In reality, this led to a repetitive confusion between the role of the state and the process of socialization, which caused the 'institutional hypertrophy' of the whole socio-political system. The notion of socialization had an impact on the sphere of defence, particularly in the form of the official Yugoslav defence doctrine, which was a variation of the Marxist defence concept of the people-in-arms, based on the broadest possible participation of the population in different segments of the defence system.[3]

The Yugoslav defence system had two main functions:

a) to assure deterrence and protection from the potential aggressor in peacetime,
b) preparedness to harmonize the activities of the whole society in case of war.

The Yugoslav federal state had, in the postwar period, gradually shaped its constitutional and legal system. The last constitution, adopted in 1974, granted all competence in the sphere of defence to the federal state and the federal military headquarters (i.e. Federal Secretariat for National Defence-FSND). This competence encompassed the whole organization of the defence system as well as the leadership and command of the SFRY armed forces.[4]

The SFRY armed forces were composed of two parts, defined by Article 240 of the 1974 constitution, the YPA and Territorial Defence (TD). While the YPA was a multinational federal standing army (composed of professionals and conscripts), the TD was a militia army (composed of a small core of professionals and large reserve units), organized on the level of individual republics, communes and some larger enterprises.

The TD was not legalized until 1968. It represented in fact a subsidiary local component of the Yugoslav armed forces, which was in the military sense subject to the FSND. The most important reasons for the introduction of the TD can be found in the context of world military events (e.g. the 1967 Six Day War in the Middle East, the invasion of Czechoslovakia in 1968, etc.), which made Yugoslav military headquarters believe that the state had to be prepared to face a possible conventional attack on its territory and a prolonged struggle against occupation.

The Yugoslav military headquarters had never recognized the TD as an equal partner in the defence of the country. This was shown in many ways. The TD was armed with out-moded weapons and obsolete military equipment. Their units were composed of recruits who no longer satisfied the necessary ability requirements of the regular army. Individual republics as constituent elements of the federal state had commanders of TD, who were as a rule active high-ranking officers of the YPA, appointed by the Federal Secretary for National Defence, who was always an active general. In the first half of 1990 the FSND embraced a new doctrine on TD ('Doktrina Teritorijalne Obrane Oružanih Snaga'), which radically changed the then prevailing conception of TD and transformed the status of the Republican Headquarters of TD from agencies of the republic into elements of the YPA, thus bringing TD under the direct control of the YPA headquarters. This dictate was followed by several practical measures: recruiting activities were transferred from the local and republican levels to the FSND, and eventually the TD was disarmed during the first multi-party elections in Slovenia and Croatia in 1990/1991.

The ultimate leadership and command of the Yugoslav armed forces in peace and war was entrusted to the Presidency of the SFRY (art. 313 and 328 of the 1974 constitution).[5] Until 1980, the role of the Commander-in-Chief of SFRY armed forces was held by the President, Josip Broz Tito, who, as the highest political authority, represented an important bond between the military organization and society, and as a charismatic leader he ensured direct civilian control of the Yugoslav armed forces. After his death, and particularly after the disintegration of the monoparty system, the Yugoslav constitutional and legal system could not adequately continue either the deceased President's personal or Communist party control of the Yugoslav armed forces. As a consequence, the YPA acquired the status of an autonomous political force within the state.[6]

The organizational, material-technical and personnel aspects of the military confrontation in Slovenia

SFRY had for a long time been considered to be one of the strongest armed forces in Europe. The size of the armed forces decreased from approximately 250,000 men in the 1970s to about 150,000 men at the end of the 1980s. Its huge stocks of arms and ammunition had been built up over the decades since 1945. They included notably around 520 combat aircraft, 2900 tanks, 2800 armoured personnel carriers, 25,000 mortars, 11,000 artillery tubes, 1250 short-range land-to-land missiles, 1.2 million rifles, etc. (Bebler, 1993, p. 29).

The military organizational structure in Yugoslavia after 1990 was composed of three military districts with headquarters in Zagreb (Croatia), Belgrade (Serbia), and Skopje (Macedonia), and one military-maritime district with headquarters in Split (Croatia). Within these military districts operative-strategic units were operating (brigades, battalions, etc.). The whole Slovene territory was a part of the military district with headquarters in Zagreb which included five operative-strategic units. A detailed analysis, comparing different data and sources, indicates that in the period from June 26 to July 18 1991 the YPA had at its disposal on Slovene territory approximately 13,000 to 14,000 men (professionals, conscripts and civilians employed by the YPA).[7]

At the time of the military intervention, an additional 600 to 1000 members of the military and federal police forces were sent to Slovenia in order to back up this operation.

As Table 4.1 indicates, the whole military force of the YPA in military intervention in Slovenia had at its disposal a huge quantity of arms, though not all of it was used. According to some estimates, approximately 2000 to 3000 men of the YPA were actually engaged in the military confrontation in Slovenia. The TD was organized into seven military regions, 27 military districts and one special brigade encompassing 35,000 men and women by 8 July 1991, the numbers having been rapidly augmented from 10 June.

Table 4.1   Armament at the disposal of the YPA and used in military intervention in Slovenia

		At disposal (number of pieces)	Used in military intervention operation
1	Tanks	299	115
2	Armoured personnel carriers	163	82
3	Field guns	100	32
4	Howitzers	310	-
5	Mortars	228	-
6	Anti-aircraft guns	294	-
7	Combat, transport & reconnoitring helicopter	1-5	20 flight missions
8	Combat aircraft	1-5	15 flight missions

Apart from TD, the police force was activated with 20,000 officers, the national self-protection force[8] with up to 20,000 participants, and civil protection and civil defence units with up to 100,000 Slovene citizens.

While the TD and police forces were engaged in combat activities such as fighting, protection of border crossings, blockade of military barracks and the obstruction of the YPA's manoeuvres, protection of communications, etc., the rest of the Slovene defence forces implemented non-combat defence activities, such as medical care, water supply, road blockades, data collecting, control of the territory and access to larger cities, etc.

Table 4.2   Armament and ammunition at disposal of the Slovene TD and police force for defence in 1991

1	Armament and ammunition belonging to infantry (rifles, machine-guns, sub-machine guns, pistols)	34,295 with 11 million rounds of ammunition
2	Minethrowers	1,024 with 2,397 mines
3	Anti-tank armament (armbrust etc.)	1,106
4	Mortars (60 and 82 mm)	6,232 shells
5	Anti-aircraft guns (20 mm)	39,900 pieces of ammunition
6	Anti-tank bombs	306
7	Anti-tank mines	1,066
8	Explosives	33,379 kg

As Tables 4.1 and 4.2 indicate, the relationship between the aggressors and defenders, so far as manpower was concerned, was in favour of the defenders, while the YPA had the advantage in armament, ammunition and military equipment.

In analysing the military confrontation between YPA forces and Slovene defence forces the following general observations can be made:

1. The YPA as a multinational conscript army was neither prepared nor motivated to perform the police function of preventing Slovene

independence. The lower units of YPA disintegrated when confronted by the Slovene TD and surrendered after being urged to comply by the Slovene authorities;

2. The YPA headquarters underestimated Slovene preparedness for defence;
3. The preparedness and high level of motivation of the TD, police units and citizens engaged in defence were a reflection of the national aspirations expressed in the referendum of December 1990;
4. Though the successful defence of Slovenia was the result of a complex series of interlocking factors (i.e. political, diplomatic, military, cultural, etc.), three basic characteristics of Slovene defence strategy have proved significant, according to the view of a large proportion of the surveyed members of the TD who were directly involved in the armed conflicts in Slovenia.[9]

These basic characteristics are:

a) the principle that Slovenia in its defence relied above all on its own forces and capacities. Support from other states was more likely to be forthcoming when Slovene's defence forces had demonstrated their success;
b) the combination of armed and non-armed forms of struggle and resistance contributed to the military success. The Slovene experience has shown that a properly conducted political and diplomatic campaign within the country as well as at the international level can play a very important role in ensuring a successful defence;
c) the effective diversion of all available resources towards defence and the ability to maintain constant opposition spread over the whole Slovene territory.

The shaping of a new Slovene defence system and regulation of armed forces

After the YPA departed from Slovenia in October 1991, the military supervision of Slovene territory was taken over by the Slovene TD and police forces. The ongoing process of the reorganization of the TD into the Slovene armed forces was integrated with the creation of a new and comprehensive defence system. The present defence system of Slovenia has its legal and political basis in the new Slovene constitution (adopted in December 1991), the Law on Defence (adopted in December 1994), the Law on Military Service (1991) and the National Security Resolution of December 1993 ('starting points on national security concept from the point of view of defence, security, protection and rescue'). The latter regulates the broadest starting points on which the entire national security system is based. This political document defines the international aspect of Slovenia's defence policy as based on the policy of defensive self-reliance and close association with NATO.

The existing defence system of Slovenia consists of the following two basic elements: military defence and civil defence (art. 3, Law on Defence, 1994). While military defence is carried out by the Slovene Army, civil defence is expected to ensure the continued functioning of the socio-political system in war and to organize the transition and adaptation of all resources and facilities to war-time conditions. It is intended to provide economic and psychological defence as well as other non-military institutional forms of defence (See Official Gazette of Republic of Slovenia, No. 82, 1994, p. 5029).

The Slovene armed forces are officially called the Slovene Army. Unlike the previous system, the Slovene Army (SA) today consists of both a standing army and dispersed territorial units. It has the following basic functions:

1. Organization and training of its units in preparation for armed struggle and other forms of military defence
2. Carrying out defence operations in case of aggression and
3. Co-operation in repairing loss or damage caused by natural disasters and other accidents (See Official Gazette of Republic of Slovenia, *ibid.* p. 5034).

On 27 July 1995, a new military defence doctrine was approved by the Slovene Government. It provides complete guidelines for military action in time of war, including organization, planning, preparation and deployment of the SA. The underlying doctrine derives from the fact that Slovenia, given its small size, cannot create an army able to wage a classical war against aggressors; its armed forces, therefore, are organized in such a way as to inflict the greatest possible losses on a potential enemy. In this respect, the SA is divided into two main parts, provisionally called the manoeuvring part and the stationary part. These two parts differ in their organizational structure, goal and presumed operations, though they are both subordinated to the General Staff. The essential purpose of this division is to ensure on the one hand units which will be organized, equipped and trained in such a way as to be able to intervene wherever necessary within the whole territory of the Slovene state, while on the other, there are units which operate within defined areas only (Grizold, 1994, p. 90).

The SA standing component represents less than a half of the former YPA's strength on Slovene territory. The total number of heavy weapons has also been reduced, particularly heavy armour and artillery. Fixed-wing combat aircraft have been eliminated altogether. The same applies to tactical surface-to-surface missiles, napalm and cluster bombs, heavy bridging equipment and other clearly offensive elements of the former YPA's arsenal (Bebler, 1993, p. 65).

The highest ranking organ of the SA in military and professional terms is the General Staff located within the Defence Ministry. The President of the Republic is titular Commander-in-Chief, while the Defence Minister holds the most influential position in the military and in the defence sphere as a whole.

The whole Slovene territory is militarily subdivided into seven regions, each having its own regional staff. Inside each region or province there exist several district staffs, each of them covering two to three municipalities. All of these staffs are composed of professionals.

There is compulsory military service of seven months for Slovenian males, producing approximately 7,000 soldiers from an annual contingent of 12 to 15 thousand conscripts. The entire military force will consist of around 10,000 servicemen and slightly over 4,000 commissioned and non-commissioned officers.

There have also been qualitative changes in the relations between military and civilian institutions in Slovenia. The erstwhile symbiosis between the military and the party has been abolished, as has the requirement for party membership of professional military personnel. All party activities have been prohibited and discrimination on the basis of religion within the military has been abolished. The political weight and role of the military has been greatly reduced. Physical control over most of the land and sea borders, previously exercised by the YPA, has been transferred to the police. The entire military corps has become more socially representative in regard to gender, social origin, and religion. The military has been placed under strict civilian control. A civilian has been appointed Minister of Defence and all defence activities have come under parliamentary control. The national security system as a whole is more transparent and accessible to parliamentary scrutiny, to the mass media and public criticism. The entire interface between the military and civil society has been subjected to the spirit of pluralist democratic values, which have become the explicitly stipulated frame of reference for the military, coupled with their assured professional autonomy (Bebler, 1993, p. 67).

Although the military and national security system in Slovenia has been evolving towards that of developed parliamentary states, there remain some unresolved problems.

In the process of shaping its new national security identity, Slovenia has not yet succeeded in developing a modern concept of national security. The existing Slovene national security system is framed within the traditional national security concept, which places greatest emphasis on the military component. For Slovenia as a small community it is important to shape a comprehensive national security system in which the balance between the military and non-military mechanisms would be ensured. Only such a national security system would reflect both the capacity of a small state to defend itself against a variety of threats, and its ability to ensure the development and well-being of its population.

Notes

1. See also Reneo Lukić, The Wars of South Slavic Succession: Yugoslavia 1991-1993, PSIS Occasional Papers, No. 2/93, Graduate Institute of International Studies, Geneva, pp. 20-22.

2. Concerning the legalistic interpretation of the military intervention two points are specially worth noting: a) the Yugoslav 1974 Constitution was at the time in marked dissonance with the social, political, economic and cultural changes which had occurred in Yugoslavia within the last two decades. The invocation of this Constitution was obviously an anachronism. b) This Constitution was the expression of the Yugoslav political system in which the YPA had completely integrated and identified itself with the ideology and politics of the ruling political force - The Yugoslav League of Communists - LCY. After the disintegration of LCY in 1989, the YPA lost its ideological coherence as well as the last vestiges of civilian (i.e. party) supervision and it acted as an autonomous political force relying on the most convenient ideological frame - Serbian totalitarian nationalism.

3. "...national defence is a social function and defence is not organized only by the state itself but by society as a whole..." Ustava SFRJ (The Constitution of SFRY), DDU, Ljubljana, 1974, Chapter VI p. 274.

4. The competence of the Yugoslav federal state, i.e. its organs in the sphere of defence, was defined in Chapter II of the Constitution of SFRY (art. 81-290). Accordingly, the Yugoslav federal state had exclusive competence in the organization and command of the defence system and the Yugoslav armed forces. Thus, the federal state was competent to take decisions on the declaration of war and negotiating peace treaties, on defence plans, mobilization, leadership and command of the armed forces, adoption of the budget for YPA, and so on. All other formal subjects of the Yugoslav defence policy (republics, communes, local communities and enterprises) were never properly involved in decision making within the sphere of defence.

5. The Constitution of SFRY (1974) granted the following competence to the president of SFRY as the Commander-in-Chief of the armed forces:

   - commanded and was in charge of the Yugoslav armed forces and determined the bases of plans and preparatory measures for the defence of the country;
   - attended to the organization and mobilization of the resources and forces of the country in the case of war and determined the tasks of the armed forces in peace;
   - appointed, promoted and relieved of duty generals and admirals and other military officers as designated by the federal law;
   - appointed and dismissed from office presidents, judges and lay judges of military courts, as well as the military prosecutors, etc. Ustava SFRJ (The Constitutuion of SFRY), DDU, Ljubljana, 1974, pp. 150-151.

6. For detailed reading see Anton Bebler, Jugoslovanska ljudska armada in razpad Jugoslavije in: Anton Grizold, Razpotja nacionalne varnosti, FDV, Ljubljana, 1992, pp. 45-57, and Ljubica Jelušič, Legitimnost vojaštva v sodobni družbi. Doktorska disertacija. Ljubljana, pp. 206-233.

7. According to the official analysis of Slovene TD headquarters, dated July 1991, the size of YPA forces available for military confrontation was much larger, amounting to 18,000-22,000 men.

8. The national self-protecting forces (NSPF) derived from the Slovene experience during the national liberation war (1941-1945), and retained a special function after the war only in Slovenia. They were a non-military formation with the following functions in case of natural hazards, war or other emergencies:

-   detection of threats and danger;
-   public alerts;
-   preparation for protection;
-   rescue;
-   repairing loss or damage.

9. It pertains to the research study: 'Slovene Soldiers-Members of the Territorial Defence in the Armed Conflicts with the YPA in Slovenia', which included 512 out of 728 respondents. This figure represents approximately 2 per cent of all conscripted to the TD at the time of the armed conflicts in June 1991. The survey was conducted over the period from 10 September to 10 October 1991 by the Defence Research Centre at the Faculty of Social Sciences, University of Ljubljana.

5 Slovenian Political Culture: Paradoxes of Democratization

IVAN BERNIK, BRINA MALNAR, NIKO TOŠ

Political culture in post-socialist societies: some general considerations

There are good reasons to designate the emergence of post-socialist societies as a complex process; it is by no means limited to political democratization but encompasses the transformation of almost all aspects of social life. To understand this process, one should focus primarily on the intricate interdependencies between the different aspects of transformation. This point is aptly illustrated in R. Dahrendorf's observation that:

> the formal process of constitutional reform takes at least six months; a general sense that things are moving up as a result of economic reform is unlikely to spread before six years have passed; the third condition of the road to freedom is to provide the social foundations which transform the constitution and the economy from fair-weather into all-weather institutions which can withstand the storms generated within and without, and sixty years are barely enough to lay these foundations (Dahrendorf, 1990, p. 93).

One may disagree both with Dahrendorf's specification of the most important societal spheres and the duration of their transformation, but it is difficult to object to his key claim that the pace of transformation of individual societal spheres is utterly different. The ensuing temporal inconsistencies of change have far-reaching consequences. Not only that the breakthroughs in one sphere cannot be stabilized until 'backed' by the transformation of other spheres, but the slow pace of transformation in one sphere can also block or even reverse changes in other spheres, e.g. the effectiveness of legal reforms can be undermined if they are not 'supported' by transformations of the economic and social structures of society. From this point of view, the central problems and uncertainties of post-socialist transformation are related to the temporal co-ordination, i.e. synchronization, of changes of different aspects of social life (see Offe, 1991).

It seems that this general analytical perspective has been at least tacitly adopted by most of the research on political culture in the post-socialist societies. This perspective implies that the research on political culture should mostly focus on the (in)congruency of political culture transformation with the democratization of the political system. This idea has been clearly articulated in Lipset's reappraisal of the social requisites of democracy. He argues that:

> the success of democracy in these (i.e. post-socialist) countries depends largely on their populations' ability to adapt to freedom, to break away from their former views on the role of the state and their willingness to accept the cyclical nature of the free-market system, and of course, on successful economic performance (Lipset, 1994, p. 13).

At the same time he stresses that the mass commitment to democracy needs ample time to emerge. Hence it follows that post-socialist societies are characterized by a considerable 'time-lag' between the transformation of the political system and the emergence of an adequate political culture. This lag can make the 'success' of democracy in post-socialist societies highly precarious. Therefore, it is not only scientifically but also politically highly relevant to examine this gap and its consequences for the stability of the new political order.

The obvious advantage of this perspective is in its ability to generate clear research questions - but this already presupposes answers to key questions of political culture theory, i.e. the 'questions about the permanence (or variability) of political cultures and the necessity of maintaining a congruence between the culture and the structure of the political system' (Dalton, 1994, p. 470).[1] It sees political culture as relatively constant in comparison with other aspects of social life and claims that congruence between political culture and political system is a necessary condition of the stability of the political order. Thus the scope of research questions which can be articulated in the framework of this perspective is considerably limited. In our study, we will draw mainly on the analytical potentials of this perspective, but at the same time we shall bear in mind that some of its presuppositions are highly contentious.

Given the fact that the post-socialist societies have established basic democratic institutions, the most relevant research question seems to be to what extent is political culture 'catching up' with the new institutional order. Or to put it even more directly, to what extent is the 'post-socialist' political culture approaching the pattern prevailing in Western democracies? However, the discussions on political culture in both Western democracies and in post-socialist societies indicate that this question can be misleading. Studies show that there is no homogeneous pattern of political culture even in individual Western societies, let alone in all of them (Kitschelt, 1993, p. 306). As there are different bases and modes of commitment to democracy in Western societies, the transformation of political culture in post-socialist societies cannot be conceived as a simple advance towards a homogeneous Western pattern.

Another point in favour of a 'multilineal' concept of political culture transformation is provided by the current discussions about the basic characteristics of socialist and post-socialist political culture. Although there were substantial differences between socialist societies, the prevailing pattern of political culture was characterized by paternalistic-authoritarian attitudes towards political authorities, feelings of powerlessness and a strong orientation on private life (Meyer, 1993, p. 3). As shown by many studies (Bernik, 1993, pp. 108-115), even during the most 'fortunate' periods of these societies, the attitudes towards political authorities were mostly based on pragmatic considerations, i.e. the acceptance of the socialist regimes was dependent on their abilities to provide the expected levels of economic and social well-being. It may be assumed that the gradual decline of socialist regimes also led to the erosion of paternalistic-authoritarian attitudes. Thus, a ground should have been created for the emergence of values and attitudes supportive of the new democratic political system. This claim also implies that the emergence of new democratic political institutions was supported or at least paralleled by a developing democratic political culture. Nevertheless, this conclusion has been dismissed by most analyses as being too simplistic. On the one hand, it has been argued that the disintegration of the old political values does not necessarily lead to the emergence of new ones but to the protracted absence of any consistent political values and expectations, i.e. in a state of anomie (Kolarska-Bobinska, 1990, pp. 281-2; Ziemer, 1994, p. 493). On the other hand, it has been shown that this vacuum can be filled with political values and attitudes which can by no means be termed democratic (Vainshtein, 1994, pp. 251-52).

One of the most provocative arguments in favour of the latter claim has been presented by P. Sztompka. He argues that the post-socialist societies are characterized by 'civilizational incompetence' (Sztompka, 1993). Whereas the post-socialist societies have achieved some breakthroughs in both the economic and political spheres, in the cultural sphere traditional value patterns have come to the fore. According to Sztompka, this indicates that despite their revolutionary rhetoric, the socialist regimes covertly also relied on these cultural patterns. In other words, in post-socialist societies the burden of the past is most obviously felt in the cultural sphere. For this reason, the post-socialist societies are, according to Sztompka, culturally relatively incompetent to cope with new developmental challenges.

The gist of Sztompka's argument strongly resembles points brought up more than 20 years ago in the discussion about the 'egalitarian syndrome' (Župan, 1970, pp. 21-39) in Yugoslavia.[2] In the centre of this discussion was the claim, elaborated by J. Županov, that the prevailing cultural matrix in Yugoslav society was characterized by a specific mix of egalitarian and authoritarian values and expectations. Although this cultural matrix was rooted in tradition, it was functionally incorporated into the socialist society; the political regime was able to win mass support by fulfilling the egalitarian expectations of the majority of the population. Whereas this 'merger' of egalitarianism and authoritarianism was functional for the stability of the political regime, it was, as especially stressed by Županov, highly dysfunctional for the modernization of Yugoslav society.

These accounts not only suggest that the possible transformations of political culture are multilineal, but they also indicate that they take place in a broad 'space', to be defined by traditional cultural sediments, i.e. mostly by values and attitudes clustered around authoritarian paternalism on the one hand, and different forms of emergent democratic political culture on the other. Most of the accounts also suggest that post-socialist societies are characterized - due to the high resistance of political culture to change - by incongruence between cultural change and change in other spheres.

The structure of this imaginary space gets increasingly complicated when one takes into account the differences between the post-socialist societies. According to authors who argue that tradition exerts an important influence on political culture, the major differences can be explained by different cultural backgrounds. One of the main divisions should be between societies with Catholic and Orthodox religious traditions (Adam, 1989). In contrast to this view, Evans and Whitefield argue that the political process in post-socialist countries is on a national level primarily determined by three variables - 'economic development, levels of ethnic homogeneity and the historic status of the state' (Evans and Whitefield, 1993, p. 539). The societies with higher economic growth, with a high level of ethnic homogeneity and not preoccupied with nation-state building have more chances of achieving political stability than the others. Their list of variables can be supplemented by at least one more - the pace of political transformation. It is to be expected that the countries experiencing gradual political transformation have more chances of developing the prerequisites for a stable political order than the countries whose political systems were transformed in revolution-like events.

In our study, this outline of determinants shaping the stability/transformation of political culture will be taken as a general framework in which the leading hypotheses regarding the change of political culture in Slovenia and its function in the consolidation of the new political system will be specified. Before embarking on this task, a brief description of the 'Slovenian way' from socialism seems necessary.

The Slovenian case: democratization and state-building

Although strongly interrelated, the processes of democratization and state-building in Slovenia have not been entirely simultaneous. The former has been much more gradual and predictable than the latter. The third important process, the transformation of the economy, has also lagged behind the political transformation, but it has been speeded up by the separation of Slovenia from Yugoslavia. The claim that the post-socialist transformation is a complex set of interrelated but not necessarily temporally harmonized and co-ordinated processes obviously holds true for the transition in Slovenia.

The course of Slovenian democratization has been, at least in some respects, similar to the Hungarian 'negotiated revolution' (Bruszt, 1990) and different from the more revolution-like democratization in Czechoslovakia and in East Germany (Ash, 1990). The first steps towards transformation of the political system were initiated by political nonconformism, which re-emerged at the beginning of the eighties, following its suppression during the seventies. Although it was limited to relatively small groups of intellectuals (mostly social scientists, philosophers and writers) the political nonconformism profoundly influenced the political discussions with two radically new sets of ideas - that the socialist system could not be reformed, but that it should be transformed by following the example of Western democracies and that in the course of this transformation the position of Slovenia in the Yugoslav federal state should be redefined in favour of more autonomy.[3] The influence of new ideas was enhanced by the indecisive reaction of the Slovenian political elite, which faced an increased erosion of legitimacy. The attempts to retain some public support compelled the ruling elite to adopt an increasingly conciliatory stance towards the new ideas and their proponents. Thus, at the end of the eighties a basic consensus about the further course of democratization and autonomization was achieved without any formal negotiations between the new political actors and the old political elite. This consensus enabled the transformation of diffusely organized nonconformism to legalized political opposition, and its differentiation into different political parties, on the one hand, and the transformation of the Party to a party on the other. This development culminated in the democratic election in spring 1990 which led to the reversal of the main political roles. Although at the election the former Communist party emerged as the strongest individual party, it was sent into opposition and the parties which grew out of political nonconformism formed the ruling coalition.

The demand for a redefinition of the position of Slovenia within the Yugoslav state strongly influenced the course of Slovenian democratization. As this demand was met by an increasing rejection on the part of other Yugoslav elites - especially of the Serbian one - it facilitated the emergence of the basic consensus on the agenda of democratization among all political forces in Slovenia. Nevertheless, the outside pressure did not prevent a gradual formation of a relatively differentiated political scene. Once accepted by all political actors, the idea of autonomy was no longer an important political issue and the political conflicts increasingly focused on internal problems, especially on the modalities of economic transformation, at the beginning of the nineties.

Another circumstance which facilitated the political differentiation and formation of a 'normal' spectrum of political parties was the ethnic homogeneity of Slovenian society.[4] There were no structural preconditions in Slovenia to organize political parties on an ethnic basis. In the absence of institutionalized negotiating mechanisms at the federal level, and amidst growing tensions among the proponents of centralization and decentralization of the Yugoslav state, the break-away option prevailed in Slovenia in 1990. Although some preparatory steps were taken before the proclamation of independence in 1991, the new state was confronted both with the problem of internal consolidation and accommodation to the new political and economic environment. Thus, the proclamation of independence signalled the transition from the 'heroic' phase of democratization, which was characterized by grand political decisions, such as the scrapping of the authoritarian political order, the proclamation of independence, and broad consensus to the 'prosaic' one (Bernik, 1994, pp. 123-130). The political events, especially the perturbations on the political scene, have shown that the prosaic problems have sometimes been much more divisive and difficult to solve than the ones with historic flair.

On the basis of this brief account of democratization in Slovenia and in the analytical framework presented in the previous section the leading hypotheses of our study of political culture in Slovenia can be explicated. The first one regards the relationship between the pace of democratization and the configuration of political culture. It can be hypothesised that the gradual and rather consensual democratization enabled the formation of a political culture supportive of democratic institutions and procedures. To put it concisely, it is to be expected that authoritarian attitudes are on the decline, whereas libertarian attitudes are growing. This hypothesis also suggests that no indicators of pronounced anomie are to be expected, but at the same time a highly consistent political culture cannot be envisaged because the transition is far from being completed. Given the important redistributive role of the socialist state, one may assume that large parts of the population will support an active role for the state in securing social welfare.

The second hypothesis is related to the role of nationalist sentiments in the process of democratization. It may be assumed that because of the strong interdependence between democratization and state-building the role of these sentiments has been significant. Nevertheless, one can also expect that their role has been declining following the completion of the 'heroic' phase of democratization. This means that attitudes towards the new international environment are to be characterized by high levels of openness. They should differ sharply from attitudes towards the former environment, i.e. the Yugoslav federal state, which were obviously characterized by a high level of ethnocentrism. Thus it can be hypothesised that one of the important aspects of change in the political culture is the growing importance of attitudes supporting the inclusion of Slovenia in processes of European integration.

Finally, because of the relatively slow pace of transformation and high levels of consensus on both democratization and state-building, it may be hypothesized that the majority of the Slovenian population has not only adapted to the new political order but also accepted it as legitimate. This implies that the support for democracy should be largely unconditional and thus independent of its immediate economic and social effects. If this hypothesis proves to be true, it may be argued that the new political order has already reached a relatively high level of consolidation (see Linz, 1990, pp. 157-160) and that Slovenia has entered - at least as far as political order is concerned - the post-transitional stage.

These hypotheses are conceived as guiding hypotheses and our analysis should provide an assessment of their empirical relevance. This means that no definite answers to the questions implied in these hypotheses are to be expected. There are at least two reasons for the fact that the results of our analysis will be relatively modest. The first is related to the fact that the transformation of political culture is a long-term process; that is why it would be premature to come to any far-reaching conclusions on the basis of present studies. The second is related to the quality of empirical data on the transformation of political culture in Slovenia. There is a long tradition of opinion research in Slovenia, but, of course, most of the data collected by opinion surveys are related to a 'mass response' to the societal changes (see Rose and Haerpfner, 1994, p. 3).[5] These data provide an important insight into the change of attitudes of respondents towards the political system, but they are not systematic and thorough enough to enable validation of complex hypotheses regarding the transformation of the political culture. Because they mainly concentrate on political attitudes, they cannot provide information on all aspects of political culture, which also consists of values and expectations (Meyer, 1993, p. 3; Street, 1994, p. 107). Moreover, our data do not provide enough information on those aspects of political culture which can be considered as 'deeper' than attitudes and more invariable. We hope, nevertheless, that this study will provide some basic information about the state of political culture in Slovenia and indicate which questions should especially be focused on in future research.

Do democracy and the market make a difference?

The first aspect of the 'mass response' to the political and economic transformation which is relevant from the point of view of our analysis is related to the question of how the differences between the old and new order are perceived by the respondents. The data on the perceptions of these differences can provide us with some rough information on the mass support for the new order and on the basis for this support, provided that there is any.

Recent Slovenian opinion surveys indicate that respondents perceive both the new political system and economic system to be preferable to the old ones. Asked to evaluate the differences between the socialist economic system and the emerging market system on a scale running from +100 to

-100, in a 1994 survey the respondents 'marked' the old regime with one positive point and the new one with 4.3 positive points. Most critical towards the old economic regime were the respondents with the highest levels of education, whereas the positive evaluation of the new one is higher among the younger respondents. As far as the political system is concerned, the differences in evaluation are more pronounced. In the same survey the old political regime was ascribed 14.8 negative points, whereas the new one scored 9.8 positive points. It is worth noting that in 1992 the evaluation of the old regime was less negative (minus eight points) and the new one less favourable (plus 3.5 points). Both the negative attitudes towards the old political system and those favourable towards the new one are positively correlated with the educational level of the respondents.

The perceived differences between the old and new political and economic order are smaller than one may expect on the basis of our previous claim that the transition in Slovenia was necessitated by the declining legitimacy of the old system and a broad national consensus on the agenda of radical changes. These findings are complemented by the data gathered by annual surveys in the last ten years. Although substantial changes occurred in this period, the data show no clear break in the evaluation of the performance of the economic and political systems. The surveys show that since 1984 more than 60 per cent of the respondents perceived that the economic situation had deteriorated in comparison with the situation about five years ago; this percentage has remained almost unchanged even after the first free election and the ensuing economic transformations. In 1984, 24 per cent of respondents felt that the decision-making processes were getting less democratic than before. This percentage grew slightly in the next few years to decline in 1990 to 18.6 per cent. But in the following years it rose again to reach 25.9 per cent in 1993. The share of those who believed that the law is less respected than before reached its peak in 1988 (37.2 per cent), declined in following years and grew again up to 33.6 per cent in 1993. In this context it is also worth noting that after the first democratic election in 1990 the share of those who believed that an ordinary citizen did not have enough opportunities to influence important decisions remained on the level which was characteristic of the eighties (about 60 per cent).[6]

Although the stability of the data regarding the evaluation of the 'day-by-day' performance of the political and economic systems is, at least partly, due to the growing aspirations of the respondents, these data show that the perceived differences between the old and new system are surprisingly small. It seems that the gradual and consensual transition to democracy and market economy has prevented the majority of the population from perceiving differences between the old and new order - and also from evaluating the latter as clearly superior. This conclusion can be relativized by the data related to the respondents' evaluation of the expected performance of the new economic and political system in the near future, i.e. in five years time. Compared with the evaluation of their present performance, the evaluation of their prospects is clearly positive. According to the 1994 survey, both political and economic systems were ascribed - on the same scale as above - 29.9 positive points.[7] The most optimistic were highly educated respondents.

These data unambiguously show that in the perception of respondents the difference between the old system and the present functioning of the new one is less pronounced than the difference between the current performance of the new system and its prospects. In other words, the democratic political system and market economy are, according to respondents, worth believing in not so much because of their present benefits but because of their potential which will be realized in the near future. If we accept Rose and Haerpfner's proposition that 'as long as the level of approval of the future remains higher than of the past, then this will be a sign of the popular support for the market economy (or democratic system, respectively)' (Rose and Haerpfner, 1994, p. 16), then the above data can be understood as an unambiguous indicator of the respondents' support for both the new political and economic order. Nevertheless, before accepting such a far-reaching conclusion it seems necessary to examine on what expectations the respondents' positive evaluation of the future of the new order are based.

The basis of support for democracy

The optimistic evaluation of the future of democracy in Slovenia suggests that the respondents have a relatively clear notion of democracy and its benefits. The data from the 1991 survey do not speak unanimously in favour of this supposition; up to 40 per cent of respondents on lower educational ranks chose the 'don't know' option in responding to the question whether and how strongly political freedom, social equality, equality before the law, reduction of unemployment, improvement of economic conditions and a multiparty system were related to the democratic political order. Nevertheless, more than 50 per cent of all respondents saw the above items strongly or at least significantly related to democracy. Most of the respondents (76.1 per cent) saw political freedom as an indispensable ingredient of democracy. Political freedom was followed by a multiparty system, equality before the law, improvement of economic conditions and a reduction of unemployment (61.2 per cent and 60.2 per cent respectively), whereas only 52 per cent of them saw social equality related to democracy.

If we leave aside the fact that about 15 per cent of the respondents chose the 'don't know' option, it could be argued that the popular notion of democracy includes a rather pragmatic understanding of the concept. In this perspective, democracy is viewed as an effective means for providing for the economic and social well-being of the citizens. This understanding of democracy is congruent with the relatively high expectations regarding the future performance of the new economic and political system, mentioned in the previous section. It seems that these expectations are based on the assumption that it is only a question of time for democracy to demonstrate its practical benefits. Instrumental understanding of democracy has also clear evaluative implications - in this perspective democracy is worth believing in because it promises an improvement of economic and social well-being. In other words, the instrumental understanding of democracy is intrinsically linked to an instrumental acceptance of democracy.

The survey data indicate that the instrumental understanding and acceptance of democracy also imply specific preferences regarding the role of the state in regulating the economic and social processes. In general, the respondents accept the basic principles of a market economy, but they favour a relatively strong regulative role for the state. The comparison of 1989 and 1991 data has shown that the proportion of respondents who favour a strong role for the state in providing social services increased considerably. International comparisons have shown that the attitudes of Slovenian respondents towards the regulative role of the state are basically similar to the attitudes of respondents from most of the other post-socialist countries, but Slovenians are more inclined than the others to support an active role for the state in reducing income inequalities and securing full employment (Rus, 1992, pp. 51-55).

As already indicated, the prevailing acceptance of the new political order is based on the belief that democracy is a promising, if not the best, way to maximize individual and public well-being.[8] It is obvious that in this case a long-term support for democracy is strongly dependent on the ability of the political system to provide the expected benefits. But if democracy is not able to provide these benefits, an alternative, supposedly more efficient, means can be opted for. Of course, at the time when democracy seems very promising these options are distant. An indication that this possibility is not entirely hypothetical provides the response to the statement that a small number of resolute leaders would contribute to common welfare more than many conferring and debating democrats. In the 1991 survey 50.9 per cent of the respondents agreed with this statement. In the same survey 64.7 per cent of the respondents also approved the statement that it does not matter who rules as long as 'things are going well'. Nevertheless, in general the respondents showed high support for the democratic political system. The prevalence of these attitudes is most obviously demonstrated by the fact that, according to the 1992 survey, 80 per cent of the respondents would oppose abolition of the parliament and of political parties.

This generalized support for democracy is in obvious discrepancy with the findings that both political parties and parliament enjoy a low level of public trust. According to the 1994 survey, of all the most important societal institutions the political parties enjoyed the lowest level of trust and the parliament also ranked low. In general, all institutions which are immediately 'responsible' for economic and social well-being (enterprises, trade unions) and political stability (political parties, government) are at the bottom of the trust scale, whereas the ones which bear less direct responsibility (courts, president of state) are on the top of the scale.[9] These findings can be related to the evaluation of the present and the future state of economy and politics. As shown in the second section, the respondents' evaluation of the current performance of the new economic and political system is relatively low. In consequence, the institutions which are engaged in the day-by-day running of the economy and politics are not highly trusted. But a low level of trust in the key institutions of the new system does not imply that the system itself is put into question by respondents. The trust in the political system is grounded in the respondents' high expectations about its future performance and not on its perceived present performance. On this basis, the respondents are able to reconcile high general support for the new political system with comparatively low trust in its basic institutions.

This discussion offers at least a preliminary assessment of our first hypothesis. There is ample evidence that the new political and economic systems have been generally accepted by the majority of the population. This also implies that there are no signs of widespread anomie, but the above data show that the attitudes towards the new order are characterized by many inconsistencies. At the same time, the data do not support the claim that the slow pace of transformation has been an important factor conducive to the formation of general support for the new order. The data presented so far do not indicate that the existence of relatively broad support for the new political order necessarily means a prevalence of libertarian attitudes over authoritarian ones. To assess the changes in political culture, it is not enough to establish that a general support exists for the new political order, but it is necessary to explore the basis of this support.[10] Although our claim that the prevailing acceptance of democracy in Slovenia is instrumental needs many clarifications, it indicates, nevertheless, that this type of support for democracy includes some deep contradictions. The most obvious one is that this support can be withdrawn if the democratic system fails to provide the expected benefits and some 'functional alternatives' can be endorsed. That is why the question of whether an instrumental acceptance of democracy necessarily presupposes a clear shift from authoritarian to libertarian attitudes seems very relevant. In the next section, we will try to discuss some aspects of this question.

Old ethnocentrism in new circumstances: The stability of latent authoritarianism

The claim that openness both on the societal and personal level is strongly related to the political democratization and marketization of economy has been extensively theoretically and empirically elaborated in the framework of modernization studies (Sztompka, 1993, pp. 69-78). Having in mind the general findings of these studies, there are good reasons to assume that post-socialist societies will be characterized by an increased tolerance towards internal differences (ideological, ethnic, etc.) and a growing openness towards their relevant social environment. Nevertheless, it would be wrong to expect that the emergence of a democratic political system and the institutional preconditions for a market economy is necessarily paralleled by the emergence or strengthening of attitudes in favour of internal and external openness. As stressed by Evans and Whitefeld (1993, p. 539), this attitude change can be especially difficult in those post-socialist societies which, following their break-off from broader state entities, have embarked on nation-state building. It is to be assumed that the nation-state building might not only slow down the formation of 'modern' attitudes towards internal and external differences, but might even foster the resurgence and strengthening of ethnocentric attitudes. This is why the analysis of these attitudes could provide a good basis to answer some aspects of the question about the stability of an authoritarian orientation in post-socialist societies.

Although the course of the transition to democracy in Slovenia has been strongly influenced by the breakaway from Yugoslavia, we have, nevertheless, assumed that it has not prevented the gradual shift from ethnocentrism towards attitudes of openness. There are at least two factors which make this assumption plausible - the relatively high ethnic homogeneity of Slovenian society which gives little room for internal primordial cleavages on the one hand and the relatively high level of openness (compared with other socialist regimes) of the old regime to Western influences on the other. One should also bear in mind that the breakaway of Slovenia from the federal state was explicitly legitimated by a desire to approach Western standards and to enter the Western forms of integration. In the following paragraphs, we will try to examine whether the assumption about the shift from ethnocentrism to openness can be validated by empirical evidence.

Opinion surveys leave no doubt about the mass support for the change of the position of Slovenia within Yugoslavia. Already in the 1987 survey 59.1 per cent of respondents agreed with the statement that Yugoslav federal republics should have higher levels of autonomy and more than half of them believed that the development opportunities of Slovenia would improve outside Yugoslavia. Nevertheless, the idea of a radical breakaway from Yugoslavia seemed, at that time, still a distant one; in 1988 slightly more than one quarter of respondents agreed that this idea should be taken seriously. In the same year 58.5 per cent of respondents supported the view that for the future economic, political and cultural development of Slovenia it was most important to cooperate with West European societies. This attitude pattern remained relatively stable, only the support for a radical break with Yugoslavia grew steadily; whereas at the beginning of 1990 the majority of respondents still believed that a confederal state was the most viable option, in the second half of the same year the majority of them opted for an independent state. At the same time the respondents indicated that they were not ready to pay a high price for the achievement of this goal; the majority of them were ready to 'work harder', 30 per cent would accept a fall in income and 20 per cent would be ready to fight for independence.[11] Moreover, the majority of them expected that in the longer run the breakaway from the federal state should pay off in an increase in living standards. Of all the respondents, the highest expectations were held by the less educated ones.

These data suggest that the support for a radical break with Yugoslavia was fostered mainly by pragmatic and not 'ideological' considerations. It is fair to assume that the prevalence of pragmatism diminished the role of ethnocentrism in the process of separation from the federal state. Pragmatic attitudes towards the old environment would also facilitate the adaptation to the new environment. Nevertheless, the survey data does not support this conclusion. The period in which the mass support for a radical break with Yugoslavia was gaining ground was also characterized by a growing ethnocentrism; surveys show both growing ethnic distance towards other Yugoslav nations and towards immigrants in Slovenia (Klinar, 1992, pp. 70-76). This indicates that the movement for Slovenian political independence was not based on solely pragmatic considerations, but was also underpinned by strong ethnocentric and xenophobic feelings. The fact that independence was not just a matter of reason but also a matter of heart explains why the endeavours to establish an independent nation-state were met by broad and firm support in Slovenia. But one may claim that after this point (i.e. after the establishing of the Slovenian nation-state in 1991) the ethnocentric and xenophobic attitudes lost their positive functionality and it is to be expected that they have been in decline since then.

Surveys have confirmed this expectation as far as the growth of general attitudes of openness towards the new international environment is concerned. In a 1994 survey about 70 per cent of respondents believed that Slovenia should follow the West European model. Almost the same percentage of the respondents (64.7 per cent) would also support Slovenian membership of the European Union. But more precisely formulated questions shed some doubt on the depth and consistency of these attitudes. It is worth noting that 60 per cent of respondents supported the statement that Slovenian independence was more important than the prospective benefits of integration into Europe and nearly the same percentage of them also agreed that Slovenia should organize its own defence, even when this led to additional costs. These replies indicate that the attitudes of openness towards the new situation melt down when the openness, in the opinion of the respondents, could endanger national sovereignty and its symbols.[12] Although respondents on higher education levels showed more openness, their attitudes did not differ substantially from the attitudes of other respondents.

Two explanations of these attitudes seem plausible. The first one is based on the assumption that political sovereignty is perceived by the majority of Slovenians as a guarantee of future improvement in economic and social well-being. That is the main reason for the obvious inconsistencies in their attitudes toward the new international environment; on the general level openness is perceived as an undisputed value, but when related to specific problems this attitude is 'profaned' and relativized by pragmatic calculations. In effect, openness is accepted as an undisputed value as far as it promises clear benefits. The second explanation views these inconsistencies as a sign of latent xenophobia which is not directed solely to the old environment but also to the new one. This explanation suggests that the acceptance of openness as an abstract value is repudiated on the practical level not only because of its possible disadvantages but also because it conflicts with deeply entrenched ethnocentric attitudes.

Although the opinion surveys provide no conclusive data, there is some evidence which speaks in favour of the second explanation. Almost 70 per cent of the respondents in the 1994 survey agreed with the statement that Slovenians should prefer buying Slovenian products and 65 per cent of them believed that Slovenian agriculture should be protected from foreign competition - even at the cost of higher prices for agricultural products. These attitudes are not limited just to the economic sphere, they also prevail in the sphere of ethnic relationships. The majority of respondents (63.7 per cent) believed that one should be cautious and reserved in contacts even with friendly disposed nations. The xenophobic attitudes were even more pronounced when the respondents were asked about their attitudes towards minorities in Slovenia. In the 1993 survey, 70.8 per cent of respondents entirely or mostly agreed with the statement that in a situation of growing unemployment the immigrants should be made redundant first. Almost the same number of respondents also agreed that the legal procedures for granting Slovenian citizenship to immigrants should be reviewed - and some already granted citizenship have it withdrawn. Finally, 43 per cent of respondents supported the idea that people should take things into their own hands if the state would not protect the interest of native Slovenians. The lowest level of ethnocentric and xenophobic attitudes was to be found amongst the younger respondents and the highly educated ones.

Although the available data are not thorough and systematic, they show that the emergence of broad support for the democratic political system in Slovenia has not been paralleled by any substantial shift in the attitudes regarding ethnocentrism and xenophobia. It is obvious that support for democracy can coexist with attitudes having clear authoritarian connotations and that general support for democratic rules does not necessarily exclude the endorsement of discriminatory measures towards ethnic or other minorities. The data also indicate that these attitudes show a high level of resistance to change. The levels of ethnocentrism and xenophobia which were found by the surveys in the late eighties have been also found in more recent surveys (see Klinar, 1994, pp. 44-46).

The data presented in this section provide additional support for our claim that the political culture in Slovenia is characterized by many inconsistencies (see also Toš, 1994, pp. 207-217). But they do not validate our hypothesis that the building of a nation-state has been paralleled by a decline of nationalist sentiments. It may be argued that, under the new circumstances, these sentiments have become more covert. At the same time, general attitudes of openness towards the new environment have become more manifest. Nevertheless, the data show that the underlying pattern of attitudes has not changed substantially and that support for openness is mostly based on pragmatic considerations, i.e. the majority of respondents supported it only as far as it 'paid off'. When the respondents perceived that openness towards the new environment could lead to undesired effects, they were ready to resort to ethnocentrism. Whether these attitudes and the ones we discussed in the previous section do form a favourable environment for the stabilization of the democratic political system in Slovenia will be examined in the next, concluding, section.

Conclusion: political culture and political stability

As already indicated, the available data do not allow us to test our guiding hypotheses systematically, but only to assess their empirical relevance. It means that our analysis cannot provide a thorough account of the transformation of political culture in Slovenian society. Nevertheless, it indicates major changes in politically relevant attitudes and enables us to draw some preliminary conclusions about their functions in the stabilization of the new political and economic system.

In general, the data show that in Slovenia the transformation of the political and economic order has not been accompanied either by broad anomie nor by an upsurge of traditional values amounting to the 'civilizational incompetence' of the main social actors. On the contrary, the majority of the population has been able not only to adapt to the systemic change, but also to support it actively. This was partly due to the fact that the slow pace of institutional change has given pro-democratic attitudes ample time to emerge. In other words, the change of politically relevant attitudes has been gradual and thus much more characterized by continuity than a radical break. Taking into account the level of explicit support for the democratic institutions (and new economic institutions alike) one may argue that change in political attitudes has contributed considerably to the consolidation of the new order.

Nevertheless, our analysis also shows that this conclusion has to be qualified in many respects. The most important qualification is related to the fact that our hypothesis stating that the circumstances in Slovenia enabled the development of relatively unconditional support for the new political order has not been confirmed. As shown in the third section, the framework of support for the new political order is an instrumental acceptance of democracy. Democracy is highly valued by the majority of the population because it is perceived as the best way of promoting individual economic and social well-being. If the difference between values and interests is in the fact that the former enable people to distinguish 'right' from 'wrong' behaviour and situations and the latter to distinguish what is 'advantageous' or 'disadvantageous' (see Smelser, 1994, p. 155), our analysis shows that there is a high degree of parallelism between both aspects, i.e. the new political order is believed to be right because it is perceived as at least potentially advantageous. Or to put it more directly, the support for the democratic regime has been much more a matter of 'rational choice' than of 'moral choice'. The main paradox of this type of support for democracy is that it can, in certain circumstances, put heavy strains on the political system which can eventually lead to its destabilization. It is the essence of conditional support for a political system that it can be withdrawn when the political system is perceived as not sufficiently efficient in fulfilling expectations.

It cannot be overlooked that the main paradox of the instrumental acceptance of democracy is related to the high expectations it generates. In other words, this type of acceptance implies a specific notion about the functions of democracy. This is well reflected in the fact that the Slovenian respondents ascribe to the political system broad prerogatives in regulating the economy, especially in ameliorating its deficiencies such as unemployment or high income inequalities. The respondents obviously prefer a system which has been aptly termed 'political capitalism' (Offe, 1990, p. 284), i.e. capitalism which is stimulated or kept under control by political intervention. Thus, the democratic system is related to expectations which could largely extend beyond its capacities. In these circumstances, to retain mass support, 'new democracies need efficiency - particularly in the economic arena, but also in the polity' (Lipset, 1994, p. 17). But the question remains, whether they command the resources needed for high efficiency.

The second qualification of the claim that changes in political attitudes have significantly contributed to the consolidation of the new political system is related to the inconsistencies in the political culture. Some aspects of these inconsistencies are already included in the preference for 'political capitalism'. This preference combines support for the basic institutions of the market economy and relatively strong 'statist' attitudes, i.e. the broad economic prerogatives of the state are not seen by respondents as incompatible with the principles of a market economy. Moreover, the strong regulative role of the state is seen as desirable as long as it promotes individual well-being and upholds certain standards of social justice.[13] But these two expectations, i.e. expectations regarding economic well-being and those regarding the implementation of social justice standards are not easy to reconcile - especially in less affluent societies.

Another, even more important, inconsistency is generated by the fact that attitudes of general support for democracy are not 'followed up' by changes in other politically relevant attitudes. Our analysis of attitudes related to inter-ethnic relations has shown a high persistence of ethnocentric and xenophobic attitudes in Slovenia. The stability of these attitudes is in obvious contrast to the high flexibility of the population as far as active support for the new political system is concerned. In other words, our analysis has not confirmed the claim that general support for democracy is, as a rule, related to growing tolerance towards social differences and growing openness towards the international environment. One cannot help asking whether the persistence of these attitudes does not diminish the importance of overt support for democracy - even leading to the long-term destabilization of the democratic political order. The latter is related to the possibility that the authoritarian values which constitute the background of ethnocentric and xenophobic attitudes would encourage support for authoritarian solutions when democratic solutions are perceived as inefficient.

To conclude, there are, as far as political culture is concerned, two general factors which can influence the stability of democracy in Slovenia - the conditional acceptance of democracy and internal inconsistencies in politically relevant attitudes. As already indicated, the way that democracy is accepted may make support for the new political order volatile just when it could need strong 'moral' support, and the existence of latent authoritarianism could render other (i.e. non-democratic) options attractive. Although one has to consider these possibilities, it would be wrong to argue that these factors should sooner or later lead to the destabilization of the new political system or even to the restoration of the old regime.[14] Our analysis provides no evidence in favour of the claim that a high degree of congruency between political culture and political system is a necessary precondition for a democratic political system to achieve its consolidation. It seems that the functioning of a democratic political system is not directly dependent on its cultural environment and that the emphasis on cultural determinism, which is characteristic of most political culture studies, is not justified. In other words, the influence of political culture on the consolidation of the democratic political system seems to be mediated by many contextual factors which are out of the scope of political culture research.

Notes

1. It seems that the question of whether the 'notion of political culture actually provides a good basis for explaining what happens in the political process' (Street, 1993, p. 105) also belongs to the list of the key questions of political culture theory. But Street's analysis indicates that there are no disagreements about the general answer to this question. Of course, there are disagreements about the modalities of influence of political culture on political structures.
2. In retrospect, this discussion seems to be by far the most valuable contribution to the study of political culture in the former Yugoslav society. There were also other theoretical and empirical studies of political culture, but almost all of them were limited to the question of to what extent the official 'political culture of self-managerial socialism' permeated the masses (see Lukšič, 1992, pp. 16-20).
3. Although the political nonconformism was necessitated by internal circumstances, the nonconformist ideology was strongly shaped by external influences. Even the demands for Slovenian autonomy in Yugoslavia, and later for independence, were legitimated as a necessary step to join processes of transnational integration in Europe. The key reasons for the strong reliance on foreign examples were the absence of significant pre-socialist democratic traditions and the relative economic and cultural openness of Yugoslavia towards Western societies. In the later stage of democratization, there were attempts by some political parties to stress their allegiance to pre-socialist political tradition. But the long period of political discontinuity and a radical change of social structure (e.g. before the second world war Slovenia was mostly agricultural, now only about ten per cent of the entire population is still active in agriculture) have made these attempts unproductive.
4. According to the 1991 census, 87.7 per cent of inhabitants of Slovenia declared themselves to be ethnic Slovenians. The others were mostly immigrants from the former common federal state.

5. In Slovenia, annual opinion surveys on a representative nationwide sample (Slovenian Public Opinion) have been conducted without interruption since 1968 by the Institute for Public Opinion and Mass Media Research at the Faculty of Social Science in Ljubljana. Our analysis will be based on the data collected by these surveys.

6. Between 1968 and 1989 the respondents were asked whether the policy of the Party was congruent with the interests of the majority of Slovenian population. Only in the last year (1989) was the percentage of those who believed that it is entirely or at least partially congruent slightly under 50 per cent, whereas in all previous years their share was above this mark. Moreover, in the first half of the eighties, about 75 per cent of respondents believed that the Party served the interests of people fairly well. If the responses to this question are taken as a rough measure of the legitimacy of the old political regime, one may argue that it enjoyed a relatively stable and high level of popular support - even in the initial period of democratization. This reflects the ability of the old Slovenian political elite to adapt to the changing situation and to defend, on the federal level, the interests which were perceived by the majority as legitimate Slovenian national interests.

7. In the New Democracies Barometer, a comparative survey conducted in 1991 and 1992, Slovenian respondents were amongst those who most highly evaluated the economic and political prospects of their respective countries in five years time (see Rose and Haerpfner, 1994).

8. This claim implies that at least in Slovenia the primary source of the mass dissatisfaction with the old regime and support for its abolition was its declining economic performance and not its authoritiarian political nature. The data on growing dissatisfaction about the state of the economy since 1984 and on relatively stable mass acceptance of the Party's policy support this claim.

9. These data are roughly similar to the data from Czech Republic, Slovakia, Hungary and Poland (see Rose and Haerpfner, 1994, p. 18). Only in the cases of the church and the army are there some obvious differences. The church, that is highly trusted in all the above countries, except the Czech Republic, is in Slovenia among the less trusted institutions. The army is better regarded than the church, but is not at the top of the Slovenian trust scale.

10. The importance of differentiating between these two questions is aptly demonstrated by R.J. Dalton's study of political culture in the former East Germany. The 1990 survey 'finds a broad similarity in the democratic attitudes of West Germans and East Germans' (Dalton, 1994, p. 477), but a close examination of the basis of East German pro-democratic attitudes shows that 'support for democratic norms is strongly linked to the lure of Western affluence and the perceived demise of the GDR economy' (Dalton, 1994, p. 491).

11. It is worth noting that only 8.6 per cent of respondents believed that the impending disintegration of Yugoslavia would end in violence and war. After the Slovenian breakaway the great majority of respondents (78.5 per cent) would again have supported this decision even if they had known that this act would have led to a short violent conflict and economic troubles. This decisiveness is in sharp contrast with the cautious mood before the proclamation of independence. This twist of mood has been undoubtedly related to the fact that the costs of independence have been relatively low.

12. It is possible to note an interesting parallelism between the attitudes towards the old and the new environment; there has been, on the one hand, strong support for reducing all those contacts with the former federal state which could limit Slovenian autonomy and, on the other hand, support for intensification of those links with the new international environment which Slovenian sovereignty can 'tolerate'.

13. This is not to say that this discrepancy is a characteristic of Slovenian political culture only. It is to be expected that it can be found not only in other post-socialist societies,

but also in well established democracies. It is also not necessarily the case that it has detrimental effects on the stability of the democratic political order.

14.   It is highly unlikely that new authoritarianism, which would be made manifest because of the perceived economic and social inefficiency of the democratic order, would imply support for the re-establishment of the old system. It would mean opting for a system from which support was withdrawn just because of its inability to provide the expected economic and social benefits.

Appendix to Chapter 5[1]

Table 5.1   Respondent's assessment of economic and political system in Slovenia

(mean score on -100.........+100 scale)
-100 lowest scale
+100 highest score

	1992	1994
socialist economic system	-7.6	1.1
present economic system	-32.7	4.3
economic system 5 years from now	28.7	29.9
socialist political system	-8.1	-14.8
present political system	3.5	9.8
political system 5 years from now	37.2	29.9

Table 5.2   How would you evaluate the democratic nature of the decision-making process compared to the situation five years ago?
(% response)
(all interpretations refer to 4+5 sums)

1 - now much better
2 - now better
3 - the same
4 - now worse
5 - now much worse
9 - don't know

	1	2	3	4	5	9
1980	11.7	49.7	20.1	4.4	0.5	13.5
1982	5.5	31.3	36.8	8.1	1.2	17.2
1983	3.2	18.0	40.0	18.9	3.0	16.9
1984	2.0	12.4	43.7	19.1	4.8	18.2
1986	2.5	16.3	44.1	18.5	3.8	14.7
1987	2.5	18.2	34.0	24.9	6.8	13.6
1988	2.6	24.7	26.6	25.6	6.6	13.9
1990	10.2	43.2	16.4	14.8	3.8	11.8
1991	5.6	37.6	19.4	18.8	5.0	13.6
1992	5.8	37.2	18.8	17.5	3.9	16.8
1993	6.6	32.7	17.9	20.6	5.3	16.9

Table 5.3   How would you evaluate respect towards the law compared to the situation five years ago? (% response)
(all interpretations refer to 4+5 sums)

1 - now much better
2 - now better
3 - the same
4 - now worse
5 - now much worse
9 - don't know

	1	2	3	4	5	9
1980	7.7	47.6	23.6	5.9	0.6	14.5
1982	2.2	18.2	42.9	10.9	3.1	22.5
1983	1.2	12.1	43.4	17.5	3.9	22.0
1984	1.2	8.6	47.5	17.1	5.6	19.2
1986	1.0	10.4	46.7	18.0	5.0	18.9
1987	0.6	9.3	38.2	24.5	9.2	18.1
1988	0.7	9.6	34.0	27.8	9.4	18.6
1990	1.9	20.0	36.9	18.5	5.1	17.6
1991	1.3	14.0	36.1	22.1	6.0	20.6
1992	0.8	14.3	35.6	20.1	5.4	23.7
1993	1.0	12.3	28.6	25.1	8.5	24.5

Table 5.4   Does an ordinary citizen have enough opportunity to influence important political decisions? (% response)

	1	2	3	4	5
1983	8.3	26.3	47.3	7.1	11.0
1984	5.4	22.0	53.3	10.5	8.7
1986	7.2	25.0	44.8	14.0	9.0
1990	3.3	16.6	53.8	16.2	10.1

**Table 5.5   How strongly are the following items related to democracy?
(% response)**

1 - strongly related
2 - fairly related
3 - a bit related
4 - not related at all
5 - don't know

	1	2	3	4	5
political freedoms	44.0	32.1	6.6	2.5	14.9
growing social equality	22.0	30.0	22.9	8.0	17.1
political decentralisation (regionalism)	20.0	35.0	16.9	4.1	24.1
fighting corruption	23.6	25.2	19.1	8.9	23.2
moral/sexual freedom	17.2	29.9	21.1	9.3	22.4
equality before law	37.9	28.0	13.7	5.4	15.0
state control over banks and big private enterprises	17.2	27.6	21.9	10.8	22.6
equal rights for women	40.2	30.2	11.5	3.4	14.7
reduction of unemployment	35.4	24.8	16.8	8.7	14.3
improvement of economic situation in the country	36.6	24.8	16.8	7.6	14.3
multi-party system	48.1	24.1	8.7	2.6	16.5

Table 5.6   How do you see the future of Slovenia? (% response)

	January 1990	December 1990
as a Yugoslav federal republic	15.2	5.3
as a part of a Yugoslav confederation	50.2	32.5
as an independent state	23.5	52.3
don't know	11.1	9.8

Survey responses referred to in text (year of survey in brackets). All figures refer to % response

Question 1

A few resolute leaders would contribute to the common welfare more than many conferring and debating democrats (survey 1991)

1 - agree	........................50.9%
2 - disagree	........................49.1%

Question 2

As long as things are going well, I don't really care who is in power (survey 1991)

1 - agree	........................64.7%
2 - disagree	........................30.8%
3 - don't know	.... 4.5%

Question 3

Would you be for or against abolition of parliament and political parties in Slovenia? (survey 1992)

1 - for	........................15.0%
2 - against	........................80.0%

Question 4

How much do you trust the following institutions in Slovenia? (survey 1994)
(mean score on 1.........7 scale)   1. don't trust at all 7. fully trust

- political parties	........................2.77%
- courts	........................4.12%
- police	........................3.91%
- state bureaucracy	........................4.05%
- government	........................3.64%
- army	........................3.81%
- media	........................3.79%
- parliament	........................3.51%
- catholic church	........................3.38%
- trade unions	........................3.23%
- president	........................4.05%
- patriotic societies	........................4.04%
- private enterprises	........................3.35%
- foreign economic counsellor	........................3.48%

Question 5

How should Yugoslavia be arranged in the future? (survey 1987)

1. Yugoslav republics should have
   greater autonomy 59.1%
2. more decisions should be made on federal
   Yugoslav level 8.8%
3. things should remain as they are 18.0%
4. don't know 14.1%

Question 6

What would be in your opinion Slovenia's development opportunities outside Yugoslavia? (survey 1987)

1. no development opportunities for Slovenia
   outside Yugoslavia 18.9%
2. new development opportunities for Slovenia
   outside Yugoslavia 52.9%
3. don't know 28.2%

Question 7

In your opinion, does it make sense to discuss Slovenia's independence in the present situation? (survey 1988)

1. makes sense 28.9%
2. undecided 26.9%
3. makes no sense 44.2%

Question 8

Please choose the most important region for Slovenia to co-operate with, regarding Slovenia's future economic, cultural and political development (survey 1988)

1. Other Yugoslav republics 18.4%
2. Industrialized Western countries 58.5%
3. East European countries 1.7%
4. Developing countries in Asia,
   Africa, Latin America 1.5%
5. Neighbouring countries (Austria, Italy) 10.8%
6. don't know 9.1%

Question 9

Would you personally be prepared to do some of the following to contribute to Slovenia's independence? (survey 1990)
(the percentage of 'Yes' answers for each item)

1. work harder	68.3%
2. suffer drop in living standard	29.5%
3. face poverty, unemployment	6.5%
4. live under stress	6.8%
5. fight for independence	19.5%

Question 10

Which of the two statements do you favour?
(A) Slovenia's development should follow the West-European model
(B) Slovenia's development should be based on its ethnic tradition (survey 1994)

1. strongly in favour of A	34.8%
2. in favour of A	34.6%
3. in favour of B	17.8%
4. strongly in favour of B	12.8%

Question 11

Would you support Slovenia's joining the European Union? (survey 1994)

1. strongly support	17.3%
2. support	57.4%
3. reject	3.1%
4. strongly reject	0.3%
9. don't know	21.9%

Question 12

Slovenians should favour purchasing Slovenian products (survey 1994)

1. strongly agree	38.5%
2. agree	31.2%
3. disagree	23.0%
4. strongly disagree	6.5%
9. don't know	0.8%

Question 13

Slovenian farmers should be protected from foreign competition (survey 1994)

1. strongly agree 29.1%
2. agree 35.8%
3. disagree 24.4%
4. strongly disagree 9.4%
5. don't know 1.4%

Question 14

One should be cautious and reserved towards other nations (survey 1993)

1. strongly agree 19.8%
2. agree 43.9%
3. undecided 12.6%
4. disagree 14.1%
5. strongly disagree 5.9%
9. don't know 3.7%

Question 15

Immigrant workers should be made redundant first in a situation of growing unemployment (survey 1993)

1. strongly agree 38.7%
2. agree 32.1%
3. undecided 12.3%
4. disagree 9.1%
5. strongly disagree 4.3%
9. don't know 3.5%

Question 16

Legal procedures for granting Slovenian citizenship should be reviewed and some already granted citizenship withdrawn (survey 1993)

1. strongly agree 35.5%
2. agree 34.5%
3. undecided 10.8%
4. disagree 8.0%
5. strongly disagree 4.0%
9. don't know 7.1%

Question 17

People should settle things by themselves if the state would not protect the interest of native Slovenians (survey 1993)

1. strongly agree 20.2%
2. agree 22.7%
3. undecided 16.8%
4. disagree 19.4%
5. strongly disagree 11.9%
9. don't know 8.9%

Notes

1.   All data in the paper was obtained from 'Slovenian Public Opinion' data sets and refers to a general national representative sample (N = 1050 +/- 15 cases). The Slovenian Public Opinion survey has been conducted yearly since 1968. The head of the Slovenian Public Opinion project has been, since 1968, Professor Niko Toš.

6 Establishing State Authority

FRANCI GRAD

The status of the republic in the Yugoslav federation

The Yugoslav Federation after 1974 had many unusual aspects which distinguished it from other modern federations. The 1974 constitution in many ways brought the Federation closer to the idea of a confederation in its last period, even though it retained all the general characteristics of the federal state. What is important is the position of the federal union and the relationship within it between the federated units and the federal government. It is in this respect that the Yugoslav Federation differed from other modern federations, since it had highly distinctive confederal elements which were absent or rudimentary in other federations. Those confederal elements included the need for unanimity in the approval of constitutional changes and of laws in the Assemblies of the Republics and Regions; parity of the chambers of the Yugoslav Parliament; parity within the Presidency of the SFRY and some other important federal organs; the inconsistently asserted supremacy of federal law over the laws of the Republics; and the inability of the federal government to assert constitutional supremacy over the Republics.

Some other peculiarities of the federal constitutional order were important for the process of Slovene independence as well as for the disintegration of the Yugoslav Federation as a whole. The basic relationship between the Republics and the Federation was defined in such a way that the Republic was the residual bearer of state authority and the Federation's powers rested on the authority invested in it by the federal constitution.

The federal constitution had undergone changes according to the consensus of all the Republics (and autonomous regions). The position of the Republics in relation to the Federation was constitutionally affirmed on the one hand but, on the other, this principle could be interpreted in such a way that the Federation was not the source of authority which delegated powers to federal units, but that its own authority was derived from the original authority of the Republics on the basis of the federal constitution.

The debatable nature of the Federation was accentuated in the basic principles of the Yugoslav Constitution of 1974, which explicitly emphasized that the Yugoslav Federation was formed by the voluntary and consensual union of the Yugoslav nations, and resulted from these nations' right to self-determination, and included the nations' right to secede. The right of self-determination of a nation and the right to secede were the main arguments which supported the thesis that the consensual formation of the Yugoslav Federation was not only relevant to its foundation, but also in the same manner to any possible secession.[1] The right of secession (*ius secessionis*) is characteristic of confederal and not of federal provisions, and this right was one of the most important confederal elements in the Yugoslav federal regulations.

In spite of the fact that during the existence of the Yugoslav Federation there was a large gap between the normative provisions of the constitution and the realities of the current conditions, these confederal elements made the independence process of the individual Republics much easier, when political and economic conditions in Yugoslavia called for it (Jambrek, 1992; Ribičič, 1992). These provisions enabled the formation of statehood by the Republics from within the legal federal constitutional regulations, which was of great importance for the later formation of completely independent states. It became evident that the Federation, except for the federal army, did not have any means to prevent the independence of the Republics.

The process of Slovene independence

From the beginning, the main characteristic of the process of Slovene independence was the view that the process should be legally established and regulated. This resolution was of great importance not only for the establishment of relations with the Yugoslavian Federation but also for the legitimacy of the process itself in the eyes of the world. During the Slovene independence process many acts of a 'legal constitutional' nature were adopted, providing the constitutional foundation for the independence process.[2] These acts defined in a legal form the Republic's different levels of independence and its separation from the federal legal order and federal state organization. These acts were neither the acts of an independent state nor were they the acts of the federal body and that is why their legal constitutional nature is sometimes not clear.

The first steps toward independence were made by the Republic of Slovenia (formally and by declaration) within the framework of valid federal constitutional regulations, even though individual constitutional solutions deviated from the nature of the federal regulations. The first serious conflicts with the federal state appeared during the acceptance of changes to the federal constitution between the years 1987 and 1988. The first tendencies towards the democratization of the political system in Yugoslavia had started a few years earlier, while at the same time the federal government showed a tendency towards greater centralization. These trends became more obvious during the process of the acceptance of the federal constitutional amendments in 1988, which Slovenia opposed. Slovenia based its legal position on the fact that the lack of consensus on the constitutional changes prevented their acceptance.

After the imposition of the federal amendments, during the period when the acceptance procedure of the Republican constitutional changes took place, relations between the Slovene and federal governments became more and more strained due to the increasing democratization of political life in Slovenia and the resulting demands for basic changes to all social regulations. Similar procedures were not found in other Republics, but there were demands for political change expressed through a so-called anti-bureaucratic revolution, which led only to the replacement of some people in high positions though not to changes in the political system as a whole. All this distanced Slovenia even more from the other Republics. At the same time, in Slovenia the movement towards independence started to appear and the disturbances in the other Republics made this movement even stronger. The federal government threatened, with varying degrees of concealment, that they would re-establish order in the Republic. This created a suspicion that it would invoke the common interest of all the Republics and that they would claim to be acting within the framework of the valid federal constitutional provisions.

The Slovene authorities based their position on specific legal constitutional provisions. These were the amendments to the Republican Constitution which were accepted in 1988, especially the LXII amendment (and the related XLVI amendment) and the LXIII amendment. It was stated in the first of these amendments that the Republican Assembly is obliged to protect the constitutional position of the Republic when and if the federal organs interfere with their decisions contrary to their constitutionally regulated competencies. This is the so-called claim for the nullification of federal decisions (*ius nullificationis*), which is characteristic of a confederation but not a federation. The second amendment also contains the right of nullification and it states that without the agreement of the Republican Assembly of that Republic, a state of emergency cannot possibly be decreed. These constitutional solutions were not on the whole formally congruent with the federal constitutional provisions but were, as a response, understandable, given the circumstances inside the federation. The Slovene authorities tried to secure the position of the Republic before the centralists threatened it constitutionally because it had no power to interpret the federal constitution in the way that it had the Republican Constitution. The constitution could not give an absolute guarantee against federal authority, but the constitutional structure of the federal authority and the division of functions between the federal state and the Republic prevented the federal authorities from asserting the superiority of the federal over the Republican constitution by any legal means.

The situation during this time was contradictory because, on the one hand, there was, normatively speaking, the independence of the federal unit inside of the Yugoslav Federation, which was much greater than that of any other comparable modern federation and, on the other hand, the circumstances were at the point where there were no guarantees from the federal authority that it would actually act in accordance with the constitutional regulations.

Further decisions on the constitutional path of independence for Slovenia more or less followed from these starting points. At first sight, from the federal relationship point of view, the less important constitutional change in amendment XCI, which was accepted in the spring of 1990, with the word 'socialist' being eliminated from the name of the federal unit, meant direct opposition to the valid federal constitutional order which still proclaimed the socialist social system valid for the entire state. Thus, the above mentioned constitutional change allowed for the introduction of a completely different political system inside the Republic which was incompatible with the rest of the federation. The constitutional changes were the result and at the same time the consolidation of the process of democratization of the political system in Slovenia which reached its peak with multi-party elections. That was reason enough for political life as well as political regulations in Slovenia at that time to differ significantly from positions in other Republics, and it was no longer possible to talk about a unified political system throughout Yugoslavia.

The transfer of authority during the elections in the spring of 1990 was of great importance and perhaps even crucial for the future development of relations between the Republic and the federal state. The elections themselves, which were multi-party, were a crucial change in the political order, and not only in political life itself. Political forces which sought the complete change of the social order came to power. They wished for a complete or at least greater independence of the Republic in relation to the federation and accelerated the process towards independence after assuming power. Points of view concerning the method of gaining independence differed significantly. The question was: should the Slovene state simply take over the state functions of the federal state or should this process of assuming authority be legally regulated and grounded? The principle which emphasized the importance of an adequate legal basis in the process of independence prevailed. This was promoted as the only way to achieve statehood with a valid legal order. This meant that every new step on the path to independence needed to be legally grounded and protected by legal means. The new authority took over the extant system and directed it towards the realization of independence through changes to the Republic's constitution which became progressively more radical.

The acceptance of the XCVI amendment to the Republic's constitution in the autumn of 1990 was very important for relations with the Federation.

The amendment used the right of nullification as a starting point concerning relations between the Republic and the Federation, which had been very limited in the previous amendments of 1989. It stated that in the Republic of Slovenia, any constitutional provisions of the SFRY which were not in accordance with the constitution of the Republic of Slovenia were not valid, and that in the future federal laws were valid in the Republic of Slovenia only when the Republic's Assembly approved. The pre-existing federal laws explicitly stated which provisions did not apply to the Republic of Slovenia. The Republic itself did not break off relations with the federation - it placed them on a different ground. An unregulated and undefined situation - legally speaking - arose; on one hand the Federation persisted in asserting the pre-existing valid federal relationship based on the federal constitution, while the Republic on the other hand persisted in the relationship which the Republic itself had created, and within which it still considered itself formally a part of the Yugoslav Federation.

What that actually meant was that the Republic recognized federal authority only to the degree that it was still in accord with the political processes in Slovenia. This was the starting point for the formation of the independent Slovene state and its own legal order. A large gap between the normative and actual situation resulted because the federal system was still operating on the territory of the Republic regardless of the will of the Republican authorities and was, through its agencies, still supervising some federal operations. The Republican authority was unable to prevent that at that time.

Negotiations on the formation of a Yugoslav confederation took place at the same time. This suggestion was proposed by Slovenia and Croatia, but in the other Republics and in the federal organs there was a counter-proposal for a more centralized federation. As a result, an agreed dissolution of the Yugoslav federation was not expected and consequently the Slovene authorities decided to follow their own path, supported by the decision of the Slovene people in a plebiscite.

In the plebiscite, held on 23 December 1990, the people of Slovenia voted to become an independent and autonomous state. After the plebiscite Slovenia's constitutional relation to the Federation was even more radically restructured. All ties with the Yugoslav federation were broken off at the constitutional level (in principle). The XCIX amendment, adopted at the beginning of 1991, declared that functions which had been assigned to the Federation by the federal constitution should be taken over by the Republic in addition to its existing functions.

The Republic of Slovenia legally seceded from the Federation with this amendment, but this constitutional resolution was not immediately put into effect. The amendment included a temporary provision which allowed the Republic of Slovenia to regulate relations with the other Republics of the SFRY and with the organs of the SFRY in the framework of the valid pre-existing regulations.

The XCIX amendment was not so radical concerning the organization of the state because it did not interfere with the cooperation of the Republican representatives in the federal organs of authority. It is clear that the Republic kept its representatives in the federal organs because it was still dependent to a large degree on the federal state and the federal legal order and wanted to continue its involvement in federal decisions.

Regardless of this, the final assumption of the state functions of the federation was in principle already achieved, and Slovenian independence was effectively accomplished - even though it was not declared as such. In reality it was impossible to carry out these fundamental decisions. The federal government was still very strong and the processes of independence had barely begun in the other Republics. That is why some time had to pass before the actual application of these fundamental decisions. It was expected that political conditions in the other Republics would change, bringing about the collapse of federal authority. In these circumstances the authority of the Republic could be consolidated and enforced. This strategy was extremely hazardous because it relied on expectations rather than certainties.

The Law on Plebiscites (Official Record of the Republic of Slovenia, No. 44/90) stated that the Republican assembly must accept any constitutional and other acts and measures necessary for realizing independence within six months from the day of the proclamation of the decision of the plebiscite. In accordance with this law, the Republican assembly passed a few acts of a constitutional nature and importance by the end of that term and with these acts it confirmed the Republic of Slovenia on a legal basis as an independent and autonomous state and at the same time carried out the declared legal separation from the Yugoslav Federation. The act entitled 'The basic constitutional document concerning the independence and autonomy of the Republic of Slovenia' was passed. Slovenia was proclaimed an independent and autonomous state for which the constitution of the SFRY was no longer valid. In accordance with this, Slovenia assumed all of the claims and duties which had been delegated by the constitution of the Republic of Slovenia and those previously granted by the constitution of the SFRY to the organs of the SFRY.

In order to carry out this restructuring, a basic document of constitutional law was accepted which in detail regulated the way in which state functions in different areas of society would be taken over, and which until then had been regulated by the Federation through its own organs. The transfer of federal legislative functions to the Republic was readily achievable but in relation to the executive functions a smooth transition depended on the co-operation of the federal authorities, which were patently hostile.

Consequently, a state of emergency was declared according to provisions established earlier by the XCIX amendment though not previously invoked. This marked the culminating stage in detaching the Republic from the Federation. Henceforth, relations between the two entities were regarded as being between two independent states engaged in external relations rather than components of a federation re-negotiating their relationship.

The acceptance of the new constitution

Having asserted its independence, it was thought essential for the establishment of a new legal and constitutional order that the Republic of Slovenia should adopt a new constitution. The constitution it had inherited was no longer in accord with social developments. It was additionally derived from the constitution of a federal unit and not of a unitary state. Many areas were not legally regulated on a suitable basis without involving disputes about interpretation. The existing constitution also presumed very different political conditions. On symbolic as well as practical grounds it was necessary to provide an entirely new set of legal and state forms.

The direction of political developments in Slovenia made it clear that the new constitution should take as a guide comparable constitutional provisions around the world, especially in Western Europe. The existing constitution was a singular one geared to the specific conditions of the Yugoslav Federation and was quite inappropriate to the new circumstances of Slovenia. It was decided that formulation and adoption of a new constitution should follow the procedure which was prescribed for changing the previous constitution. There was a certain element of continuity between it and the new constitution.

The basic concern in the preparation of the new constitution was that it should not be ideological and that it must strictly and according to international legal standards regulate constitutional rights and privileges, and in the area of state regulations must be based on the principle of the separation of powers. It was clear that when preparing the draft of the constitution it would be necessary to be guided by the constitutions of other democratic states, especially the ones which belonged to the same cultural tradition as Slovenia. At the same time the special nature of the Slovene situation and its traditions had to be taken into account and that is why a mere mechanical adoption of foreign models was not possible (Jambrek, 1992b).

The most significant departure from the previous constitution concerned the regulation of state power. The old constitution had been regulated according to the specificities of the socialist self-management system and so differed substantially from other modern formulations. The assemblies as the representative organs at the Republic level and the local regional governments were composed of three chambers, designed so that each of them represented some special social interest, and, as a result, legislatures as a whole were not considered properly representative of the entire population.

During the post-war period in Yugoslavia (including Slovenia) the constitutional principle of the unity of authority was put into effect to a greater or lesser degree, and this principle was strongly supported in practice by a system which transferred actual power from the assemblies to their executive councils even though power was formally allocated to the assembly. This arrangement persisted in Slovenia until the enactment of the new Slovene constitution, and was one of the most important factors in that period's constitutional regulation. It is not surprising that it was subjected to strong criticism during the discussions on the new constitution.

Instead of the principle of unity of authority, the new demand was for the separation of powers. From the very beginning of the formulation of the new Slovene constitution it became clear that a political consensus existed, and the principle of the separation of powers was introduced into the Constitution as one of the basic foundations of all state regulations. In the general provisions of the Constitution of the Republic of Slovenia (second paragraph, third article) it states that power and authority were assigned following the principle of the separation of powers to the legislative, the executive, and the judicial branches.

The question which was controversial at first was whether a parliamentary system or a mixed parliamentary-presidential model should be adopted. Both possibilities were included when the constitution was still in its draft version. The first option leaned towards the German model of a parliamentary system which ensures a more stable government, especially through the institution of the so-called constructive no confidence vote. The second one to a higher degree tied the government to the president of the republic, with executive powers, similar to the French parliamentary-presidential model. Both versions stem from the belief that a more stable and strong government should be established and that the government should not have to be dependent on the ever-changing relations between the political parties in the parliament. In the early stages of the discussion on the draft version of the constitution, the second option was defeated and the parliamentary system suggested in the draft version was accepted.

The main reason for such a decision was stated in the political debates which emphasized that a strong President could inhibit the nascent democracy. One of the reasons for such a decision was undoubtedly the fact that by the time the preparations for the acceptance of the new Slovene constitution started, the first multi-party elections had already been held.

These elections brought many parties into the parliament and the dominant view was that it would not be much different in the future. The people preparing the new constitution were in favour of a more stable government in the parliament because in the classic parliamentary system it is the government which is threatened when there are many parties with seats in the parliament.

The first draft of the constitution was ready in the autumn of 1990, and it was finally accepted on 23 December 1991. The constitution has 174 articles and is almost half as long as the previous Republic constitution. The legislative function is performed by the State Assembly in accordance with the new constitution (80th article), and has 90 members. All members are elected directly on the basis of the universal and equal right to vote, by secret ballot. The members of the Italian and Hungarian national communities are specially represented in the State Assembly because every designated national community has one member in the Assembly regardless of the size of its population. The State Council, inside of which some special social interests are represented, has some particular competencies concerning the performance of the tasks of the legislative branch.

The Head of State is the President of the Republic, and is directly elected for a five year term. The President of the Republic represents the state and is at the same time the Commander-in-Chief of the army and has other competencies usual for the head of state in parliamentary systems. The president does not have any authorization to interfere with the competencies and functions of other state organs.

The seat of executive power is the government, which is composed of ministers nominated by the State Assembly based on the President of the Government's suggestion. The President of the Government is elected by the State Assembly according to the suggestion of the President of the Republic. The relations of the State Assembly with the Government are roughly speaking similar to that of a conventional parliamentary system. The stability of the Government is ensured as in the German pattern, through the so-called constructive no confidence vote. Some departures were instituted, which especially in practice strengthen the role of the State Assembly in its relations with the Government, and to a lesser extent the State Council.[3] It was not possible for all the steps to be taken simultaneously. The process was especially difficult because the existing Assembly in its structure and way of operating differed from its replacement. The sequence of changes depended greatly on first instituting the new State Assembly.

For these reasons the law on the implementation of the constitution, which was accepted at the same time as the constitution, established a transitional term of one year during which the transition would be completed. During this period the elections to the State Assembly, the State Council, and of the President of the Republic were to take place. The main problem was the sensitive and contentious question of the most appropriate electoral system for the formation of these bodies, especially the State Assembly. The determination of the electoral system was not resolved by the constitution but left to the passage of a special law requiring a two-thirds absolute majority.

The formation of an independent legal order in Slovenia

The change of the constitutional position of the Republic of Slovenia from a federal unit to an independent state had a major influence on the legal order in the Republic. While the Republic was still a part of the Federation there had been two valid legal orders on its territory - the legal order of the Republic and the legal order of the Federation. The independence of Slovenia ended the validity of the federal legal order on the territory of the Republic. A large vacuum opened up in all areas of society that had until then been regulated by the federal system. It is understandable that the Republic could not fill the legal vacuum immediately, which was caused by the sudden lack of validity of federal authority and legal order on its territory. The establishment of a new legal order in such expansive areas, which previously had been administered by the federal state, was a very demanding and long task. In these circumstances and until the new laws were adopted, the old federal regulations continued in use, to the extent that they were not in conflict with laws of the Republic. The fact that Yugoslav law had been applied until recently made its continuation relatively easy until it could be supplanted gradually by new legislation (Grad, 1991).

The conversion of the legal system was facilitated by constitutional events. The XCVI amendment of October 1990 asserted the priority of Slovenian law but permitted the continued application of federal law and the federal authorities still had the authority to enforce it. The promulgation of the XCIX amendment extended the competence of Slovenian law but federal law was retained to regulate its relations with the other Republics. With the assumption of complete independence all federal laws still in application were absorbed into Slovenian law until such time as they were replaced and to the extent that they were not unconstitutional. The new Republic was thus able to implement a fully-operational legal system. A major difficulty arose from the question of the constitutional compatibility of the existing laws, given the very different circumstances of their generation. A solution was provided by extending the validity of existing laws for two years.

During that time the possibility of a legal challenge would be excluded - even though they might be ostensibly opposed to the new constitution. The only exception to this legal constitutional protection was for regulations concerning human rights and basic immunities. The time limit of two years turned out to be too short even for the adjustment of the most important laws, not to mention the full scope of the legal system, but the State Assembly decided not to prolong the period.

Despite the intensive legislative activity of the new Assembly, it was clear that the task of re-working the entire set of statutes is an enormous one and not likely to be easily achieved. In addition, some of the new laws are themselves subject to challenge before the Constitutional Court, which further impedes the pace of reform.

There are difficulties in securing an orderly and accepted transition from the previous constitutional and legal system, particularly where it is required to underwrite changes of a most momentous kind. However, the Slovenian insistence on a careful progression, producing the new system in conformity with the requirements of the old, has guaranteed that the transition has had a sound basis and that challenges to its validity have been minimal.

Notes

1.   The Yugoslav theorists had very different views of the meaning and nature of the constitutional regulation of self-determination. Theorists from Serbia especially claimed that the right of self-determination had been consumed during the consensual foundation of the Yugoslav Federation. See: Kristan I. (1990), Right of Self-determination, Zbornik znanstvenih razprav vol. 1, Ljubljana.

2. About the meaning and the role of these acts from the legal constitutional point of view see: Grad F. Constitutional Acts in the Process of the Independence of the Republic of Slovenia, Legal practice No. 18, Ljubljana.
3. The state regulations of Slovenia with regard to the new constitution is more precisely dealt with in: Kristan I., Ribičič C., Grad F., Kaučič I., State Organization of Slovenia (1994), ČZ Uradni list RS, Ljubljana.

7 Changes and Adaptations of Formal Control

JANEZ PEČAR

The formal control mechanisms of a state by which society maintains the necessary conformism have always been subjected to radical transformations, especially in times of regime change and particularly when it comes to changes of the socio-political system as a whole. Slovenia has experienced such a transformation twice in the last 50 years; at the end of the second world war and in the current process of securing independence.

Slovenia is confronted with the question of how to provide for its external and internal security in the most appropriate and optimum way. Since external security depends on factors out of the control of Slovenia, it is much more feasible for it to focus on its internal security, which is entirely in the care of the state itself and its repressive mechanisms; among them, the police and other law enforcement agencies play the most prominent role and all other mechanisms only follow them. However, all of them have to protect human rights and civil freedoms, since this is one of the basic conditions to be met by Slovenia in order to join some international, particularly European, associations.

This period is one of radical change for Slovenia, producing difficulties, pressures and conflicts, and causing not only political but also moral and often material damage. Many things occur which have no benefit for society and its morals; the values of yesterday become anti-values, and those which are emerging cannot be a guide to action in the future. So it is said that people live in transition, characterized by social disorganization and anomie, which have an equally detrimental impact on social relations as on the formal controls of the state. This has had to be reorganized in the face of the already existing 'controllers' of conventional mechanisms, which was quite controversial in itself. Similar reasons have given rise to calls for political revenge and purges or 'lustration'; namely, those who acted in accordance with the law in the past are no longer considered suitable to perform their duties according to new norms, in spite of the professionalism of most of the control professions. This was one of the reasons for social instability, although 'repression' cannot be considered to be a key factor in the maintenance of social cohesion. In any case, people have to be prepared to meet the demands of the future, which will be economically, socially, culturally, politically and, in terms of security, quite different from the present ones. But since politics has always determined state control, it is important to perceive its meaning, role and style in a social community in this context.

Self-protection ideology of the former Yugoslavia

After the meeting of the Central Committee of the Yugoslav League of Communists, held at Brioni in 1965, at which the Minister of the Interior of Yugoslavia was removed from official and political positions, and following the events of 1968, when some of the socialist countries occupied Czechoslovakia, a system of so-called self-protection was gradually established in Yugoslavia. It brought radical changes to the concept of internal security, particularly in regard to the question of what security tasks should be performed by state organs and how to involve citizens in these tasks. They were intended above all to provide security within work organizations and in the communities where they lived. The movement to self-protection, however, soon manifested certain shortcomings, as well as raising questions about the concept of 'internal security'.

The political authorities of this time determined that 'self-management mechanisms' had to be partially responsible for security issues in their environment. This triggered a certain measure of detatization of some of the roles traditionally assumed by security organs, and conferred these tasks on non-state agencies. The responsibilities of 'self-management' were thus assigned some new competences for security, which clearly indicated the decentralization of some state functions. At the same time, 'security' began gradually to become a significant 'value' and to gain corresponding political weight.

Despite 'social self-protection', which was basically a political-security concept and aimed at protecting the social system, becoming gradually more and more bureaucratic and normative, it nevertheless contained numerous elements of the 'new policy of Social Defence' of Philipo Gramatica and Marc Ancel. Both social self-protection in Yugoslavia and the new policy of Social Defence relied, in addition to state repression, also on the non-state mechanism of an attack on deviancy. They both passed from normative activities to professional tasks within individual disciplines, and from professional handling of deviancy to the lay performance of such duties and to voluntary participation in providing security. Both concepts emphasized that the responsibility for deviancy lay in the environment in which it arose and both sought the participation of the community in deviancy control, above all by agents in the immediate environment. In spite of this concept, the state never denied its ultimate responsibility for legal enforcement.

This has produced a dichotomy of state and non-state control and given prevention the same weight as repression. This was also the beginning of detatization of certain, particularly marginal, state control roles.

In spite of contemporary views on the virtues of 'social self-protection' in relation to the control of deviancy and crime, this nevertheless proved ineffective, especially because it:

- was too politicized, generalized and normative;
- was focused too much on the protection of the state and much less on individuals and small groups;
- was regulated according to the needs of the state and its organs;
- did not take into consideration people's motives and was thus imposed on people even where there was actually no need for it;
- did not take sufficiently into account professional knowledge concerning the contemporary struggle against deviancy.

New circumstances - new control needs

With the break-up of the former Yugoslavia and the foundation of a new state of Slovenia, socio-political conditions and views on the role of the state began to change. This included the selling off of socially-owned property to private ownership in pursuit of policies of denationalization and privatization. It has generated processes of stratification and the formation of a different social structure, with changes in the distribution of wealth and, consequently, of power. There has been the development of new forms of crime, new moral standards, and different social practices, and these have produced scandals, a decline of authority, aimlessness, anomie and social disorganization. Past values have vanished while new ones have not yet been established. In brief, at this moment, society in Slovenia seems politically divided and in the process of disintegration. Organized crime, (such as arms and drug trafficking) which was practically non-existent before, has emerged as a major concern. There is also an increase in violence, in armed robberies and the use of arms in the commission of other crimes. Business crime, in a diversity of forms, is a feature of the new economic order. Within the political sphere there is an abuse of power and the pursuit of revenge against opponents. In addition, Slovenia has to cope with high levels of unemployment, a significant number of company bankruptcies, relatively low productivity, a rising retired population, a large number of refugees from the other republics of the former Yugoslavia and an increase in conventional deviancy.

In regard to external security, Slovenia is confronted with many problems too: the police have to protect 1218 kilometres of border (includingly 546 kilometres of border with Croatia) and 16 nautical miles of coast; Italy is making unacceptable demands on Slovenia and in the meantime obstructs its integration in the European Union. Slovenia does not have any external friends, nor has it an elaborated concept of a foreign policy. The situation is therefore extremely complex and indicates a need to strengthen control in order to protect what has already been achieved.

In view of the need to establish security arrangements based on an adequate concept of criminal policy, it is appropriate that Slovenia should try to create suitable strategies of state policy which would guarantee not only the necessary level of legality but would also provide efficient security services that were not too expensive. This requires an assessment of security needs, a greater integration of security mechanisms, including reform of the judiciary, as well as the integration of the new types of control mechanisms which have been instituted by the state. Their operation requires functional co-ordination, good performance, problem orientation, high professional skills and a capacity to react at the right time. The new circumstances require a revision of the concept of state-performed control.

Regulation of control issues

The most necessary changes which are required are:

- to nullify the federal legislation of the former state of Yugoslavia
- to make a new determination of the laws and regulations relating to different aspects of national existence.

The need for centralization and etatization arises in many regards from the smallness of Slovenia and from the legal void caused by the transition from one system to another, thus creating the need for different regulations. Thus, the new state needed, in addition to its Constitution, a law on citizenship (Slovenia has granted citizenship to more than 170,000 people from other republics of the former Yugoslavia who have, consequently, dual citizenship), laws on personal names, on the register book, on associations, on political parties, on public assemblies and performances, on arms, on the protection of data, and numerous others. In the sphere of internal security policies, the most urgently needed laws were: a law on defence, on foreigners, on passports, on the supervision of the state border, on road traffic, etc. In this context, it is particularly important to mention also the 'Resolution on Conceptual Starting-points of National Security', a document containing views concerning the security of the Slovene state, and consideration of what to do and how to act in the future in this field.

Laws which are equally important for the operation of control mechanisms in Slovenia and which have given rise to very vigorous public debates, especially in Parliament, are the criminal code, the law on criminal procedure, the law on the implementation of penal sanctions, the law on detective activity, the law on the courts and the law on the state prosecutor and social attorney. In addition to these, there are various others, such as the law on public security (i.e. the police law), the law on intelligence activities, the law on the Slovene security and intelligence agency, which are still in preparation.

The need for the establishment of standards and regulation of behaviour and control issues reminds us of the dictum of Tacitus that 'the more a state is corrupt, the more laws it needs'. However, the Slovene police law is only in its beginnings and, in addition, the legislation adopted requires further modification if it is not to operate in too discretionary and selective a way.

Parallel with the regulation of the operation of control mechanisms, there has also emerged the need for other changes concerning not only financial and personnel issues but also professional and political questions. In Slovenia, as often in history, groups have tried to interpret control issues in their own interest and to usurp control mechanisms in certain areas of criminal policy, reflecting on their view of society and the place of the mechanisms of control within it.

Changes in organization and personnel

Socio-political changes, especially if they are so radical that they introduce new values, bring about many organizational and personnel changes and require the adjustment of control mechanisms to the needs of power, or at least compliance with the consensus reached among the political forces of a given society. This has been particularly noticeable in all the societies of Eastern Europe following the fall of real-socialism. In this connection, Fogel (1994, p. 7) states that some of the 'lustration laws' in Czechoslovakia, Poland and Bulgaria caused such political cannibalism that it surpassed even the French Revolution in regard to terror and pogroms, especially in the secret services and police.

In Slovenia adaptations in political control have resulted in three changes in the position of Minister of the Interior within four years, three directors of the criminal investigation agency, three chiefs of the uniformed police and four directors of the Slovene security and intelligence service, even the name of which has been changed twice. Judicial and prosecution agencies have been far less affected by these changes, since they were less visible or given less political importance. People nevertheless have left these agencies too, in search of more promising employment prospects in the economy or at the bar.

The processes of transition have had a basically negative or even destructive impact on Slovene control mechanisms, in spite of individual codes of conduct adopted by the police, judiciary and other agencies. Thus, control will continue to be an extremely important problem in terms of organization and personnel, especially because the police are far from being satisfied with their salaries, their working conditions and new workload. So, independence has not only brought many new problems, but also a greater demand for their solution.

Depoliticization of control mechanisms

In contrast with the former socio-political system, which required political appropriateness from personnel serving in the control agencies, as well as professional ability, the present system has entirely rejected this criterion as extremely undesirable, and has proceeded to prohibit it. Thus, police officers, according to the Constitution, are not allowed to be members of political parties, while a draft law on public security (the police law) even goes so far as to threaten those who become politically engaged with the loss of employment. In other control agencies (with the exception of the army) the political activity of 'controllers' is not legally regulated and depoliticization is not mentioned so radically.

In many respects the alleged depoliticization is a sham concealing 'sharing of the spoils of power', based on the electoral performance of individual political parties. Therefore, genuine depoliticization has penetrated only certain levels of the hierarchy of control agencies. Thus, the appointment of ministers has always been a result of the struggle for power between political parties, and when political changes at the top bring new ministers, then deputy ministers, as the professionals responsible for individual sectors, have to resign in order to let new ministers appoint new deputy ministers, not necessarily according to their professional capacities but rather on the basis of their political affinity. Such politicization will then proceed downwards to the lower levels of power, causing incessant political changes in individual state agencies when political control of the ministry changes. These circumstances are encapsulated in the Latin saying *Cui licitus est finis, etiam licent media* (those who are allowed goals, are also allowed means). Such a politicization presents a constant threat to professionalism, continuity, a systematic approach, rational and economic management, and everything that has been considered necessary to a good and efficient organization, from Max Weber onwards. Anticipation of constant change gives rise to fear, uncertainty, anomie, disinterest, dissatisfaction and other negative reactions in personnel, which can lead to a subculture of deviancy. This has recently been observed in the police and customs service (Findlay and Zvekić, 1993, p. 242), revealing that the police rely more on propaganda, prejudice and deterrence than on the correct application of legal rules.

For this reason, Slovenia is making considerable efforts towards the professionalization of individual control activities, which includes also various specializations and the application of a professional deontology in the performance of control tasks. The practice of lustration (or purging) by rules, the aim of which is to restrict the rights of individual groups of people who exercise certain public duties (for example, work in the sphere of detective activity or in the judiciary) has been introduced in Slovenia only to a limited extent and not so radically as in some other ex-socialist countries.

The old and new control mechanisms

Some new control mechanisms have emerged in Slovenia in recent years which did not exist before and which have been instituted alongside the traditional mechanisms. In concept, they are similar to systems of control in Western countries, i.e. in societies with parliamentary systems of a long-standing tradition. The level of regulation reveals also relatively new views on social control which are given considerable emphasis in the social sciences, especially with regard to deviancy.

The new control mechanisms include six parliamentary investigation commissions and some corresponding boards; the office of the Ombudsman; a financial court; an agency for money payments, supervision and information; an office for the prevention of money laundering; VOX - a service within the office of the president of government, responsible for citizens' complaints against irregularities committed by state organs; the former social attorney of self-management, now transformed into the social attorney; the newly-created labour and social courts have begun to operate alongside the ordinary courts; and municipalities have been allowed to establish their own constable services. The reform of the judiciary has also commenced.

These new mechanisms invigilate the operation of other control agencies, such as the police, public prosecutor's office, judiciary, administrative organs dealing with petty offences, inspections, correctional institutions, customs services and other agencies of state administration in general. Thus, the network of control, even in such a small country, becomes ever more extended, a phenomenon known as 'net widening'. This can either indicate a mistrust of existing traditional organs or the need for new mechanisms to cope with an actual and threatening situation in the state. In any case, it certainly does not represent the rational and efficient management of control, especially because it has proved necessary at the same time to fill gaps in the existing mechanisms with new forces, to reorganize them and provide them with equipment. Furthermore, other agencies are to undergo specific changes, including the district and higher courts and the corresponding state prosecution agencies, as well as the Supreme and Constitutional Court.

New circumstances have brought new views on needs for control mechanisms, as well as a different institutionalization of control. The usual adage *Quis custodiet ipsos custodes* (Who controls the controllers) can be reformulated in this situation to produce the question: 'Who controls those who control the controllers?' As state control is widened and deepened the questions of how much it costs and what benefits it gives to society are never asked. Since a state exists, mechanisms for its protection and control appear to be an urgent need, something which is entirely self-justifying. The present organization suggests state centred regulation of control mechanisms in which the nascent local self-government will not have an important role and in which the need for service delivery will be decided only by the state.

Deviancy in control mechanisms

If we accept the view that control of a given society cannot be better than the society itself, then it is quite clear that we must expect the appearance of some excesses and incidents which are undesirable in this activity. Slovenia at this time of transition is being influenced by the most diverse currents which are in many regards unfavourable to it. The negative and crimogenic factions arising from new social circumstances have a marked impact on the control agencies. It means heavier burdens for them, with the need for a greater striking force and mobility, higher demands for providing equality, justice, and the preservation of social standards from criminal threats and unfavourable influences from the outside. Control mechanisms in Slovenia are thus confronted with relatively new phenomena, such as corruptibility, a legal system unequipped to deal with current societal needs, dubious transactions connected with 'social property' which is being privatized, the concealed flow of capital abroad, improper enrichment etc. The changed circumstances have prepared the ground for the rise of a new deviancy, including an increase in violence and various other kinds of abuse. Judgements have to be made about the priorities of various social interests. The increasing awareness of enrichment by dubious means generates in control agencies dissatisfaction with work and its environment. There have been strikes by the police in pursuit of better salaries, more effective organization and greater security of employment. All this has led to indiscipline in control agencies, various violations and scandals (some of them political). There has even been participation in criminal activities by the special forces of the Ministry of Interior and Ministry of Defence.

For this reason, the 'pathology of control' has to be understood as a concept covering irregularities. These may include operational anomalies, including a variety of illegal and unethical actions, arbitrary and unjustified infiltration, the planting of evidence, selling of records, unlawful use of force, creation of rules and principles *ad hoc*, delayed and unsolved cases, and uninvestigated crimes, which contribute to a distrust of state control and, consequently, of state authority.

Formal control and the 'new' democracy

Since the state is expanding its control mechanisms, Slovenia urgently needs a democratic vision of how to deal with deviancy and the threat of it, and how to shape its control mechanisms. For this reason, it is necessary to have, in addition to a concept of national security, an appropriate criminal policy. It is not only the state but also the most diverse para-state, extra-state and entirely civil and private mechanisms for the maintenance of public peace and order, justice and security, that must be integrated. These strategies may be repressive or preventive, educational or social. At present, Slovenia is rapidly expanding state control. It is not ready to reduce its control mechanisms and activities, but is rather trying to spread them, in spite of talking extensively about freedom and democracy. Thus, control mechanisms, instead of being services at the disposal of people, become menacing by making demands on them for obedience and conformism. This indicates at the same time the deficiencies of the political culture, since the elimination of deviants is the rule rather than the exception and their integration into the social community the exception rather than a rule. All this presents a threat to democracy, since it reflects a social climate which, despite democratic claims, can in reality often prove to be quite different. Thus the state becomes more and more politicized and alienating, which makes its citizens less and less willing to participate in it.

Private security as a potential competitor

As well as a tendency to centralize the state on the one hand, and endeavours to establish local self-government on the other, there is a movement towards privatization, with the restoration of private property and the encouragement of private enterprise. This has led to the development of detective activity and private security firms. This private sector activity requires state regulation and the development of a working relationship between state control and private security, since the two security sectors can develop side by side and complement each other or be in a conflicting relationship.

The state in Slovenia has also begun to accept a different approach in the struggle against deviancy. However, it still remains relatively reserved in its attitude towards populist self-protection. This is undoubtedly a result of past experience, when this area was relatively well developed but too extensively regulated by legal rules and politicized. Although the negative experiences from the past are to be avoided, it is nevertheless important to emphasize that, without private security and the voluntary participation of the public, Slovenia cannot expect to have an adequate criminal policy for the control of deviancy. Since state control agencies are less responsive to public needs, people are often better served by private security institutions. They provide services for a fee and often compete with the state or even become adversaries. Both parties engaged in the control/security function have so far been relatively cautious, and are still seeking their way. The 'security market' is gradually expanding and 'security' is becoming a 'commodity' in Slovenia, rather than the 'value' understood by state control. In this way, 'criminal policy will now have to protect the interests of a private subject with equal due attention as it protects a state one' (Szabo, 1991, p. 298).

Satisfaction with state-performed control

It is difficult to generate satisfaction with the operation of a state control which represents above all 'repression', even though it also has some more positive roles. The increase in crime, the emergence of new forms of deviancy, the use of weapons in violent crime, the internationalization of crime and terrorism produce a demand for intervention but the politicization, corruption and other abuses of the control agencies place in question their ability to deal satisfactorily with the situation.

This dissatisfaction with formal control therefore creates the need for alternative control models. It encourages the institution of private security, with the privatization of protection. It encourages vigilantism in self-protection associations of those who feel threatened, and demands for the suppression of threats. This has led to the development of new security technologies, and new methods of protection, justified in the interest of security. Seen from this perspective, deviancy has also a positive social function, because it generates vigilance, makes society organize and inspires a range of positive reactions, from legislative activity to the invention and use of security devices.

Slovenia has been slowly following the lead of the more developed Western world, in which crime is regarded as reaching dangerous levels. The crime already existing in Slovenia inspires fear and indignation, as well as mistrust of the police and judiciary, and makes people critical towards the situation in which they live. This situation has slowly led to a growing demand for 'quality control', 'quality circles', 'outcome measurement', 'performance indicators' and 'customer relations' in the control agencies (Holdaway, 1993, p. 61). This means, however, that 'maintenance of order, application of laws, protection of people's life and property as well as protection of conditions granting basic human freedoms, constitute an absolutely necessary condition for the existence of any democratic society ' (Szabo, 1979, p. 2). Since Slovene formal control has not yet achieved such a situation the public continues to express dissatisfaction.

Integration in international organizations and activities

As a new state, Slovenia had to make serious efforts to become internationally integrated in numerous activities including those of formal social control. Certain obstacles to the cooperation of Slovenia with international organizations have been overcome by joining these organizations, through para-state, civil or professional associations. However, the most serious difficulties are expected in attempts to integrate Slovenia with the European Union and other key international and European organizations.

It has made some progress in international integration. It has become a member of the United Nations and its agencies and, in the field of control activities, Slovenia was admitted to Interpol, at the 61st General Assembly of Interpol in Dakar, 4 to 10 November 1992. The consequences of its membership in Europol are, as yet, unknown, but in order to deal with problems arising from tourism, migrants, refugees, borders, traffic, citizenship, international crime, terrorism, counter-terrorism, etc., numerous bilateral and multilateral agreements have been adopted, especially with neighbouring countries. In fact, the participation of Slovenia in the security provisions of Europe is an absolute necessity in view of its situation in the middle of the continent and particularly with regard to the war situation in the Balkans. With this in mind, Slovenia has organized numerous international conferences dealing with human rights, economic crime and the development of the police in the next century. It has prepared joint programmes of cooperation, assistance, education and research in numerous areas and established various consulting teams. In addition, it has conceived numerous strategies and documents, made plans for training at a high level, and designed projects of quality management of human and material resources by using all available information sources. It has already set goals for the future in some areas, by taking into consideration the new circumstances arising in Slovenia from the processes of transition. Some of these goals concern human rights and civil freedoms, which seem to be the most threatened by the state and its control mechanisms. In brief, Slovenia is in the course of the most intensive processes of integration in a variety of international associations.

Control for the future of a state

Even in normal conditions of social development, control mechanisms have to constantly adjust to the expectations of political parties and the general public. These expectations, however, depend upon the extent of deviancy, the state of public law and order, and the security situation in general. Since security is not only an objectively measurable, but also an emotionally determined category, views of it tend to be conflicting. In this connection, there always arise such questions as: who makes norms of conduct, for whom are they made, what are the criteria which determine them and to what extent are they applied in a discretionary and selective way?

Slovenia, as a small country, is likely to be constantly menaced in its internal security by organized crime, civil dishonesty and social violence. For this reason, Slovenia will have to think about establishing an appropriate culture to support its control mechanisms. This will have to be done in such a way as to protect, on the one hand, individuals from the aggressiveness of the state and to reduce the fear of its control mechanisms, and to preserve, on the other hand, its security and national identity which is crucial to a small nation threatened by stronger neighbours.

Modern management of control agencies requires a recognition of the many parameters by which it would be possible, especially in the contemporary information society, to predict tasks evolving in the future. In this perspective, the quality of performance, adequate interpersonal relations, responsibility and readiness are important features for the realization of the long-term goals of control agencies.

Slovenia has consolidated its state control and strongly centralized it. In regard to its internal security, the question therefore arises as to what extent Slovenia, as a small entity, can allow itself detatization and decentralization? Unless the less important behavioural issues and control over them is left to non-state and informal mechanisms of control, Slovenia is likely to become increasingly authoritarian, if not totalitarian, particularly because its society is still not very integrated. Formal toleration of private security indicates a certain degree of openness and pluralism in the domain of behaviour control and is an important step towards democracy.

Attempts at preventative measures and the introduction of specific methods in crime prevention do not indicate any particular spirit of inventiveness of Slovene society. The supervision of state control agencies seems inadequate and the numerous measures to remedy this cause rather more harm than good, due to ideological antagonisms. This developmental stage should not last long enough to cause unfavourable consequences for the mature Slovene state. However, the present attitude of politics towards state control can best be expressed by Gogol's famous thought: 'Don't be angry with the mirror if your face is ugly'.

The new penal law has provided the state with the necessary instruments for an effective response to deviancy. However, legal regulation of deviancy is only one element in a range of possibilities for dealing with what is wrong with society. All the rest has yet to be established, designed and created, perhaps by emulating others, particularly those who have already undergone these stages of development. This should be undertaken with proper and careful verification, because society is sensitive to external influences. It is clear that 'cultural values are those crucial variables which either accelerate or impede integration in Europe' (Holdaway, 1993, p. 53).

In the present decade, many of those responsible for control agencies and power-holders in general are looking beyond the year 2000. This applies particularly to those societies in Europe which are at present undergoing transition, including Slovenia and the other former socialist countries. Slovenia can expect to be confronted with more serious difficulties than those generally expected by strategic planners. There is a greater need for voluntary participation by the public, professionalization of control organization and activities, transparency of control, and a client orientation. This can be met by various forms of operation, adjusted to the given situation, and includes privatization of some aspects of control. What is, however, particularly important for Slovenia is to reduce the costs of security and control activities on the one hand, and to increase their efficiency on the other.

8 Changing Patterns of Social Partnership

IGOR LUKŠIČ

Introduction

The term social partnership refers to a mode of conflict-resolution and the regulation of social, industrial and labour policy by means of relevant interest organizations representing labour and capital, that is employees and employers, working in concert. This article will describe the process of the reforming and creating of new interest organizations involving employers and trade unions in Slovenia in the second half of the eighties and in the beginning of the nineties. As an introduction, some historical details and an outline of the political background will be presented.

History

Social partnership is an important dimension of the corporatism that has always been one of the most powerful political doctrines in Slovenia. After the encyclical Rerum Novarum of Leo XIII a powerful peasant movement emerged, which was called 'Krekovstvo', (Žižek 1987, pp. 9-60) after its leader, Janez E. Krek. Its main goal was to protect the Slovene language and the Slovene people, who were mostly poor peasants. The movement was organized mostly by peasants, but workers were involved too in cooperatives. They promoted the corporatist ideas of the Christian community, unity and nationalism. The movement was anti-liberal and anti-capitalist.

In the 1930s, after the encyclic Quadrogesimo Anno of Pius XI, Christian intellectuals promoted the idea of the corporatist state involving a major role for corporations (Zver, 1992, pp. 37-47).

After the second world war corporatism took on a socialist form. Yugoslavia practised self-management, which was a kind of social partnership on the basis of 'social ownership', especially after the Constitution of 1974. The Parliament of each Republic comprised three Chambers: the Chamber of Communes, the Chamber of Associated Labour (where all questions concerning economic and social policy were to be discussed), and the Socio-Political Chamber. For every vital social interest, a special so called Self-Management Interest Community was organized,[1] with an equal number of representatives of 'producers' and 'consumers'. Each of them could participate in a session of the Parliament as a 'fourth Chamber' on a matter considered to be within their competence.

In the Chamber of Associated Labour, representatives of workers and managers were elected for every vital branch of the economy and social services. In addition to articulating their respective economic interests, they could also speak in the Socio-Political Chamber through a trade union delegation. The delegations of the League of Communists and the Youth Organization also had a keen interest in economic questions. The Chamber of Commerce (Gospodarska zbornica) had a special status when an economic matter was on the parliamentary agenda. It also had a direct relationship with the government.

Within the self-management structure there existed a developed system of self-managing agreements and societal compacts which served as a model of co-operation between the socio-political communities (commune, republic) and the interest and economic organizations. This was designed to replace, on the one hand, the anarchy of market forces and, on the other, the rigidity of state interventionism. These agreements and compacts were made at federal, republic and communal levels.

State council

This self-management type of social partnership has survived in the new Slovenian Constitution of 1991 in the form of the State Council.[2] Article 96 of the Constitution defines the State Council as 'the representative of the bearers of social, economic, professional and local interests'.[3] On this Council are represented the main, vital interest organizations of labour (the trade unions), of business (the Chamber of Commerce), of agriculture, of trade and the free professions, of the social services (those involved in medicine, the universities, social policy, education, science, culture and sport) and 22 representatives of local interests. The Council has 40 representatives in all and they are elected indirectly through electoral colleges, which are formed by representatives of the relevant interest organizations and councils of communes for local interests.[4]

Four representatives of trade unions and four representatives of employers' organizations are elected to the Council. Councillors from trade unions are elected by an electorate representing the eleven trade unions which registered to participate in the elections. Three of these Councillors are from the biggest Trade Union, the Federation of Free Trade Unions of Slovenia and one belongs to the Trade Union of Education and Science. All Councillors on the employers' side are elected from the Chamber of Commerce. Councillors from trade unions and employers' organizations have the most active role in the Council. The main problem is that the Council has limited competencies: the ability to remit laws back to the parliament for further consideration as well as the ability to initiate laws and referendums and to call for the establishment of a Parliamentary Inquiry.[5]

Trade unions

Before 1990 only one trade union existed, which was, in fact, an Association of Trade Unions. It was more or less the cipher of the state and of the dominating League of Communists. In fact its main function was to stabilize the political and social system as a whole. The trade union was to represent the working class as the ruling social formation and was not intended to further the interests of the actual workers in this or that factory. In the second half of the 1980s many strikes broke out, and in the majority of cases the trade union was not on the side of workers but on the side of the directors. On the other hand, the experience of the Polish trade union Solidarity and its role in the democratization of politics had a great impact on Slovene radicals, especially amongst young intellectuals. As a consequence, the Youth Organization made a proposal to establish an independent trade union in the name of the real interests of the working class, a trade union which would organize workers in the fight against the state and the directors. Pluralization of trade unions was seen as a means of revitalizing the idea and practice of self-management in a period of increased centralization in Yugoslavia. Workers' opposition would give a new energy to the process of decentralization and lead to a strengthening of the autonomy of enterprises.

One of the most important strikes erupted in December 1987 in Litostroj, one of the biggest metal enterprises in Ljubljana. This also had a symbolic meaning as Litostroj was also called 'Tito's establishment' (Titovi zavod). The strike committee dissolved the old trade union and established a new structure. At the same time the strike committee took the initiative in establishing a Social Democratic Party at the beginning of 1989.

The first alternative trade union was established in December 1989 in Ptuj after long preparation inside the Socialist Youth Organization. It was called the Independent Trade Union of Slovenia, and it continues as one of the minor Slovenian trade unions.

With the emergence of new parties the initiative for creating alternative trade unions changed. Some of the new parties recognized the need to create their own trade union. One month before the first multi-party elections since the second world war the Youth Organization lost the initiative in terms of the creation of a federation of alternative trade unions, which passed to the Social Democratic League. DEMOS, an association of newly created parties, established its own Trade Union called Independence - the Confederation of New Trade Unions of Slovenia. Its major goal was to fight against the rival old-established trade union, but also to further the interests of its attached party. While DEMOS was in government Independence acted as a typical governmental trade union, but when DEMOS lost power in 1992, Independence become more labour orientated. But the political origin of Independence still generated conflict between its political and industrial roles and obstructed a more unified presentation of labour interests.

Soon, after the establishment of the first politically strong alternative trade union, various new trade unions emerged, almost all on the basis of opposition to the old trade union regime.

The original socialist trade union had been reviewing and revising its activities. The first step was made when considering the constitutional possibilities for trade union pluralism. It determined that its main role should be as workers' advocate and not as a system-maintaining organization.[6] Its new position was confirmed by the Congress of March 1990. It was renamed the Association of Free Trade Unions, and was committed to autonomous operation, including independence from state organs and parties and the furtherance of the interests of labour. The subsequent election of one of the previous leaders has brought into question its commitment to these new aims and resulted in many branches leaving the Association.

The new law on trade unions gave encouragement to the creation of trade unions in the name of pluralism. As a result nineteen Trade Unions (almost all at a national level) are recognized. There are four major federations or confederations of Trade Unions with the renewed AFTUS as the most powerful Trade Union, covering about two thirds of employed labour in Slovenia.

Table 8.1   Membership of trade unions

Trade Unions	no. of members[7]
Association of Free Trade Unions of Slovenia	439,850
Independence - Confederation of New Trade Unions of Slovenia	163,000
Confederation of Trade Unions '90 of Slovenia	49,512
Confederation of Trade Unions PERGAM	31,286

AFTUS has 20 representative branches and is recognized as being politically on the left. It has some relations with the Associated List of Social Democrats. The Independence - Confederation of New Trade Unions of Slovenia includes 19 branches, but only eight of them are recognized as being representative, and this union is placed politically on the right. It has some connections with the Social Democratic Party of Slovenia. The other two confederations have no special political identity, but they are regarded as being more inclined to the right. PERGAM includes eight branches, with five of them as representative branches and Trade Union '90 has ten representative branches.

Beside these four major trade unions the Ministry of Labour also recognized as representative fifteen autonomous Trade Union branches.

Employers' organizations

The most powerful organization on the employer's side is the 140 year old Chamber of Commerce which was modernized in 1992. Membership of the Chamber is obligatory[8] for all enterprises. Incorporated in the Chamber of Commerce is the Association of Managers (Združenje manager). Also within the Chamber of Commerce are the Association of Enterprises (Združenje podjetnikov), which represents small businesses and small industries, and the financially and profoundly autonomous Chamber of Tradesmen of Slovenia. The OGISTA association was created for the protection of the interests of tradesmen as employers. In 1994 the employers established an Association of Employers of Slovenia on a voluntary basis. The Association includes only five per cent of total enterprises, but it has 65 per cent of capital investment and more than 50 per cent of the total number of employees.

All of these organizations are based in the capital Ljubljana. In Maribor only one such organization was established - the Association of Employers - which has no legal status and therefore has no involvement in the system of social partnership.

In early 1995 there have been open discussions about re-organizing the Chamber of Commerce and the other organizations of employers. They are aimed at creating a more efficient and financially viable organization which will be appropriate to the process of privatization.

Tripartite organs

After the elections in 1990 a tripartite body was established in the Ministry of Labour to deal with employment policy. Trade unions and the Ministry of Labour suggested that the creation of a tripartite body would be more independent from the government and parliament. Both the 1990 government and that of 1992 tried to organize the economy according to the Anglo-Saxon model, that is with a strong commitment to the free market. As a result there were 124,000 unemployed, strikes, growing poverty and a considerably worse overall economic situation compared to that before 1990. After elections in December 1992 a new government was established - a grand coalition of Liberal Democrats, Christian Democrats, Social Democrats and the Associated List of Social Democrats. The Associated List was given control of (among others) the Ministry of Labour and the Ministry of Economy, which are the two most important for the creation of the system of social partnership.

It was not until the creation of the Association of Employers of Slovenia (AES) at the beginning of 1994 that the idea of a tripartite organ acquired a strong supporter on the non-labour side as well. In April 1994 a tripartite agreement on wage policy for 1994 was adopted and signed by representatives of six Trade Unions, the AES, the Chamber of Commerce of Slovenia (CES) and the Chamber of Tradesman of Slovenia (CTS) and by the President of the Government. This agreement is referred to as the Social Pact.

The Economic-Social Council (ESC) (Ekonomsko-socialni svet) which was established by that agreement is made up of fifteen members, that is five from each group. The government delegation[9] consists of the Minister of Economic Relations and Development, the Minister of Labour, Family, and Social Questions, the Director of the Institution for Macroeconomic Analysis and Development, the State Secretary of the Ministry of Finance and a member of the Office of the President of the Government. The delegation of employees[10] consists of the President of the Association of Free Trade Unions of Slovenia (AFTUS), a member of the executive of the AFTUS, the President of the Trade Union PERGAM, the President of the Independence - Confederation of New Trade Unions of Slovenia and the President of the Confederation of Trade Unions '90 of Slovenia. The delegation of employers[11] is constituted of the President and Vice President (for small scale industry) of AES, a member of the Executive Committee of AES (for large industry), the President of the Chamber of Commerce, and the President of the Chamber of Tradesmen. Each member has a substitute to permit fully attended sessions. Up to the present, representatives of the trade unions and employers have consistently attended, but on the government side, widespread absenteeism, especially by the Minister of Economic Relations and Development, has been the norm.

The main purpose of the ESC is to consider policy concerning economic and social matters. It is guided in this by the elements of the social pact[12] and it is expected to invigilate its implementation.

The Council has adopted standing rules which determine its fundamental areas of concern and these are:

- the social pact,
- social rights,
- employment and working relations,
- the system of collective agreements,
- taxes and prices,
- economic policy,
- juridical security,
- cooperation with the International Labour Organization and the Council of Europe.

The Council is empowered to produce statements, initiatives, proposals and recommendations and send them to the organs and organizations in charge: the Government, the State Chamber, the State Council, and to release them to the public. Unanimous (each member has one vote) conclusions of the ESC are binding on all organs and the working bodies of all three social partners. The ESC is financed by the state budget.

Up until mid-January 1995 the ESC had thirteen sittings, discussing the standing rules and nature of the ESC, and legal questions arising from collective agreements, workers' participation, the minimum wage and wage policy for 1995. It also debated the budget and the social pact for 1995.

The new urge to pluralism has often created ideological conflict and there is a real possibility that this will weaken the labour side and consequently complicate the work of the whole ESC.

The general conclusion of expert observers is that the government leans towards a liberal policy and that is not in favour of social partnership. According to the main actors, the ESC was reluctantly agreed to by the government following strong pressure from the Trade Unions, the AES and the Ministry of Labour. So far, it is clear that the government has no interest in promoting social partnership and only observes what is going on between other partners and within them. It is claimed by AFTUS that the government deliberately generates conflict, because it put in process, in July 1994, amendments to the law on labour participation without previous consultation with trade unions or discussion with the ESC. The same happened with the budget memorandum, a document which determines the most important public expenditure. The government sent this to the parliament without discussing it beforehand in the ESC.

All of the parliamentary parties are in favour of social partnership and the creation of a social pact, but most have little understanding of the situation. The only exceptions are the Associated List of Social Democrats and the Slovenian Christian Democrats (who have a labour faction in the party and an officer responsible for labour policy and social partnership.) Parties on the right of the political spectrum stress that the biggest trade union and the Chamber of Commerce are still 'red' and they are not the proper representatives of workers and employers. They suggest that a viable social partnership depends on the reform of the participating groups.

Parties seek to influence trade unions and employers' organizations, but the former have rejected close formalities, merely seeking their assistance when they need access to the law-making procedures in the State Chamber.[13] AFTUS disclaims that it is the Associated List's trade union, despite the fact that leading officials are members of the Associated List and that their President is also a member of the Presidency of that party.

All partners, especially the biggest two trade unions, have excellent knowledge of how the concept of social partnership functions in Austria. Some of them also have knowledge about the models operating in Cyprus, Scandinavia, Italy and Germany and they invoke them as possible patterns for creating structures of social partnership in Slovenia. The most important influence comes from Austria, because of similarities in social structure between Slovenia and Austria, and because Austria is a major practitioner of the concept of social partnership.

Conclusion

The process of constructing organizations in the field of social partnership has not finished yet. On the side of labour, trade unions are trying to find a common position to advance their course in confrontation with the government and employers' organizations. Politics and party orientations still play a very important role, but it must be stressed that such influence has become less visible. On the side of the employers the most important obstacle is the uncompleted process of privatization. After a clearer structure of ownership is in place it should be easier to define the roles of management, employer and owner, which would permit the better differentiation of organizations.

The Economic-Social Council plays an important role as the political forum where discussions about vital social and economic questions take place. It is likely that the ESC will, in the near future, strengthen its position as a problem-solving, stabilizing and depoliticizing organ in keeping with the established Slovenian traditions of social partnership.

Notes

1. To mention only a few of them: Self-management Interest Community for: Culture, for Science, Sport, Forestry, Social Care, Medical Care, Transport etc.
2. It should be stressed that such a kind of second chamber, composed of representatives of interest groups, exists also in the Republic of Ireland and in the Free State of Bavaria. A similar representative organ exists also in Hong Kong.
3. *Ustava Republike Slovenije* (Constitution of the Republic of Slovenia) (Ljubljana: Mladinska knjiga, 1992), 37.
4. It should also be noticed that the Council of RTV (Slovenian State Television) is made up of representatives of relevant interest organizations such as the Association of Employers of Slovenia, the trade unions, pensioner associations, writers, film producers, journalists, invalids etc.
5. Constitution of the Republic of Slovenia. Article 97. Časopisni zavod Uradni list Republike Slovenije, Ljubljana 1992.
6. That guarantee was made with Clause 27 of the IX amendment to the Constitution of Socialist Republic of Slovenia in September 1989.
7. Trade unions assume continuing membership and do not adjust their figures for wastage. That means that these numbers include also unemployed and deceased persons. The numbers are taken from report of Mandatory Commission of the Council of RTV Slovenia (October 1994), when trade unions elected their members of the Council.
8. A judgement of the Constitutional Court stating that compulsory membership in the Medical Chamber is not in contradiction with the constitutional freedom of association has been very important for strengthening the power of the Chamber of Commerce. Compulsory membership has become a constitutional norm.
9. The idea of both the employers' and employees' side was that the Prime Minister should be a member of the ESC, but he refused. The Minister of Labour suggested that a delegation should include three ministers in order to show the other two partners that the government is serious about social partnership, and respects the ESC. Even that proposal failed to come to fruition.
10. Trade unions made an agreement that the criterion for the number of members in the delegation is the number of union members. According to this criterion the trade union with two thirds of members of all trade unions has the right to two mandates in the delegation.
11. All members were appointed by AES.
12. To create a social pact is the main task of the ESC. Actors also stressed this task as their primary one in interviews. They stress that the agreement to the minimum budget for 1995 should be seen as a kind of social pact for that year.
13. The Association of Free Trade Unions for example has invited all parliamentary parties to a meeting to let them know what are the conclusions of their Second Congress in 1994. The trade unions also hope that all parties would strengthen their labour and wage policy.

9 Interest Organizations in the Policy-making Process

DANICA FINK-HAFNER

Introduction

The aim of this paper is to present some characteristics of interest group development and the role of interest groups in policy-making processes in Slovenia, with respect to modernization theory and to the policy network concept (Jordan and Schubert, 1992). Key characteristics of interest group influence at four levels (parliament, state council, executive power and constitutional court) are presented on the basis of empirical data from three parliamentary surveys (1991, 1992, 1994), interviews with selected interest groups and governmental representatives as well as from official statistical data.

Social pluralism vs political pluralism

In the theory of political modernization as well as in the literature on democratic transition, increasing popular participation in politics is treated as one of the key characteristics of democratization (LaPalombara and Weiner, eds., 1966; Welch, 1967, pp. 7-8; Finkle and Gable, 1968; Huntington, 1969; Eisenstadt, 1967, 1971; Higgot, 1980; Kabashima and White, 1986, p. 95; Leftwich, 1990; Linz, 1990). The experiences of democratic transitions in European post-socialist countries have shown that this 'iron law' of democratization does not work automatically or parallel to the formal change in a political system. At the same time we cannot say that organized interests are now developing out of *tabula rasa* (Wiesenthal, 1995. p. 1).

On the basis of our research into the Slovenian experience we will illustrate the disproportion between the development of social pluralism and the development of political pluralism in the context of interest group competition and influence on the policy-making process.

It is obvious that there were interest organizations of a kind within the old political system, although they were not autonomous and a lot of them were not even voluntary organizations. In the process of democratic transition the number of non-party, autonomous and voluntary organizations has been increasing. These phenomena had been developing during the whole decade of gradual liberalization and democratization in Slovenia (Table 9.1).

Table 9.1   Number of organizations[1] in Slovenia 1980-1992

year	enterprises	social organizations	societies	societies & social organizations	organizations (all)	enterprises & organizations
1980	-	45	5,261	5,306	16,304	-
1981	-	1,539	5,715	7,254	17,111	-
1982	-	1,623	6,266	7,889	18,002	-
1983	-	1,704	6,627	8,331	18,480	-
1984	-	2,037	6,793	8,776	18,903	-
1985	-	3,783	5,444	9,227	19,292	-
1986	-	8,600	899	9,499	19,177	-
1987	-	9,484	407	9,891	19,716	-
1988	-	9,651	417	10,068	19,614	-
1989	-	9,827	430	10,257	19,177	-
1990	14,597	10,073	450	10,257	15,967	30,564
1991	23,348	10,398	494	10,892	15,587	38,936
1992	36,448	10,865	588	11,453	15,731	52,179

Source: Zavod za statistiko RS, Statistični letopisi 1977-1994.

We have to stress that these figures do not mean that the number of all existing organizations is at the same time representative of the number of interest groups which play the role of policy actors. People are still learning to be active citizens. Some very active single-issue groups have been established like the Angry Savers and the Syndicate of Renters of Denationalized Flats. Basically, they are groups of educated people who are fighting for their rights as consumers or as citizens. Similarly, some other associations were founded which also express citizen activism but so far in a more silent way (such as the Society of Tax-payers, the Parents' Club for Better Schools, the Society for Equal Opportunities for Men and Women, the Forum for a Cultural Policy Programme). Some regional interest groups were formed to struggle against the centralism of the newly formed state (the Forum of Slovenian Štajerska, the League for Primorska). Additionally, some internationally well-known organizations started to create organizational units in Slovenia (the Rotary club, the Lions). It also seems that some groups, raised out of the social movement cycle from the eighties, still exist, although they are rarely visible in public life (local and regional green groups, regional feminist groups, the 'Pro Life' movement).

The groups and organizations mentioned above do not have the resources to act continuously as policy actors that policy-makers would highly respect. Besides them there is a relatively small number of organizations which are able to act continuously and on the basis of (at least some) material, technical and personnel resources (such as the trade unions, the Chamber of Commerce and other lobbies coming from the economic sphere, the League of Consumers of Slovenia, and the students' organization in Ljubljana).

Therefore, it is obvious that interest groups in Slovenia differ from each other in many ways - according to their character (remaining 'core-members' of the new social movements, different corporate interest groups, professional associations, single issue groups, regional interest groups, economic interest groups), to their size (some of them are basically small core groups, others like trade unions have a membership which is bigger than the membership of all combined political parties), to the model of their internal and external organization, to the breadth of their main interests and goals, to the longevity of their activity and to the amount of their material resources.

So, on the one hand, we can say that society is pluralizing, that civil society subjects are starting to develop in a modern way. But, on the other hand, we cannot really say that the structure of political intermediation in Slovenia is already completely modern, that groups and organizations regularly behave as policy actors. All groups and organizations are not interest groups or pressure groups by definition (Wilson, 1990; Grant, 1989; etc.). The proportion of interest/pressure groups is still relatively very small, but according to our parliamentary research (Centre for Political Research, FSS-ISS, Ljubljana) this proportion is growing relatively quickly.

Influencing the parliament

The role of interest groups in a policy-making process

Our research in the Slovenian parliament (1991, 1992 and 1994) has shown that only a relatively small section of interest associations do act as interest groups and try to influence the policy-making process. Social organizations and societies have mainly remained hidden in a civil society sphere and have become interest intermediators between society and policy-makers. What usually drives them to become active in policy-making is the experience that they have to intervene into the policy-making process if they want their interests to be heard and respected in the creation of laws.

Organizational ecology (Atkinson and Coleman, 1992, p. 157) in Slovenia is not as crowded an interest area as in older democracies which have a highly developed participatory political culture. Our empirical research has shown that only a relatively small number of interest associations are active in policy-making. Usually, only certain social groups are able to organize themselves into interest groups. Their main characteristics seem to be a high level of education and/or a long professional tradition and an ability to organize professional associations of their own quite effectively (social groups such as doctors, dentists, lawyers, and teachers in secondary schools) or in rooting themselves into an important economic or public service sphere.

In spring 1992, interviewed members of the Slovene parliament estimated the power of bureaucracy and interest group influence on the policy-making process in the following manner (the per cent shown is those MPs who estimated the influence of bureaucracy or the named interest groups as great or very great) people in government departments (47 per cent); professional associations (27 per cent); large research institutes (25 per cent); medical doctors (25 per cent); 'managers' lobby (24 per cent); universities (21 per cent); the Chamber of Commerce (20 per cent); the expropriated (19 per cent); the Church and religious organizations (15 per cent); cooperative associations (13 per cent); feminist groups (13 per cent); large public utilities such as railways and the post office (13 per cent); tradesmen - excluding their influence through parties (13 per cent); trade unions (12 per cent); intellectuals in a cultural field (12 per cent); the Ljubljana banks (12 per cent); large economic organizations (11 per cent); teachers (11 per cent); pensioners (ten per cent) the 'atomic lobby' (eight per cent); farmers - excluding their influence through parties (eight per cent); foresters (five per cent); the peace movement (five per cent); employees on public estates (two per cent).

In Spring 1994, when we interviewed MPs about their perceptions of the most influential interest groups in specific policy fields (parliamentary working bodies) we obtained the following picture (Table 9.2)

Table 9.2   **Interest groups which are most important in policy fields where respondents (MPs) are active most***

Interest groups	No. of MPs who mentioned the i.g.	% of MPs who mentioned the i.g.
- trade unions	19	13.9
- farmers	13	9.5
- the disabled	13	9.5
- chamber of economy	11	8.0
- institutions & organizations in the field of health care	10	7.3
- local communities	9	6.6
- the retired	9	6.6
- economic organizations	8	5.8
- universities	7	5.1
- organizations in the field of sport	6	4.4
- cultural organizations	5	3.7
- students	4	2.9

*73 out of 90 MPs responded in the survey of Spring 1994.

Beside the 12 interest groups mentioned 74 others were mentioned by fewer than four MPs. Altogether only 86 interest groups were mentioned, while in Great Britain (as Richardson reported) there are more than 1000 of them in separate policy fields. The number of groups mentioned by Slovenian MPs seems to be very small compared to the official number of all organizations in Slovenia. In December 1993, 52,179 such enterprises and other organizations were officially registered (Source: Zavod za statistiko RS).

From Table 9.2 it is obvious that the most influential interest groups are those which have a longer organizational tradition, at least a basic level of professionalization and at least some continuous financial background. This fact could explain why the most influential interest groups are not those newly created in the process of democratic transition, but those which have roots in the previous system.

The interest group picture in Slovenia presented is probably just temporary. It seems that in future we can expect a dynamic development in this field. In the Spring 1994 parliamentary survey, 71 per cent of MPs estimated that the number of organizations, associations, societies and groups which want to influence policy making in the parliament is growing. Even now MPs are experiencing quite lively contacts with interest groups (Table 9.3).

Table 9.3   Frequency of contacts between MPs and interest groups

Frequency	% of MPs
daily	11.0
weekly	37.0
monthly	35.6
less than monthly	9.6
no answer	6.8

Attitudes of MPs toward interest groups

Political parties in Slovenia, as in other East Central European countries, are still dominating policy-making processes (Agh, 1994, p. 296; Judge, 1994, pp. 25-31). But it seems that parliamentary parties have started to think of other policy actors as relevant policy agents and even as possible political allies. On the one hand, parliamentary parties have already obtained the support of certain interest groups. On the other hand, MPs have been asked by interest groups to advocate their policy proposals in the parliament.

According to the parliamentary survey of 1994, 69.9 per cent of MPs do not think that the influence of different organizations, associations and groups can jeopardize democratic policy-making, but 19.2 per cent of MPs still think this may happen. They connect this attitude to their experience with some interest groups' practices which MPs consider to be a misuse of power in influencing the parliament. Otherwise, at least half of them were ready to declare that they felt close to a certain interest actor (Table 9.4).

Table 9.4   The proportion of MPs who feel they are personally linked to a certain organization, association or group

Existence of personal linkages	% of MPs
- yes	49.3
- no	38.4
- cannot say	9.6
- no answer	2.7

The most powerful links seem to be professional ties, links developing out of MPs' leisure-time interests and links to their home-place or region. (Table 9.5).

Table 9.5   The nature of the personal link between MPs and interest groups

Types of personal linkages	% of MPs
- profession	39.7
- home place	24.7
- personal interests (culture, sport, hobbies...)	24.7
- other linkages	6.8
- no answer	46.6

It is interesting that in the 1992 survey MPs from governmental parties statistically significantly (sig.= 0.0008) noticed fewer interest groups than the parties in opposition.[2] We can say that the position of MPs within the government/opposition cleavage in the parliament significantly influences their attitude toward interest groups. As in other countries, political opposition is more interested in contacts with interest groups. In our research from 1992, 69 per cent of oppositional and 42 per cent of MPs from governmental parties shared the opinion that interest groups affected by concrete policies should be consulted more often. Probably this is because interest groups can act as an opposition's allies in the criticism of a government.

Influencing the executive

The role and the level of interest group influence on policy making does not run automatically and in parallel to the political system change from a monistic to a pluralistic one. It is, for instance, a fact that the new government has so far shown relatively little readiness to accept interest groups as partners in the formation of the key public policies. The examples of the trade unions and farmers who have used strikes and demonstrations as forms of pressure on the government in order to force direct negotiations have clearly shown that they cannot get space in a policy-making area without struggling for it with the presently dominant policy actors.

It is interesting that big interest groups which were also active within the old political system (presently the biggest trade unions, the Chamber of Commerce, the League of Cooperatives) feel that there is a large gap between the accessibility of the old and new political elite. Government is now much more closed to interest groups and it is very difficult to get an appointment with certain ministers and especially with the Prime Minister. They feel that this is partly due to ideological reasons. The Chamber of Commerce, for example, became known as a 'red' (communist) institution. For similar reasons, interest groups in the field of agriculture such as the Union of Cooperatives which used to be strongly allied with the Ministry of Agriculture and Forestry, are now excluded from policy processes in that field. But even completely new interest groups whose interests favour the transformation process (as in the case of the Owners of Expropriated Property) are faced with the problem of exclusion from (for them) very important decision-making. The interest groups which existed already in the old regime also feel that they now have to put much more effort into preparation before possible meetings with government officials. They are expected to come forward with very strong and analytical arguments, prepared in advance. These preparations have become a necessary pre-condition for negotiations and talks with the government. Within the old political system government officials were very open and always ready to meet representatives of at least those corporate organizations mentioned. So interest groups representatives felt that the vertical information-flow in both directions was very good. Now they feel that they are no longer recognized as an important voice which should be heard and included in public policy-making and implementation.

Besides the ideological arguments in favour of interest group exclusion on the government side, one further argument was put forward in interviews with government officials. In the case of agriculture it was said very clearly that the interest group arena is very fragmented and that the government side does not see any representative organization which would really represent a substantial proportion of this social group. This is why they do not consult any of the fragmented interest groups in the field which are all in competition among themselves.

Of additional importance is that interest groups now find the parliament more accessible than the government. This is one of the reasons why MPs are their important lobbying targets. Another important reason for this is that the Slovenian parliament does not just formally accept the bills prepared by the government. Cases when the parliament completely changes the bill prepared by the government are not rare. Even more, the MPs from governing parties are not disciplined in voting for government proposals and may help the opposition to defeat governmental proposals. MPs also have a right to propose a bill and there were cases when they used that right quite effectively - even tabling alternative proposals to an already existing governmental bill. All these facts at least partially explain why the legislature is an important locus of power in the functioning of the Slovenian political system and is therefore also an important area for interest group activities.

The constitutional court as a target of interest group activity

During the last few years interest organizations have started to exert pressure in the field of judicial power. The official statistics of the Constitutional Court of the Republic of Slovenia reveal a fast growing tendency towards using this channel of influence (Table 9.6). The proportion of cases initiated at that court by enterprises, societies and organizations had risen from 9.5 per cent in 1989 to 39.1 per cent in 1993. At the same time it is interesting that in 1993 the proportion of issues concerning laws and regulations was as large as 50.3 per cent. More thorough empirical research is needed to analyse how much interest organizations are active in putting these issues on the Constitutional Court's agenda in comparison with other actors, and how and when they decide to use this channel for fulfilling their interests.

Probably there are at least three important reasons for interest groups targeting the Constitutional Court. Firstly, the fact is that the new Slovenian parliament has adopted an enormous number of laws in a very short period of time. Under pressure of time it often happens that bills are not very well prepared. This is why the phenomenon of correcting laws soon after they have been adopted is not rare in practice. It is possible to achieve that by political means but also by means of decisions of the Constitutional Court. Secondly, consultative politics has not been given an important place in the process of policy-making. This is why many laws do not reflect all the relevant problems concerning the area they regulate. Interest groups concerned try to postpone their implementation and achieve their correction by all means that are available to them. One of these means is indirect pressure through initiatives at the Consitutional Court. Thirdly, in all the cases when interest groups try to change the laws or at least prevent their implementation the political elite is not prepared to change its decisions - this is especially true when interest groups do not have substantial sources of power. The power of the interest groups might be strengthened by the decision of the judicial power.

Corporatist arrangements - institutionalization of corporatism in the form of the state council

Corporatism is not a new phenomenon in Slovenia. It has some roots in national history as well as in the former system of self-management. This was particularly evident in relationships between trade unions and privileged agricultural interest organizations on the one hand and the old political elite on the other. Functional representation of other interests was also included in the institutional structure of the old political system.

After a break caused by the change in the political elite and by changes in civil society, elements of neo-corporatism are now clearly re-emerging in the new political context. Firstly, one mode of this type of arrangement is a direct one and based on personal networks between a certain corporative organization and a certain Ministry. As analysis by Igor Lukšič (1994) has shown, a corporatist type of policy network is gaining more and more resources in Slovenia through the establishment of modern corporative organizations, such as chambers after 1990, and by giving them specific competence in creating and implementing public policies. This is shown in the case of the Medical Chamber and health-care policies. Secondly, a more institutionalized form of corporatism, the State Council, is a part of the constitutionally defined political system. And thirdly, new corporatist institutionalism is also developing in the form of specialised councils. Therefore we can talk about emerging neo-corporatism in Slovenia although it would be difficult to compare it with West European experiences as defined by Wiesenthal (1995, pp. 9-12) and Reutter (1994, pp. 1-2) directly.

Table 9.6   Cases coming before the constitutional court of the republic of Slovenia in the period from 1988 to 1993 according to the type of initiators (% in brackets)

Initiators	1988	1989	1990	1991	1992	1993
-proposal-makers (the Court, Chamber Economy)	0 (0.0)	0 (0.0)	2 (2.6)	4 (4.9)	7 (4.5)	6 (3.4)
-the Court of Associated labour	4 (3.9)	6 (6.7)	1 (1.3)	0 (0.0)	1 (0.6)	0 (0.0)
-public attorney	0 (0.0)	0 (0.0)	0 (0.0)	0 (0.0)	0 (0.0)	0 (0.0)
-social attorney of self-management	5 (4.9)	5 (5.6)	4 (5.2)	1 (1.2)	0 (0.0)	0 (0.0)
-local community assembly, public account agency	1 (1.0)	1 (1.1)	4 (5.2)	2 (2.4)	12 (7.8)	6 (3.4)
-enterprise, org. of assoc. labour	3 (2.9)	5 (5.6)	5 (6.5)	9 (11.0)	11 (7.1)	38 (21.2)
-local community	1 (1.1)	3 (3.4)	3 (3.9)	4 (4.9)	0 (0.0)	0 (0.0)
-other self-management organization	4 (3.9)	2 (2.2)	0 (0.0)	0 (0.0)	0 (0.0)	1 (0.6)
-citizen	62 (60.2)	52 (58.4)	42 (54.5)	43 (52.4)	80 (51.9)	89 (49.7)
-worker	16 (15.5)	7 (7.9)	8 (10.4)	4 (4.9)	1 (0.6)	6 (3.4)
-society, organization	4 (3.9)	4 (4.5)	2 (2.6)	8 (9.8)	28 (18.2)	32 (17.9)
-other initiators	1 (1.0)	3 (3.4)	6 (7.8)	5 (6.1)	13 (8.4)	1 (0.6)
-anonymous	1 (1.0)	0 (0.0)	0 (0.0)	2 (2.4)	0 (0.0)	0 (0.0)
-own	1 (1.0)	1 (1.1)	0 (0.0)	0 (0.0)	1 (0.6)	0 (0.0)
Total (N)	**103**	**89**	**77**	**82**	**154**	**179**

Source: Annual Report of the President of the Constitutional Court 1992, 1993.

As we have mentioned, the State Council is one of the forms of corporatist arrangements in Slovenia. It is an institution, composed of 22 representatives of local communities and 18 representatives of functional interests (Table 9.7).

Table 9.7   The formal structure of the state council (representatives of interests)

Interests to be represented	No. of seats
local communities	22
employers (business)	4
employees (labour)	4
farmers	2
tradesmen	1
free professions	1
universities and high schools	1
education	1
culture and sport	1
medicine	1
social services	1
Total	**40**

The State Council acts as a kind of an advisory body with the right to demand that parliament reconsiders a certain bill which has already been passed by parliament. This right has already been invoked, and where two-thirds of MPs do not vote for the bill again it is abandoned. In some cases this practice appeared to be a temporary veto on the parliamentary decision. A recent change of thought is that the State Council should be more active in the process of decision-making before the bill is passed in the parliament.

So far, the State Council has not gained a clearly defined and influential position in the total policy-making process. This is the main reason why it has not also gained a high priority on an interest group list of lobbying targets.

Other developing corporatist arrangements: the economic and social council

The Economic and Social Council is a tripartite body which was proposed after the 1990 elections on the initiative of the trade unions and the Ministry of Labour under a former communist.[3] It was to comprise representatives of trade unions, employers and the government. The initiative suggested that the body should deal with employment policy and act independently from the government and parliament. All governments (the two created after the 1990 elections and the one created after the 1992 elections) were inclined to give a strong role to free market arrangements in the economy and were therefore not very much interested in creating the tripartite body. Problems with growing unemployment and the gradual consolidation of the three partners and their supporting political agencies made the establishment of the Council possible in April 1994.

The Council involves three delegations representing the three partners with five members from each. It is focused on issues of economic and social policy.

Its statements, initiatives, proposals and recommendations are sent to the government, the parliament, the State Council and the public. Unanimous conclusions of the Council are binding on all organs and working bodies of the three social partners. As Lukšič reports elsewhere in this book, by mid-January 1995 the ESC had had thirteen meetings discussing the standing rules and nature of the ESC, some bills concerning collective agreements, workers participation and the minimum wage as well as the 1995 wage policy, the 1995 budget and the social pact for 1995.

Although the Council is functioning, there are a lot of obstacles to its effective operation, such as the strong liberal orientation of the government, the still not completed process of organizational development on the civil society side and the domination of the political process by parties. It is also very interesting that consensual decisions of the ESC, at least so far, have not modified parliamentary decision-making in the policy fields involved. This practice again differs from the description of West European neo-corporatism by Reutter (1994, p. 8). Namely, in Slovenia all the key decisions reached in the ESC go through the parliamentary procedure in the State Assembly.

Patterns of interest group involvement in a policy-making process

We cannot talk about one common pattern or structure of relationship between policy actors in all policy fields in Slovenia. As Table 9.8 shows, policy sectors may differ a great deal in this aspect.

It is interesting that the most influential cross-sectoral policy actor seems to be the state bureaucracy and that in certain fields experts have gained a relatively great influence. Twenty-nine per cent of MPs interviewed in 1992 estimated the influence of experts in the defence field as being great or very great, and twenty-seven per cent of them thought that the same was true for the role of experts in the field of international relations.

Table 9.8   The number of all interest groups mentioned in a certain policy field and the number of influential groups (survey in the Slovenian parliament in 1992)

policy field	no. of interest groups mentioned	influence of interest groups		
		1-3 dominant	several more influential	lack of influence
-health care	15	X		
-research & technology	15	X		
-employment, social policy	14	X		
-economy	13		X	
-defence	13			X
-int.relations	13			X
-credit-monetary policy	12		X	
-education, culture, sport	11	X		
-agriculture	10		X	
-home affairs	9			X

As survey results from 1992 have shown, the number of all interest groups mentioned in certain policy fields is generally very low. It is interesting to see what kind of interest groups are estimated by MPs as the most influential. Interest groups (and experts) mentioned in specific policy fields are as follows:

1. Health-care: the Slovenian Medical Association, the Business Association of Health-care Organizations, the Medical Chamber;
2. Agriculture: the League of Cooperatives, the farmers' organization within the Slovenian People's Party;
3. Education, culture, sport: the teachers' syndicate, the trade union of employees in the field of education, the state office for education;
4. Economy: the Chamber of Commerce, economic branches, the farmers' lobby;
5. Employment, social policy: trade unions, organizations of the retired, organizations of the disabled;
6. Defence: several groups like foresters, women's groups, the League of Veterans, local communities (mentioned rarely and as actors with little influence) + influential experts;
7. International relations: several groups like the Chamber of Commerce, the trade unions, the ethnic minorities, the United Nations Society, professional associations (mentioned rarely and as actors with little influence) + experts;
8. Home affairs: several groups like the Chamber of Commerce, the trade unions, the professional association of lawyers, associations concerned with human rights, movements - such as 'Pro-Life' (mentioned rarely and as actors with little influence).

Of course, the picture of interest groups involved is a very dynamic one. Therefore it is really valid only for the period when the research was being conducted. Similarly, this is true for patterns of relationship between interest groups and other policy actors.

Our 1992 research has shown four patterns of relationship between the policy actors:

a) Domination by a small number of influential interest groups in a more numerous interest group environment + relatively important influence of governmental representatives (health care, employment, social policy, education, culture, sport, research and technology).
b) Several interest groups with a dispersed and smaller influence in a more numerous interest group environment + relatively important influence of governmental representatives (economy, agriculture, credit-monetary policy).
c) Important influence of experts + relatively important influence of governmental representatives in the policy field + several rarely mentioned and not really influential interest groups (defence, international relations).

d) Underdeveloped interest groups + relatively important influence of governmental representatives in the policy field (home affairs).

The dynamic re-creation of Slovenian society, politics and policy space is still very lively, therefore additional empirical research should be done to explore changes in the structure and patterns of relationship between the policy actors which meet in concrete policy fields.

Methods of interest group influence

Our 1992 parliamentary research shows that interest groups in Slovenia try to influence policy-makers in different ways. The most important methods used for lobbying parliamentary bodies (listed in the order from most to less frequent) are:

- attending sessions of parliamentary working bodies,
- forwarding material to members of parliamentary working bodies,
- forwarding suggestions to them, public presentation of opinions and statements,
- personal contacts with MPs or even directly through a political party (farmers have organizations of their own within two political parties in Slovenia - the Christian Democrats and the Slovenian People's Party).

Some interest groups (such as medical doctors, pensioners, the Chamber of Commerce, banks, trade unions, universities and large research institutes) try to maximize their pressure by using several channels and methods at the same time.

Empirical data on lobbying was also obtained by interviewing representatives of some interest groups (the biggest Trade Union, the League of Consumers of Slovenia, the Chamber of Commerce, the Owners of Expropriated Property, the League of Cooperation, the students' organization). These have shown the importance of using the following additional methods: sending letters to all MPs; inviting all MPs to special meetings where an interest group tries to explain the social problem from its own point of view and suggests solutions; creating direct personal linkages between the interest group and the political party by an MP being at the same time also a member of the executive body of the interest group; using personal contacts with selected MPs who feel close to certain interest groups and are prepared to act as their speakers in the parliament; establishing close personal contacts with administrative staff in the parliament and within Ministries; using a network of informal contacts between important persons, where with the help of one person the interest group can gain easier access to information and to politicians; several interest groups (the League of Consumers of Slovenia, the Association of Owners of Expropriated Property) also forwarded some cases of violations of consumers' and citizens' rights to the Court.

In the 1994 survey, 97.3 per cent of MPs indicated that they had already been asked by an organization, association or group to present an initiative for preparing or changing a certain legislative bill or were asked to give their opinion on the possibilities of passing a certain legislative bill in the parliament. 57.5 per cent of MPs also confirmed that their party/parliamentary club had already sought out an alliance with a non-party organization, association or group. So, we cannot really talk about a one-way relationship, but more about a process of exchange between interest groups and parties.

Naturally, Slovenia is also experiencing a negative side of lobbying by interest groups and their direct connections with the government. For example, the proportion of MPs who experienced (according to their opinion) illegal or even violent methods of pressure seems to be growing very quickly (Table 9.9).

Table 9.9   Unacceptable methods of lobbying in the Slovenian parliament - perceptions of MPs in 1992 and 1994

	1992	1994
-% of MPs with exp. of unacceptable lobbying	14%	31.5%
-'unacceptable' methods according to MPs perceptions	an attempt of corruption; 'persuading without arguments'; threatening and insulting letters; demonstrations, boycotts, 'politization'	attempts of corruption; threatening and warning letters; threatening with publishing unpleasant information in mass media; blackmailing and pressures; intrusiveness without arguments

The growth of MPs' perception of 'unacceptable' methods of lobbying raises at least two questions which need normative answers. The first one is what can be defined as 'unacceptable methods of lobbying' since MPs have very different opinions and ethical criteria about this concept? For example, in our survey some MPs thought it was unacceptable even to be given a free railway ticket or to be invited to dinner or lunch. Others (22 per cent of them) just did not answer the question. And secondly, what rules of behaviour and sanctions for unacceptable behaviour need to be created in order to prevent and/or punish the unacceptable behaviour?

Additionally, some scandals caused by publishing information on the misuse of administrative and ministerial positions in favour of certain enterprises have stressed the problem of clientelistic relations in the new context.

The role of interest groups in the linkage of society with the state

The case of Slovenia is an illustrative example of the present democratic deficit in post-socialist countries. People in these countries can to some extent rely upon elections and strikes as mechanisms for influencing the political sphere, but not upon (as in old democracies) more conventional forms and mechanisms of interest mediation (Table 9.10).

Table 9.10   The most effective ways for influencing governmental decisions in Slovenia - answers of the first order and a sum of the first three orders (in %)

	I	I+II+III
- elections	43.5	54.8
- strikes	10.3	28.6
- demonstrations	3.7	17.5
- by political parties	3.0	21.0
- by MPs, members of govt.	3.9	24.6
- citizens' initiatives	1.4	10.0
- different societies	0.6	8.7
- publishing letters in mass media	1.0	14.6
- nothing is influential, people don't have any influence	21.5	65.3
- don't know, no answer	11.1	54.7

Source: Niko Toš, Slovenian Public Opinion, November 1993

Democracy has a future if it brings a real change in people's everyday life (Linz, 1990, p. 159). In the first few years of the nineties a majority of people in Slovenia estimated the social changes as a decline in the quality of their life. There had been a danger that pessimistic perceptions could become an autonomous factor of social and political instability producing a passive resistance to change or, more seriously, uncontrolled social conflicts.

Although during the last two years more people seem to have been improving their quality of life, in November 1994 58 per cent of respondents still estimated that they were worse off or much worse off than two years ago (Source: Toš, Slovene Public Opinion Poll). The dissatisfaction of a large part of the population encourages the survival of the old political culture. People still mainly expect that the state will solve all social problems as it used to do within the socialist political system. Weak intermediary structures go along with a strong 'protest syndrome' - direct protest actions seeking immediate state intervention to solve the specific problem of unemployment caused by the closing down of a factory or a problem of low salaries in enterprises or even in the public sector (such as the police) and so on. So, it is not political participation itself which is seen as a goal, but the solving of the acute problem of economic security, well-being, social status and mobility opportunities (Huntington and Nelson, 1977, p. 161).

It is obvious that interest groups are generally not seen by the public as links or mediators between the society and the state. They are seen mainly as actors linking very specific groups or organizations with those who make decisions in the policy-making process. Even in cases of bigger interest groups such as trade unions, a (possible) growing influence of the trade unions cannot automatically solve the problem of alienation, because trade unions are losing the trust of their members and the public in general - a similar trend with all the main political institutions in Slovenia, such as the government, parliament, political parties, and President of the Republic. As experiences in older democracies have shown, creating stable policy networks, where interest groups can play an important role, does not always and automatically mean more democracy for individual citizens. So bringing interest groups into policy-making would not automatically mean more democracy from the citizens' point of view. It could also bring about two processes: firstly, the process of colonization of the state on behalf of lobbies and secondly, the process of colonization of the civil society on behalf of political parties and the state.

Conclusions

In political science, pressure groups and therefore pressure politics are widely regarded as a largely modern phenomenon, a product of the modernization process (Rush, 1990, p. 4). It seems that the trend towards an increasing number and different forms of interest groups, and their pressures on public policy-makers, is an inevitable aspect of the modernization process. Those authors who are interested in the social roots of modern political participation (Lipset, 1959; Rothman, 1960; Huntington and Nelson, 1977) tend to present the relationship between socio-economic development, development of social structure on the one hand and political participation on the other, as positively correlated. Huntington and Nelson (1977, p. 43-45, 166-167) stress the following correlation: the more people become literate, educated, prosperous and the more they work in middle-class occupations the more they become political participants. Additionally, the growing complexity of the economy leads to a multiplication of organizations and associations, an expansion of the functions of government, as well as the building of the nation-state. So, in the long run, the economic and social forces feeding the expansion of political participation seem to be automatically developed and inexorable. Differences in forms and variations of levels of participation are thought to be primarily the product of the decisions of political elites (Huntington and Nelson, 1977, p. 170-1).

Political scientists have thought that post-socialist countries are exceptional in this sense and that we could not expect real interest group development or that only particular economic interests would be developed there (Marsh, 1993, p. 32). The case of Slovenia does not really confirm these expectations. For example, Slovenia has had for a long time some of the basic social preconditions for political participation. Slovenia is an industrialized and urbanized country, with nearly no illiteracy, with a developed education system, with a relatively small but existing so-called middle-class strata, with the highest GNP per capita among all former socialist countries of U$6000. It also has an enormous number of interest organizations as well as an old corporatist tradition. It is true that only a small number of the existing groups now behave as modern interest groups in the policy-making process, but we can already talk about the 'multi-actor political system' (Agh, 1994, p. 297).

Since an interest group system had not been developed immediately and in parallel with the introduction of the new political system, researchers thought that it could not really develop in these specific circumstances. According to our empirical research, modern interest groups in Slovenia are in the process of formation and gradually they are gaining some role in a policy-making process. Contrary to expectations (Marsh, 1993, p. 32), the case of Slovenia shows that the number of interest groups which are active in policy-making is growing and that the most influential extend beyond the usual economic groups. Additionally, the corporatist tradition is revitalizing the political culture and new institutions. Some sectoral cases in Slovenia have also shown that more personally determined networks are gradually developing into quite stable and even formally defined relationships between dominant policy actors (monopolistic interest groups and the relevant Ministry). In general, it seems that this is happening in the fields where the corporatist tradition is most strong.

Some important processes like the process of privatization, denationalization, and the general process of extending the operation of the market are still taking place and are reconstructing the social structure and dominant values. Additionally, citizens, groups, organizations and the new political elite are re-socializing and learning how to behave effectively in the new circumstances. It seems that the learning process has so far been going in the direction of a broadening of interest group activity in the policy-making process and in all branches of power, legislative, executive and judicial. The parliament seems to be much more open to interest groups than is the case with the executive power, but interest groups still often feel helpless.

Beside this general picture we should also stress the variety of sectoral experiences our empirical research has shown. The fact is that in different policy fields in Slovenia different types of policy network concepts are applicable, most notably in a multi-interest group context. After all, some types of policy networks developed within the old democracies, where the concept was created, include only a few policy actors (Van Vaarden, 1992, pp. 39-41).

Ultimately, the testing of theories and concepts concerning interest groups and their stabilizing role in a policy-making process in post-socialist countries will only really be possible after a longer period of time. We cannot expect that social and political phenomena, which have been developed in old democracies through decades, will be fully developed in new democracies in just a few years. Neither can we say, on the basis of the present situation, that this phenomenon will not become a highly significant one.

Notes

1.   Definitions of Organizations:

> Enterprises...profit organizations active in economic or non-economic fields;
> Societies...voluntary association of citizens for fulfilling of special interests;
> Social Organizations...special official category in the Slovenian social system. Examples of social organizations are the Red Cross, Firemen Societies, Hunters' Societies, Fishermen Societies, Motoring Societies, the League of Reserve Military Officers;

Organizations...organizations in all spheres of social life (before 1990 also self-management economic organizations included).

2. In the case of our research from 1992, 76 per cent of government MPs identified only one or two interest groups in 'their' policy field and only 24 per cent of them noticed three or more interest groups. In contrast only 12 per cent of opposition MPs identified one or two interest groups and 68 per cent three or more interest groups.

3. An account of the Economic and Social Council is provided by Lukšič in Chapter 8 of this book.

Appendix to Chapter 9

Table 9.11 Trust in organizations and political institutions in Slovenia (in %)

	totally/a lot	little/not at all	don't know
trade unions			
SPO1991 (1)	15.2	70.2	14.6
SPO1992 (2)	16.2	67.8	16.0
SPO1992 (3)	13.1	66.9	20.0
SPO1993 (1)	11.3	71.3	17.4
SPO1994 (4)	12.0	71.9	17.1
political parties			
SPO1991 (1)	12.2	76.9	10.9
SPO1992 (2)	11.3	78.3	10.4
SPO1992 (3)	7.7	77.2	15.1
SPO1993 (1)	3.2	86.6	10.2
SPO1994 (4)	4.7	85.1	10.3
government			
SPO1991 (1)	42.6	52.2	5.2
SPO1992 (2)	32.5	61.3	6.2
SPO1992 (3)	34.3	59.1	6.6
SPO1993 (1)	13.3	79.0	7.7
SPO1994 (4)	14.3	79.4	6.3
parliament			
SPO1991 (1)	36.8	52.4	10.8
SPO1992 (2)	33.7	54.5	11.8
SPO1992 (3)	20.2	64.3	15.5
SPO1993 (1)	15.0	71.7	13.3
SPO1994 (4)	15.0	71.2	13.3
President of Republic			
SPO1991 (2)	67.8	26.2	6.0
SPO1992 (3)	59.2	32.8	8.0
SPO1993 (1)	46.6	47.3	6.1
SPO1994 (4)	45.3	46.7	8.1

SPO=Slovenian Public Opinion Polls
Source: Niko Toš, Slovene public opinion (SPO), longitudinal project, Centre for Public Opinion and Mass Communication, Research Institute for Social Sciences, Faculty of Social Sciences, Ljubljana.

Table 9.12   **Membership in trade unions which took part in elections to the state council in December 1992**

Trade Unions	no. of members
Association of Free Trade Unions of Slovenia	435,716
Independence - Confederation of New Trade Unions of Slovenia	162,000
Confederation of Trade Unions '90 of Slovenia	41,557
Trade Union of Education & Science	30,062
Trade Union of Medical & Social Care	23,573
Confederation of Trade Unions PERGAM	18,392
Trade Union of Bank Workers of Slovenia	9,500
Trade Union of Railway Workers	7,429
Trade Union of Policemen	5,096
Trade Union of Dentists & Doctors	2,070
Trade Union of Workers of the University of Ljubljana	950*
Trade Union of Journalists	807
Trade Union of New Researchers	215*

Source: Report of the Election Commission of the Parliament of the Republic of Slovenia, December 1992.

*Reported by Igor Lukšič (1994, p. 210) on the basis of an interview with the secretary of the Trade Union.

Table 9.13   Membership of four Slovenian federations or confederations of trade unions

Trade Unions	no. of members
Association of Free Trade Unions of Slovenia	439,850
Independence - Confederation of New Trade Unions of Slovenia	163,000
Confederation of Trade Unions '90 of Slovenia	49,512
Confederation of Trade Unions PERGAM	31,286

Source: Report of Mandatory Commission of the Council of RTV Slovenia, Oct. 1994, when Trade Unions elected their members of the Council (as quoted by Lukšič, forthcoming).

Note: Trade Unions do not always de-register departed members.

Table 9.14   Membership of trade unions in Slovenia - results of a telephone survey in September 1994 (in %)

trade unions	reported membership (%)
Association of Free Trade Unions of Slovenia	22.1
Independence - Confederation of New Trade Unions of Slovenia	5.3
Confederation of Trade Unions '90 of Slovenia	1.0
Confederation of Trade Unions PERGAM	0.8
a member of any other Trade Union	10.7
a member of a Trade Union, but does not know of which one	5.9
a member of no Trade Union	54.2
TOTAL (%)	100.0
(N)	506

Source: Stanojević and Omerzu (1994, p. 122)

10 Development of a Party System

DANICA FINK-HAFNER

Key processes of multiparty system development in Slovenia in the eighties and in the beginning of the nineties

The development of the democratic party system in Slovenia has been closely related to two key processes of political modernization which occurred at the end of the eighties and at the beginning of the nineties.

Firstly, there was a gradual process of liberalization and democratization. This resulted from social and political struggles between the old Slovenian political elite and the emerging civil society, which by the end of the eighties also produced the new opposition parties. In this respect, it was a process of democratic transition such as might be found in an independent national state (compare Dahl, 1971, pp. 40-41).

Secondly, the process of democratic transition coincided with the process of nation building, including that of state building. Therefore, it could also be seen as a transition characteristic of 'dependent' states (Dahl, 1971, pp. 40-41). Namely, the establishing of competitive politics and the introduction of a market economy in Slovenia meant a radical cutting of the umbilical cord with the old system and also with the federal Yugoslav state, which had not yet been prepared for the reform. In the beginning, the emergence of political parties in Slovenia was an expression of political modernization, but it soon became closely related to the process of national integration and state-building. Parties became agents of the formation of the Slovenian state as well as 'prisoners' of that process.

In this paper we are going to present the key processes and characteristics of a multi-party system development in Slovenia from the following aspects:

- Political modernization and the adaptation of the old elite in Slovenia;
- Political pluralization within the old Yugoslav political elite and the formation of 'national' communist parties in the republics and autonomous provinces of the former Yugoslavia;
- Development of new political parties in Slovenia;
- Organizational and social sources of parties in the newly emerging party arena in Slovenia;
- Parties' search for social roots and identity;
- Key characteristics of development of the new party arena;
- The 'partyness' of the new democracy in Slovenia.

Political modernization and the adaptation of the old elite in Slovenia

The socialist political system in Slovenia (and the former Yugoslavia), with its emphasis on self-management, had one key characteristic in common with the mainstream East European political systems. Namely, the leading role of the communist party had never really been limited by self-management. The main obstacle to the development of modern competitive politics was a restriction on the freedom of association. This obstacle was systematic and was even included in the constitution (Article 153 of the Constitution of the SFRY, 1974).[1] Thus, the realization of the freedom of association was closely related to the realization of all other politically relevant rights - freedom of speech, of public assembly, voting rights, etc. (Zupančič et al. 1989, p. 5, Bertalanić 1990, p. 1).

The first stages of the transition, in the middle of the 1980s, involved the acceptance of the existence of an opposition. In Autumn 1989 the monistic Slovenian Constitution was amended to permit pluralism. The new pluralism was entrenched by the new democratic Constitution of 1991.

Political modernization in Slovenia was relatively peaceful, although the old Slovenian political elite used various repressive measures against individual opponents, but excluded the massive use of physical violence. The process of political modernization came into existence in three major forms of political change which were required to create a systemic change.[2] Firstly, there was the mobilization of new social groups for concrete political goals, especially those social groups previously excluded by the socialist monistic system, such as farmers-peasants, craftsmen, private entrepreneurs, the young, the religious or ideological dissidents; secondly, by the political tolerance of social protest; and thirdly by the process of reform from 'above'.

The internalization of modern democratic values involved a long-term process in society as well as the conversion of the old political elite. A very significant indicator of a gradually changing political consciousness is clearly seen in the successive statements on the role of the League of Communists inside the political system. The long-term survey project, the 'Slovenian

Public Opinion Poll' (SPO) gathered data on a representative sample of the adult population (18 years and over) of Slovenia and in the period before 1986. This had clearly shown strong support for the League of Communists to remain the leading party. Only after 1986 did support for a multi-party system start to spread among the majority of the adult citizens (Table 10.1).

Table 10.1 Comprehension of social role of LC - the league of communists (in %)

		agrees entirely	agrees almost entirely	doesn't know- undecided	mostly doesn't agree	doesn't agree at all
a) LC should be only one of	SPO86	21.4	24.4	28.7	14.3	11.2
the political parties - each	SPO88	30.8	25.8	27.0	9.8	6.7
individual should decide freely which party to support	SPO89	48.8	26.3	18.0	4.7	2.2
b) LC should be the only	SPO86	19.1	26.3	25.9	19.2	9.5
political power in our	SPO88	8.4	10.4	26.1	38.0	17.0
society	SPO89	4.9	7.6	19.3	26.7	41.6

SPO86 - SPO89...'The Slovenian Public Opinion Poll'. Research in the years 1986, 1988, 1989 - taking a representative sample of the adult population of Slovenia.

In the year 1986, 45 per cent of those questioned agreed entirely or substantially with the view that multi-partyism should be introduced, but by the year 1989 this percentage had risen to 74 per cent. The gradual and uncertain acceptance of party pluralism among ordinary people is not surprising if we take into account the old elite's strategy of proposing a 'social contract', as well as using ideological instruments and repression for maintaining the old regime.[3]

Opinion leaders drawn by the Slovenian Public Opinion Poll from a wide variety of target groups showed differing attitudes to political change. The 'non-conforming intellectuals' (namely in the literary, artistic, spiritual, humanitarian and health-care areas) had the most well-defined positive attitudes toward multipartism. In 1989 they were more radically in favour of political pluralism than the 'average' population of Slovenia. On the other hand, another segment of opinion leaders principally drawn from local politicians were even more conservative than the 'average' population of Slovenia and continued to adhere to a monistic socialist type of political culture.

It is interesting that the old political elite at the national level was much more adaptive to the new circumstances than the local political elite. (Fink-

Hafner and Kranjc, 1988). In 1986, the liberal segment gained the upper hand, and the conservatives became marginalized in the Slovenian League of Communists. Two of the important factors in that victory were the democratization of the Slovenian League of Communists' statutory rules and the fact that the new LC leadership, headed by Milan Kučan, was elected by secret ballot at the eighth congress in 1986. The Slovenian political leadership found itself in a dilemma; there was domestic pressure toward political pluralization, democratization and economic reform on the one hand and resistance towards these reforms with growing threats of repression by 'Yugoslav' forces on the other. The decision of the Slovenian political elite to support their nation and republic appeared to be decisive for further development.

During the eighties the conservative political elite used different strategies in its conflict with the developing civil society. There was repression and stigmatization of individual and collective supporters of these alternatives. Such persons were kept under surveillance, and there was a strategy of co-option into an unchanged or only partly corrected system. When social and political opposition became so strong that it could only be subdued by violent repression, the political elite agreed to abandon the LC's monopoly position. Thus, the Slovenian political elite's official political stance evolved from a rejection of the legitimacy of political pluralism, to agreement with a quasi-pluralistic formula termed 'non-party pluralism', and thereafter towards a normal conception of multi-party political pluralism in which the LC would be only one political party among others and without any special privileges.

One of the important results of this process was also the development of an element of pluralism within the framework of the existing and formally monistic political institutions. The transforming segment of the old political elite even took over some key civil society initiatives, though with an important time-lag. In the middle of the eighties, the Socialist Youth Alliance of Slovenia and later also the Socialist Alliance of the Working People[4] became vehicles for the initiatives of some new oppositional political parties. Similarly, the Socio-Political Chamber of the Slovenian National Assembly became a venue where the self-transforming Socialist Youth Alliance of Slovenia was able to undertake initiatives on behalf of the emerging autonomous civil society. It is also important to note that the Slovene legislation of Autumn 1989, which introduced multi-partyism to the Yugoslav framework of what was formally still a one-party system, was adopted by the existing Slovene 'monistic' parliament of Slovenia.

The controversial and ambiguous situation of the 'old' Slovenian political elite in the transformation process raises the question of whether this elite had the function of reproduction and/or transformation of the socialist political system in Slovenia. We can say that major political transformation was inevitable as an autonomous civil society evolved during the eighties and as there emerged a growing cleavage between the Slovenian and other political elites in the former Yugoslavia. It was the reaction of the old political elite in Slovenia that made this transition relatively smooth and peaceful. Indeed, as pressure from Yugoslav sources increased, the Slovenian political elite even became an ally of the emerging civil society. A symbol of that alliance was, for example, the demonstration of common symbolic resistance to repressive Serbian nationalism in the Slovenian National House of Culture, in 1989. Had the Slovenian political elite chosen the option of cooperation with the monistic forces in the former Yugoslavia, it would have lost its national legitimacy and therefore also its dominant position. Sharing power with the opposition became the necessary condition for its survival.

Paradoxically, the Slovenian political elite acted as its own grave-digger in order to ensure a continuing role in the emerging pluralist political system. It would, however, be incorrect to consider the political elite as the main generator of change. It was, more precisely, a contributing factor rather than an initiator of the gradual, non-violent democratic transition. The old elite's adaptive behaviour was rewarded with the significant success of the former communists at the first free elections in 1990. They won the highest percentage of votes of any individual party and the former president of the Slovenian League of Communist, Milan Kučan, was elected President of the Republic with a big majority.

Political pluralization within the old Yugoslav political elite - the formation of 'national' communist parties

Research conducted in the former Yugoslavia in the eighties (Šiber, 1989; Grdešić, Kasapović and Šiber, 1989; Jambrek, 1989) has shown that it was undoubtedly possible to speak of national communist parties existing within the former Yugoslavia at the end of the eighties. During the second half of the eighties communist parties in different republics and provinces clearly developed a concept of responsibility to 'their societies' rather than to the federal entity. In fact, political pluralization occurred within the old socialist paradigm, but in the form of a cleavage between republics and provinces of the former Yugoslavia. The social and political background of the 'nationalization' of communist parties was deeply rooted in a cleavage between traditionalism and modernism. Therefore, political pluralization in the former Yugoslavia involved the 'nationalization' of the old political paradigm. After 1990 only some of the former republics and provinces left the old paradigm and started to develop modern democracy, while others just continued the old regime with a new image and 'by other means'.

So, what were the most important ideological and political differences between communist parties in the former Yugoslavia at the end of the eighties? In 1989, the organizations in the separate republics and provinces had clearly different attitudes toward the basic questions of economic and political development - particularly those concerning the changes of the political system inaugurated by the 1974 Yugoslav Constitution. Gradually, the common ideology started to diverge along national lines. Two key views on the transformation of the political system could be discerned at this period: the real-socialist (or conservative) and the reformist. Research has shown that there was a distinct correlation between regional variables and attitudes towards political pluralism (Table 10.2). In the Spring of 1989, members of the Slovenian League of Communists openly strove for a radical transformation of the political system and for the setting up of a pluralist and competitive political system. Others were not so in favour of democratization.

Table 10.2   Republics/provinces allegiance and attitude towards political pluralism (only a clearly supportive attitude (in %))

Problems	MG	SER	VOJ	BIH	MAC	KOS	CRO	SLO
Striving for a multi-party pluralism	6	9	10	12	14	16	19	36
Acceptance of existence and activity of new political league	9	8	12	14	14	24	19	44
New leagues' mass media	12	10	14	18	16	24	24	46

Source: Šiber 1989, p. 29.

There were also considerable differences of opinion on the possible re-construction of the Yugoslav federation. The views of LC members ranged from those supporting a centralist arrangement to those seeking a pluralist political arrangement (Figure 10.1). The Slovenian preference was clearly in favour of a pluralist, decentralized solution (Šiber, 1989, p. 29). The Slovenian membership gave the highest priority to economic reform, the establishment of the rule of law and political pluralism (Šiber, 1989, p. 33).

Figure 10.1 Continuum from a centralist to pluralist political arrangement

centralism   decentralization

| SER | MG | VOJ | MAC | BIH | KOS | CRO | SLO |

monism   pluralism

Source: Šiber, 1989, p. 84.

Deep differences between the republican and provincial League of Communists were shown in the contents of discussions at the first conference of the Yugoslav League of Communists in May 1988. A content analysis of discussions (Grdešić et. al., 1989, pp. 75-6) has shown that communists from Croatia and Slovenia were in favour of reformist socialism. In their discussions they expressed their support for the reform of the LC, for a market economy and for the legalization of a plurality of interests. Communists from other federal units (BIH, MG, SER, MAC, KOS, VOJ) were in favour of traditional socialism. In their discussions they stressed support for the renewal of the LC, for more responsibility and a better personnel policy, for the maintenance of democratic centralism, for the equality of economic actors and for central regulation. Kosovo moved closer to a more decentralist strategy because of its special problems with Serbian repression of the Albanians.

The differences among the constituent units of the Yugoslav League of Communists were finally manifested in a definitive split, when the Slovenian delegates demonstratively walked out of the Fourteenth Congress of the Yugoslav League of Communists on 21 January 1990. It is interesting that members of the former Slovene communist leadership tried to postpone the final split as long as possible in the hopes that a compromise solution might be found and the split avoided. They only took the step when members of the traditionally orientated party elites openly told them that it was time for the Slovenes to leave. The walkout of the Slovenian communists met with a round of applause by the majority of delegates at the congress. The Slovenian League of Communists, having broken its ties with the old political system, started the real process of transformation into a modern political party which would be able to compete with other parties in a democratic way. With the disintegration of the Yugoslav League of Communists, the Yugoslav People's Army became the only really federal institution remaining.

Development of new political parties in Slovenia

Factors of party development

The development of modern political parties in the context of the democratic transition in Slovenia can be analysed and understood on the basis of several different theoretical approaches developed in political science with respect to historical experiences in Europe and in the United States of America. The *modernization approach* could help to explain structural factors of party development in Slovenia at the end of the eighties as well as the earlier emergence of parties in Slovenia in comparison with other republics and provinces of the former Yugoslavia. Research conducted in the eighties in the former Yugoslavia reveals that different patterns and levels of modernization had developed in different federal units. In the eighties Slovenia had reached the point where the introduction of a market economy and a multi-party democracy became necessary preconditions for further social development, including political development. Although modernization theory explains the structural factors producing democratic development it cannot entirely explain the final timing of the change.

Here a *crisis theory* is valuable in stressing the processes of delegitimization of the old regime and cyclical crises as factors in creating oppositional parties and also re-creating the old socio-political parties. The socialist regime had undergone several serious crises in postwar Yugoslavia. From the sixties onwards tendencies towards political modernization became obvious, but had been suppressed by repressive and ideological measures. After 'the iron seventies', Tito's death in 1980 and in the context of a growing economic crisis at the beginning of the eighties, a new cycle of delegitimization of the old regime started to emerge. Delegitimization of the old economic and political system peaked in the second part of the eighties. This was the time when the first embryonic oppositional parties were organized in Slovenia.

The *institutional approach* could partially explain and describe party system development in Slovenia - especially after the first free elections in 1990. The newly created parliamentary parties were to a great extent composed of core groups of new politicians sitting in the parliament. Parties were financed by the state budget as well as being supported by the parliamentary and governmental administration, all of which helped the parties to strengthen their organization and create an organizational network in Slovenia as a whole. Therefore, we could conclude that several different factors initiated and supported party development in Slovenia from 1988 till now. Parties which evolved from the old socio-political organizations had far fewer problems with resources and development/maintaining of their organizational network.

Stages of party development

In Slovenia the development of new political parties passed through several stages. *Firstly*, they emerged as embryonic parties within the one-party system framework and found a legal space within the existing socio-political organizations, especially within the Alliance of Socialist Youth. The first such parties were established in Spring 1988. *Secondly*, at the end of the eighties multi-partyism was legalised within the framework of the one-party system. At that time and especially just before the first free elections in 1990 multi-partyism started to flourish and oppositional parties declared their intention of taking over full political power. *Thirdly*, parliamentarization of the most influential parties after the 1990 elections has helped the new parties to develop their organizational structure throughout the Republic of Slovenia. The *fourth* stage, which is still ongoing, is marked by the consolidation of the party system and the individual parties' search for social and economic roots.

Resources of organizational development

As in other cases of transition from a totalitarian to a democratic political system a deep political change was expressed by an eruption of new political organizations. It is interesting that the majority of new political organizations (54 per cent of the 124 organizations registered by 31 December 1993 on the basis of the Act on Political Organizations of December 1989) were registered in the capital of Slovenia. This was probably the result of the concentration of oppositional intellectuals and movements in Ljubljana.

Political parties had developed from different social and organizational bases as follows:

- the old socio-political organizations (Alliance of Socialist Youth of Slovenia - now Liberal Democracy of Slovenia, Slovenian League of Communists - now United List of Social Democrats);
- new social movements (the Greens of Slovenia);
- social opposition to the old regime such as the Writers' Association, a group focused around 'Nova revija' - the New Journal... (the Alliance of Intellectuals, later renamed the Slovenian Democratic Alliance);
- mobilization of existing social groups - farmers, craftsmen (new parties which at least at the beginning presented themselves as 'class' parties - Slovene People's Party, Slovene Craftsmen's Party);
- political organization of formerly apolitically organized social groups such as the retired (parties of the retired);
- political expressions of regional interests (like the Alliance of Haloze, Party of Slovenian Štajerska, Alliance for Primorska);
- religious (Catholic) milieu such as Revija 2000 - The Journal 2000 (Christian Socialists);
- on the basis of ethnicity (such as Alliance for Equal Rights of Citizens, Alliance of Romi - Gipsies, Communita Italiana).

In the context of the first free elections in 1990 we can observe parties with very different organizational origins - those primarily organized in Slovenia, branches of parties primarily organized in the former Yugoslavia, branches of international parties and organizations of national minorities within Slovenia.

From recent developments it has become obvious that organizational strength is related to the original resources. Only the successfully transformed socio-political organizations brought strong organizational networks into the new party system. A few newly organized parties consolidated their organization successfully (the Christian Democrats, the People's Party, the Slovenian Social Democrats). Others have been having serious difficulties due to a lack of personnel and scarce financial resources as well as splitting and reorganizing themselves politically. It is also of note that branches of parties primarily organized in the former Yugoslavia as well as branches of international parties disappeared very quickly.

Development of organizational networks

Most of the parliamentary parties succeeded in developing their organizational network throughout Slovenia. The transformed socio-political organizations abandoned their economic branch network. This was a consequence of the political decision adopted under pressure from the political opposition at the end of the eighties to 'free the economy from politics'. In the new political system, party organizational units are allowed only on a territorial principle.

With some exceptions (such as the Slovenian National Party) parties have developed several organizational levels including those at a national, regional and local level. The most important motivation for a territorial organizational network was a struggle for votes in the years 1990 and 1992. Territorial penetration by the 'centre' which controlled, stimulated, or directed the development on the 'periphery' (Panebianco, 1988, p. 50) was therefore a dominant pattern of their organizational development. This pattern was only partly combined with territorial diffusion in the sense of the spontaneous germination of party associations which were later integrated into a national organization (Panebianco, 1988, p. 50).

Parties' organizational networks still differ according to the level of party development. Successfully transformed socio-political organizations such as the former communists and the Alliance of Socialist Youth of Slovenia are in a much better position than the newly formed political parties since, to a great extent, they have kept their old networks of communal and regional units. They can still use a lot of facilities from the old regime and function with a core of their original personnel as well as with many of their old members. In contrast to this, new political parties had to start creating the whole organizational, personnel and activist network from scratch. That is also true for the still emerging parties and for some of the parties which are emerging from party splits.

Organizational complexity

Another aspect according to which parties in Slovenia differ is organizational *complexity*. It is interesting that in 1992 right-wing parties were generally much more complex than left-wing and centre-orientated parties. For example, the Slovene Christian Democrats had about five ancillary organizations, the Slovene 'People's Party' eleven, others had one or two (usually youth and women's organizations). Exceptionally, the Slovene National Party has no ancillary organizations. The Party of Social Democratic Renewal was an exception on the left in that it had a variety of interest organizations, which had the status of autonomous entities within the party. Interest groups were not clearly defined in the party's statutory rules and could not be easily counted without more thorough research. After 1992 it seems that some ancillary organizations became much less active or even disappeared. Some of them also left the party because they were unhappy with shifts toward centralization within 'their' party. New ancillary organizations have also developed to integrate specific target groups into parties. This was especially apparent in small parties with big political ambitions who started to give special space to groups like the religious, farmers, potentially wealthy interest groups (like owners of disappropriated estates) and business managers. This has happened even in cases when these groups were not their 'natural' allies (such as in the case of a new ancillary organization of the religious within the new social democratic party). Obviously, the internal organizational structure of parties is still in a process of dynamic change. The main factor influencing organizational development in all aspects remains the struggle for votes. Therefore we can expect a new wave of organizational adaptation in the forthcoming election period for the 1996 elections.

Types of parties

With respect to parties' relationship towards the civil society and towards the state we can say that practically all the parties in Slovenia act as *elitist* parties. Internal democracy has not been developed in any real sense. We can even talk about very big differences among parties. If some of them recognize internal democratic procedures at least in their statutory rules, others (such as the Slovene National Party) do not even prescribe them but give the whole power to the individual party leader. Some events, such as the decision to abandon the right to autonomy of auxiliary organizations within parties, have even shown some steps backwards in the development of intraparty democracy. Parties which in the beginning expressed an intent to develop internal democracy now ignore it. Therefore, it is not a surprise that Slovenes mainly see parties as run by egoistic party elites for their personal interests.

At the same time we could also say that Slovenian parties try to follow the pattern of *'catch-all'* parties, targeting as many voters as possible without providing for a narrower 'class' orientation. At the same time *clientelistic* organizations based on coalitions between business and political parties are developing. So the key characteristics of parties in Slovenia in the middle of the nineties would be: close ties with the state, clientelism, domination of personal networks and weak ties between voters and parties.

Parties in search of social identity

Instability of voters preferences

Slovenian political parties are still in the process of building up their identity. As Slovenian public opinion polls during the first two years of democratic transition have shown, the voting preferences of Slovenes are still very unstable (Toš 1992, 1992c). Most voters have not yet developed a firm attachment to any of the existing parties. For example, about 50 per cent of people surveyed in the Slovenian Public Opinion Polls between 1990-1992 did not know which party they would vote for at the next elections.

From the ideological aspect we could say that Slovenes are to a large extent left or left-centrist orientated. In several public opinion researches in the period from June 1991 to February 1992 about 69 per cent of those interviewed said that they would position themselves in the left-centre part of the left-right continuum and only 31 per cent of them would locate themselves on the right. Both extremes of self-identifications were marginal, covering only a few per cent each.

There are also some social characteristics which affect the building of party-identification in Slovenia. Left or left-centrist orientation is more common among people with higher education and among officials with high education. More rightist orientation could be found among farmers, workers, the religious and the otherwise more traditionally orientated people.

According to Slovenian Public Opinion Polls between 1990-1995 party identification is relatively stable only in the case of the Party of Democratic Renewal (former League of Communists). Public opinion polls 1990-1992 had also shown that about 50 per cent of voters who voted for the Slovenian Farmers' Party, the People's Party, the Slovenian Christian Democrats and the Greens of Slovenia at the first free elections declared that they would again vote for the same party at the next elections.

This did not prove to be a good indicator of stabilizing party identification, since at the 1992 elections some parties (like the Greens of Slovenia) gained far fewer votes than they had expected, and a completely new party, the Slovene National Party, got as much as ten per cent.

Many key determinants of party identification, such as the structure of the party system, the positioning of voters on the left-right continuum, and party self-identification are still in a process of dynamic change. Probably identification will not stabilize for some time, but an analysis of the Spring 1994 Slovenian Public Opinion Poll data has shown that the upper classes are much more orientated toward the transformed parties from the old regime (Table 10.3). The new parties seem to be able to attract more voters from the lower social strata.

Table 10.3   Party identification according to self-perceptions of interviewer's own class status (in %)

	CLASS		
parties	low	middle	upper
old	12.3	17.6	36.3
new	28.1	28.5	28.4
don't knows	59.6	53.9	35.3

signif.= 0.00000
C= 0.15245
Source: Niko Toš, Slovenian Public Opinion Data, Spring 1994

Party self-identification and voters' perceptions of parties

It is extremely difficult to define parties in the Slovenian post-socialist context on the left-right continuum. One cluster of problems implies difficulties with the operationalization of 'left/right' criteria and the other cluster of problems contains confusions with an inconsistent (self) definition of parties.

Nearly all the parties tend to present themselves as 'centre' parties, with the exceptions being the Socialist Party of Slovenia, which at 1990 elections presented itself as a party of the 'left centre', and the Party of Democratic Renewal which declares itself to be 'a party of the European left'. Only the Greens of Slovenia clearly stated that they were 'a holistic party' which could not be considered in left-right terms, before splitting along left/right lines. It is interesting that three parties avoided expressing their left-right identity for a long period of time. These were the Slovenian People's Party, the Slovenian Christian Democrats and the Slovenian National Party.

At the beginning of 1995 it is obvious that the majority of parties still tend to present themselves as being centre, centre-left or centre-right parties. Events within the ruling coalition and pressures from one former coalition partner (Social Democratic Party of Slovenia) seem to have pushed the Christian Democrats and the Slovenian People's Party more towards the right - especially in pre-election periods. Otherwise it is impossible to predict more long-term and permanent shifts in the ideological structure of the party system in the future. Four main factors support a thesis that the 'old' left-centrist parties have the most promising basis for the future. These factors are: good economic results and relative social peace under the present government, which is predominantly led by the left-centrist parties; domestic and foreign experts' estimation that Slovenia has very good prospects for further relatively stable economic development; a relatively stable dominant left-centrist orientation among Slovenian voters; and the far reaching and promising social and economic resources of the two successfully transformed 'old' left centrist parties.

Membership

At the end of the 1980s membership figures of political organizations were declining because of the growing freedom of association and because of the growing criticism of the political organizations of the regime - although at least some of them had already started the process of democratic transformation. We can also say that people did not readily decide to join the newly formed political parties. Data from Slovenian public opinion polls has shown that the percentage of adult citizens who are members of political parties is declining; in January 1991 it was 9.1 per cent, in December 1991 6.1 per cent, in March 1992 5 per cent and in November 1992 4.5 per cent. At the end of the 1980s and just after the first free elections it seemed that the percentage of adult citizens involved in party political life would approximate to the percentage of adult citizens who had been members of the League of Communists, but today we can observe a growing membership crisis. It is interesting that this tendency has not become a public issue. Its salience for parliamentary parties has been reduced by the introduction of state funding.

Participation in party life

Another aspect of citizens' participation in party life is of course their involvement in party activities. Only a few per cent of adult citizens attend political meetings and demonstrations and according to SPOP data this was 4.5 per cent in November 1992. Party life is dominated by the activity and interests of party elites, and citizens increasingly see parties as institutions which only serve the interests of their leaders. SPOP data demonstrate this belief in elite dominance: in January 1991 it was 32.1 per cent, in December 1991 36.1 per cent and in March 1992 41.1 per cent. Politicians are mainly seen as people who misuse politics for their own benefit (56.6 per cent of SPOP respondents in November 1992 agreed with that opinion). About half of the adult citizens (51.7 per cent of respondents in the SPOP just before the elections in December 1992) did not feel close to any party.

Ideological structure of the Slovenian party arena

The building of ideological identity and links with European party groupings

Initially, newly emerging parties did not declare clear continuity with parties existing on the territory of Slovenia before the second world war. Gradually they have expressed a more precise affinity towards certain party groupings of the West European tradition. Therefore, ideological characteristics are at least partially visible from party names, key ideological orientations and party links with international groupings. According to these three indicators and on the basis of Lane and Ersson's classification, we could distinguish the following types of parties which appeared in Slovenia in the context of democratic transition:

- religious parties (like the Slovenian Christian Democrats, the Christian Socialists);
- ethnic parties (like the organizations of the Italian and Hungarian minorities, Romi/Gypsies);
- rural-agrarian parties (like the Slovenian Farmers Union - now the People's Party);
- socialist parties (like the United List of Social Democrats, the Social Democratic Party of Slovenia);
- liberal parties (like the Liberal Democratic Party, the Liberal Party);
- ecological parties (like The Greens of Slovenia, The Greens - Social Ecological party);
- regional parties (like The League for Primorska and several others);
- at the 1992 parliamentary elections also a typical charismatic party appeared (the Slovenian National Party).

Although we are able, at least approximately, to distinguish political parties according to their main ideological principles, we cannot say that these idiosyncrasies clearly express the social and political cleavages in Slovenia. Empirical research has shown so far that the main cleavages in the party arena are still along the line of communism/anti-communism and along the line of traditionalism/modernism. From time to time a cleavage between the centre and the periphery also becomes important - especially in the context of discussing regionally related issues in Slovenia.

Party programmes - issues of democratic transition and state-building

On the basis of a content analysis of 1990 party programmes (Podmenik, 1993) it is very difficult to establish differences between parties. Party programmes at that time were to a great degree uniform. The goals of democratic transition became common to all parties. The majority of parties declared the following political goals: respecting human rights and freedoms, supporting parliamentary democracy, political pluralism, social security and welfare state, integration into the international community and Europe, encouraging entrepreneurship and the market economy, supporting ecology, social diversity and the pluralism of interests. There were differences of emphasis and some covered special issues such as science, technology, demilitarization, protection of minorities and also in their definition of Slovenian sovereignity.

The question of national integration was a strong concern of the new parties, especially in the years 1989-1991. Concern with the fate of the Slovene nation were often expressed in party names with the addition of the adjective 'Slovenian'. In the beginning, party proposals for solving the dilemma of whether to remain within the former Yugoslavia or to leave it, differed substantially. The Liberal party and the Party of Democratic Renewal supported the idea of a Yugoslav confederation; the Socialist Party of Slovenia and the Slovenian Democratic Alliance went for both confederation and for an independent Slovenian state; the Social Democratic party of Slovenia, the Slovenian Christian Democrats and the Greens of Slovenia were explicitly in favour of the completely sovereign Slovenian state; the Liberal Democratic Party opted for a democratic nation state, 'in which male and female citizens sovereignly decide about the state' (Podmenik, 1993, p. 56). In the final result, all the parliamentary parties acted consensually at the time of the declaration of an independent Slovenian state in June 1991.

The 1990 election results had shown that an identifiable, clear and consistent party programme did not play an important role in the voting process. The Slovenian Farmers' party did not even produce a programme, but it won 12 per cent of votes. It seems that emotions, perceptions of social identity and the images of party leaders were much more influential.

In the run-up to the 1992 elections parties became more aware of the need to present themselves to the public and all tried to campaign using the mass media. As a content analysis of the 1992 party programmes has shown (Podmenik, 1993), priorities in programmes were the economy, international relations, and social policy. Instead of issues concerning statehood and the political system, other issues appeared such as culture, unemployment, agriculture, science, the army and privatization. Less frequent issues mentioned were local self-government, workers' participation, youth policy, immigrants and refugees, housing policy, regions and regionalism, trade unions and others. Party programmes tended to avoid conflictual issues and issues which could not gain broad support.

It is interesting that while on the one hand party programmes are very 'moderate' and 'centrist', on the other hand parties in every day politics engage in conflict - mainly on the basis of the polarization between the parties which emerged from the organization of the old regime and those from anti-communist opposition. The conflict hinges on the interpretation of history and elite competition for political power. On one issue there has been near unanimity among parties and that is the allocation of privileges to the political elite.

The development of the new party system

The process of transition has gone through several stages as follows: from a monistic structure which tolerated the newly emerging opposition; through the bipolar structure (anti-communists, reformed-communists); to the multi-party structure and then to a revival of a bipolar structure on the basis of a cleavage of old/new political parties. It seems that at the moment the Slovenian party arena is hanging between polarized pluralism and moderate pluralism as defined by Sartori (1976, pp. 131-45, 173-85).

We can find some elements of both types of pluralism in a mixed form. A prime indicator of *moderate pluralism* is the number of parliamentary political parties which have political relevance. As a result of party integration and splitting the number has been reduced from eight or nine in the early stages of the transition to five or six in 1995, which is characteristic of moderate pluralism (Table 10.4). A willingness to govern in coalition has given stability to Slovenia since 1990 and recently it has become obvious that a smaller number of parties is needed to form a coalition (Table 10.4) and that more varied coalitions are possible. Some opposition parties, which in the past used to be competitors, have started to occasionally collaborate. An index of fractionalization (Table 10.4) is similar to that in other democracies. (Sartori, 1976, p. 314), and it has declined after the second elections in 1992. Accordingly, the aggregation index expressing the relation between the share of the largest party and the number of parties (Lane & Ersson, 1987, p. 158) has logically grown.

It is difficult to claim that there are explicit anti-system elements in the party system which would create a polarized pluralism, because there are no calls for changing the new system. Few parties deny the legitimacy of a democratically elected new political elite which contains an important segment of the old. There are some indicators of polarized pluralism such as a considerable ideological distance between the communist successors and the anti-communists, a deep distrust between parties, conflict between parties mainly on the basis of ideology ('ideological fever' - Sartori, 1976, p. 137), and 'bilateral' opposition, where opposition parties fail to cooperate.

Table 10.4   Key characteristics of the party arena at the 1990 and the 1992
               elections

party arena	1990	1992
no. of all competing parties at elections	17	33
no. of parliamentary parties	9	8
% of valid votes for old parties which entered the parliament	37.1	37.0
% of valid votes for new parties which entered the parliament	54.8	45.3
% of valid votes for four biggest parliamentary parties	57.4	61.6
% of 'lost' votes (not represented in the parliament)	8.06	17.69
-index of fractionalization (Fp)	0.873	0.840
index of aggregation (Ia)	0.01994	0.3125
no. of parties in the governing coalition	6	4*

Fp= index of fractionalization as defined in Sartori, (1976, p. 307)
Ia= relation between the share of Seats of the largest party and the number of parties in this parliament.
*...the SDPS left government in April 1994, and the United List in January 1996 leaving only two parties in the coalition.

There are some indicators of *consolidation in the party system* having already taken place but there is still further consolidation possible while party organizations are still dynamic and all the major parties have an organizational network throughout the whole of Slovenia. By adopting a new law on political parties in Autumn 1994 a strong move toward public financing of parties was made. A renewal of the discussion about election laws suggests that major parties will try to adopt new election laws for the 1996 elections designed to keep smaller parties out of the parliament, especially by introducing a relatively high threshold.

The 'partyness' of the new Slovene democracy - a challenge for democratic consolidation

There are several indicators which support a hypothesis about the complete domination by parties of political life and especially the 'partyness' of elections in Slovenia. The 'partyness' in Slovenia can be mainly treated as a special situation[5] arising from the role of party elites in the political process. The most important factors in creating this phenomenon are:

- the monopolization of politics by party elites;
- the relatively poor roots of political parties in Slovene society;
- the very loose and fluctuating party identification of voters;
- the concentration of human and technological facilities and resources at a national level;
- the relatively low level of interest of party members (real and potential) in participation in party life;

- the strongest interest of members of party elites in obtaining professional political advancement.
- the lack of a democratic political tradition and culture, which give substantial room to party elites to act inventively;
- the ability of party elites to maintain and regenerate their privileged position without being required to cultivate their voters or demonstrate that they produce benefits for the whole of society.

The distrust of Slovenes for political parties and politicians results from a perception that politics is mainly a matter for elites. In its turn, this lack of trust is a consequence of the observable practices of an egoistic and ideologically overburdened party elite.

'Partyness' is a phenomenon which finds fruitful ground in the context of a democratic transition where some classical democratic conditions are very weak - relationships between parties and voters, between party leaders and party members, political leaders and voters. Although some corporatist elements are included into the new political system, corporatist groups have not developed into 'natural' political actors yet. In some cases party elites even try to strengthen party positions by the personal unification of two important political positions, like being a member of government (a minister) and at the same time a party president (at the moment in the case of the SDPS).

There are also some factors which do not sustain the 'partyness' of government. For example, parliamentary groups are led by MPs who do not have the highest positions in the party leadership, so that they don't concentrate as much power as in, for example, the Norwegian case. The Slovene political system also recognizes the separation of offices between parliament and government. It is still unclear how the reform of local government will affect the development of the growing 'partyness' in Slovene politics.

It seems that the factors supporting 'partyness' are at the moment more powerful than the factors indicating its limitation. At the same time the social and economic conditions of the democratic transition are still difficult. Probably this is the main reason why Slovenes are more and more sceptical about politics, parties and their role in Slovene political life. More and more people are convinced that party leaders and politicians in general try to pursue only their own interests and not the interests of the voters and society.

It seems that the process of democratic consolidation is tightly linked to the improvement of the quality of every day life, to a building up of the rule of law and a more thorough formulation of legal norms and public control in the field of party life. Of course, the creation of an interest group system as a parallel mediating system would help to limit party power - but would it help to create an influential position for citizens at the same time? The problems of the consolidation of democracy have opened some old questions about democracy and its actors. In post-socialist countries like Slovenia it is impossible to predict whether the conditions for the limitation of 'partyness', in favour of democratic politics and its legitimacy, will be created soon enough and strong enough to prevent the complete dominance of parties over political structures and processes.

Table 10.5   Percentage votes by parties which gained parliamentary seats in 1990 and 1992

* Elections, April 1990, for Socio-political Chamber, proportional system, no. of seats: 80 (78 for parties + two for representatives of national minorities)
** Elections, Dec. 1992, for State Assembly, proportional system (d'Hondt's System), no. of seats: 90 (88 for parties + two for reps. of national minorities)

Party	1990*	1992**
Party of Democratic Renewal United List (Party of Democratic Renewal, Workers' Party, Social Democratic Union, Democratic Party of Pensioners)	17.3	13.6
League of Socialist Youth (LSY) Liberal Democratic Party (former LSY)	14.5	23.5
Slovenian Christian Democrats	13.0	14.5
Slovenian Farmers' Party - People's Party (SFP-PP) Slovenian People's Party (former SFP-PP)	12.6	8.7
Slovenian Democratic Alliance (SDA) Democratic Party (a part of SDA)	9.5	5.0
The Greens of Slovenia	8.8	3.7
Social Democratic League of Slovenia (SDLS) Social Democratic Party of Slovenia (former SDLS)	7.4	3.3
Socialist Alliance of Slovenia	5.4	not in parliament
Liberal Party	3.5	not in parliament
Slovenian National Party	not formed yet	10.0

Table 10.6   Party composition of governments in Slovenia in the period from May 1990 till 20 June 1995

Period	Party of PM	Other Parties	Status
16.5.1990-14.4.1992	SCD	SDA, SFP-PP, SDPS, GS, LP	Majority
14.5.1992-12.1.1993	LDP	DP, SDPS, GS, PDR	Majority
12.1.1993-April '94	LDP	SCD, SDPS, PDR/ULSD*	Majority
April '94-26.1.1996	LDP	SCD, ULSD**	Majority
26.1.1996 -	LDP	SCD	Minority

*   SDPS left the Government in April 1994. In May 1993 PDR integrated with three other socialist orientated parties and formed a new party with the name United List of Social Democrats (ULSD)

**   In January 1996 ULSD left the Government

Abbreviations used in text:

BIH   Bosnia and Hercegovina
CRO   Croatia
DP   Democratic Party (part of former SDA)
GS   The Greens of Slovenia
KOS   Kosovo
LDP   Liberal Democratic Party
LP   Liberal Party
MG   Montenegro
PDR   Party of Democratic Renewal
SCD   Slovenian Christian Democrats
SDA   Slovenian Democratic Alliance
SDPS   Social Democratic Party of Slovenia
SER   Serbia without provinces
SFP-PP   Slovenian Farmers' Party-People's Party
SLO   Slovenia
SNP   Slovene National Party
SPP   Slovene People's Party (former SFP-PP)
ULSD   United List of Social Democrats
VOJ   Vojvodina

Notes

1.   'Freedoms and rights of man and citizen are limited only by equal freedoms and rights of others and by the interests of the socialist community, which are defined by the Constitution' (second section of Article 153 of the 1974 SFRY Constitution, anthology 'Protection of Human Rights', p. 520).

2.   Ekkart Zimmerman, 'Evolutionaerer und revolutionaerer Wandel', in Klaus von Beyme, Ernst-otto Czempel, Peter Graf Kielmansegg, Peter Schmoock (eds.), Politikwisenschaft (Stuttgart-Berlin-Koeln-Mainz: Beltz Verlag, Weincheim, Basel und W. Kohlhammer Gmbh, 1987), p. 253.

3.   E.g., in Slovenia the attitude towards the policy of the League of Communists was measured during the period from 1968 to 1988. It is true that the percentage of people who agreed with the attitude that its policies were in accordance with the interests of the majority changed greatly in favour of a more critical opinion (during the period of political stability the percentage varied between 20 per cent and 50 per cent and dropped to only 5.8 per cent in 1988). But at the same time more people started to agree with the estimation that the policy was partially in accordance with the interests of the majority (even at the end of the old regime this percentage was 44.1 per cent). Only about one fifth (18 per cent in 1988) of Slovenes estimated it as a policy which was not in

accordance with the interests of a majority. Source: data of Slovene Public Opinion Research 1968-1988, Centre for Public Opinion, Faculty of Social Sciences, Ljubljana.

4. The Socialist Alliance of the Working People was an organization embracing all citizens as individual members and having as collective members all the socio-political organizations including the League of Communists, which was dominant.

5. For the concept of 'partyness' see Katz, 1986.

11 The Changing Political System

DRAGO ZAJC

Introduction

The Slovenes established an independent state relatively early. They were freely electing their dukes in their ancient state of Karantanija ('Civitas Carantania') in the last centuries of the first millennium. They were unable to preserve their independence, because of the location of their territory at the crossroads of very different interests, and their small number. There is no tradition left from that time, but the spirit of that state and of its democratic procedures has remained alive through history.[1]

The Slovenes, as part of the Austrian Empire, had no autonomy, no national church nor a national economic policy. What they had was a written national language, codified by 16th century Protestant reformers (the Bible was translated into Slovene in 1584) and a vivid sense of their ethnic and cultural identity, separate from all neighbours. Their national consciousness matured when the poets, writers and historians began to write in the national language. The brief period of French rule in the Illyrian Provinces (1809-1813) spurred the development of their political consciousness, but its expression was blocked by the Metternich regime. Like other 19th century nationalists, the Slovenes developed a political program, called The United Slovenia, which was their unique contribution to the revolutions of 1848 (Kann, 1950, pp. 294-304). In the second half of the 19th century they were one of the smallest nations within the Austrian empire (only four per cent of the population), and were divided into six administrative units (crownlands). They had a majority only in Carniolia, placed in the middle of their territory. The Assembly of Carniolia could be considered to be a genuine 'Slovene' parliament in the broadest sense, though the powers of the Assembly were extremely limited (their functions were more or less advisory). Moreover, until 1907, the representatives were elected to it (as well as to the all-Austrian parliament in Vienna) on the basis of the curia system, giving an incommensurate number of representatives to the city dwellers, while the great majority of rural peasants were poorly represented (Mason, 1985, p. 39; Melik, 1965, pp. 53-81). In spite of their efforts and very skilled parliamentary tactics in the Vienna parliament (where they had 24 deputies), the Slovenes in the Austro-Hungarian Empire could never realize their main political goal from the political program of 1848, i.e. the unification of the whole Slovenian territory in one country, having one representative body for themselves.

When the Austro-Hungarian Empire collapsed at the end of the first world war, the Slovenes were pleased to leave, but they were also surprised at the loss of large parts of their western and south-western territory to Italy as a reward for joining the Allies in 1915. The Slovenes had only a very small army and were therefore vulnerable to the threats from Italy. This obliged them to unite (together with the Croats, who were exposed to the same threats from Italy) with Serbia to form a new South Slav state, called at first The Kingdom of Serbs, Croates and Slovenes, then renamed as Yugoslavia in 1929. Great national tensions were provoked in this new centralized state when Slovenes, and other nations, were expected to have no more than second class status to Serbians, who dominated the new state. The only representative institution was the parliament in Belgrade, where the influence of Slovene deputies was minimal. In 1929 the constitution was abolished and parliamentarism was replaced by the authoritarian rule of the monarch. Twelve years later, Yugoslavia became an easy prey for Nazi and fascist forces. Slovenia was occupied and divided between Germany, Italy and Hungary.

Between 1941 and 1945 a strong Slovenian resistance against the occupiers was organized by the Liberation Front, which was a coalition of several political groups and parties, including the Communist Party of Slovenia. Other parties did not want to take the risk of openly opposing the resistance.   The Communists, with experience in underground activities and armed fighting, slowly became the most important political force, finally forcing the rivals to accept their leadership. Nevertheless, the resistance attracted people of all possible political persuasions with only one wish - to liberate the country at all costs and to re-establish Slovenia - in what they saw as its historical frontiers. The first and most important step in this direction was taken after the capitulation of Italy in 1943, when the Slovene partisans liberated large parts of Slovenia. The first all-Slovenian parliament was convened in Kočevje in October 1943, when 572 deputies made important decisions about the building of national statehood on the basis of the right of self-determination of the Slovenian people (Šnuderl, 1950, p. 284). In the same year, the Slovene delegation to a meeting of the all-Yugoslav anti-fascist front in Jajce (Bosnia) voted for a federal system in postwar Yugoslavia. At the time the question of the nature of the political system remained unresolved and was left to be decided after the final liberation.[2]

After the second world war, the Slovene Communists fell under the total domination of the central Communist leadership in Belgrade. Many achievements from the war period in Slovenia were lost, including its own partisan army, police, independent currency, and the possibility of a revival of a coalition government. Yugoslavia was reconstituted in 1946 as a Socialist Federative Republic and political and economic life was quickly reorganized following the soviet model. (The federal constitution of 1946 was a copy of Stalin's soviet constitution of 1936). The possibilities for political pluralism, though formally permitted in the first years, could not exist in practice. Ordinary life became strictly controlled and some typical soviet-style trials were organized to frighten the intelligentsia and eliminate every thought of political opposition to the new regime. On the other hand, the individual nations and republics were granted a number of autonomous rights, which were explicitly written into their individual constitutions. The Slovenian Assembly was established as a successor to the assembly convened in the war period.

The introduction of a very authoritarian and centralized style of political and economic leadership did not suit the level of social and economic development of Slovenia. By the end of the sixties, a more liberal wing began to form among Slovenian Communists under the leadership of the President of the Slovenian government, Kavčič. His group was ousted in 1972 and orthodox Communists returned and remained dominant until the mid-eighties with the appearance of Milan Kučan. In a new ideological attempt to co-opt liberal ideas, in 1974 Yugoslavia adopted the final federal constitution which turned the strictly centralist organization into a loosely bound federation with some elements of confederation. The Slovene constitution of the same year incorporated again the provisions for self-determination.[3]

In the second half of the eighties, the Slovenian branch of the Communist Party was the first in the former Yugoslavia to recognize the need for a change in the political system and contributed to a rather smooth transition to democracy within Slovenia. Elements of political pluralism were introduced even before they broke with orthodox communist ideas (the Slovene delegation walked out on the all-Yugoslav Communist party congress in Belgrade in January 1990). By that time, the opposition to the League of the Communists was already playing a decisive role and exerted heavy pressures on the leading political elite to 'dismount' from political power. Thus the conditions for the establishment of a parliamentary system in an independent Slovenia were finally created, independence being the prerequisite for further democratization.

Characteristics of the 'socialist' political system

The socialist revolution had partially taken place during the war and made the Yugoslav Communist Party the only political power after the war, when Yugoslavia was reconstituted in 1946 as a socialist federal republic. The Communist Party as a leading power wielded a strong central authority based on a supranational ideology with one main political goal - the creation of a classless society, where all antagonistic interests based on private property would be abolished. In the first years after the war the party identified itself with the state apparatus, transforming - in a way similar to the Soviet Union - all other organizations (trade unions, youth leagues, professional and other organizations) into mere transmitters and instruments of its own will. By assuring both ideological domination and massive support, mainly through the all-embracing People's Front (later renamed The Socialist Alliance of Working People), it maintained a more or less total monopoly on decision-making in the elected representative bodies.

There is little doubt that the conflict with Stalinism in 1948 was highly influential in orientating the Yugoslav Communist party to re-conceptualizing the whole idea of socialism. Trying to develop a consistent theoretical standpoint against the Stalinist centralist model of government and revolutionary social practice, it started with a critique of the 'statist' conception of socialism and its connection to the idea of alienation. From the early fifties, a special socialist self-management system was developing, gradually embracing all spheres of production of goods and services (the first workers' councils were created in 1950).

The new Yugoslav political and social concepts were built on several very provocative presumptions. The main one was that self-management interests could replace the political interests of the people in an industrial society, political parties becoming thus unnecessary. It was also believed that such a political system could be built even in a poorly developed country with extremely great differences in productivity and in national income among its constituents. Finally, the Communists supposed that the question of national identity of nations, even with very different political cultures and historical experiences, had inevitably become obsolete in a socialist system.

Starting in 1953, special efforts were made to spread self-management in the enterprises, institutions and local territorial units and to achieve the integration of the whole society by building a specially designed assembly system at the levels of the commune, the republic and the federation. The idea implied, firstly, the replacement of classical political representative bodies with the multi-cameral structure of the assemblies at all levels, which made it possible for the various spheres of labour and social life to be represented in decision-making. Secondly, there was the special character of the mandate of the deputies. In order to prevent the alienation deriving from the classical view of representation, the deputies remained firmly linked with their jobs and working organizations and thus became delegates. (After 1974, the delegates were appointed to the communes' assemblies separately for each session, depending on the question under discussion). Thirdly, there was the role of the executive - in order to prevent the concentration of state power in the hands of government, the executive functions became a part of the direct competence of the assembly itself. So, the government became an 'executive council' as a special committee of the assembly with formalized responsibilities (Pašić, 1970, p. 23).

Until 1974 the assembly system underwent many experiments with different numbers of 'self-management' chambers, but the chamber for the representation of 'general' interests (elected through general elections by all citizens) still retained its importance. In the short liberal period at the end of the sixties and the beginning of the seventies the Assembly of Slovenia, especially its 'general' chamber, though elected on a politically non-pluralist basis, suddenly became very critical, with obvious tendencies towards becoming a more independent centre of decision-making. Consequently, the Communist party decided to prevent the ordinary citizens from having a voice and succeeded in instituting new changes to the assembly system (Kardelj, 1973, p. 176; 1978, p. 18b). Based on these premises, Slovenia's political system in the period 1974-1990 was a unique mixture of a non-pluralist political system and an assembly-style self-management system, stemming from the basic units of 'associated labour' on the one side and from territorially organized communes on the other. The assembly of the federated republic of Slovenia was composed of three chambers - the two self-management chambers were the Chamber of Associated Labour, made up of the delegates of employed citizens, and the Chamber of Communes, composed of the representatives of local communities. The third was the Socio-political Chamber, composed of the delegates of the leaderships of the five constitutionally recognized socio-political organizations (League of Communists, Socialist Alliance of Working People, Socialist Youth, Trade Unions and War Veterans) (Ribarič, 1983, pp. 276, 302, 333). As a special chamber it was actually introduced in order to replace the former 'general' chamber, but formally to assure 'the right measure in finding the common and general social interest' (Ribarič, 1983, p. 302). The close linkage of the idea of self-management in the social base with the assembly system also expressed itself in another very particular solution - the two self-management chambers at the level of the communes and republics were composed of the delegates of the 'basic delegations' elected in the enterprises and local communities, i.e., their delegates were indirectly elected. At the federal level, the Federal Chamber had the same composition, while the Chamber of Nations was composed of delegates elected by the assemblies of the republics.

The three chambers, composed of very different numbers of members, made the more important decisions collectively: some decisions were within the competence of two chambers and some decisions were made by a single chamber. If there was no consensus between the chambers, the issue went through a co-ordinating procedure. Such cases were rare, because the real centres of political power were the various organs of the League of Communists, which intervened when there appeared to be the possibility of a disturbance either within the republic of Slovenia or between the republic and the federal agencies. But conflicts between the republic and federal authorities were more and more likely to occur because of the poor problem-solving capacity of the self-management system in general and the growing tendency to strengthen the central government. Such a centralization might be intended for the benefit of those republics which were lagging behind in economic development and it could be used to obtain more influence on the federal budget.

The role of the so-designed Assembly of the Republic of Slovenia was very different from the representative institutions of the parliamentary type. It was supposed to be not only a legislative body passing laws and supervising the work of the government through ministerial responsibility, but also to function as a territorial organ of self-management, i.e. co-ordinating and integrating various activities. But the incorporation of self-management into the representative body resulted in great complications and lack of efficiency. It was an inevitable result of the fact that the self-management system could never be realized at the level of the social base because the elitist power structure in work organizations did not change (Županov, 1987, p. 178). The whole idea of the gigantic self-management community, embracing all units producing goods and services and taking over the responsibilities of the state, could not survive because of the lack of co-ordination. The multitude of micro-decisions could not replace the central decision-making, which remained politically directed.

It also had negative effects on the functioning of the Assembly. The three chamber system had great difficulty in solving concrete and urgent problems. The legislative work was concentrated in the Assembly, the standing committees not being organized to undertake legislative review and thus speed up the legislative procedure. The gap between the normative and the real was evident in the organization of the standing committees. The eight committees had very broad competencies, dealing with nationalities, war veterans, international relations, legislation, the judicial system, social control, citizen complaints and public information. They had no control over the executive.[4] At the same time the executive council of the Slovene republic retained a very diversified structure with 23 secretariats corresponding to the departments or ministries of conventional governments. The practice of changing delegates after each session of the assembly also contributed to the supremacy of the executive power.

The insufficient influence on Yugoslav economic policy, combined with great differences in the national income between north and south (as much as seven to one in the case of Slovenia and Macedonia), proved that the self-management assembly system did not facilitate problem-solving. Instead of accelerating development it was hampering it. The Assembly of the Republic of Slovenia was unable to pursue a continued long-term policy and bear the responsibility, especially regarding policies at federal level. It was also subjugated to external sources of power, only regaining some of its real responsibilities at the very end of its existence.

It became clear that the basic right to social and economic self-management granted by the Constitution of 1974 differs radically from the classical rights to freedom and independent action inherited from the bourgeois revolutions (Erlich, 1982, p. 213). By exercising the basic and inalienable right to participate in decision-making within the working organizations and communes and to elect the delegates for the assemblies, the citizens had no influence over the decision-making process at the level of the republic and the federation. For the Yugoslav self-management theorists, often referring to the heritage of the Paris commune of 1871 and the Soviet Constitution of 1918, the self-managing democracy was synonymous with the dictatorship of the proletariat, where there was no place for the 'obsolete' bourgeois rights and 'futile' parliamentary procedures. The final decision about what is in accordance with the basic ideas of socialism was primarily in the hands of the organs of the Communist party on the statewide level, which retained not only supreme ideological control but could take quite unpleasant measures towards political opponents seeking more freedom of expression or advocating the principle of governing by the consent of the people.

The 'scientifically' perceived idea of self-management was mixed up with social utopian ideas from the past, according to which society can start to function as an 'association of producers'. This idea, totally opposed to democratic principles based on the individuality of man, endowed with the inalienable *'ius resistendi'* to the unjust government, became even more obsolete as the Slovene society was reaching the end of the 20th century. The self-management assembly system, as much as it aspired to introduce direct links between basic workers' organizations and assemblies, obviously fell victim to modern politics, based on individual rights and representative democracy. Thus, the abolition of the means of mediation between the citizens and the state, i.e. the political parties, 'created a paradox that could be called single party direct democracy, which is precisely what one wants to avoid...' (Bobbio, 1987, pp. 81-84).

Key elements and issues in the process of political system change

The actual level of economic and social development in Slovenia also influenced political development in the period after the second world war. In the eighties, Slovene civil society started to assert its autonomy, opposing state interference and ideological censorship. The consequence was the mobilization of all kinds of traditional and new social groups (farmers, craftsmen, the young, intellectuals, private entrepreneurs, writers, ideological dissenters, etc.) seeking specific political goals (Fink-Hafner, 1994, p. 387).

Human rights became the key issue in these processes, since it became obvious that the new rights of self-management could not replace classical political rights and freedoms. The possibility of an independent action did not exist in practice since all political activities had to be channelled through existing socio-political organizations. Establishing an opposition was also impossible since the government at both federal and republic levels exerted tight control over citizens. The institutions of repression (the military and the police) were outside the control of the parliament. In Slovenia a particularly strong protest against limitations on rights and freedoms arose after government officials admitted the existence of a 'parallel' law system, consisting of secret regulations.[5]

Contrary to trends in other parts of Central and Eastern Europe, the developments in the former Yugoslavia took an unexpected direction. In reaction to the growing demands for political freedoms and human rights, especially in Slovenia, the centralization of all decision making was attempted, first in the clandestine shifting of responsibilities from the republics to the Federal Assembly. There was also an illegal transfer of the responsibilities from the Chamber of Nationalities, which made decisions by the consent of all republics, to the Federal Chamber. In these processes the organization of territorial defence under the command of the republics was abolished, consistent with the objectives and interests of the Serbian-dominated officer corps of the army. These attempts first took the form of a proposal to change the structure of the Federal Assembly by introducing a third chamber of 'associated labour' composed of representatives of the 'united Yugoslav working class' with power over fiscal policy. The second and more important was the proposal to change the federal constitution by transferring many of the responsibilities of the republics to the federation. For Slovenians, this produced the occasion for combining demands for human rights with demands for the right of self-determination (Zajc, 1992, p. 443).

The amendments to the federal constitution, finally adopted in 1988 after great pressure from the federal level, meant the significant erosion of the sovereignty of Slovenia (Kristan, 1989). But the transfer of about forty responsibilities to the federal authorities provoked great public resistance and endangered the legitimacy of the old political elite in Slovenia. It became much more responsive to the demands of the people, seeking their consent for decisions, but also increasingly depending on their support against growing pressures from the federal government and the central party organization in Belgrade. This was also the time when the Slovene Assembly finally lost its subservient position in the political system and became a real representative body of the Slovene people. But several steps had to be taken in order to establish the democratic principles of government and to implement the constitutional right of self-determination.

The first step was taken in September 1989 when the Slovene Assembly adopted a number of amendments to the Slovene constitution (IX-XC), re-affirming first of all the right of the Slovene people to self-determination (Amendment X). Other amendments opened the door to political pluralism (Amendment XLV) and to private ownership (Amendment XXVII), thus dividing former Yugoslavia into two separate and opposed political systems - one socialist and the other democratic, with the establishment of parliamentary democracy. Three months later, at the end of December, the Law on the Elections to the Assembly of Slovenia was passed on the basis of these amendments, which guaranteed the free competition of political parties.

The second important step in political modernization was the acceleration of the preparation of the new Slovene constitution, based on the idea of full sovereignty of the Slovene state and on the classical rights and freedoms of citizens. It actually became the most important task after the victory of the Demos coalition in the first democratic elections to the Assembly of Slovenia, in April 1990. The Demos coalition won a majority of seats (approximately 55 per cent) in the assembly. The runners-up were the Party of Democratic Renewal (former Communists), the League of Socialist Youth - Liberal Party and the Socialist Party of Slovenia. A mandate to form the government was given to the Slovene Christian Democrats as leading members of Demos. Premier Lojze Peterle also recruited members from other parties. At that time the Assembly of Slovenia still retained the three chamber structure (with 80 delegates in each), sharing decisions equally.[6]

The next step was the adoption of a Declaration of the Sovereignty of Slovenia on 2 July 1990, by the Assembly of Slovenia. It explicitly stated that the federal constitution and federal laws would be in force in Slovenia only if they did not contradict the constitution and laws of Slovenia. All the federal laws adopted after this Declaration were valid in the Republic of Slovenia only by the consent of the Slovene Assembly.

The fourth step was the plebiscite for an independent Slovenia, which took place on 23 December 1990. Before the plebiscite the Slovene Assembly adopted The Statement of Good Intent, making clear its desire to become a sovereign parliamentary democracy, by stating that 'the establishment of the independent Slovenian state is not directed against anyone either within Yugoslavia or beyond its frontiers. Slovenia recognizes the same right of other peoples living within SFRY.'[7] The results of the plebiscite for the independence of Slovenia held on 23 December 1990 re-affirmed the legitimacy of the Slovene government and demonstrated clearly the level of popular support for the idea of independence of Slovenia (turnout was 93.5 per cent with 88.5 per cent in favour of independence). On the basis of these results the Slovene assembly adopted on 2 February 1991 a Proposal for the Consensual Dissolution of the Socialist Federative Republic of Yugoslavia, stating that the process of dissolution would be based on the principle of mutual interest, and pledging itself to future cooperation on the basis of good will.

The first democratically elected Slovene assembly decided to implement this policy on 25 June 1991, thereby attaining the main goal of Slovene self-determination. The aggressive response of the Yugoslav Army, which still remained under the control of the Central Committee of the League of Communists in Belgrade, proved to be irrational and unnecessary. It only complicated the process of dissolution of the former federal state and the settlement of questions of succession.

The main dilemmas and constitutional choices

There was no question for the public at large or for Slovenian scholars at the end of the eighties that Slovenia must become a sovereign and independent state. A group of prominent lawyers, social scientists and philosophers, nominated by the constitutional committee of the Slovene Assembly in 1990, proceeded from the standpoint that its own constitution is the supreme legal document for its territory and not that of the federal Yugoslav government. They also adhered to the idea of total separation of powers, that principle having been abolished in 1953 by constitutional law. The first draft, prepared in 1990, contained various ideas and constitutional arrangements as a result of the fact that expert arguments were inadequate on their own and political solutions were needed too. Some of the basic dilemmas at the beginning were whether to implement a parliamentary or parliamentary-presidential system; whether the parliament should consist of one or two chambers; and whether the government should be responsible only to the parliament or co-jointly to the parliament and state president (if the combination of a parliamentary and presidential system were chosen). In a purely parliamentary system the president would have a more representative role, with the possibility of a suspension veto on the laws passed by the chamber. Dealing with these dilemmas the drafters of the new Slovene constitution also sought to provide a system of state organization which would ensure relative government stability and prevent government crises. A major difference from the previous system would also be in the role of the constitutional court, which would judge the validity of legislation.

The new constitution of the Republic of Slovenia was ratified by the Parliament on 23 December 1991. It has many characteristics of the constitutions of newly sovereign nations - particularly in stipulating the linkage between individual freedoms and national aspirations. It states that 'The SFR Yugoslavia is not a state which observes the rule of law but rather grossly violates human rights, minority rights and the rights of constituent republics and autonomous provinces'. The Republic of Slovenia hereby 'assumes all rights and obligations which, by the Constitution of the Republic of Slovenia and Constitution of the SFRY, had been transferred to the federal authorities of the SFRY'.[8] At the same time it acknowledges that '... we Slovenians created our own national identity and attained our nationhood based on the protection of human rights and freedoms, on the fundamental and permanent right of the Slovenian people to self-determination and as a result of our historical and centuries long struggle for the liberation of our people'.[9]

Similarly to many other modern constitutions, the new Slovenian Constitution asserts that 'Slovenia is a democratic republic' (Art. 1) and 'a state governed by the rule of law and is a social state' (Art. 2). It is also 'a state of all its citizens and is based on the permanent and inalienable right of the Slovenian people to self-determination' (Art. 3). In a way typical of post-Communist constitutions, human rights and fundamental freedoms are carefully protected in the large second part of the constitution (Arts. 14-65). Equality before the law is proclaimed (Art. 14) and the direct exercise of human rights is guaranteed (Art. 15). Protection of personal liberty, of human personality and dignity are also guaranteed (Arts. 19 and 21), as well as equality in the protection of rights (Art. 22). Other clauses guarantee due process of law, the right to legal remedies (Arts. 23 and 25) etc. Protection of the right to privacy and of personal rights, and the privacy of the means of communication are guaranteed, as is freedom of expression (Arts. 35, 37 and 39). A significant number of the articles deal with participation in political life - the right of peaceful assembly and free association, voting rights and the right to participate either directly or through elected representatives in public affairs (Arts. 42, 43 and 44).

At the same time, most of the welfare rights of the previous socialist system remained practically unchanged, like the right to social security (Art. 50) and the right to health care (Art. 51). Very important are the articles dealing with marriage and the family, with the rights and obligations of parents, freedom of choice in child-bearing and the rights of children (Arts. 53, 54, 55 and 56). The freedom to work is guaranteed (Art. 49) and the state is made responsible for the creation of opportunities for employment and work (Art. 66).

The constitution of 1991 is based on the principle of the division of powers and provides for checks and balances between the three branches. Written mostly in the European continental tradition, it attempts to require the utmost responsibility of the government to the governed. The constitution establishes the popularly elected National Assembly (Državni zbor), consisting of 90 deputies (Art. 80). The deputies of the National Assembly are representatives of all the people (Art. 82). The National Assembly adopts the laws and makes other decisions by majority vote of those deputies present and voting (Art. 86). The constitution also provides for a second chamber, The National Council (Državni svet), composed of the 40 representatives of different social, economic, trade, and professional groups, as well as of local government (Art. 96). The powers of the National Council are limited. It may propose laws and express its opinions about the matters within the jurisdiction of the National Assembly, and may require that the National Assembly reconsider the adopted laws prior to their proclamation. It may also require a referendum (Art. 97).

In order to ensure government stability the so-called 'constructive vote of no confidence' was introduced, connected with a proposal for a new Prime Minister (Art. 116). The government is composed of the Prime Minister and ministers of state and is accountable to the National Assembly (Art. 110). A candidate for the position of Prime Minister is nominated to the National Assembly by the President of the Republic, after consultations with the leaders of the various political groups within it. The Prime Minister is responsible 'for the political unity, direction and administrative program of the government and for the co-ordination of the work of various ministers of state' (Art. 114). The ministers, who are appointed and dismissed from the office by the National Assembly upon the nomination of the Prime Minister, are collectively responsible for the work of government, each of them responsible for his own ministry (Arts. 112, 114). The National Assembly may depose a Prime Minister by the vote of no confidence (Art. 116). But the Prime Minister may himself propose a confidence vote in the government (Art. 117). The control by the National Assembly over the government is further assured by the interpellation 'with respect to the work of the government or of an individual minister' (Art. 118).

The President of the Republic is elected in a direct general election for a term of five years and may be elected for a maximum of two consecutive terms. His function could be considered as merely representative, although he is empowered to nominate a prime minister and even to dissolve the National Assembly and call new elections when no candidate for prime minister obtains the requisite majority of votes (Art. 111). He can also call for new elections whenever a vote of confidence in the government fails to carry a majority of all elected deputies and the National Assembly does not either elect a new prime minister or express its confidence within thirty days (Art. 117).

The courts are the third branch of the government and are entirely separated from the executive and legislative branches. The independence of the judiciary is stated expressly in the way that judges exercise their duties and functions in accordance with the constitution and with the law (Art. 125). The biggest change in comparison with the previous socialist system is that judges have life tenure. (Art. 130). Judges may not simultaneously hold any other government position on any level, nor may they hold any party position (Art. 133). Another major difference is in the role of the Constitutional Court, which not only judges the validity of legislation but also mediates disputes concerning competence between practically all state bodies.

The organization of the government

The writers of the new Slovene constitution had a strong parliament in mind and an independent but fully responsible government. But the transformation of the 'executive council' into an effective government was embroiled in controversy and re-opened some basic dilemmas of the political system. According to one concept, decision-making should be firmly in the hands of the parliament. Every side step was considered an attack on constitutional principles. The other approach was to take into account the developmental trend in the relationship between parliaments and governments in modern democratic states, which showed a strengthening of executive power. The government should be therefore in the centre of all processes, endowed with considerable responsibilities. The parliament would control the government by legislation, budgetary measures and by the traditional means of exerting parliamentary control. By the Law on the Government, passed by the National Assembly in January 1993, the government, composed of 15 ministries, is responsible for the implementation, co-ordination and control of policy, as determined by the National Assembly.[10] Since the government still considered its role to be limited and also too different from the role of governments in more developed countries, it soon proposed some changes to secure greater independence from the parliament.

The composition and functioning of the parliament

The transformation of the old tri-cameral type of parliament based on functional premises into a modern representative parliament demanded first of all the establishment of a body representing all citizens, where all public matters would be ventilated and basic disagreements resolved. Its basic function would be in preparing and passing legislation. There were many who argued that Slovenia should have one main legislative chamber. But the relatively strong ties of the political system with the civil society provided also for the establishment of the 'non politically' composed National Council (Državni svet). In spite of its corporativistic character and its weak position relative to the National Assembly, it is possible to speak of a 'limited' two chamber system (Grad, 1992, p. 59). These choices have decisively influenced the new democratic institutions, especially the role and mode of operation of the National Assembly (Državni zbor).

The new Slovene parliament, especially its main chamber, the National Assembly, composed, in the main, of representatives of political parties, has met some serious problems in adapting to the new situation of permanent confrontation between the government and the opposition, primarily because the new political parties have not had time to develop appropriate conventions. The parties had to master the arts of coalition formation and to learn how to behave either as the government or as the opposition. There were several models of coalition experienced, including the coalition of the new democratic parties (Demos), the 'small coalition' in the period after the collapse of Demos at the end of 1991 and the 'grand coalition', composed of the renewed and new political parties, belonging to very different 'families of political ideas'. This second coalition was brought into being after the second elections to the National Assembly in December 1992 by the Premier dr. Janez Drnovšek, President of the largest political party, Liberal Democracy of Slovenia. Because of its composition, which is important for the stability of Slovenia, there are obvious disagreements among these political parties. At the same time, many issues which had been suppressed by the previous regime suddenly entered the political arena and burdened political discourse.

The National Assembly was confronted by an extremely difficult task in re-organizing the whole social, economic and political life of Slovenia. Dealing with these problems was intensive and demanding legislative work. Each law was changing a set of old values and enforcing new rules of behaviour, frequently resulting in a synthesis of the old and the new. The volume of legislation in Slovenia is excessive when compared with the legislation in other states, even those with recently established democratic parliaments. The National Assembly became overloaded and society sometimes seems to be unprepared to adapt to the changes. The volume of new laws produces a further problem when the administration cannot implement them properly. It is important to understand that the Slovenian National Assembly underwent many changes itself in the process of the social transformation. The three chamber system has been replaced. In July 1993 the new Standing Orders of the National Assembly were passed and the standing committees were re-organized so that they corresponded to the ministries of the government.

Table 11.1 The legislative output of the Slovene parliament 1990-1994

Proposers	The assembly of RS May 1990 - Nov. 1992	The national assembly Dec. 1992-Dec. 1994
Government	160	167
Deputies	12	51
Others	1	1
Total	179	219

These 22 standing committees (dealing with economic policy, environmental policy, agriculture and forestry, monetary policy, budget, foreign policy, administration and justice, defence, science and technology, health and social policy, culture, education and sport, electoral and administrative matters, certification and immunity, standing orders, nationalities, local administration, petitions, womens' policy, control over security and intelligence services, privatization, and handicapped policy) are endowed with substantial powers to amend bills. Their reports can be very influential in the final outcome.

Conclusion - evaluating the stability of the new system and predictions for future development

Slovenian history is the story of a small nation which experienced many forms of foreign domination, from cultural and economic to political, constantly expressing the will for the right of self-determination. Through their political development, Slovenes have experienced many different political systems and institutions, always as part of other states.

As a very small nation incorporated into the greater Austrian Empire, it struggled for greater autonomy, political administrative unification and its own representative body, a goal that could only be reached outside the Empire. Joining with Croatia and Serbia into a new state after the first world war brought them a measure of protection from foreign domination, but it also brought a new experience of inequality among the constituent nations. It was during the second world war, when the Slovenes organized a strong and efficient resistance against the occupiers, that they finally succeeded in establishing the fundamentals of their own statehood on the basis of the right of self-determination. At the same time they tried to create a new modern and democratic federation with the other nations of prewar Yugoslavia. But the reality of the Communist domination of the resistance movement and the logic of political relations among the partners of the winning coalition in the second world war produced a result very different from the wishes of a great majority of Slovenians.

Despite the new Yugoslavia being founded as a federative state, securing a substantial degree of autonomy for its constituent nations, the elementary human rights and principles of democratic parliamentarism were never respected. Self-management socialism as conceived in postwar Yugoslavia remained in fact a form of the 'dictatorship of the proletariat' and never became an all-embracing economic democracy. In spite of frequent institutional changes and corrections, the system never succeeded in operating independently. The idea of a self-management assembly system without proven results did not serve the needs of a relatively developed modern society and only enlarged the great gap between the normative and the real, until it became obvious that it simply could not work.

Theoretical explanations of the decay of political systems often generalize without taking into account the particular case. The process of democratization in Slovenia must be considered in the context of the global crisis of socialism even though it has many distinctive characteristics. Its uniqueness was determined by the fact that the process of democratization became strongly intertwined with the process of regaining national sovereignty. It was the people who reacted against the unjust government, considered at the same time as foreign and hostile.

In the process of democratization constitutional choices have been made, creating for the first time a modern parliamentary system, which contrasts with many other old and new East European states, which have adopted relatively strong semi-presidential systems (Croatia, Serbia, Poland). These new democratic institutions, based on the premises of total sovereignty and political self-responsibility are much more likely to endure the challenges of future development. The new democracy, if it is as sound as is hoped, will not permit radical and untested changes.

In spite of the difficulties, the process of the democratization which has been accelerated after the independence of Slovenia can be considered successful since the parliament and other institutions are quickly learning through experience. Democratization is, of course, only one aspect of modernization - political modernization also depends on the modernization of other areas, such as the economy, technology, etc. There are signs that the economy is making good progress. If we believe that economic prosperity is a prerequisite of political stability, then we can expect that Slovenia will gradually consolidate its position as a liberal democratic state.

Notes

1.   The ancient ritual, by which the free people transmitted their sovereignty, had impressed the humanist Eneas Picolomini, known as Pope Pius, II, who travelled in the middle ages through Slovene lands and described it in his 'Cosmographia Pii Papae De Europa' (1509). Later, the French historian Jean Bodin presented the ritual in 'Six Livres De La Republique' (Paris, 1576) as an original example of the idea of sovereignty 'without comparison in the world'. It is supposed that Thomas Jefferson was inspired by this example of democratic contract between the people and a sovereign when he was drafting the American Declaration of Independence. See also: Sergej Vilfan, Pravna zgodovina Slovencev (The History of Law Among Slovenes), Slovenska matica, Ljubljana, 1961, p. 57.

2.   In 1944 an agreement between the NKOJ (the 'internal' government of Yugoslavia) and the King's government in exile determined that the form of government would depend on the choice of the people after the war, but the Communist leaders considered the agreement to be purely tactical.

3.   The Constitution of Slovenia of 1974 stated: 'Based on the right of every nation to self-determination which includes also the right of secession, the Slovene nation... has united with other nations and nationalities in a federal republic of free and equal nations...'. (See Constitution of SR of Slovenia, 1974, Basic principles, Article I).

4.   See: Poslovnik Skupine SRS (Standing Orders of the Assembly of the SRS), Ljubljana, 1982, art. 172.

5.   The existence of the secret federal laws and other regulations was discovered by a group of deputies in the Slovene assembly, leading to a special investigation about the circumstances and consequences of the so-called 'process against the four' at the military court trial in Ljubljana in 1989 (their report to the assembly was presented on 21 June 1989).

6.   See: Ustavni amandmaji k ustavi Socialistične republike Slovenije (Amendments to the Constitution of the Socialist Republic of Slovenia), Uradni list SRS (Official Gazette of SRS), 22/1989.

7.   The new Slovene independent constitution was needed, though the possibilities of a confederation of the states were still discussed. See: Tine Hribar, Ustavna prelomnica (The Constitutional Breakthrough), Demokracija, 17/1989.

8.   See: The Statement of Good Intents, adopted on 6 December 1990, article 2.

9.   Basic Constitutional Charter on the Independence and Sovereignty of the Republic of Slovenia, Constitution of the Republic of Slovenia, edt. by Constitutional Commission of the Parliament of the Republic of Slovenia, Ljubljana 1993, pp. 11, 13.

10. *Ibid*, p. 15.

Appendix to Chapter 11

Table 11.1 The changes in the composition of the Slovene parliament

1986 - 1990		
Chamber of Associated Labour 150 delegates	Chamber of Communes 68 delegates	Socio-Political Chamber 50 delegates
1990 - 1992		
Chamber of Associated Labour 80 deputies	Chamber of Communes 80 deputies	Socio-Political Chamber 80 deputies
27 December 1992		
	National Council 40 councillors	National Assembly 90 deputies

Table 11.2 The changes in the structure of the government

Former Government	New Government
1. Ministry of internal affairs	1. Ministry of internal affairs
2. Ministry of foreign affairs	2. Ministry of foreign affairs
3. Ministry of finance	3. Ministry of finance
4. Ministry of defence	4. Ministry of defence
5. Ministry of transport & communications	5. Ministry of transport & communications
6. Ministry of culture	6. Ministry of culture
7. Ministry of education & sport	7. Ministry of education & sport
8. Ministry of science & technology	8. Ministry of science & technology
9. Ministry of environ. & physical planning	9. Ministry of environ. & physical planning
10. Ministry of agriculture, forestry & food	10. Ministry of agriculture, forestry & food
11. Ministry of justice & administration	11. Ministry of justice
12. Ministry of health, social affairs & family	12. Ministry of health
13. Ministry of industry & civil engineering	13. Ministry of economic activities
14. Ministry of small scale economy	14. Ministry of economic relations & development
15. Ministry of energy	15. Ministry of labor, family & social affairs
16. Ministry of tourism	
17. Ministry of commerce	
18. Ministry of planning	
19. Ministry of labor	
20. Ministry of veterans & handicapped	
21. Ministry of Slovene emmigrants	
22. Ministry of legislation -	Government office for legislation
23. Ministry of information -	Government public relations & media office

12 The New Electoral System

FRANCI GRAD

The development of the electoral system in Slovenia

Until the end of 1989 the development of the Slovene electoral system cannot be treated apart from that of the former Yugoslav federation. Subsequently it has followed a separate path. A radical break came with the first multiparty elections in the Yugoslav federation since the second world war which took place in Slovenia in spring, 1990, following legislation at the end of 1989 which made such a development possible.

The development of the political system in Yugoslavia had taken a very different course in comparison with similar contemporary systems and this had a significant bearing on the development of the electoral system, especially after 1953, which brought the introduction of the system of self-government. The basis of the conventional electoral system is the election of the representatives of the people to parliament in which the elected representatives freely and independently make decisions on behalf of the electorate. The electoral system as it developed in Yugoslavia, however, was not based on the idea of representation of the people as a whole, but of different interest groups. Initially these were only the so-called direct manufacturers; subsequently other professional groups were added. As the system developed, representation of local communities was also established. However, for the whole period after the second world war until 1990 the elections were dominated by a single party, the League of Communists.

This development was completed with the adoption of a new constitution in 1974, which established an Assembly consisting of three chambers in each of the republics (as federal units) and in the local communities, whereas the Federal Assembly, in keeping with the federal principle, consisted of two chambers. The three chambers of the Assembly represented the three basic interest groups in the society: the Chamber of Associated Labour represented the interests of all working people (employees and the self-employed), the Chamber of Communes represented the local interests and the Socio-Political Chamber represented the different interests of the various Socio-Political organizations which were general political organizations, resembling in some respects political parties, but not competitive in their character. None of these chambers, not even all three together, represented the interests of the people as a whole.

In this unique political framework a unique electoral system developed, the so-called delegate system, which introduced, instead of a traditional representative mandate, a greater dependency of the delegate (the Member of the Parliament) on his constituency (the delegate base) and, instead of direct elections, indirect elections at different levels. Only the delegations (the collective bodies) were elected directly in the various organizations and communities (local governments), these delegations directly or indirectly nominating their representatives to the appropriate Assembly. In this system, the Members of the Assembly were not seen as representatives of competing political interests, but were regarded as representing the collective interests of different segments of society. This concept was not compatible with the operation of competing political parties within a conflictual electoral system. Therefore, the process of electing the candidates was adapted to this kind of electoral system, and the candidates were usually nominated at voters' meetings, which were organized by the Socialist Alliance or by the general trades unions.

This attitude towards elections has resulted in many peculiarities which are unknown in other contemporary electoral systems. These peculiarities existed especially in the fact that the elections were not based on the vote of the individual but on the decision of a corporation; they were not direct, and the mandate of the representative was a mixture of the imperative and representative mandate.

The electoral system of the Yugoslav Federation was increasingly criticized. Most of the criticism was directed at the fact that voters did not have a direct influence on who was going to be elected into Parliament, and that it did not permit the promotion of different political views. This criticism resulted in a demand for direct elections and subsequently for multiparty elections.

The change of the electoral system and, with it, the change of the political system, began at the constitutional level with amendments to the federal constitution in 1988, which reinstituted direct elections. Nevertheless, the electoral system, in general, still remained within the former framework. The amendments to the Slovene constitution in the following year represented a more radical break with the former system. The political developments in Slovenia, including the emergence of parties, brought a demand for a closer approximation to liberal democratic political systems. It had become clear that the next elections, which had to take place in spring 1990, could not be conducted within the existing electoral system, but would need to acknowledge the reality of political pluralism.

During this time, very tense negotiations between the public authorities and the newly developed political parties took place. These mainly concerned the extent to which the new political parties would be allowed to participate in the elections and how parliamentary seats would be distributed. A constraining factor was that the existing federal and republic constitutional arrangements continued for the time being and these retained the three chamber assembly and the delegate system.

The electoral system in 1990 therefore was still incorporated within the framework of the former political system and retained some of its main features. This caused complications, since the existing constitutional arrangements had not been designed to cope with the features of a liberal democratic electoral system.

The distribution of seats in the parliament was the most controversial question. The interests of the ruling government and newly developed parties differed significantly: the ruling government saw greater potential for success in the majority electoral system, whereas the new political parties favoured the proportional system. It is interesting that the three chamber structure of the Assembly of the Republic and the delegate system formed the basis for a political compromise. The result of that compromise was that different electoral systems were adopted for the different chambers of parliament: the Chamber of the Associated Labour was elected according to the plurality system, the Chamber of Communes was elected on the basis of the majority system and the Socio-Political Chamber was elected on the basis of the proportional system (Grad, 1990).

The majority of votes in the 1990 election was gained by the Demos coalition of parties, which was hostile to the existing political elite and aimed at the abolition of the existing political and social system. Political parties which had developed from the former socio-political organizations were forced into opposition after these elections. As a result of the state of flux in the political situation a large number of parties contested the elections and nine of them gained seats in parliament. There were, in addition, a substantial number of independent candidates who were successful.

Further changes in the legislation regulating the electoral system became necessary in 1992 following the adoption of a new constitution. The Constitution of Slovenia as an independent state, which was adopted in December 1991, produced a radical re-organization of the state. In place of the tri-cameral legislature there was instituted a bi-cameral parliament with a National Assembly as the principle legislative and representative body and a National Council as the second chamber. Instead of the previous collective Presidency there was to be a President of the Republic with powers similar to those usual for a head of state in a parliamentary system.

The new electoral provisions had to take account of the party system which had been produced by the 1990 elections. None of the political parties was strong enough to obtain a majority in its own right and there was an emphasis on coalition-building. There was a continuing proliferation of political parties and, despite the very different names of individual parties, they had programmes which seemed to be very similar.

For the debate on the new electoral system it was evident that a pure plurality or majority system would not be adopted, though this still left a wide range of possibilities.

Most of the parties were firmly in favour of a proportional representative system, with a smaller number in favour of combining the proportional system with some elements of the plurality system to provide correctives to the perceived weaknesses of pure proportionality. A compromise was necessary, since the legislation concerning the new system of elections had to be passed by a two-thirds majority in Parliament.

On the basis of these considerations the law on elections to the National Assembly was only adopted after long negotiations between the various political parties and after many procedural obstacles. A law on elections of the National Council and another on elections of the President of the Republic were also adopted. The drafting procedure for the adoption of the above-mentioned laws was begun in January 1992, and the laws were passed by the end of the same year.

The law on the election of the President of the Republic was adopted in August 1992 and published in the Official Journal of the Republic of Slovenia, No. 39/92. The Laws on elections to the National Assembly and to the National Council were adopted in September 1992 and published in the Official Journal of the Republic of Slovenia, No. 44/92.

Basic characteristics of the new electoral system

General features of the electoral system

The Constitution determines only the general principles of the elections of the National Assembly and the President of the Republic, and it contains no provisions concerning the National Council. However, the Constitution provides that the electoral system for the National Assembly as well as for the National Council shall be regulated by law, with the special provision that they have to be adopted by a two-thirds majority of the Members of the Parliament to ensure a broad political consensus.

The most important law concerning elections is undoubtedly the law on elections to the National Assembly. It contains three basic requirements:

1. the seats should be distributed according to the proportional system,
2. there should be a link between the elected members and the voters, and
3. the stability of the legislative and executive power should be ensured as much as possible.

The basic principles which are introduced by the new law therefore are:

- The distribution of the mandates according to proportional representation modified by the application of an electoral threshold and the possibility of voting for the individual candidate.
- The Members of Parliament are elected in multi-member constituencies which are determined in a manner which produces a correspondence between the number of voters and the number of elected Members in Parliament.
- The seats are first distributed in the constituency according to the method of the Hare quota. The additional seats which could not be distributed in the constituencies are distributed at the national level proportionally using the d'Hondt formula.
- The procedure for the selection of candidates is mainly in the hands of the political parties. However, the law also provides for the nomination of candidates by the voters themselves.
- In order to implement the principle that the elected representatives have a close connection with the voters, votes are not cast for the lists of candidates as a whole, but for individual candidates on a list. For that purpose, the electoral districts are divided into smaller electoral units. Their number corresponds to the number of seats allocated in an electoral district. This produces eleven electoral units in an electoral district. The votes given to candidates in each electoral unit are aggregated to determine how many seats the list is entitled to receive. The votes for candidates of a given party are totalled and given to the list as though they were votes for a list. This should give the voter the possibility of voting for the individual candidate and the political party he belongs to at the same time.
- The personalization of the elections is not only provided for by giving the voter the possibility of voting for the individual candidate, but also by distributing the seats which were gained by a list not in accordance with the party's ranking, but according to the number of votes the individual candidates on the list received in the electoral unit. The system is effectively an 'open list system' and is similar to the electoral system in Finland.

This electoral system was mainly expected to give the voter a greater influence on who is to be elected into Parliament, but also had regard for the predominant influence of parties on the outcome. It is already evident that voters are exercising discretion in the election of the individual candidates, since candidates heading party lists have failed to be elected.

This system is expected to provide an obstacle to the domination of the political system by parties. It is an expectation that has been fulfilled only in part. There are still eight parties represented in Parliament and their power has in many respects increased. The strongest party is the Liberal Democrats, which obtained 22 seats in the National Assembly, while the other parties obtained smaller numbers of seats - the Christian Democrats 15, the

Associated List (which derived mainly from former League of Communists) 14, the Slovene National Party 12, the People's Party ten, the Democrats six, the Green Party five and the Social Democrats four seats.[1]

The law on elections to the National Council introduced the indirect election of members. They are elected by electoral colleges from different associations representing various interest groups. The allocations of seats is determined according to the principle of the plurality system. By putting into place a system of indirect elections it was expected that the influence of the political parties on the composition and work of the National Council would be much reduced. The National Council should represent the interests of various interest groups and not party interests. This has not been wholly achieved, but from the work of the National Council so far it can be discerned that the influence of the political parties is not too intensive and that the interests of the represented interest groups do prevail.

The law governing election to the Presidency determined that the President should be elected in direct elections in accordance with the principle of absolute majority. If such a majority is not gained by any of the candidates, there is a second ballot, in which the voters choose between the two candidates who gained the most votes in the first ballot.

The right to vote and other characteristics of the electoral system

After the second world war the right to vote in Slovenia as well as in the former Yugoslavia has always been a universal right since it has never been limited by any restrictions except, of course, by reaching voting age. The same conditions applied to the eligibility to stand for election.

The new Slovene Constitution and its attendant legislation provide for a universal right to vote in National Assembly elections, once the age of eighteen years is attained and Slovene citizenship is held.

The principle of equality of voting is breached by the allocation of an additional vote to the two minorities. As in the previous system, the Italian and Hungarian minorities have a special vote for their own representatives on condition that they are registered members of the minorities. They also have a vote in the general election for the National Assembly.

There is an even greater breach of equality of voting in the case of elections for the National Council. The right to vote for the National Council and eligibility for election is attached to membership of the nominated special groups. A person who does not have an appropriate attachment is denied a vote, while another person may belong to more than one group and thus attracts a plural vote.

The actual number of National Council Seats allocated to a special interest group is not related to the size of the group. There are four representatives of employers, four representatives of employees, four representatives of farmers, self-employed and small business and trade representatives, six representatives of the public services and 22 representatives of the local communities.

The right to vote is a personal right, which may be exercised, or not, as the case may be. In exercising the right to vote, freedom of choice is guaranteed to the voter and this is further protected by the criminal law.

Nobody can be held criminally responsible for voting in a certain way. It is a criminal offence to force somebody to vote for a certain party or candidate, to vote at all, or to vote against a policy. It is also a criminal offence to demand information about how somebody voted. The use of the secret ballot underpins these requirements.

Legal rights in connection with the electoral process can be pursued before electoral commissions and courts, before the National Assembly and ultimately they can be appealed to the Constitutional Court.

In respect of the nomination of candidates for election the changes introduced in 1990 returned the initiative to the parties although groups of voters may also nominate candidates. According to the new legislation the candidates can be proposed either by the political parties or by the voters. The process of nominating candidates by a political party is closely regulated. Candidates can by nominated by a party in three different ways:

- it can place lists of candidates in all constituencies, where supported by at least three members of the National Assembly;
- it can place the lists of candidates in each constituency separately. In this case the list of candidates has to be determined by the members of the political party, who have the right to vote and live within the constituency. In addition to this, the list has to be supported by at least 50 voters who have their residence in the constituency.
- it can nominate the list through the agency of the voters only. In this case the list of candidates has to be supported by at least 100 voters who have their permanent residence in the constituency.

A list of candidates can be produced by voters without party affiliation. Such a list of candidates has to be supported by at least 100 voters registered and permanently resident in the constituency. In practice, this method of nominating the candidates has been much invoked.

The pre-independence electoral system, with its emphasis on interest representation, did not provide rules for the geographic determination of constituencies. In the new electoral legislation the principle has been introduced that each representative represents an equal number of voters.

There are eight constituencies for the election to the National Assembly and eleven members of the National Assembly are elected from each. Each constituency is further divided into eleven electoral units, corresponding to the number of candidates to be elected for the constituency. The law, namely, sets the rule that in each electoral unit voters vote for one candidate.

There are, in addition, the special constituencies in the territories where the ethnic minorities live. One representative is elected in each of them.

In the electoral legislation adopted in 1992 the method of voting significantly changed. In spite of the electoral system being proportional, the voter did not vote for a list of candidates, but for an individual candidate on the list. Because the constituency is divided into eleven parts, the political parties or any others who proposed a list of candidates, have to decide which candidate from the list will stand in a particular electoral unit in the constituency. In each electoral unit only one candidate from the list can compete. Therefore, the voters in the electoral unit vote for individual candidates from different lists of candidates. In fact, they also vote for the whole list of candidates, since the votes which are gained by the individual member of the list in all electoral units, are aggregated and attributed to the list for the whole of the constituency. In this way, the votes for individual candidates are transferred to the lists of candidates.

The allocation of seats

The electoral system used in 1990 applied several systems of allocating seats. The plurality system was used in the elections of the Chamber of Associated Labour and the majority system in the elections of the Chamber of Communes. The seats in the Socio-Political Chamber were distributed according to the proportional system. The seats were first distributed in the constituency on the basis of a Hare quota and the remaining votes were finally distributed on the national level between the lists of candidates according to the d'Hondt system. The distribution of seats according to the electoral system adopted in 1990 was consequently very complicated, which made the whole election procedure very difficult for the voters as well as for the electoral officers, since both lacked previous experience.

The constitution adopted in 1991 did not have any provisions in respect of the allocation of seats and this matter was left to be regulated by the law on elections. The distribution of seats is proportional to a high degree. The seats are distributed on two levels: at the constituency and at the national level. The second level was introduced as a corrective to the disproportionality which necessarily arises if the seats are distributed only in the constituencies. In order to ameliorate the possible negative effect of the proportional electoral system on the stability of parliament, a threshold was introduced.

In the first round the seats in the constituencies are distributed using the Hare quota. In this way only half of the seats in the 1992 elections were distributed. This seems to imply a great equality of the different parties which participated in the elections. The rest of the seats are further distributed at the national level on the basis of those votes which remain unused in the quota distribution in the districts. In this distribution all lists of candidates are taken into consideration, except those lists of candidates which were proposed only in one constituency and those lists of candidates which would not be able to gain at least the threshold level of three seats.

When distributing the seats at the national level the d'Hondt system is used. The seats gained in this round are distributed to those lists which have the largest remainder vote in their constituency.

The personalization of the elections is secured by the fact that those candidates from the lists are elected (in accordance with the number of seats that were gained by the list as a whole) who gained the most votes in the electoral unit where they stood. This, of course, is the result of the fact that the voters in the electoral units voted for individuals and not for the lists of candidates as a whole. However, this rule does not apply to all the candidates on the lists. Not more than half of the seats which are being distributed at the national level can be distributed to the candidates, irrespective of the number of votes which they gained, according to a ranked list which is determined by the parties themselves. This, of course, means that the voters cannot influence the choice of the political party in this part of the election and that the distribution of seats in this case is left to the preferential list of the political party. The seats that are distributed in this way do not exceed a quarter of all the seats since only half of the seats that are distributed on the national level can be distributed this way. This exception to the rule of individual election is the result of the intervention of almost all political parties, which were apparently keen on ensuring some seats for their party leaders.

Local elections

The new constitution introduced also the new system of local government, which is profoundly different from the previous one. In that system the commune was one of the three forms of socio-political communities, together with the republic and the federation, but it had very few elements of genuine local government. Even the structure of the communal authorities was a mirror of the republican authority. There was an assembly, composed of three chambers and an executive council. The assembly was elected on the basis of the same delegate system as the assembly of the republic. This system of local government lasted till the end of 1994 when the new local government was established. The new communes are smaller in comparison with the previous ones and consequently the number of communes in Slovenia grew from 62 to 147.

The new system of local government is now comparable with the western systems of local government though it has some important differences. There are two elected bodies, the communal council and a mayor. The new regulation of local elections is based on the same basic principles as state elections such as universal and equal franchise, free vote, secret ballot, etc. However, the regulation of local elections is adapted to the special characteristics of local communities. For that reason, the electoral system of communes differs in some respects.

The communal council is elected directly by the residents of the commune. There are two systems of distribution of seats in the communal council. In smaller communes the council is elected on the basis of a plurality system, since the role of political parties is not expected to be so significant. In the larger communes elections are on the basis of a proportional system by voting for a list of candidates. Preferential voting is also allowed. The seats in the commune council are distributed on the basis of the d'Hondt formula.

The regulation of the nomination of candidates is, in principle, the same as in state elections though it is simplified. Thus, the candidates can be nominated either by political parties or by voters themselves.

As in state elections the legislation provides that the Italian and Hungarian minorities have the right to vote their own representatives into the communal councils in the area where the minorities are concentrated. They also have the right to vote for the other members of communal councils in the same way as other citizens of Slovenia.

The mayors of the new communes are elected directly. The mayor has to be elected by an absolute majority of votes, which may require a second ballot if this is not obtained in the first round.

The first elections to the new communal councils were held in December 1994. Though the local elections are obviously less important than state elections the political parties expended a great deal of effort and money on them. The distribution of party seats is different from that at state level. Some political parties with small parliamentary representation have won a considerable number of seats at the local level while some of the larger parliamentary parties have done much worse. A problem which results from the direct election of mayors is that the mayor may not be a member of the same political party or coalition of parties as the ruling majority in the communal council, causing problems of 'cohabitation'.

Conclusion

The electoral system of the new Slovenia has brought a radical departure from the practices of the previous regime. While the general principles of free and fair elections prevailing in the liberal democracies were agreed, there has been a keen debate on the manner in which the vote is translated into representatives. The system devised is a peculiarly Slovenian one and it has so far delivered a working parliament and a relatively stable government. There is an awareness of the fact that the electoral system can substantially affect the fortunes of individual parties and there are certain to be demands for further change. However, the requirement of a two-thirds majority to amend the electoral law means that further radical change will be unlikely while the major parties gain advantage from the current provisions.

Notes

1.   More details can be found in the Report of the Republic Electoral Commission on the results of the elections of the Members of the National Assembly held in December 1992 (published in the Official Journal of the Republic of Slovenia, No. 6/92).

13 Local Government and State Administration

JANEZ ŠMIDOVNIK

The recent situation as the baseline for the new order

In the year following the promulgation of the Constitution of the newly-created state of Slovenia in 1991, all the necessary central bodies were created. Parliament and the President of the Republic were elected at direct, general and secret elections. Parliament appointed the government and its ministers, defining by law the ministries which took over the administration of a wider range of government activities. Others, however, remained with the so-called 'communal system'. This system derived from the earlier socialist form of government whereby central and local government were inseparably linked. Its basic institution was the municipality (občina), which was designated a 'commune'. This was not the usual continental municipality, which is primarily concerned with specifically local affairs and their administration; it primarily acted as the agent of central government and dealt with local matters only secondarily. It is estimated that about 80 per cent of its work was concerned with state administration and only 20 per cent with local affairs. In terms of status it was an independent public entity, which had a directly elected representative body and functioned relatively autonomously. Thus, the municipality or commune undertook the bulk of administrative tasks in the field, and the central government had few agencies of its own. The entire territorial, functional and organizational structure of the commune was therefore adjusted to the needs of the central administration. Territorially, the commune was very large; on average it encompassed an area of 326.7 sq. km. and had 32,250 inhabitants, which exceeded by far the average size of municipalities in other European countries. In size of territory and population as well as in its competencies it was closer to the typical second tier of European local government, such as the German districts (*Landkreise*), or the first tier of state administration in the field, such as Austria's administrative districts (*Verwaltungsbezirk*).

This municipal system could not be dismantled by a dictate overnight. An Enabling Statute passed simultaneously with the Constitution extended the lifetime of the communes until the new local government system could be established. This took a long time, for local government had to be totally reformed concurrently with the extensive reform of the central administration. The reform of local government itself usually requires a period of up to a decade or more.[1] In the Slovenian case its reform had to be carried out in parallel with the reform of central government. Dismantling the existing municipalities was something like Siamese-twin surgery; the operation to separate local government and the central administration could not be performed in stages, only simultaneously. It was then a demanding, prolonged, technically and politically delicate operation which moreover had to be conducted under the difficult conditions of a new-born country which had more urgent priorities in dealing with economic, political, and especially foreign policy matters.

The constitution and the law as the foundations of the new system

Slovenia's constitution is modelled on those of parliamentary democracies. It lays down local government as a cornerstone of the political order which is carried out in the municipality. Local affairs come within the municipality's domain, are managed by it independently, and are defined as those affairs that concern only its residents. Parliament must have the municipality's prior consent before devolving functions to it, and must also assure the finance for them. The Constitution accords special status to urban municipalities which, in addition to matters of local significance, may assume various duties originating in the state's domain which are relevant to their development. Municipalities are, in principle, self-financing; those unable to provide fully for the execution of their duties owing to economic underdevelopment must be provided with additional finance by the state in accordance with principles determined by law. Under the Constitution a municipality encompasses one or more settlements which are interlinked by matters and interests common to their residents; it is constituted by law, which also defines its territory; prior to that the will of the local residents to have a municipality within a particular area has to be determined by referendum.

The Constitution also refers to 'wider' local government entities, mentioning provinces explicitly. However, these are not obligatory; they are treated as a form of voluntary interlinking by municipalities over a wide area in order to conduct local affairs of broader concern.

On the basis of the above constitutional provisions the Law on Local Government elaborates the complete mechanism of competencies and operation of local communities.

The very first analyses of the text of the Constitution indicated that the provisions cited above confine local government to a very limited scope. The constitutional formulation of the functional scope of the municipality restricts it to purely local affairs; these are matters 'which the municipality can regulate independently' and which 'are of concern to its residents alone'. The Slovenian municipality then conducts only local affairs in the narrowest sense of the term.   It is almost impossible, given this constitutional formulation, to speak of the duties which elsewhere in Europe the state may delegate from its own domain to the municipality; for under the Constitution the parliament may by law devolve particular administrative functions to the municipality only with its prior consent (that is of each municipality separately) and provided that it secures the funding for these duties.   Thus, Parliament cannot of its own accord devolve anything to the municipalities - even by law.   In practice this means that for every law that it prepares, Parliament has to obtain the approval of the municipalities for each provision that devolve a central government function to their domain.   It is difficult to imagine how the concurrence of all the municipalities could be reached in practice.   On the other hand, it is also hard to conceive that a law may devolve certain responsibilities to a limited number of municipalities, that is, only to those which have given consent.

Just how narrow the confines of local government are in Slovenia is evident when the system is compared with others in Europe.   The Slovene Constitution obviously proceeds from the concept of the complete separation of the central state and local government.   In all other European countries the execution of these functions is intertwined in various ways, although it remains clear which are state and which local.   Local agencies carry out a great part of government administration that is relevant for their residents, although under specific state supervision.   No matter how correct the strict distinction drawn by the constitution between state and local government may seem on the theoretical level, in practice it impairs and downgrades local government.   Namely, the average citizen perceives the whole fabric of public powers he has to deal with as a single complex.   He has official contacts with state administrative agencies more often than with the local government.   From his standpoint, a municipality that conducts solely local affairs and does not handle any administrative tasks seems less important and interesting than would otherwise be the case and than it actually is in other European countries.   This is a radical departure from the previous system: a move from the extreme decentralization of state functions to the municipality to their extreme centralization in state government organs.

The assessment that the ambit of local government is narrow is further confirmed when the constitutional provisions for wider local government entities are considered.   Although the constitution mentions them it also negates them with the provision that municipalities may independently decide whether or not to link up and form wider local government bodies. Given this legal basis wider local bodies cannot operate autonomously. The voluntary linking of municipalities can produce only various forms of inter-municipal cooperation, that is, organization at the municipal level and not entities such as the provinces or regions of numerous European countries. The latter are not organizations of municipalities but distinctive local government entities established in the same way as municipalities: that is, by legislative enactment. Only Parliament may grant broader local entities the powers of government and thereby guarantee their existence and functioning. A municipality, on the other hand, may at any point withdraw from a body it has established by voluntary association; this would spell the end of the body.

This means it is extremely unlikely that there will be wider local government bodies in the Republic of Slovenia. This is an additional drawback for the status of local government in the country. Many matters of broader local significance and relevance which exceed the area and capacities of the municipality, which could be dealt with by these wider local bodies, will have to be handled by the central government. When it is reduced to the municipality alone and especially to one with a very circumscribed domain, local government is consigned to the margins of public interest.

The formation of new municipalities

The creation of a new local government system alongside the new system of central administration proceeded from these factual and legal premises. It should be noted that, from the beginning, the reform of local government lacked the impetus of similar reforms in West European countries instituted in the second half of this century. The latter reforms were based on a broad national consensus both regarding the goals as well as the solutions that were to be attained. For all the general objective was the empowering of the local community to assume increasing and more demanding responsibilities which devolve to its domain through an open process of decentralization. This reform process encompassed most European states. It was set off by the formation of the European Community, which was then counterbalanced by the political principle of subsidiarity. The subsidiarity principle requires lower level territorial units to conduct all public affairs which are within their capacity; thus, all such responsibilities should devolve to their domain. The extreme concentration of public responsibilities in the field of macro-economics was counterbalanced by the principle of extreme decentralization to the micro-level of public interest. However, the local community was not equipped to perform these new tasks without radical territorial and functional re-organization.

No such consensus regarding reform of local government has ever been achieved in Slovenia. Here, reform was essential as a consequence of the general changes in the system and because the Constitution foreshadowed the re-establishment of conventional local government, though it was never clearly defined in the substantive sense. Whereas elsewhere in Europe small municipalities were fused to form larger territorial units, in Slovenia a reverse process of reform was necessary to break the large municipalities down into smaller ones, even though to some this appeared uneconomic and senseless. The general public did not understand why the existing municipality's administrative competencies had to be revoked; it meant that residents could not have the same range of their administrative tasks handled by the new municipality and would instead have to travel to the more distant centres where the state administrative offices and services would be located. The general public then was, in the main, opposed to the reform.

The political parties, including those in the governing coalition, did not initially consider the reform a major political issue; it was only when preparations were nearing completion and fierce partisan battles were already raging over practically every other issue that had to be settled in the new state that the municipality was seen as a potential political grass-roots stronghold. Two clear-cut currents emerged amongst the parties towards the end of these preparations: one, which was composed predominantly of right-wing parties, saw their chances maximized in small municipalities and so championed this model; the other, made up predominantly of left-wing parties, saw their best chances in large and urban municipalities and consequently advocated them. It was this question of generating political support that became the dominant issue of the local government debate and which ultimately affected the geography of the new municipalities.

Naturally, the criteria for the definition of the new municipalities were determined by law. In the main it determined the minimal infrastructural capacities of the area which could comprise a municipality. The central criterion was that a municipality could not have fewer than 5000 residents, even though this criterion was ignored when the municipalities were finally demarcated. Instead, political criteria prevailed in line with the interests emerging directly in Parliament when it passed the law on the new municipalities at the end of 1994. Of the 147 new municipalities formed, more than a third have fewer than 5000 residents and are too small according to the official criteria. A relatively high number, approximately one fifth, retained the territorial boundaries of the former communes and consequently exceed the intended limits. Further, contrary to trends in other European countries, there are eleven urban municipalities with a special status giving them extended powers. Elsewhere in Europe the distinction between ordinary and urban municipalities is being abandoned in favour of a uniform system.[2]

The final territorial layout of the municipalities suggests that the framers sought to evade the legally-prescribed model in order to garner a more favourable foothold for themselves. The bigger municipalities, with their greater territorial compass and economic concentration, contrast with the functional insignificance of the ordinary version. Moreover, they partly bridge the gap looming between the central government and the municipality owing to the absence of the province as a broader, intermediating locally-governed community and they are prevalent in the more developed part of the country. The small municipalities, with less than the required minimum population, will doubtless seek special status as upland or less-developed areas as defined by the law. The large urban municipalities, merely by dint of their status, will be in a more favourable position than the ordinary ones in both functional terms and financing. Thus, more than a half of the new municipalities have a different, more advantageous position than the ordinary standard municipality. This certainly is not a good omen for the newly-established system of local self-management.

The Constitutional Court itself found the structure of the new municipalities to be questionable when it was swept by a wave of protests around the country against the new municipalities; people were embittered particularly by the failure to respect their will as expressed at referenda held on the new municipalities. The Constitutional Court received a submission from 80 plaintiffs questioning the constitutionality of the Law on the Establishment of New Municipalities and Definition of their Territory and ruled that the new municipalities were unconstitutional because they did not fulfil the legally-determined criteria derived from the Constitution. It instructed the Parliament to reconcile the territorial layout of the municipalities with the spirit of the Constitution according to the criteria set down in the Law on local government by the next elections in 1996 at the latest. Hence, it may be said that a Damoclean sword now hangs over all the new municipalities and their territorial integrity, and eventually their very existence.

State administrative units

In parallel with the establishment of the new municipalities the central government also had to establish its own territorial units in the field to assume all the state functions which earlier had been carried out by the communes. There were three issues to be resolved here:

a) the territorial boundaries of the administrative units;
b) the legal status of these units; and
c) the allocation of the former municipalities' responsibilities between the new ones and the state administrative units.

These issues would not have arisen had wider local government communities - provinces or similar communities - been introduced in Slovenia, and particularly if their territories had been reconciled with those of the first-tier state administrative agencies, as is usually the case in Europe (the French *department*, or the Italian, Spanish, Dutch *province*, and the German *county*, etc). However, since they have not been introduced and most likely will not be whilst the present constitutional order of local government is in force, an institutional arrangement operative in neighbouring Austria presented itself as a solution. This is the institution of the state administrative county (*Verwaltungsbezirk*) which is the first-tier organ of state administration handling all general administrative matters and, at the same time, constituting the supervisory and advisory agency for local government. It is familiar in Slovenia because it had a similar system until 1945, when the socialist state was instituted. However, because there are constitutional constraints precluding such an institution, the administrative county was not adopted directly. A new territorial unit has been formed, described simply as a 'state administrative unit' (SAU) with no special name, whose organization and status, however, is very similar to the Austrian county. It is the first-tier organ of general state administration, attending to all affairs that are not the province of special state services (such as the customs and tax services). It brings together at the first tier the competencies of most of the central ministries. It is headed by a director appointed by the national government to whom he is accountable. The SAU works under the supervision of the central government and its ministries.

Initially, the SAU assumed all the statutory administrative functions of the former commune with the exception of the geodesic service, administrative supervision, and defence functions. The latter duties have been assumed directly by the respective ministries. This means that the Parliament has stripped the municipality of all the duties it had previously vested in it by law and transferred them to the SAU, with the exception of those which have explicitly been transferred to the responsible ministry. In time, of course, the SAU will acquire by law new duties deemed as suitable for execution at the local level. However, as far as duties devolved by the state are concerned, the new municipalities start from zero.

Political pressures were so great that no rational solution was possible regarding the sites of the SAU. Their most appropriate location would have been in provinical centres. A political compromise was instead struck and the SAU were put in the same sites as the former communes, which, although too large for the conduct of local affairs, were too small for the conduct of state administrative tasks. Instead of ten to twelve SAU there are now 59, which means that on average one unit covers only two and a half new municipalities. The number of SAU may be expected to shrink substantially in the coming years and gradually approach the lower figure.

Problems with the new organization

The new municipalities became operative on 1 January 1995, and the parallel state field administrative agencies immediately confronted a number of problems resulting from deficiencies in the reform process. This will necessitate further reforms, over and above the territorial reshaping of the municipalities required by the Constitutional Court ruling referred to earlier.

The main problems will derive from the fact that there is no coverage by either municipalities or state field agencies of the inter-regional or provincial level. A vacuum will develop in the intervening space between the national government and the municipalities, which will adversely impact on the operations of both local and central government.

Many local matters cannot be conducted effectively within a small municipality because it is too narrow territorially, too weak financially and inadequately staffed. The business arising from the common interests of people in their locality do not stop at the borders of the municipality but pass beyond them into a territorial unit that is wider even than the former commune. Unless there is an agency to conduct this business it will be neglected. This will make the system inactive precisely in the place where the best conditions exist for its dynamism. Only a small part of this business could be dealt with effectively by the new bodies.

The central administration will also suffer as a result of this vacuum because it has no foothold in a space which European comparisons indicate is the most important for performing many state services and particularly for the first tier of state administrative authority. These functions will have to be organized at the very centre of the state, which is unquestionably the least productive way of conducting public affairs.

As a consequence of the strict separation of central state and local government or the municipality, the latter remains severely limited to local affairs and so will be socially devalued, not just in relation to the former commune, which performed a large number of state services, but also in relation to the conventional European municipality with its growing importance as a factor in the public sector and a major counterweight to powerful state and supra-state formations. The previous extreme decentralization of the communal system will be supplanted by extreme centralization in national government organs. The outcome of this will be systemic sterility in the conduct of public affairs, as well as the generation of increasingly difficult political problems: on the one hand the country's peripheral areas will create linkages with neighbouring areas on the other side of the national borders; on the other there will be constant pressures on the national government, which is already over-burdened.

The existing provisions for Slovenian local government were pre-determined by the Constitution, particularly Articles 121, 140 and 143. It may be argued that these articles did not derive from any deliberate political programme but were more an expression of the personal proclivities of the framers of that part of the Constitution. Although they plainly wanted to create a centralized state with undivided authority, they apparently were not aware of all the ramifications of their formulations. The flaws in these formulations became especially evident during the drafting of the Law on Local Government which magnified the constitutional errors and in some places carried them to absurdity, particularly in regard to the province. Actual practice will continue to bring them to the surface and sooner or later necessitate new solutions at the level of the Constitution. Until these and certain other constitutional provisions are amended, it will not be possible to achieve an effective division of governmental responsibilities between central and local authorities.

Notes

1. See for example the report of the Council of Europe in the research journal no. 28, titled *Reformes des collectivités locales et régionales en Europe,* Strasbourg, 1983.
2. *Ibid.*

14 The Public Sector in Transition

MARKO LAH AND ANDREJ SUŠJAN

Introduction

The aim of this paper is threefold. Firstly, we will try to compare the Slovenian public sector before and after the secession from Yugoslavia in 1991. Secondly, we will analyse the dynamics and the structural trends of the Slovenian public budget (revenues, expenditures, public deficit and public debt) in the transitional years 1991-95. Finally, we will try to indicate some perspectives on the future Slovenian public sector.

The budget constraints on Slovenia as a republic of Yugoslavia

Following the political and economic changes in the former Yugoslavia after its 1945 constitution there were, roughly speaking, two different periods in the economic relations between the republics and the federal state which also had an influence on public sector financing. In the period of the administrative *socialist command* economy the republics were integrated into the successive centralist time plans of the federation. Although the centralist pressure was gradually declining, the republics had very restricted autonomy in their economic policy. The second period began with the revised constitution of 1974, which introduced two basic economic changes. The first was the 'orientation' from a socialist command economy towards a market economy and the so-called *market socialism* as the political authorities tried to stimulate production in the socialist enterprises. The second change was even more important as far as the public sector is concerned, since federal republics acquired limited fiscal authority over their 'national' economies. Republics were obliged to participate in the budget of the federation but they were able to create their own economic policy and had significant economic (and also political) independence.

However, it is not easy to give a clear empirical picture of the economic conditions and the public sector financing of republics in the years before the Slovenian secession. The official statistics of Yugoslavia, and of course Slovenia, used Marxist terminology, which divided budget expenditure into 'general' consumption (state administration, police, defence) and 'collective' consumption (extensive health insurance, pensions and also expenditure for various 'socialist purposes' such as infrastructure and residential investments). This 'consumption' was financed by firms through various contributions and in a very rough approximation we could equate it with a public sector.[1]

In addition, the official data for the last years before the secession are incomplete. The last Statistical Yearbook of the former Yugoslavia was published in 1990 and it includes the data up until 1989. Under the new system the Statistical Yearbook of Slovenia has been using a changed methodology since 1991 and therefore the items and the figures are not compatible.[2] Also, the growing hyperinflation (up to 1,406 per cent in 1989) in the final years of the federal state implies that the empirical data for that period are even less reliable.

With these limitations in mind we divided the total public expenditure of Slovenia for the years 1986-88 into internal and external (see Table 14.1). The internal expenditures were 'consumed' for the benefit of the republic of Slovenia, while through the external expenditures Slovenia participated in financing the functions of the federation (defence, law and legislation, diplomacy).

Table 14.1 Internal and external public expenditures of Slovenia as a federal unit (1986-88)

	1986		1987		1988	
	millions of dinars	%	millions of dinars	%	millions of dinars	%
Internal	212.6	91.2	498.6	91.2	1,686.2	92.3
External	20.5	8.8	48.3	8.8	141.1	7.7
Total	233.1	100.0	546.9	100.0	1,827.3	100.0

Source: Statistical Yearbook of Slovenia, 1991, pp. 136-7.

The receipts of the Slovenian budget (and also expenditures, as the budget was balanced) amounted to about 60 per cent of the GDP in 1986.[3] According to Table 14.1 the external (federal) obligations of Slovenia were 8.8 per cent of its public receipts (5.3 per cent of the GDP).[4]

Table 14.2 The structure of the federal budget of Yugoslavia (1986-89)

	1986		1987		1988		1989	
	millions of dinars	%	millions of dinars	%	millions of dinars	%	millions of dinars	%
Total Revenue	137.5	100.0	300.9	100.0	813.1	100.0	11,376.5	100.0
Import duties & taxes	32.4	23.6	78.9	26.2	239.6	29.5	3,240.9	28.5
Receipts from republics	102.4	74.5	216.0	71.8	522.2	67.9	7,810.9	68.6
Other	2.6	1.9	6.0	2.0	21.3	2.6	324.7	2.9
Surplus	0.0	0.0	0.0	0.0	53.4	7.0	549.6	5.0
Total Expenditure	137.5	100.0	300.9	100.0	759.7	100.0	10,826.9	100.0
Social Security	21.4	15.6	58.5	19.4	118.4	15.9	1,105.8	10.2
Federal administration	7.4	5.4	14.8	4.9	45.4	6.0	1,163.4	10.7
Defence	96.8	70.4	197.1	65.5	524.7	69.1	6,112.5	56.5
Funds for less dev. reg.	-	-	-	-	-	-	1,579.1	14.6
Other	11.9	8.7	30.5	10.1	68.2	9.0	866.1	8.0

Source: Statistical Yearbook of Yugoslavia, 1990, p. 191.

At the central level, the federal budget of Yugoslavia had two basic revenue sources as shown in Table 14.2. The first were federal taxes and import duties collected by federal authorities, which amounted to about 23.6 per cent of total federal revenue in 1986. The other major revenue source of the federal budget was contributions from republics (74.5 per cent in 1986). Their contributions depended on their GDP. Therefore Slovenia, as the most developed republic in the former Yugoslavia, contributed relatively the largest part. With about eight per cent of the population of Yugoslavia, Slovenia contributed almost 16 per cent of the federal budget (Škerjanc, 1989, p. 99).

The expenditure section of the federal budget shows that the most important item was defence - in 1986 this was 70.4 per cent of total federal expenditure. Federal administration consumed only 5.4 per cent of the federal budget.[5]

The dynamics of the Slovenian budget (see Table 14.1) show that between 1986 and 1988 there were no significant changes in Slovenian participation in financing the federal budget.

Neither were there significant changes in the dynamics of the federal budget between 1986 and 1989 as shown in Table 14.2. In 1989 a substantial part of total federal budget expenditure (14.6 per cent) was directed to the less developed regions. Before 1989, the allocations for this purpose were collected through the so-called 'fund for the less developed republics and provinces', which was not a part of the federal budget. This fund, which was intended to reduce the economic disparities between the republics, ceased to exist in the late eighties, as the political situation worsened.[6]

Although the official data show that budgets (both at a republic and federation level) were more or less balanced, the economic policy of Yugoslavia and also Slovenia was a 'soft budget constraint' policy. It is necessary to observe fiscal policy in connection with monetary policy (fiscal monetary mix) as the federal central bank (National Bank of Yugoslavia) did not follow an autonomous monetary policy.[7] In the late eighties fiscal policy was accompanied by an enormous rise of the money supply and consequent hyperinflation: this was the so-called 'political endogenous creation of money'. The political authorities had the power to interfere formally or informally in the banking system and the credit allocations of the commercial banks were influenced, sometimes even determined, by political intervention. The federal central bank was under pressure from the republican and federal political authorities, which were in fact 'the lender of last resort'. The policy of easy money as a cause of hyperinflation and redistribution of income between the republics and the federation accelerated the independence process in Slovenia.

Although the economic system was not very transparent, we can nevertheless say that in the years 1986-89 the fiscal federal pressure was permanent and constant.[8] Besides the federal pressure and economic voluntarism, the main reasons for Slovenia's secession should be found in the political, cultural and ethnic differences that had gradually been building up since the beginning of the eighties.

However, the decision of the Slovenian government in autumn 1990 that Slovenia would not pay federal taxes and import duties initiated a strong federal reaction which, in combination with other hostilities, culminated in the ten day war in the summer of 1991. Although Slovenia declared political independence in June 1991, it was still a part of the old monetary system until October 1991 when a new currency was introduced. This date should be taken therefore as the actual beginning of Slovenia's fiscal and economic independence.

Public sector financing in transition (the budget of the independent state)

The impact of economic transition on the Slovenian public sector

The transition of the Slovenian economy has been determined by at least three important characteristics:

1. a decline in real GDP, due particularly to the loss of the Yugoslav markets;
2. economic restructuring with the aim of adjusting Slovenian production to western standards and improving its competitiveness on the western markets and;

3. the privatization process aimed at establishing a normal structure of company ownership as a substitute for the so-called 'social ownership'.

During the past five years all three characteristics have directly or indirectly affected the dynamics of the Slovenian public sector. Growth recession (see Table 14.3) has severely worsened the conditions for a smooth economic transition by reducing the disposable income needed for financing the transition process. Establishing a state apparatus in the functions which Slovenia took over from the federation (defence, diplomatic service, etc.) has represented a considerable item among the Slovenian budget outlays of the past five years. Because of the lower GDP this burden has been even heavier.

Table 14.3 Macroeconomic performance in Slovenia (1991-94)

	growth rate of GDP (%)	unemployment rate (%)
1991	-9.2	8.2
1992	-6.1	13.2
1993	-1.0	15.4
1994	1.0	14.2

Source: Bulletin of the Parliament of Slovenia, No. 32, 1993, p. 10; Macroeconomic Trends in Slovenia, 1994, p. 51.

Economic restructuring has put additional pressure upon public expenditures in two ways:

1. directly, through heavy subsidies, which have been a part of a comprehensive incentive scheme, aimed at stimulating entrepreneurship and promoting technological modernization and investment and;
2. indirectly, through transfer payments, required to alleviate the problem of unemployment, which is a normal by-product of the process of economic restructuring.

A significant pressure upon the budget has been imposed by privatization. A considerable number of ex-socialist firms (with a large number of employees and technologically uncompetitive production) were not able to adapt themselves to the post-socialist circumstances, characterized by restrictive monetary and fiscal policies. They ran up high debts and withdrew from privatization schemes. Because of the large number of jobs at stake, a 'shelter' for these firms had to be provided by the state either by guarantees for bank loans or by direct support from the budget. In either case these firms have contributed to a rise in public expenditures.

On the revenue side the main problem has been to find sources to cover the increased public spending. As a republic of the socialist Yugoslavia Slovenia could, by endogenous creation of money (mentioned earlier), promptly balance any potential public deficit. With secession this practice came to an end. Slovenia had to start balancing its budget by raising taxes and by internal and/or external borrowing.

The structural dynamics of the Slovenian public sector in the years 1991-94

The general dynamics of the Slovenian public sector after 1990 are shown in Figure 14.1. We can see that the aggregate public expenditure has been rather successfully balanced by public revenue. A moderate growth in the public deficit has been stabilized at around two per cent of GDP, which is comparable with the situation in the more highly developed market economies.

Figure 14.1   The dynamics of the Slovenian public sector (1991-95)

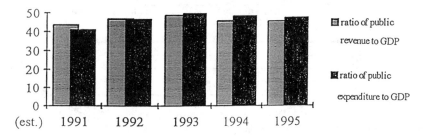

Source: Bulletin of the Parliament of Slovenia, 1993, No. 32, pp. 11-7.

The structure of public sector receipts for the period 1991-94 is shown in Table 14.4a. The most important sources of public revenues are taxes (corporate taxes, sales taxes, individual taxes, import duties), which contribute around a half, and social security contributions (pension and health), which provide over 40 per cent. Other sources (various fees, tariffs and tolls) provide between six per cent and nine per cent of public revenues.

Sales taxes represent around a quarter of revenue and almost 50 per cent of tax receipts. This share is likely to rise in the future because the government plans to increase sales tax rates for a number of specific goods (e.g. alcohol, cigarettes, petrol).

Next to sales taxes in their importance for financing the budget are individual income taxes. They provide around 14 per cent of public sector revenues. In 1994 the individual tax rate scheme was modified to distribute the burden of income tax more equally across the population.[9]

The importance of corporate tax has been relatively small and declining (from 1.4 per cent of total public revenue in 1991 to 0.9 in 1994), which is the result of a comprehensive government supply-side programme which reduced corporate tax rates in order to stimulate investment and growth.

The share of social security contributions in total public revenue has been gravitating towards 40 per cent.

Table 14.4a Slovenia: The composition of public sector revenue (1991-94)

	1991		1992		1993		1994	
	% of total	% of GDP	% of total	% of GDP	% of total	% of GDP	% of total	% of GDP
Taxes	48.3	21.1	46.2	21.7	47.7	23.3	50.0	22.9
Corp-orate taxes	1.4	0.6	1.3	0.6	0.9	0.4	0.9	0.4
Individ-ual income taxes	15.4	6.7	14.9	6.9	14.3	7.0	13.1	6.0
Sales taxes	23.3	10.2	23.0	10.8	24.6	12.0	27.7	12.7
Import duties	8.2	3.6	7.0	3.3	7.8	3.8	8.3	3.8
Social Security contrib.	44.8	19.6	48.4	22.7	46.0	22.5	40.1	18.8
Pension insur-ance contrib.	32.1	12.9	29.7	12.5	30.3	13.4	25.9	11.9
Other	6.9	3.0	5.4	2.6	6.3	3.0	9.1	4.2
Total	100.0	43.7	100.0	46.9	100.0	48.8	100.0	45.9

The structure of public expenditure for the same period is presented in Table 14.4b. Among the budget outlays at the state level the share of public administration has been the most important and has also experienced the highest growth (3.1 per cent of GDP in 1991, 6.1 per cent of GDP in 1994). The explanation for this could be found in a rising number of employees in state administration, in material costs and investments in state offices and in a gradual expansion of the diplomatic network, which, particularly for a small economy, represents a very high expenditure.

Another relatively high (and rising) share in budget outlays belongs to defence. In 1991 Slovenia organized its own armed forces and started establishing basic systems of national defence, which had to be financed from the budget. It should be noted that although these amounts are high (more than four per cent of total expenditure and 2.1 per cent of GDP in 1994) they are still considerably lower than those Slovenia used to pay to the federal budget for the Yugoslav army.

The share of social transfers in total public expenditure has been relatively constant. Despite the continually rising unemployment rate, it has remained at around eight per cent, which could be explained by the fact that in 1993 the government tightened the criteria for entitlement to unemployment benefits.

The share of public investments (both in relation to total expenditure and as a percentage of GDP) appears to have been rather stagnant. However, it should be noted that a rising proportion of public investment has been directed for improving traffic infrastructure, particularly for highways. A ten year programme of highway construction is planned to be accomplished by the year 2000.[10]

The share of government subsidies has been gradually declining (from 6.3 per cent of total expenditure and 2.8 per cent of GDP in 1991 to 3.3 per cent and 1.6 per cent in 1994), which is the result of the government's decision to dispense with the old socialist practice of subsidizing unprofitable firms. In the past, government subsidies led to grave structural distortions and the survival of some outdated, uncompetitive sectors (e.g. the steel industry). Since the production of these sectors is labour intensive, the government, in order to prevent social unrest, decided on a gradual programme of restructuring.

Two more items among budget outlays are worth mentioning. The increasing share of interest payments in total expenditure is due to the rise in public sector borrowing. And there has been a rising share of guarantee payments. Namely, one of the ways of 'rescuing' the ex-socialist firms (those which have been considered to have profitable projects) has been to provide governmental guarantees for bank loans granted to these firms. Apparently, governmental estimates were mostly wrong, and consequently the burden on the taxpayer has increased.

In 1991 there was still some financing of the federal functions, which represented 0.9 per cent of the Slovenian GDP, but this item has since disappeared.

Although the budget outlays at local level since secession have been declining in relative terms, the new legislation on local authorities (starting in 1995), according to which the number of local units (communes) has more than doubled, will probably cause a considerable boost in budget outlays in the years to come.

Pension insurance payments represent around 27 per cent of total public expenditure and around 13 per cent of GDP. Since the Slovenian population is getting 'older' (as in many other European countries) the number of pensions is rising (435,000 in 1994). If the growth of GDP remains stagnant, the amount of pension insurance payments might significantly increase the burden on the tax-paying active population in the following years.[11]

The share of medical insurance in total public expenditure has been constant, with the exception of the year 1991, at around 15 per cent (seven per cent of GDP). However, during the past four years a comprehensive reform has been carried out within the medical insurance system. While the contribution rate has remained more or less the same, there have been radical restrictions of services. Medical services are confined to what is essential from a medical point of view and several benefits are no longer provided. For additional services, patients are required either to pay a large portion of the costs themselves or to participate in non-compulsory medical insurance schemes.

Table 14.4b   Slovenia: the composition of public sector expenditure
(1991-94)

	1991		1992		1993		1994	
	% of total	% of GDP	% of total	% of GDP	% of total	% of GDP	% of total	% of GDP
Budget outlays - state level	42.4	17.5	45.6	21.2	45.8	22.8	45.1	21.8
Public admin-istration	8.1	3.1	12.5	5.8	13.2	6.6	12.6	6.1
Defence	2.6	1.1	3.9	1.8	3.0	1.5	4.3	2.1
Education, Science, Culture	4.6	1.9	4.3	2.0	4.1	2.2	5.6	2.7
Social transfers	8.3	3.4	7.5	3.5	8.9	4.4	8.7	4.2
Subsidies	6.9	2.8	6.1	2.9	4.7	2.3	3.3	1.6
Investment	6.4	2.6	5.4	2.5	4.7	2.3	4.6	2.2
Interest payments	0.8	0.3	1.0	0.5	3.1	1.6	4.1	2.0
Guarantee payments	0.0	0.0	2.0	0.9	0.7	0.4	1.5	0.7
Refugees	-	-	0.3	0.1	0.3	0.2	0.4	0.2
Federation	2.1	0.9	-	-	-	-	-	-
Budget outlays-local levels	16.5	6.8	10.4	4.9	10.4	4.8	10.1	4.9
Pension insurance	26.9	11.0	27.5	12.8	27.6	13.7	26.4	12.8
Medical insurance	12.2	5.0	15.7	7.3	15.9	7.9	15.1	7.3
Other	2.0	0.8	0.8	0.4	0.3	0.5	3.3	1.6
Total	100.0	41.1	100.0	46.6	100.0	49.7	100.0	48.4

Table 14.4c   Slovenia: budget surplus and deficit (1991-94)

	1991		1992		1993		1994	
	% of expend.	% of GDP	% of expend.	% of GDP	% of expend.	% of GDP	% of expend.	% of GDP
Surplus (+) or deficit (-) of public sector	+6.4	+2.6	+0.7	+0.3	-1.8	-0.9	-1.5	-2.5

Source: Bulletin of the Parliament of Slovenia, 1993, No. 32, pp. 11-7; Rupnik, 1994, App.

Public debt and public deficit

After the secession Slovenia followed restrictive monetary and fiscal policies in an attempt to decrease inflation, which led to a budget surplus in the years 1991 and 1992. Inflation has been considerably reduced and so the government opted for a slight deficit in the years 1993 and 1994 (Table 14.4c).

The Slovenian public debt amounted to 25.7 per cent of GDP in 1993[12], which is relatively low when compared to most European countries. However, its nature is specific. It did not originate 'normally' (by gradual and continuous governmental servicing of the budget deficit) but had emerged as a consequence of Slovenian secession and the change of the political and economic regime.

We must distinguish two different sources of the public debt: the 'external' and the 'internal'. Total external debt, estimated at about six per cent of GDP in 1993, is indebtedness to various foreign commercial banks, international financial organisations and foreign governments. It emerged in the seventies and eighties in the former Yugoslavia and can be further divided into two parts. The first consists of the loans that were used directly by legal entities located on the territory of Slovenia. This, the so-called 'allocated' debt, was recognized as a fixed obligation (a primary deficit) of the new Slovenian state and amounts to US$1.8 billion.[13] But there are still ambiguities about the size of the second, so-called 'unallocated' part of the former federal debt, as the negotiations about the succession of Yugoslavia are not concluded so far. According to the IMF formula for the distribution of assets and liabilities, Slovenia would have to take over some US$510 million (i.e. 16.4 per cent of US$3.1 billion of federal, unallocated debt). This would bring the Slovenian external debt to a level of about US$2.2 billion. Even by assuming this percentage of unallocated debt, Slovenia would still have a debt to export ratio around 20 per cent, which means that its debt burden is significantly below that of any other republic of former Yugoslavia and also below the corresponding ratios of practically all other countries of Central and Eastern Europe (Mrak, 1994, pp. 30-3).

The second source of the Slovenian public debt is internal. Internal debt, estimated at 19.7 per cent of GDP in 1993, originated when the state decided to transform the 'questionable' assets (mostly credits to unprofitable ex-socialist firms) of commercial banks into public debt. This step was necessary in order to enable the monetary and real sector of the economy to rid itself of the burdens of the past.

The government chose the usual fiscal and monetary techniques for financing its debt. The central bank (Bank of Slovenia) issued different kinds of government bonds which covered about 80 per cent of the internal public debt. As the Slovenian financial market is very small with insufficient effective demand and with few foreign investors, only 0.5 per cent of the issued bonds were sold. The majority entered the asset side of the commercial bank balances as a long-term claim on the Slovenian government.

Some positive economic indicators of the last two years (trade balance surplus, revival of industrial production, relatively low inflation rate, growing foreign exchange reserves, a slight decline of unemployment) and a relatively low level of public debt in relation to GDP lead to the conclusion that Slovenia should not have any major difficulties in servicing both the external and internal part of its public debt in future.

Perspectives

The public budget is always the expression, reflection and the consequence of the broader political and economic situation and it must be considered in relation to it. Slovenia as a small country can only adjust its own economic policy to political and economic trends which are created elsewhere.

There are two extreme medium-term 'scenarios' of future Slovenian economic performance. The pessimistic scenario is connected with the possible expansion of the war in Bosnia (and in some other ex-Yugoslav republics). This scenario, of course, implies a very uncertain situation with unpredictable changes in public budget financing. The other, more plausible scenario, is a 'peace' scenario. Accordingly, Slovenia will become increasingly integrated into the European Union, proceeding (by associate membership) to eventual full membership.

Therefore, in the medium run the crucial targets for Slovenian fiscal and broader economic policy should be fulfilling the criteria for associate membership (Essen Treaty)[14] and full membership (Maastricht Treaty) of the EU. As far as fiscal criteria are concerned, Slovenia fulfils both criteria from the Maastricht Treaty, as its public debt is lower than one third of GDP and its public deficit is lower than three per cent of GDP.[15] However, Slovenia does not fulfil Maastricht monetary criteria in respect of inflation and interest rates, which also have some budgetary implications.[16]

The projections of public expenditure in relation to GDP predict a gradual fall in the forthcoming years to about 45 per cent of GDP. This, however, does not mean an absolute fall of public expenditure as this trend should be accompanied by the growth of GDP. Two preliminary projections were made by the International Bank for Development and by the Institute for Macroeconomic Research and both are very optimistic. Growth rates of GDP predicted by the first projection are four per cent in 1995, 4.5 per cent in 1996 and five per cent annually for the period 1997-2000. Growth rates of GDP predicted by the second projection are two percent in 1995, four per cent in 1996 and 4.5 per cent annually for the period 1997-2000.[17]

Consequently, we can in the medium run predict a relative fall, but absolute growth, of public expenditure with a small budget deficit.

Conclusion

Due to the differences in methodology there is no definitive empirical answer to the question of whether the public expenditures of Slovenia as a new state are larger than they were in the former Yugoslavia. We can conclude that the transition of the public sector in Slovenia was quite smooth. Parallel to its political transition, Slovenia followed a gradual 'fine tuning' of fiscal measures. On the revenue side of its public sector the tax system has been converging to match the tax systems of the member states of the European Union. On the expenditure side of the public sector the only radical changes have been brought about by the requirements of the new state apparatus. Continuation of this harmonization with the fiscal system of the European Union can be expected in the future.

Notes

1.   There was also hidden taxation. The most significant example is defence expenditure, which was not financed solely through the budget. There were a number of laws which obliged firms and different organizations to cover defence expenses (for example war shelters) similarly to fixed production costs. Real expenditure for defence was therefore much higher.
2.   The last year before the secession (1990) represents a statistical gap.
3.   The year 1986 is considered to be the last relatively stable year before the economic and political situation in the former Yugoslavia destabilized in the late 1980s.
4.   According to Flajs (1993, p. 64), who uses the SNA methodology (System of National Accounts of the United Nations), in 1986 11.7 per cent of the Slovenian GDP was not consumed in Slovenia.
5.   However, it must be pointed out that federal expenditures (especially for military equipment) were spent mostly in industrially developed republics. In this way Slovenia 'received back' at least a part of its contributions to the federal budget.
6.   The fund was established in the middle of the seventies, especially for the development of Kosovo, the least developed region in the former Yugoslavia. However, since Kosovo was an administrative part of Serbia as a federal unit, it gradually turned out that this fund mostly benefited Serbia, which was thus able to get additional resources from other federal units. Obviously with the disintegration of the fund in 1989 a substitute was found in the federal budget.
7.   Increases in government expenditures can be financed in three ways. The first is raising taxes, the second increases in external borrowing and the third increases of money supply (fiscal monetary mix). While in the seventies the Yugoslav government relied on external borrowing (and accumulated an enormous external debt), in the eighties there were frequent money supply increases required by the political authorities in order to finance various 'priorities' determined by political and not economic criteria.
8.   This conclusion is also supported by Flajs (1993, p. 65). According to him the external contributions of Slovenia were (in per cent of GDP) 11.7 per cent in 1986, 11.2 per cent in 1987 and 11.5 per cent in 1988.
9.   According to the new tax rate scheme more income tax is paid by the population in higher income brackets. Additionally, some new forms of property tax are planned to be introduced in the following years, which will also affect the wealthier population.
10.   The value of planned investment projects in the area of infrastructure (highways, railroads, airports, telecommunications, ecological generation of electricity) in the next six years amounts to US$2-3 billion. Of course, not all the projects will be budget financed; various measures are in preparation to attract foreign direct investors.
11.   In order to reduce the pressure on the pension insurance system and since raising the contribution rates would be a strong disincentive for the economy, the government plans to support various forms of non-compulsory pension insurance schemes.
12.   See Bulletin of the Parliament of Slovenia, 1994, No. 10, pp. 74-85.
13.   The total medium and long-term allocated debt of former Yugoslavia (according to the data of the former National Bank of Yugoslavia) was US$12.0 billion. It was allocated to the federal units (i.e. six republics and two autonomous provinces) in the following volumes: Serbia - US$3.2 billion, Croatia - US$2.7 billion, Slovenia - US$1.8 billion, Bosnia

and Herzegovina - US$1.5 billion, Vojvodina - US$0.8 billion, Kosovo - US$0.7 billion, Macedonia - US$0.7 billion and Montenegro - US$0.6 billion (see Mrak, 1994, p. 31).

14. The Essen Treaty gives only political (and offers some technical) suggestions for the countries that would like to achieve associate membership in the EU. Economic criteria are not defined.

15. According to Maastricht amendments the ratio of government deficit to GDP and the ratio of government debt to GDP should be less than three per cent and 60 per cent respectively. Slovenia thus has the possibility of raising both the public debt and the public deficit.

16. Monetary convergence criteria defined by the Maastricht Treaty are: (1) consumer price index (CPI) must not exceed by more than 1.5 percentage points the CPI of the three best performers; (2) the average nominal long-term interest rate must not exceed by more than two percentage points the interest rates of the three best performing member states in terms of price stability. Additional criteria are normal fluctuation of margins and no currency devaluation for at least two years.

17. See Industrial and Development Policy of Slovenia, 1994, p. 15.

15 Costs and Benefits of Secession

JOŽE MENCINGER

The economic disintegration of Yugoslavia

The economic aspects of the disintegration of Yugoslavia have been overshadowed by political and ethnic considerations. In fact, disintegration started with the end of economic growth in the early eighties. The political vacuum after Tito's death, the rise of oil prices, the tightening on the world financial markets, and the breakdown of the so-called contractual socialism had given the first impulses for what, in the early eighties, developed into a deep economic, social, and political crisis. This prompted attempts at a new economic reform. However, for the first time, and despite a proven ability to adapt systems, re-evaluate Marxism, and redefine socialism to daily needs, Yugoslavia found it difficult to move in any direction. The country had apparently reached the point at which an economic reform unaccompanied by a political system change could only increase the inconsistencies between the economic and political systems. A radical economic reform would require above all a separation of political and economic power, while political considerations permitted only modest changes.

The reform attempt in 1982 therefore produced a long-lasting stalemate. Finally, in 1988, when party ideologists and economists persisted in speculating on new types of socialism, the federal government, comprehending its inability to deal with economic problems within the existing system, launched a new reform. It began with the premise that the system of property rights was the root cause of economic problems and urged the abandonment of the so-called non-property philosophy of social property. 'The Enterprise Act' passed in December 1988 also formally abrogated socialism; as a result, the 'self-management relationships' were replaced by the 'capital relationships'.[1]

In December 1989, the federal government launched a 'shock therapy' stabilization programme. Fixed exchange rate, tight monetary policy, and wage controls were to be the pillars of this policy. However, an overvaluation of the dinar, the weakness of wage controls, and fiscal overhang existed from the very beginning. In the first two quarters of 1990, economic performance was satisfactory; in April 1990, the rate of inflation was actually negative. In June, fatal mistakes were added to those of December 1989. Policy makers started to pump money through selective credits to the agricultural sector and nearly doubled the salaries of federal employees. This triggered a general race of wages. The programme was left without nominal anchors; the burden remained solely on a fixed exchange rate. Private and public sector spending increased dramatically during the summer and stayed high, while economic activity plummeted. This made price stability unsustainable; in the third quarter the economy was pushed into critical illiquidity, large scale bartering, and a recession without deflation. Exports dropped, imports grew, and the trade deficit soared. In October, the run on the banks, to withdraw deposits in foreign exchange, began and foreign exchange reserves, the last resort of the stabilization program, decreased dramatically.

The development both in the systemic and economic policy spheres prompted the economic disintegration of the country. In short, at the end of 1990, i.e. long before its political disintegration, Yugoslavia ceased to exist as a viable economic entity; taxes were not collected, money was 'printed' by republics, tariffs and special levies were introduced for 'imports' from other republics, and republics started to build up new economic systems.

The 'economic history' of secession

The real economic arguments for the secession of Slovenia differ substantially from the populist notion of 'being exploited' by other republics. Instead, they are related to the prospects of a transition to a market economy. Independence became 'the emergency exit' condition for macro-economic stabilization, supply side restructuring, and systemic transition, and the potential benefits of secession became higher than its economic and social costs.

Slovenia was better placed than the rest of Yugoslavia to establish a 'normal' economic system, adapt to European standards, and adhere to sound economic policy measures. Furthermore, disintegration gave a better prospect for integration with Europe. Slovenia had the advantage of the early market orientated reforms in Yugoslavia, and had some further advantages of its own: a homogeneous, socially-stable population; highly skilled workers; a well diversified manufacturing sector dispersed over the country, which would require less restructuring than in the rest of Yugoslavia, and which, as a consequence, would diminish social tensions during the transition; the rather supple responsiveness of a homogeneous economy to economic policy measures; well established economic links with western markets; and its geographical position were among them. Furthermore, Slovenia had never been fully integrated with the Yugoslav economy; it was autonomous in infrastructure (access to the sea, pipelines, railways, communications, electricity transmission, etc.), and the trade patterns with the rest of Yugoslavia resembled those with foreign countries. Because of its small size, the proximity of developed countries, and its relatively efficient manufacturing sector, almost 50 per cent of GDP originated from exports and about 70 per cent of exports and imports were with the European Community and EFTA.

Table 15.1   The Slovene economy at independence 1991

Output & Demand in millions of US$			
Area (in 000km)	20.2	GDP at market prices	11,778
Population (in 000)	1,996	-exports (goods & services)	5,828
Employment (in 000)	823	-imports (goods & services)	5,269
Unemployment (in 000)	85	Total consumption	7,562
GDP/capita (in US$)	5,900	-private	6,019
External Debt		-general government	1,543
-long term (in millionUS$)	1,814	Gross Domestic Investments	2,992
-short term (in million US$)	141	-in fixed assets	2,238
-debt/export ratio	0.31	-change in inventories	754
-debt/GDP ratio	0.15		

There were negative aspects to independence and the more predictable ones included:

a) a reduction of the market; a diminished supply of raw materials and of cheaper finished products from the rest of Yugoslavia;
b) the termination of the foreign trade links which Slovenia had through Yugoslav companies and vice versa;
c) a likely. loss of the property of Slovene companies in other parts of Yugoslavia;
d) the lessened interest of foreign investors in a smaller market.

The legalization of political parties in 1989 created the necessary conditions for free elections and parliamentary democracy. Pre-election campaigns, elections, and the transition of power from the old to the new governments were conducted in a calm atmosphere. The results of the elections, however, divided Yugoslavia into two parts; communist/socialist type systems in Serbia and Montenegro, and Western type systems in the rest of the country. This, together with the emergence of nationalistic governments, the quickly growing animosity between Croats and Serbs, and the collapse of economic reform, finally led to the breakdown of the country.

The political future of Slovenia - to be a member-state of the Yugoslav federation or confederation, or a wholly independent country - was, after the elections, still not clearly determined. The actual development toward full independence was therefore a result of spontaneous responses to unpredictable events rather than of a well-designed blueprint. Only at the end of 1990, when the leaders of Demos, the party of government, decided to organize a referendum and were supported by the opposition parties, did 'independence' replace a rather unclear notion of 'sovereignty'.[2]

The Slovene government installed after general elections in 1990 also realized that the prospects of transition to a market economy within Yugoslavia were worsening due to mistaken economic policy, an unsuitable economic system, and a federation facing political turmoil. It therefore focused on pragmatic adjustments to the economic policy measures of the federal government, a gradual construction of a 'normal' economic system, acquisition of policy tools, and preparations for eventual independence. They needed to adjust quickly to highly uncertain political developments.

The government acted at two levels: the 'underground' and the official. Monetary issues were dealt with at the former level, fiscal issues constituted the bulk of operations at the latter.

At the very beginning, the Slovene government implicitly supported the federal stabilization programme by imposing relatively efficient wage controls and by reducing public consumption (both compared to the rest of Yugoslavia). Increasing discrepancies in federal economic policies which most badly affected the exporting sector, however, soon prompted demands for changes in the stabilization programme.[3] They included devaluation of the dinar, reduction of taxes and government spending at the federal level, efficient control of wages, corrections in monetary policy, and redemption of the Iraqi debt by the federal government. The federal government ignored these requests, which left the republic's government with only a limited range of economic policies. Prevention of bankruptcies by postponement of tax payments, export subsidies and partial redemption of the Iraqi debts by government bonds was introduced during 1990.

In June 1990, Slovenia suspended its contributions for less developed regions. In retaliation, Serbia imposed special levies on Slovene and Croat firms and on all payments to these two republics. When, in October 1990, Serbia ceased to forward sales taxes to the federal government, Slovenia followed. Finally, in December 1990, Serbia 'broke' into the monetary system. This prompted Slovenia to request new changes in economic policy by presenting a new Memorandum on Economic Policy and refusing federal proposals for centralization.[4] The proposals on economic policies for the first time encompassed principles for the division of financial and non-financial assets and liabilities between Slovenia and the rest of Yugoslavia. They were again ignored. When the National Bank of Yugoslavia ceased to intervene in the foreign exchange market Slovenia reacted by introducing its own 'quasi' foreign exchange market with a flexible exchange rate and the Slovene ECU as a measure of account.

The approach to systemic changes was cautious as well. They were to be introduced by two types of statutes:

1. those facilitating functioning of a market economic system and
2. those needed for the transition to a market economy.

In the first group, the system of direct taxation introducing simple, transparent, uniform and non-discretionary taxes was passed in December 1990. The first normal budget of an independent country was presented to the Parliament in February 1991, and the new system of simple indirect taxation was prepared.

The search for monetary independence began in mid-1990 and concentrated on three issues: the consequences of unilateral decisions for the functioning of the financial system and for relations with other countries and international institutions; possible arrangements for a monetary system in a confederation, which was still considered a choice; and the prospects for monetary independence. After the Serbian raid on the monetary system in December 1990, the discussions shifted to the name, the pattern, and the most appropriate moment for the introduction of a Slovene currency.[5] The statutes regulating the monetary and financial sector such as the 'Law on The Bank of Slovenia', 'The Law on the Banks and Saving Institutions', and 'The Law on the Rehabilitation of the Banks and Savings Institutions' were prepared in the beginning of 1991. They were passed together with the 'Declaration of Independence' and statutes regulating citizenship, passports, control of the border, customs procedures and foreign relations at the end of June, 1991.

Establishing a monetary system involved a choice between a fixed and floating exchange rate. The former surrenders the control of money supply, the latter control of the exchange rate; economic theory does not provide an answer as to which is preferable. A majority of experts support the view that the fixed exchange rate system suits countries in transition better (Meltzer, 1992), or propose the crawling peg as an intermediate possibility (Bomhoff, 1992). Slovenia, contrary to these beliefs, opted for a floating rate after an abrupt drop of foreign exchange reserves in October 1990. The drop revealed that the fixed rate could not be defended. The exchange rate system debates continued, encompassing major theoretical quandaries known from the debates on the optimum currency policy that are summarized by Ishijama (1975). The issues, the relationship between the real exchange rate and macro-economic stability, and the anchoring role of the nominal exchange rate, divided the participants. Theoretical arguments were used to defend different positions and much less attention was addressed to the actual arrangements in other countries (Mencinger, 1993).

During the search for a definitive solution to the currency question, preparations on a functional level continued; before the end of 1990, for example, provisional notes were printed. At the same time, temporary solutions to handle the repercussions of a fixed overvalued dinar and to cope with advancing hyperinflation were explored and introduced if found suitable. These efforts are well illustrated by 'The Law on the Introduction of a Parallel Currency' drafted on 4 February 1991, which proposed a parallel currency as a measure of account and an auxiliary means of payments. It envisaged a parallel monetary unit, pegged to the Austrian Schilling, that would enter circulation through foreign transactions and float against the dinar. The idea was abandoned because a rent-seeking 'certificate of import privileges' offered a much simpler and less risky solution. It would not expose Slovene banks to the likely angry reactions of the federal authorities. With the 'certificate', Slovenia was able to effectively establish an independent currency area within the Yugoslav fixed exchange rate system. It functioned in the following manner: an exporter who, for example, sold foreign exchange to a bank at the official exchange rate, obtained a certificate that was saleable and would allow the bearer the access to foreign exchange. The fixed rate plus the price of the certificate equalled the flexible rate. The black market for foreign exchange was also abolished by its tacit legalization. Finally, the 'Slovene ECU', a measure of account, to which the parties in economic transactions could adhere, was introduced in May 1991, less than two months before the proclamation of independence. Its value was to be determined by the average weekly price of the 'certificate' on the Ljubljana stock exchange.

Pragmatism and gradualism proved successful in coping with the consequences of the federal economic policy by establishing sovereignty in the fiscal and foreign exchange systems and preparing institutional settings for a 'new' country long before the proclamation of independence.

The costs and the benefits

Standard economic theory considers state disintegration a hindrance to economic development; the costs are stressed, the benefits are ignored. In reality, the disintegration cannot be disentangled from the overall transition, which affects the allocation of costs and benefits. While the costs of disintegration appear rather low for the 'NORTH' they are high for the 'SOUTH'. This can undoubtedly be applied to the Slovene case.

The Slovene economy has, despite preconditions and thorough preparations, been badly hit by the secession itself and, even more so, by the subsequent political and economic developments in the remnants of the former federation.

The 'supply shock' added considerably to inflationary pressures in the first months after independence. Slovenia also suffered damage because of hostile actions against business units in other republics, particularly because of the asymmetry of ownership. In 1990, there were 2,710 business units and 62 companies owned by Slovene companies in other republics compared to only 690 units and nine companies owned by other republics in Slovenia.

The links with the rest of the world have remained hindered by other unresolved issues such as responsibility for the Yugoslav foreign debt and foreign currency reserves, the non-financial assets, 2,500 different bi- and multi-lateral agreements on export quotas, transport licences, etc.[6] Slovenia shares collective responsibilities for the whole of the Yugoslav debt and even an agreement between the constituent parts of Yugoslavia therefore would not resolve the issue if creditors do not accept it. There were other unresolved issues as well; domestic debt emerging from foreign currency deposits amounted to 12 billion US$, out of which 2.1 billions were deposited in Slovene banks. Non-financial assets of the federation also need to be allocated and many other problems resolved.

The above-mentioned issues proved to be relatively less important. It was the near disappearance of the Yugoslav market of 23 million people that has been the most important and difficult to overcome. In 1990, the sales by Slovene companies to the rest of Yugoslavia equalled 130 per cent of exports to the rest of the world. In 1993, they amounted to only ten per cent of total exports. Though the structure of exports at the branch and even enterprise level was similar to the structure of sales to other republics (Bole, 1992), the costs of re-orientating trade from a protected market to the far more competitive European markets have been significant. Slovenia had also handled a high percentage of foreign trade for the enterprises from other republics or used their raw materials.

Table 15.2   The structure of sales and purchases in 1990 (% of total)

	Slovenia	other countries	other republics of Yugoslavia
Sales to	57.3	17.9	24.8
Purchases from	63.2	15.2	21.6

Source: Planning Office of the Government of Slovenia, 1991

Table 15.3   The estimated 'loss' of the markets in 1992

	actual	normal	loss	in %
exports to Yugoslavia	1508	5822**	4314	74.1
exports proper	5173	6371*	1198	18.8
total exports	6681	12193	5512	45.2

*Estimates based on the former 're-exports' of goods from other republics by Slovene companies which amounted to approximately one billion dollars yearly; **'normal' exports to Yugoslavia = exports proper * (24.8/17.9)

The dramatic reduction of trade with the former Yugoslav republics was the principal cause of the depression. The 'ten days' war' in June 1991 and secession in October 1991, pushed production down rapidly to a decline of 9.3 per cent in 1991 and six per cent in 1992. Employment went hand-in-hand with the decrease of economic activity; the adjustment of employment to changes in production since 1990 has been high. Thus, total employment fell by 5.6 per cent in 1992, and by 3.5 per cent in 1993. The reduction was concentrated in the business sector; there has been no significant drop of employment in the public sector. The so called restructuring of the economy consisted mainly of 'firing and retiring'. The number of unemployed nearly quadrupled in three years, total unemployment reached 137 thousand in the last quarter of 1993, the official unemployment rate exceeded 15 per cent,[7] and the number of pensioners doubled in the same period to 408,000. Both required increased social transfers. Taxes were increased and the share of the public sector in GDP increased to 48 per cent. The resulting increases of the costs of production could only partly be transferred to prices, which resulted in inflationary pressures, losses and bankruptcies.

Slovenia appears to be the least affected by the disruption in co-ordination caused by the conversion from a sellers' 'market towards a buyers' market which characterized the transition to a market system in other socialist countries (Kornai, 1993). The co-ordination of the economy has for many years been decentralized, the impact of insufficient demand prevailed over that of supply shortages already in the eighties and the notion of 'monetary overhang' was unknown. The necessity of rapid restructuring was produced more by the secession and ensuing collapse of Yugoslavia than by the transition itself.

The impact of the enormous switch in trade from the former Yugoslav to the genuine foreign market can be observed in 1992, when exports increased by 33 per cent and imports by 28 per cent. The results in 1993 were far less impressive.[8] The trade surplus in 1992 came as a joint result of increased exports as companies tried to replace the former Yugoslav market by exports, and reduced imports, which plummeted with the contraction in domestic demand and vanishing links with the rest of the Yugoslavia. The relative openness of the German market was particularly important because the demand pattern on the tiny domestic market differs substantially from the supply pattern fitted to the Yugoslav market while the structure of sales to the former Yugoslav market much more resembled the export structure. The secession of Slovenia therefore did not affect its trade patterns markedly.[9]

Monetary policy was crucial to preserving a relatively strong tolar[10] alongside the surplus on the current account. It reacted cautiously in removing initial administrative restrictions and intervened sensibly to prevent substantial nominal appreciations of the tolar that would result from supply and demand. However, monetary policy became trapped between conflicting goals (Mencinger, 1994), aiming on the one hand to lower inflation and keep it under control, and on the other to prevent the real appreciation of the tolar to preserve exports competitiveness.

While the relative stability of the floating tolar might be considered a success, it produced problems for the central bank in 1993 and particularly in the second part of 1994. Two sharp rises of the nominal rates, in October 1991 and in January 1992, were followed by a nearly constant nominal rate until the middle of 1992. Since then, the exchange rate changes have roughly matched inflation. Consequently, the real exchange rate fell by a third in the first period, recovered a little, and has since then remained relatively stable. The 'overvalued' tolar was in 1992 accompanied by a surplus in foreign trade which resulted from the economy's efforts to replace the lost Yugoslav market with a proper foreign market on the one hand, and a domestic depression which required fewer imports on the other. In 1993, exports of services and inflow of capital became the two main sources of a constant growth of foreign exchange reserves. They, at the end of 1994, reached US$3 billion; a high figure given the size of the economy and the corresponding M1, which amounts to approximately US$1 billion.

Before independence a shortage of foreign exchange and a high debt burden were endemic to the former Yugoslav economy and a major constraint on its growth. Shortage of foreign exchange, a debt burden which used to be the 'normal' state and the binding constraint on economic growth in the former Yugoslavia were among major uncertainties before independence. Yet, within a relatively short period, the situation changed dramatically, and by the middle of 1993 the country began to face an excess supply rather than shortage of foreign exchange. This sudden abundance of foreign exchange created a previously unknown problem of the so-called 'Dutch disease'.

Fiscal policies have also been weakened by the characteristics of the transition and by the size of the country. First, fiscal revenues fell because of the squeeze on economic activity, particularly of the socialist sector where the predominant part of tax revenues was generated. This has not been replaced by growth in the private sector, which has successfully avoided taxation. The depression on the other hand required an increase in social transfers. Bridging the gap by a budget deficit has been impossible. Financing by printing money is ruled out, domestic borrowing is practically impossible, and borrowing abroad would further increase the abundance of foreign exchange, strengthen the tolar, and further reduce competitiveness. With a trade-output ratio over 1.2 and a supply structure adapted to the former Yugoslav market, the tiny economy cannot rely on domestic absorption and therefore on standard Keynesian cures. A lasting stabilization with growth therefore requires reduction of costs per unit of output, modest public expenditure, wage restraint and administrative price controls on non-tradeables.

In 1993, Slovenia reached the bottom of the depression. GDP increased slightly, and turned to growth of four per cent in 1994. A brisk growth in industrial production which started in the second half of 1993 surprised both the government and the analysts. It seems to come from three sources: 'mistaken' economic policy, foreign demand, and normalization of the economic system. The government failed to implement its declared economic policy of first stabilizing the economy. Foreign demand, particularly that of the German economy, increased as well.[11] After 1991, trade shifted further towards developed market economies and the dominating position of Germany strengthened.

Inflation is currently running at an annual rate of 15 per cent.[12] Inflation at this level has been accompanied by attempts to introduce sound income policies.[13] The wages bill increased, which is explicable in terms of the traditional structural explanations of inflationary mechanisms, reinforced by the long-lasting 'pre-privatization environment' (Bole, 1993), in which enterprises are able and willing to push wages up so that employees get as much as possible before privatization is completed. Social transfers, old age pensions in particular, and the cost of a growing government apparatus in a small country make any fast reduction of the costs of production unlikely. The chosen method of privatization also does not promise to bring about the badly needed restructuring of the economy.

Table 15.4   Economic performances of Slovenia, 1991-1994 (quarterly)

	1	2	3	4	5	6
1989	-.81	73.8	-0.31	28.2	852	804
1990	-2.85	50.4	-1.02	44.6	1029	1182
1991/I	-4.70	18.8	-2.76	63.2	990	1202
/II	-3.32	30.2	-2.66	70.1	900	1034
/III	-2.95	34.5	-3.00	78.5	855	760
/IV	-4.09	66.4	-2.42	88.6	1113	1144
1992/I	-7.80	42.6	-2.21	95.1	1245	1413
/II	-3.87	18.5	-1.69	96.3	1272	1242
/III	-0.86	6.2	-1.12	104.4	1360	1239
/IV	0.50	7.5	-1.48	114.7	1295	1413
1993/I	0.02	6.8	-1.35	119.9	1251	1391
/II	-2.60	3.9	-0.68	126.0	1255	1470
/III	0.07	4.3	-0.69	133.2	1202	1305
/IV	3.86	6.1	-1.60	136.8	1345	1600
1994/I	3.39	4.0	-1.41	133.3	1319	1404
/II	1.14	4.5	-0.60	125.3	1429	1704
/III	2.84	3.8	-0.60	125.2	1427	1637
/IV	-0.42	4.8	-0.66	124.4	1636	1924

1) quarterly rates of change of industrial production,
2) quarterly rates of change of retail sale prices,
3) quarterly rates of change of employment in the business sector,
4) unemployment in 000,
5) quarterly exports in millions US$
6) imports in millions US$ (exports and imports do not include trade with the former Yugoslavia)

The macro-economic performance of the new country can nevertheless be considered satisfactory, particularly if all adverse circumstances are taken into account. Production has been growing, prices have been stabilized at a 'normal' level, the budget is balanced, public debt amounts to only 30 per cent of GDP, surplus in services outweighs deficit in trade, and foreign exchange reserves match foreign debt. The growth prospects remain uncertain; by gaining political independence, the economic independence of Slovenia decreased rather than strengthened. The tiny economy cannot rely on a small domestic market to achieve sustainable growth; it depends crucially on exports, and particularly on the development of the European economy.

After four years, the benefits of secession appear to prevail over its costs. Namely, while the costs of re-orienting trade from protected to competitive markets were significant, the secession intensified economic restructuring, produced sound economic policy, and permitted the construction of a 'normal' economic system.

Notes

1. Despite the failure of systemic changes in Yugoslavia, former constituent parts retained many advantages for economic and social transition compared to other EE countries. Most of the so-called essentials for economic transition: decentralization, price reform, openness to the outside world, and diversification of ownership were at least partly met before the country's political and ideological collapse. There was no need for decentralization and re-organization of central institutions; directive planning had been dismantled in the fifties, and in the sixties financial autonomy had been given to the enterprises. The enterprises were autonomous, planning did not exist and the government used standard fiscal and monetary policy tools. Basic market institutions existed although the notion of the so-called 'integral market' encompassing product, capital, and labour markets was not inaugurated until 1988. The liberalization of prices for certain products was the core of the economic reforms of 1965. Since then price controls were only used as anti-inflationary measures. In addition, Yugoslavia was a relatively open economy; links with the rest of the world through commodity, factor and financial markets, and the structure of its foreign trade and exchange rate systems resembled those which characterize developing market economies rather than CPEs. Convertible exports far exceeded exports to clearing areas. Land was predominantly privately owned and private ownership has been a feature of the fast-growing service sector.

2. On 23 December 1990, 88 per cent of eligible voters voted for independence. Six months were given to the government to prepare technicalities.

3. 'The Memorandum on Economic Policy in the Rest of 1990' sent to the federal government in August 1990.

4. 'The Memorandum of the Executive Council of the Assembly of the Republic of Slovenia on its Standpoints about the Re-organization of Economic Relations in Yugoslavia'.

5. In the beginning of 1991, similar ideas appeared in other Yugoslav republics, notably Croatia, which, at that time, favoured a monetary union between Bosnia and Hercegovina, Croatia, and Slovenia. The ideas of establishing a Yugoslav currency board also circulated.

6. Foreign indebtedness of Slovenia is low and the country could easily settle its commitments to foreigners. Its servicing amounts to less than ten per cent of foreign exchange inflows.

7. Things are not so bad by ILO standards; according to the latest investigation and applying ILO standards, the School of Social Sciences at the University of Ljubljana estimated the unemployment rate at slightly under nine per cent.

8. The drop in total exports of nearly nine per cent ($6,681 million in 1992 and $6,088 million in 1993) was caused by the collapse of trade with the former Yugoslavia which plunged by 37 per cent (m$1508 against m$963) while exports to other countries dropped two per cent (m$5173 to m$5125). Total imports were affected in the opposite direction, showing a growth of 5.6 per cent (m$6,141 to m$6,488). This comprised a fall of imports from former Yugoslav republics by 44 per cent (m$1218 to m$692!), while imports from other countries increased by 22 per cent (m$4923 to m$5797). Non-factor services have, however, helped in the current balance, with a large surplus in 1992 and a modest one in 1993.

9. Two easily explicable changes in trade patterns can be at a one digit level. First, the shares of exports and imports of mineral fuels increased because Slovenia has been buying crude oil and has been processing it in a foreign refinery. Second, a substantial drop in the share of machinery and equipment and an increase in the share of miscellaneous goods was caused by the switch towards Western Europe and the importance of 'Lohn Arbeit'.

10. Monetary policy was highly restrictive in the first half of 1992; real money supply between October 1991 and June 1992, decreased by 40 per cent and foreign exchange transactions became the only channel of money creation; the ratio of foreign exchange reserves of the BS and high powered money increased from 0.04 to 1.70, and the ratio of total reserves and M1 from 0.31 to 1.35. The regulation of money supply and banks' liquidity shifted from the manipulation of required reserves to open market operations and prudential regulations; the share of required reserves in total banks' reserves decreased from 0.71 to 0.08.

11. Exports surpass domestic private consumption, and exports to Germany alone surpass government consumption or investment demand. Furthermore, the demand pattern on the tiny domestic market differs substantially from the supply pattern fitted to the former Yugoslav market while the structure of sales to the former Yugoslav market much more resembled the export structure.

12. In October 1991, when the tolar was introduced, monthly inflation was 21.5 per cent. It was steadily suppressed, reached the level of two per cent monthly in the middle of 1992 and has since then remained steady until the end of 1995.

13. In the third quarter of 1993, a Wage Contract replaced the Law on Wage Bill Freeze from the beginning of 1993. According to it, an increase of inflation of less than three per cent a month is not compensated for, if prices increase by more than three per cent and less than five per cent per month or cumulatively in two months, 60 per cent of the increase is compensated for by a wage increase. If the monthly increase or cumulative increase in two months exceeds five per cent, 80 per cent of the increase is compensated for. Expectations that the Wage Contract would be a far less efficient anchor for wages and social transfers (which are pegged to average wages) proved true.

16 Re-shaping the Labour Market

IVAN SVETLIK

A prologue

The economic and political systems of the former Yugoslavia were recognized as much more liberal than those of the other communist countries of Central and Eastern Europe. This was particularly true for the economy, which was closely linked with the West European one. Germany and Italy were, respectively, the first and the third economic partners for most of the post second world war period. The relationship was not only in trade but also through direct cooperation between West European and Yugoslav enterprises.

The intensive links with Western economies had an important impact on the labour market and employment policies of the former Yugoslavia. In the 1960s, when Western economies were facing a surplus demand for labour, Yugoslavia allowed its workers to emigrate. Until the middle 1970s about one and a half million Yugoslav workers from all parts of the country found jobs in Western Europe and thus alleviated the 'growth-gap unemployment' (Addison and Siebert, 1979) which was increasing in Yugoslavia at that time. The oil crisis and a shift of Western economies towards technologically intensive production affected the Yugoslav labour market significantly. The emigration of surplus labour stopped, many workers returned back home and the unemployment problem was aggravated. Yugoslavia tried to solve this problem by means of accelerated investments on the basis of foreign loans, hoping to create enough new jobs. This turned out to be not very successful due to the application of old technologies, inefficient management and a lack of skills among employees. This strategy caused increasing indebtedness of the country.

The position of Slovenia in relation to the rest of the former Yugoslavia could be likened to the position of Western Europe in relation to Yugoslavia. Slovenia was its most developed part with a GNP per capita ten times bigger than in Kosovo. In the 1970s there was a surplus demand for labour in Slovenia which allowed for the immigration of workers from the southern regions. Every year about 15,000 workers, i.e. 1.5 per cent of new labour, arrived. The immigration to Slovenia associated with labour-intensive investments continued up to the mid-1980s when Slovenia also faced economic crisis and increasing unemployment. Unlike Western Europe, Slovenia could not stop the immigration of cheap labour, which prevented its economy from adopting technological change. This situation caused more and more frequent discussions about the burden of the economic crisis that Slovenia had to carry. There were demands to limit immigration, which was producing several side effects such as increasing social costs for welfare provision, housing, child care, educational, health care and other facilities generated by the guest workers and their families.

Another more indirect impact of cooperation between the Yugoslav and West European economies was on the structure and the functioning of social policy and employment structure. While Yugoslavia did not adopt the Western system, it created one which was much different, at least in practice, to those of other communist countries.

Officially there was neither a labour market nor a labour market policy. Employment security was guaranteed to all employees by law. Occasionally, there were discussions about employment policy, which was considered a part of economic policy. Cyclical political campaigns stressed the importance of the creation of new jobs as a result of the better utilization of labour and of decreasing labour costs. Nevertheless, employment offices were created in the 1950s. First-job-seekers could register with the employment offices, which were supposed to help them find employment. There were also unemployment benefit and unemployment assistance schemes for those who might eventually become unemployed without any fault of their own. They were mainly used by re-entrants to the labour market, since first-job-seekers were not eligible.

In Slovenia, where open unemployment was not a problem, the main activities of employment offices were occupational guidance and providing grants to students entering high schools and universities. They also dealt with those marginal to the labour market such as the disabled, ex-delinquents, alcoholics and those unwilling to work, who represented about one third of the unemployed.

It should be stressed that the administration of the employment system, like the administration of the other welfare areas, was highly decentralized in the former Yugoslavia. This allowed for adaptation to the local specific problems, which differed significantly from region to region. However, such an arrangement caused increasing difficulties of co-ordination at the federal level and at the same time eased the creation of autonomous administrations in the successor countries after the break-down of the former Yugoslavia.

The unemployment shock

Radical changes of economic and political institutions are usually caused by major crises. This applies in the case of the Slovenian employment system. However, it was the change of the economic system from a command towards a market economy rather than the separation of Slovenia from Yugoslavia which played a crucial role. Thousands of individuals, who had perhaps never thought about unemployment before, experienced it after the reform of the economic system which started in 1989.

Table 16.1   Changes of the basic unemployment parameters in the period 1984-1993

Parameter	1984	1989	1991	1993
unemployment rate %				
-registered	1.8	2.2	8.2	14.4
-according to labour force survey (LFS)	2.2	2.6	7.3	9.1
av. no. of registered unemployed	15,066	28,218	75,079	129,078
newly registered	23,364	31,200	81,566	97,722
employed by help of employment office	19,416	18,312	37,234	60,006
Laid-off workers as % of unemployed	0.0	18.2	68.0	32.2

Until 1989, unemployment in Slovenia had exceeded three per cent only in the periods 1952-1953 and 1967-1969. According to the labour force survey data, it reached 2.6 per cent in June 1989, 7.3 per cent in October 1991, 9.1 per cent in May 1993 and 9 per cent in May 1994. The data on registered unemployment reported by the National Employment Office is even higher due to the use of less strict criteria. It was 2.2 per cent on average in 1989, 8.2 per cent in 1991, and 14.4 per cent in 1993. Employment offices register individuals as unemployed with too little attention to paid or profitable work in the grey economy, and of their availability for employment. The number of unemployed individuals registered with employment offices rose from about 15,000 in 1984 to over 130,000 in 1993. Afterwards the number started to fall.

As is shown in Table 16.1 the number of individuals who register at employment offices increases much faster than the number of those who find employment through the help of employment offices. However, the situation in 1993 improved, perhaps because economic growth began again. This is shown also by the sharp increase of those unemployed who lost their job in the first period of transition and the equally sharp decline in 1993.

The two most affected groups are young job hunters and those who are unskilled. While the overall rate of unemployment in 1993 was 9.1 per cent, it was 24.2 per cent in the age group 15 to 24 years. In 1991 only three EC countries had higher unemployment in this age group: Greece (24.6 per cent), Italy (28.2 per cent) and Spain (30.5 per cent).

While the rate of unemployment for the least educated workers was not greater than that of other educational groups until 1989, it increased significantly thereafter. The data on the duration of unemployment confirm their most unfavourable position. The duration of unemployment in December 1990 was 60 weeks on average, 73.3 weeks for those with only a primary education and 149.5 weeks for those with less than a primary education. These two groups represented about 34.9 per cent of the unemployed and about 25.4 per cent of the labour force in 1994. In the light of unavoidable technological modernization, their employment prospects are minimal unless educational and training programs are utilized. The unemployment rate of university-educated individuals is rising as well. However, it remains much lower than for the other educational groups.

It is interesting to note that the unemployment rate of women is lower than for men. Such a situation can be found only in countries such as Denmark, Ireland and the United Kingdom. In Slovenia it could be explained by the higher percentage of women in services, which have not been hit by the crisis as much as the manufacturing industries where men prevail.

The reasons for unemployment

Several reasons contributed to the quick rise in unemployment. The first is the market economy which has exposed all firms to open competition. Firms now seek better utilization of all production factors including labour. The sub-employment in the 1980s, estimated at about 120,000 to 200,000 employees (Mencinger, 1983), has been transferred to open unemployment. While there were no redundant workers among the unemployed in 1984, their share rose to 68 per cent in 1991. These unfavourable conditions could continue due to the privatization process which has been in full course. Initially perhaps, the high percentage of firms in workers' ownership will put a break on radical changes, such as massive lay-offs and complete closures. The hope that self-employment would compensate for the loss of jobs was lost quickly. While self-employment was increasing quickly up to the year 1991, when it reached 14.7 per cent of the working population, it fell again to 12.3 per cent of the working population in 1994.

The number of unemployed individuals would have grown at an even faster rate if the Bankruptcy Law had been applied more strictly. However, the government estimates that the explosion of social problems associated with an even faster increase in unemployment could not be controlled. The latest announcement indicates that the government is to speed up the bankruptcy of those enterprises which do not have a real chance of survival and to assist those which have promising programs and markets. The assistance will be subjected to a time limit. This may add some additional tens of thousands of unemployed to the already large figure.

The second reason for rising unemployment is the loss of international markets. It is estimated that Slovenia lost nearly 50 per cent of its external markets in the period 1990 to 1992. The sales levels in the markets of the former Yugoslavia fell by 72 per cent in comparison to the period before 1990

(Gospodarska gibanja, No. 226). Some markets were lost because of the breaking up of Yugoslavia and the introduction of associated administrative barriers, especially in Serbia, while others were lost because of physical barriers preventing the free flow of transport. Other markets were lost because of the international blockade of Serbia and Montenegro.

Markets have shrunk also because of falling purchasing power in the former Yugoslavia and East European countries. These losses are difficult to estimate. The consequences of the loss of markets are falling industrial production and the loss of jobs. From 1989 to 1993 there was a negative GNP, industrial production and job growth. In 1991, for instance, Slovenia lost about nine per cent in employment and industrial production fell by 10.6 per cent. The situation was the worst in 1991 because of the war and the resulting poor tourist season.

Slovene enterprises are intensively searching for new markets, especially in the West, and some have been successful in only a short period of time. This is indicated by the rate of increase in exports since 1989, which continues and provides a positive balance of payments and increasing hard currency reserves, which mounted to over 2.5 billion USD in 1994 and represented about one fifth of yearly GNP. This has prevented a worsening economic situation. Moreover, it seems that in 1993 the slump has bottomed out. In 1994, national statistics reported increases of nearly five per cent in GNP and over six per cent in industrial production growth. Unemployment fell slightly.

Up to 1992 there had been no significant inflow of foreign capital to Slovenia because international recognition was only achieved in January 1992, and investment risks were considered too high. However, foreign companies that were previously in Slovenia have not withdrawn. Full international recognition of Slovenia following admission to the UN has encouraged foreign entrepreneurs to come. Economic relations are gradually being established with the EU, the European Bank, the World Bank, the IMF and the World Trade Organization. The Czech Republic and Slovenia have been identified as the most successful among East European countries.

The demographic pattern also contributes to the over-supply of labour on the labour market. The projected number of individuals who enter the labour market will significantly increase in the period 1990 to 1996, while the number of individuals who leave it will fall slightly. In addition, levels of immigration into Slovenia constantly exceed the levels of emigration. This was the case in the past because of the lack of legislation in terms of Slovene citizenship and work-permits for non-citizens and as a result of the influx of Bosnian refugees. This process could continue due to the increasing structural unemployment.

In 1993 there were over 91,000 vacancies reported and only 63,384 were filled. In spite of relatively high unemployment, some firms, such as those in engineering, cannot find enough labour in Slovenia for road construction projects. As a result, the 1993 figure of 31,600 non-Slovene citizens having work permits could increase in the future. On the other hand, the Slovenian economy must adapt its pattern of production to the demand on the most developed markets. A rapid technological change is under way, which causes additional inconsistencies between labour demand and supply. A lack of highly skilled labour and a lack of programmes which would facilitate labour mobility is becoming more and more visible. This problem has been aggravated by a rapid decline of the agricultural sector and a rapid growth in the service sector. The percentage of the working population in the agricultural sector fell from 15 per cent to 10.7 per cent and the percentage of the working population in the service sector increased from 39.9 per cent to 45.1 per cent in the two years, 1991-93.

Labour market policy

The unemployment brought about by the new institutional arrangement is not unexpected. Therefore, the new labour legislation has retained the existing passive labour market measures such as unemployment benefits and social assistance, has given new responsibilities to the employment offices and has introduced an active labour market policy. In addition, unemployment has been reduced significantly by means of early retirement. These changes have been part of a wider reform of the social security system, which includes also changes in the regulation of health insurance, social assistance, pension and disablement insurance, family protection, employee participation and work inspection.

Passive measures

All employees must be covered by unemployment insurance. For several groups of citizens, such as the self-employed, insurance is optional. With unemployment insurance, one is entitled to unemployment benefits, social assistance, training and re-training courses, transfer allowances, on-the-job training, redundancy payment, subsidy for early retirement, and health and pension assurance.

Unemployment benefits relate to the level of wages and the duration of employment. One is entitled initially to 70 per cent of the wage earned during the last three months of employment. After three months, the unemployment benefit is reduced to 60 per cent of the previous wage. However, the unemployment benefit cannot be lower than 80 per cent of the guaranteed minimum wage. Lower income groups are also entitled to special allowances for every dependent family member. The longest period for receiving unemployment benefit is two years for those with 20 years or more in the work force. Workers three years from retirement age can receive unemployment benefits until they have retired. However, those who have never been employed, or who have been employed for less than nine months, and employees who resign are not entitled to unemployment benefits. This poses a particular problem for the young seeking their first job.

When unemployment benefits are terminated one can ask for social assistance. This assistance is means tested. The period of entitlement to social assistance is three years, including the time during which one receives unemployment benefits. In May 1993 only 26.9 per cent of unemployed persons in Slovenia said that they were receiving either unemployment benefits or assistance. This was more than the average of the 12 EC countries in 1991, (i.e. 19.8 per cent). It was more than in the southern EU countries such as Greece (3.5 per cent), Portugal (6.8 per cent) or Italy (17.2 per cent), but much less than in the northern EU countries such as Denmark (67.2 per cent) or Belgium (76.6 per cent).

In cases where individuals have no means to live on, they can approach the community social work centre. There a means tested assistance is provided, partially in cash and partially in kind.

Another passive measure, introduced in the mid-1980s, was early retirement. Initially employees could choose a five year early retirement with reduced pensions. This programme did not appeal to most employees. As unemployment increased, the reduction of pensions for early retirement was abolished. Firms and the Ministry of Labour contributed to the Pension Fund for the missing working years, thus solving the redundancy problem of older employees. In 1993, 2,067 redundant workers were retired on the basis of this programme. It proved to be very expensive and widely used. Consequently, the Ministry of Labour reduced its participation, leaving enterprises to employ this option.

Under conditions of an undeveloped labour market policy without programmes orientated to older workers, there was probably not a good alternative to early retirement. It contributed to the lower unemployment figures. However, because of this programme, the activity rate fell from 68.6 per cent in 1991 to only 57.7 per cent in 1993. The activity rate is especially low in the age group of 50 to 64 years. It was only 34.7 per cent in 1993 while it was 50.2 per cent on average for the 12 EU countries. This was a sharp decline, which counteracted some advantages that the Slovenian economy had in comparison to the EU countries.

Well-developed programmes for the disabled have been in place for many years, i.e. training and re-training programmes, sheltered workshops, wage subsidies for the employment of disabled persons, subsidies for the adaptation of workplaces, etc. In 1993, 341 persons received disablement status, 639 were enrolled in training programmes, and 91 in other programmes for disabled persons. In 1991 there were 51 sheltered workshops in Slovenia.

Active labour market policy

Most of the programs of the active labour market policy are new. Before 1989, a programme for wage subsidies was given to firms employing young graduates, and it is still running. Subsidies are larger when graduates are given permanent employment but less if employment is only temporary. The subsidy applies for up to one year. In 1993, 7,072 graduates were employed with the help of this programme, which constitutes about one quarter of that generation. Employment offices have subsidized employment for 20,697 young graduates in total.

One of the first new programmes has been the Capitalization Programme. It enables an unemployed individual to receive the gross amount of entitled unemployment benefits for investment in self-employment. The same option is also offered to any employer permanently employing an unemployed individual.

To encourage self-employment among the unemployed, employment offices hold special training and consulting courses. Course teachers, advisers and consultants usually represent specialized private and public agencies. The courses' goal is to evaluate a person's interests and abilities in self-employment, to encourage some and to discourage others, to give basic information regarding the business world, to teach elementary business skills and to help individuals establish their own business and determine how to make the initial contacts needed to start in business. These courses are complimentary as part of the Capitalization Programme. In 1993, 4,353 individuals participated in these courses and 1,854 of them started their own business.

A great deal of money has been spent on training and retraining programmes. Firms which announce redundancies can apply for training money if the firm has an approved training and re-employment programme for its employees. The purpose is to prevent a loss of jobs. In 1993, employment offices gave subsidies of 50 per cent of the costs of training courses for 10,285 employees who would have otherwise been made redundant.

Employment offices also have several training programmes for the unemployed. These programmes encourage autonomous job hunting and provide skills which might be lacking. Unemployed individuals may elect to take a special educational or training programme. Employment offices cover the costs in most instances. The most popular programmes concern the use of computer software and language training. In addition employment offices run training programmes for employees who might lose their jobs. In 1993, 17,943 individuals were enrolled in various training programmes organized and paid for by employment offices.

The 'Programme of 1000 New Jobs' offers enterprises a fixed sum of money (c. U$2,200) for creating a new job and permanently employing an unemployed individual. After receiving the money, new employment should be provided within six months. Only employers who have not had redundancies in the last year can apply. This programme seems particularly attractive to the growing private sector. In 1993, 1,828 new jobs were subsidized.

In 1991, the Public Works Programme began. Its goal is the provision of temporary work and social integration for the long-term unemployed, accomplished through the cooperation of employment offices and local communities. Employment offices determine basic guidelines, approve projects and partially cover costs. Local communities propose projects, find responsible sponsoring institutions, and provide some initial money. In 1993, 671 projects were approved and 4,367 unemployed individuals in Slovenia were enrolled in the scheme. There were 188 programmes in the field of social security, 185 in public administration, education, culture and tourism, 104 in environmental protection and 197 in the maintenance of public facilities.

The projects can run for up to one year for each participant. Participation in the project is voluntary. The unemployed receive unemployment benefits or assistance, covering the costs of work clothes, travelling expenses, as well as additional incentive money. The money received may not exceed 70 per cent of the normal wage for a specific type of job. The projects are usually small, employing up to 20 individuals and covering a variety of areas such as environmental protection and improvement, building renovation, improvement of community sport and recreation facilities, home help for the elderly, assistance to families whose children have difficulties in school, child care and similar activities. In 1993 this programme provided regular employment for 410 participants.

There is no special programme to assist the most affected regions. However, the regional situation is taken into account when applying any of the labour market policy programmes. The responses of specific regions depend very much on local conditions, e.g. the activity of local employment offices and local community administration.

Most of the labour market policy programmes are designed and carried out by public employment offices. This is a new responsibility. In addition, the number of unemployed persons, who increasingly tend to register, has increased by five times since 1989. In 1984 only 41 per cent of the unemployed job seekers were registered at employment offices, while by 1993 this figure had risen to 83.3 per cent.

Such a dramatic change in responsibilities has strained the public employment offices, which have not yet adjusted to the new situation. The policy of the first democratic government prevented an increase in the number of public employees even though their relative numbers in public employment offices are only 25-50 per cent of those in developed countries. This shortcoming is partly outweighed by allowing private agencies concessions to undertake some of the public employment programmes, e.g. training and public work programmes.

It is important that public employment offices bring their services closer to the unemployed by establishing more local job centres and by encouraging a self-service approach to job-hunting. Employment information services could be improved by better utilizing computer technology. Reorganization of employment services has begun, but for the moment long queues of unemployed in front of too few employment offices prevent the provision of better services.

Summing up, in 1993 the greatest share of money allocated to labour market policy programmes was spent on unemployment benefits (57.2 per cent), on social assistance (15.3 per cent), on subsidizing new jobs (11.7 per cent), and on training and retraining programmes (6 per cent). Compared to previous years there was a shift in spending towards passive measures at the expense of active labour market measures.

An important buffer against social hardship has been 'informal' work. According to our data, 42.5 per cent of the unemployed did some paid work in the week before the inquiry in 1990. If the ILO criteria were applied, these individuals should not have been counted as unemployed. In the same year 22 per cent of the unemployed reported that they worked outside their households without being paid. On average, they performed 63.4 hours of such work per month. Another indicator of the significance of 'informal' work activities is the difference between the registered and self-reported unemployment. Because of a liberal policy concerning registration of job seekers many receive unemployment benefits while doing unreported jobs for pay or profit. As a consequence employment offices started to remove some individuals from the unemployment register. Nearly 19,000 were affected by this measure in 1993.

Epilogue

Even under the communist regime Slovenia had close contacts with Western economies. This influenced the economic and administrative systems sufficiently to make them flexible and responsive enough to adjust to the separation from the former Yugoslavia and a change of economic and political systems without an economic and social catastrophe. Quite the contrary, unemployment has been brought under control and remained below the average of the EU countries. Employment offices and several labour market policy measures had already been introduced under the communist regime and in the transition period they have been adapted to the new situation. New active labour market programmes have been introduced to deal with the increasing unemployment. These changes demonstrate the learning capacities of the social system of Slovenia, which gives hope for successful responses to future challenges.

Notes

Where not cited the data presented in this paper are taken from the following publications:

Labour Force Survey Results - Slovenia 93 - Europe 91. Results of Surveys, No. 607. Statistical Office of the Republic of Slovenia and National Employment Office, Ljubljana 1994.
Poročilo za leto 1993 (Annual Report for 1993). Republiški zavod za zaposlovanje, Ljubljana, 1994.
Statistički godišnjak Jugoslavije (1990) (Statistical Yearbook of Yugoslavia), Savezni zavod za statistiku, Beograd.
Statistical Yearbook of Republic of Slovenia (1994), Republiški zavod za statistiko, Ljubljana 1994.

17 The Future of Self-management: Reflections

ALEŠ VAHČIČ

Introduction

In this essay I would like to discuss some of the fundamental economic issues concerning the process of transition which are emerging five years after the changes in the socio-economic system in Slovenia. Particularly, I will address the question of whether the fact that Slovenia was the most developed part of former Yugoslavia and that Yugoslavia had quite a distinct economic system from the rest of Eastern Europe will have any significant impact on the future economic and social development of Slovenia. I will tentatively pose a hypothesis that due to its experience with self-management, Slovenia over time, say in ten to 15 years, will end up as a quite distinct society and will show distinctly better economic and social results than other East European countries such as Hungary, Czech Republic, Slovakia and so on. I will try to state the reasons for this prediction based on some of the recent writings in economics originating from prominent economists of quite different backgrounds and professional traditions.

In this essay I will not be able to avoid some personal remarks because, like many other Eastern European economists trained in the West, I actively took part in certain aspects of the transition process in Slovenia and was partly involved also in the debates and activities of the transition process in Eastern Europe. In my professional work I have been influenced by three quite distinct groups of western economics and business professionals. First, as a Cornell graduate student, studying economics in the class of Professor Jaroslav Vanek, I was in the small circle of economists who studied the economics of self-management based on the neo-classical paradigm. Second, I was involved with the group of development economists working in the Kuznets-Chennery tradition in the World Bank and I based my dissertation research heavily on the studies of structural change and the effects of liberalization on economic performance (Vahčič, 1976). Third, in line with some of my early findings concerning the lack of small and medium size enterprises in socialist countries (Vahčič, 1976, pp. 196-99), I became involved in the field of entrepreneurship quite early and started to study the effect of entrepreneurship on economic performance. Historically and institutionally these three intellectual and also activist traditions have been quite separate from each other and I have been trying to combine them in some kind of coherent approach to the question of economic growth and welfare.

In this paper I will argue that the key to successful economic performance of a country is competition and that capital ownership is of second degree importance for the achievement of world-class performance of companies and economies. I will also argue that some of the basic assumptions on which the old arguments on the desirability of self-management and employee ownership are still valid. There are still very important issues concerning work-place democracy, because they do not only touch deeply the question of freedom, but also have a strong bearing on economic efficiency.

Putting the question correctly

I will start my discussion with rather lengthy citations from the recent works of two economists who, each from their own perspective, raised some of the fundamental issues concerning workplace democracy relevant to countries in transition.

The first citation is from the new book by David Ellerman, *Intellectual Trespassing as a Way of Life* in which he is posing some fundamental questions on the nature of labour contracts in modern western corporations. In the chapter *Myth and Metaphor in Orthodox Economics* with the subtitle *End of the Pseudo-Debate between Capitalism and Socialism*, he says the following:

These are interesting times to think anew about orthodox neo-classical economics. With the collapse of communism, the bi-polar economic-political order is breaking down.
Suppose that the pro-slavery writers had managed to get 'The Slavery Question' posed as the question of whether slave plantations should be publicly or privately owned. Instead of being privately owned and exploited for private greed (the 'Athens model'), shouldn't the slave plantations be publicly owned and operated for the public good (the 'Sparta model')?
Public ownership of plantations would, however, be inefficient. Publicly owned slaves would be 'owned by everyone and thus by no one'. Without clear-cut property rights and claims to the residual in

the hands of an effective monitor, the slaves would shirk their duties and the plantation assets would collapse under the weight of their own inefficiency and would thus prove the superiority of 'Athenian' private ownership of slave plantations.

The Great Debate between the public or private ownership of slave plantations would finally be over.   Athens and private ownership would have won.   Pundits would declare 'the end of history'.   So-called abolitionists might speak of a 'Third Way' involving self-ownership but the slaves who have been reduced to near-starvation on the public plantations would not be able to afford some other 'experiment'. Across the long sweep of human history, the economic system with the greatest longevity and stability is slavery under private ownership. That is the verdict of history.   The slaves should forget any half-baked dreams of an untried and untested Third Way.   The public plantations should be straight-away privatized.

This hypothetical 'Great Debate' about slavery has a familiar ring to it. With the end of that pseudo-debate, the ground would be cleared for the recognition that the real question was not whether slaves should be privately or publicly owned but whether people should always be 'self-owning'.

Today, the economic systems of the world are based not on owning workers but on hiring, employing, or renting workers.   Today's pseudo-debate is over whether workers might be privately employed for private interests or should always be publicly employed for the public good. However, the real question is whether people might be rented at all (by a public or private party) or should always be jointly self-employed in their place of work' (Ellerman, 1995, pp. 49-50).

The second set of citations comes from Joseph E. Stiglitz's new book *Whither Socialism,* addressing the question of whether neo-classical economics has anything of value to offer in elucidation of the questions posed by the transition process in socialist countries and whether any practical advice can be drawn from this theory. Let us see what Stiglitz has to say about this in the preface to his book:

But the events in Eastern Europe - the collapse of socialism at a wholly unanticipated rate - raised new policy questions and revived old theoretical issues: How was the transition to a market economy to be effected?   What did these experiences have to say about the long-standing debate concerning the choice of alternative economic systems?

These questions were related to a third: What did conventional economic models have to say about such fundamental economic issues?   The conclusion that I reached went beyond the critique that the standard models had little to say about these questions. It seemed to me that the *standard models were partly to blame for the disastrous*

situation in which so many Eastern European countries found themselves (emphasis added by A.V.)...
Neo-classical economics often set itself up in contradistinction to Marxian economics. But neo-classical economics, at least in the version that became popular within the Anglo-American community, did not really provide an alternative. It provided a model of the economy that seems too distant from the underlying forces which generated support for Marxian economics and its hypotheses, its descriptions and its concerns. By arguing that we were seemingly in the best of all possible worlds did not speak adequately to the needs of those who saw economic misery all around them. Worse still, while showing the power of markets it seemed to argue that socialism could work. Market socialism could make use of markets and let the economy be spared the worst features of capitalism (Stiglitz, 1994, pp. 9-10).'

At the end of the book Stiglitz has the following to say:

My principal objective...has been to explain, from the information-theoretic perspective the inadequacies of the conventional paradigm and to suggest that the perspectives on comparative economic systems provided by the conventional paradigm are fundamentally misguided (Stiglitz, 1994, p. 255).

Stiglitz goes on and tries to provide some positive recommendations which do follow from the (correct) economic theory:

The first is to emphasize the importance of competition - not pure price competition but simply old-fashioned competition, the rivalry among firms to supply the needs of consumers and producers at the lowest price with the highest qualities. ...the difference between competition and monopoly is the distinction of first-order importance, rather than the distinction between private and state ownership...
...The distinction between monopoly and competition may also be more important than the distinction between allowing free trade or not. Free trade is important in a small economy because it provides the discipline of competition, the discipline that a country's own market may not be able to supply simply because there are too few firms. But there may be cases where there is sufficient internal competition and where apart from political economy concerns I think a convincing 'infant industry' case for protection might be made.
Thus the first objective of state economic policy is to ensure competition. This needs to be taken into account in the process of privatization or re-organizing state enterprises as well in the laws allowing the formation of firms, cooperatives and partnerships. The government must take actions to minimize the barriers to entry.

In the United States and other Western economies the governments have imposed the variety of taxes and regulations that serve as an important impediment to small firms. While these impediments have a significant cost to these small advanced countries, the cost to the former socialist economies - beginning with virtually no competitive structures - may be far greater (Stiglitz, 1994, p. 256).

Then Stiglitz goes on and notes the following under the sub-chapter *Promoting New Enterprises*:

Much of the discussion of the transition process has focused on reforming and changing old institutions. Equally or perhaps even more important is the creation of new institutions and enterprises. China presents an interesting case study in this respect. It did not focus its attention on privatizing existing state enterprises. The existing state enterprises have declined in importance as a result of the growth of new enterprises, such as joint ventures and village, township, province, and private enterprises. Institutional reforms were required to facilitate this growth. The communes transformed themselves radically, to the point where there is little resemblance between the agriculture communes of the cultural revolution and modern industrial communes (Stiglitz, 1994, p. 261).

Stiglitz continues his recommendations on what to do in the transition economies, referring now to the privatization issue:

There are some free marketeers who say that the *first step to success is to privatize the state enterprises*. Whether they are right or wrong I do not know; what I do know is that *they have no scientific basis for that conclusion* (emphases A.V.). As I argued earlier, I view competition as far more important than privatization. I see little difference in behaviour between BP and Texaco (the former appears to be far better run than the latter, but I do not want to attribute this to the large ownership share of the British government), and (perhaps more controversially) some of the major gains in efficiency at British Telecom and British Airways occurred before privatization.
Theory tells us that in both cases we will face incentive problems (principal-agent problems). The first order of importance is changing the incentive structure of managers - and this can be done while the firms remain within the public sector.
I would have liked to have said that the first order of business is putting into place new managers, but it is not obvious from where the new managers are to come and how are they to be chosen (in any case it must be recognized that there may be a shortage of competent managers in the short-run). Would a board of directors somehow elected by shareholders be any more competent at choosing new managers than would some alternative mechanism within the state

enterprise system such as the establishment of holding companies with boards of directors chosen by some other selection process (perhaps with participation by domestic and foreign banks, domestic and foreign business leaders and possibly even academics in related areas). In the interim while the privatization is proceeding it may be important to have a change in the institutional structure, such as ensuring that the state enterprises are not controlled by the ministries who formerly operated them (Stiglitz, 1994, pp. 261-262).

In continuation Stiglitz has this to say on the issue of equality:

The former socialist economies are in the perhaps unique position of being able to obtain a degree of equality of ownership of wealth unattained, and perhaps unattainable, in other market economies. The often-noted goal of a 'people's capitalism' may indeed be within their reach, in a way that most other countries cannot even remotely approach, given their concentrations of wealth. They should not lose this opportunity: the damage of the 'wealth' reform has already been done; now is not the occasion to lose the advantages that such a reform can afford: (In my earlier discussion I argued against the contention that it was possible to separate out equity and efficiency concerns; and for the advantages which are attendant upon a more equal distribution of wealth.)
From a strictly political perspective, the long-run legitimacy of democratic governments would, I suspect, be enhanced if they could succeed in maintaining a more egalitarian wealth distribution...
...One cannot obliterate the scars of communism by rolling back history: The task is to take advantage of whatever has been done, however misguided it may have been. There has been a massive wealth redistribution. That may have been a mistake. The challenge is to grasp the opportunity that it now provides to construct a more egalitarian society (Stiglitz, 1994, pp. 265-266).

At the end there is also a question on how to pose the problem correctly:

The final word of advice is, 'pose the problem correctly'. Do not see the question of 'markets' versus 'government', but the appropriate balance between markets and government, with the possibility of many intermediate forms of economic organization (including those based on a local government, cooperatives, etc.).
Imperfect and costly information, imperfect capital markets, imperfect competition: these are the realities of market economies - aspects that must be taken into account by those countries embarking on the choice of an economic system. The fact that competition is imperfect or capital markets are imperfect does not mean that the market system should not be adopted. What it does mean is that in their choices, they should not be confused by theorems and ideologies based on an

irrelevant model of the market economy. Most important, it means that in deciding on what form of market economy they might adopt, including what role the government ought to play, they need to have in mind how actual market economies function, not the quite irrelevant paradigm of perfect competition (Stiglitz, 1994, p. 267).

A final question which has to be asked is:

> Is this the best of all possible worlds? ...As a society we do not want to believe it. We cannot accept this view, if for no other reason than that the creative struggle to solve this problem has a value in itself even if we make little progress (Stiglitz, 1994, pp. 169-270).

Stiglitz in his book shows quite convincingly that the attempt to defend free market capitalism even on the narrow grounds of economic efficiency, as soon as we introduce more realistic assumptions concerning incomplete markets and imperfect information, is not valid. Therefore, it must be recognized that, at present, standard economic theory has little to offer in terms of advice on the optimal choice of economic system. In the last chapter he concludes with the following citation:

> The great socialist experiment is coming to an end: we have learned a lot from these experiments, but because they were hardly controlled experiments, what we learned remains a subject of some dispute. While government ownership is clearly no panacea, there remains scope for further experimentation. For instance, *we need to study forms of economic organization involving more worker participation and ownership* (emphasis A.V.). Not too much should be read into the failures of the worker-managed firms in the former Yugoslavia, for these involve peculiar (and obviously unsatisfactory) arrangements with respect to the transfer of property rights, as well as other institutional detail which, both *ex ante* and in hindsight, were not conducive to success. To return to the theme with which I began these speculations, the question is whether the insights of modern economic theory and the utopian ideals of the nineteenth century can be brought closer together (Stiglitz, 1994, p. 277).

Where does all this leave us? Both Ellerman, who in the Kantian manner shows that workers cannot be tools but only persons, and Joseph Stiglitz who argues in favour of some further experimentation with systems having more worker participation and ownership, in fact maintain that the economic system based on minimalist government and company organization, with external owners who control management and who, in turn, control wage workers who temporarily rent themselves to the company, is neither efficient nor desirable.

I would add that contrary to what the proponents of the liberalist, free market, private ownership system believe, i.e. that the demise of communism has proven the ultimate efficiency and desirability of the system which they promote, it has actually done just the opposite. The demise of communism has finally cleared the way to open, free discussion, unburdened by ideology, on what people really want as a good socio-economic system. Furthermore, the focus of discussion has shifted to reality, i.e. to the question of what works and what does not work, and away from the discussion of whether reality fits ideology or not. In this context it should be noted that not unlike the old communist ideologues who were proclaiming that the socialist reality, because the institutions which they had created formally fitted their ideologies, was superior to the western reality, the free trade ideologues are also claiming that the present Eastern European social and economic reality is a great success because the institutions which they helped to create in these countries somehow fit their ideologies. In reality, the performance of these countries is clearly disastrous (see Stiglitz above), and we are entering the phase of reconsidering the whole transition process. For those of us who were brought up in heavily ideologically based systems and are now slowly emancipating ourselves from ideological thinking, this scene has a clear taste of *deja vu*, except that the roles are now reversed.

I will now try to pose some more precise questions related to management and control, ownership, the future of workers self-management and the role of state.

The purpose of transition: transition to what?

First, it should be emphasized that the ultimate rational purpose of the change of the economic system from the old socialist system (which did not work) to the new one (whatever eventually it might be) is the quest for the system which would allow the countries in transition to improve their welfare and, in more narrowly economic terms, to increase the rate of growth to the level which would enable these countries to start catching up with the developed west (Vahčič and Glas, 1994, pp. 133-4).

In terms of economic theory, this problem can be posed within the framework of a branch of development economics called catch-up or convergence theory. In brief, this theory says that in principle a country which lags behind the leading country, should be able to grow faster than the leading country, if the social conditions (institutions, policies, etc.) in both countries are the same. If the lagging country does not grow faster it must be due to certain adverse social conditions preventing this country from achieving the growth potential (David and Abramovitz, 1994).

We can use this framework when interpreting the situation in Eastern Europe. The old socialist system with its particular set of policies and institutions was a major obstacle to growth and, if removed, the countries should be able to achieve a higher differential rate of growth which would enable them to catch up with the west. More concretely Slovenia, Hungary, Czech Republic, Slovakia should be able catch up with Austria, Russia should be able to catch up with Germany, China with Taiwan, North Korea with South Korea, etc. However, the realization that the old system had to be abandoned (because it did not work) is not enough. It is necessary to find out more precisely what was wrong with the old system and replace the old institutions and policies with new, better ones.

This is a general starting point when we want to discuss the economics of the transition process. We will first discuss the role of the state in transition.

The role of the state

The consensus within the mainstream economics profession was that the basic inefficiency in the old socialist system was due to the lack of market competition, excessive control of the enterprises by the state under central planning, and state ownership of companies. On the political level, the countries were not democratic due to one-party systems. So the solution seemed to be simple and noncontroversial: a multiparty system has to be introduced, markets have to be liberalized, the role of the state minimized and enterprises privatized. The pressure of world and domestic competition and the interest of private ownership would ensure that the managers would run companies efficiently and that the workers controlled by management would perform optimally. The enterprise efficiency would thus improve, return on investment increase, domestic and foreign investment would be stimulated and savings would be channelled through competitive financial markets to the best enterprises. Increased investment together with increased efficiency would lead to a high rate of growth which would lead to catching up with the west.

So far none of this has happened in Eastern Europe. The absolute level of production remains below the pre-transition levels. Russia has suffered the most. Some growth has resumed in countries like Poland, Estonia and Slovenia; in 1994 these countries showed four to five per cent rate of growth. In none of these countries has the restructuring of enterprises occurred on a major scale and foreign investment has been relatively low. Obviously the liberalization of markets and privatization were not sufficient for bringing these countries to a high level of growth.

This should be compared with the performance of China, also a country in transition, which since 1978, when the Chinese communist party started the radical reforms, became the most successful country in the world of all time in terms of GDP growth. Contrary to what the East European countries did, the Chinese entered the transition by allowing the development of entrepreneurship and competition through newly created enterprises which were not necessarily privately owned (township enterprises, communal enterprises, leasing) while at the same time they have very few privatized state-owned companies (Jeffries, 176-94). In spite of the rhetoric of free trade ideologues, who praise East European reforms, the members of the international business community are of a different opinion. They are investing heavily in the communist party controlled non-privatized but extremely fast growing Chinese economy, and the cumulative amount of foreign direct investment in China is by now U$150 billion, of which 80 billion was invested in 1994 alone.

From these facts we can conclude that the privatization of state owned enterprises obviously is not the necessary condition for successful growth in transition economies. Also, privatization and the abolition of the one-party system is not a necessary condition for gaining the trust of the international business community and attracting direct foreign investment. On the other hand, one could argue that the freeing of entrepreneurial energies *was* a necessary condition for dynamic growth. The Chinese first allowed the entrepreneurial initiative to take place in agriculture and then as greenfield operations in other sectors. This strengthened the entrepreneurial sector, which since has grown at a very fast rate, while the state sector also benefited from these developments because the demand from the entrepreneurial sector keeps the state-owned sector running. Actually, the state sector has been growing at about seven per cent a year over the past 17 years. Thus China has been successfully carrying out the transition from an inefficient, centrally planned and protected economy to an efficient market economy. The key to China's successful growth is entrepreneurial development and a gradual liberalization of the economy while state-owned enterprises remain in the hands of the state, and foreign investment is allowed by the government to enter only in a controlled manner. The Chinese are obviously not following the advice of neo-classical economists but have been able to create their own proper balance between the public and the private. In view of Stiglitz's contribution, the Chinese example clearly shows that the transition process can be very successful but it requires the choice of an appropriate mixture of policies and institutions and a correct sequencing which may be very different from those adopted in Eastern Europe. Obviously, the state has a very important role to play here and is in no way minimalist. Also, concentration on the entry of new firms rather than expending energy on privatizing existing state-owned enterprises seems to have been a much more productive way of carrying out the transition process than the one adopted in Eastern Europe.

The East European countries in transition will have to reconsider the role of the state and will have to study the experiences of successful countries rather than trying to follow the prescriptions of neo-classical economics as interpreted by western academic advisers and their domestic followers.

Management and control

Looking at the question of management and control, the purist model based on the free market private enterprise ideology would require that the majority ownership of corporations should be in the hands of outside owners. The idea is that people who save would invest in companies via well-functioning capital markets and through owning shares would control the governing body of enterprises, which would select, appoint and control the management, who in turn would run the companies by managing the employees.

This model has been ideologically pushed as the ultimate correct solution in Eastern Europe in face of the fact that even in the US, where this model is most widely used, only a minor portion of GDP is created by enterprises with such an ownership structure. A large proportion of value added in the US is produced by self-employed people, then small and medium size businesses which are owner-manager controlled and by the government sector. Among large corporations there is a significant part which is closely held by private individuals or families who take an active role in managing their companies. There is also a significant number of enterprises with substantial employee ownership. None of these economic units are controlled by outside shareholders. Even the publicly traded companies, which are majority owned by outside shareholders, are to a large extent *de facto* controlled by the management and not by the outside shareholders. This is the situation in the US. In other successful capitalist economies, particularly Germany and Japan, corporate control is even less in the hands of outside shareholders. The companies are either closely held or are cross-owned by institutions such as banks and insurance companies who exercise a very lenient control over the management. In the case of Japan and Germany the employees have also a significant stake in the running of the companies and the success of a company depends to a large extent on the interest of both management and employees in making their companies efficient.

The conclusion of the above discussion is that the success of the company depends mainly on the ability of the company to motivate employees (management and workers) to perform. In the case of Japanese companies the deal is that in exchange for job security workers are loyal to the company. In such a situation it has been possible to invest in the long-term improvement of employees' skills and so the human capital has been built for the benefit of both employees and the firm. This really means that the pure external ownership model of corporate control is neither pervasive in the west nor is it necessarily more efficient than the model of internal ownership and control. In fact there is strong evidence that just the opposite is true, as the above examples show. So the attempt to impose the pure external ownership model in the Eastern European privatization programs is rather strange and inconsistent with the realities in the west. Therefore, it is not surprising that in the course of privatization in many East European countries political pressure started to change the model of privatization from one based on pure external ownership to one based on internal ownership (Ellerman, Vahčič and Petrin, 1992). It can be hypothesized that in the countries with a stronger worker-management tradition as opposed to the countries with pervasive state control, privatization will tend to go further in the direction of employee ownership. Unfortunately, due to the war in former Yugoslavia, the only successor country which experienced a more or less normal transition from the old socialist self-management system to the new system was Slovenia. Therefore, Slovenia should be watched to see in which direction privatization will develop. The likelihood is that in Slovenia the share of employee controlled and/or owned companies at the end of the privatization process will be much higher than in other Eastern European countries. There are already strong indications that in Slovenia a large majority of privatizing companies will be eventually employee owned and/or controlled (Rop, Kusar and Mramor, 1995, pp. 405-7). In view of the world realities where the greatest proportion of GDP is produced (efficiently) by companies owned or controlled by insiders this outcome should not be of major concern.

It is now necessary to say something more precise about the cause and effect of relationships implied in the orthodox transition programs and where they have probably gone wrong. As already indicated, the welfare justification for embarking on transition is the removal of systemic obstacles to growth. The two main instruments proposed by the orthodox neoclassical advisors are liberalization of markets and privatization. Privatization preferably should take the form of mass (voucher) privatization which should ensure external control. But why should managers be more motivated to run companies efficiently when the companies are externally owned and controlled than in a situation where they themselves own a part of the company? And why should the employees work more efficiently when they are supervised by the managers rather than when they work for themselves as co-owners?

Here we do not want to enter into a lengthy debate about the merits and demerits of democratically run companies. Thousands of articles and books have been written on this question. The question of the efficiency (social and economic) of workplace democracy (self-management, worker-management, labour-management worker participation, co-determination, employee ownership, teamwork...) have been discussed by political scientists, industrial sociologists, psychologists, management scientists, economists, education specialists, etc. in great length. In the field of economics a group of economists who used to gather around the International Association for the Economics of Self-Management has studied this question for more than twenty years and held regular congresses on this question. The results have been inconclusive at worst; it could not be proven that democratically run firms lead to enterprise inefficiency. A short summary of the economics literature on the subject is reproduced below (Vahčič and Petrin, 1986, pp. 136-137).

Labour-managed economic system: theory, past experience, future

The economics literature on the efficiency of labour-managed firms takes the existing neo-classical theory of the firm and changes the assumption of maximand from profit maximization to net income per worker maximization. Under this assumption major portions of micro-economic theory, including general equilibrium theory and, to a lesser extent, macro-economic theory, were reproduced. This theory was then assumed to portray the behaviour of economies based on self-managed enterprises. In particular, this theory was taken as one which described the behaviour of the Yugoslav economy. The major finding was that in such an economy, the short time price responses of the firms could be perverse in the sense that a price increase would cause a decline in output and employment while a decrease in price would lead to increase of output and employment. Furthermore, such an economy, with profits in the short run, would lead to labour misallocation since the mobility of the labour force from lower-paying to higher-paying firms would be resisted by workers in the higher-paying firms. It was also shown that under conditions of self-financing the investment behaviour would lead to under-investment and over-capitalization of self-managed firms. From these findings one could conclude that a system based on such enterprise behaviour could not possibly be regarded as a desirable form of organization. However, theoreticians have later shown that these negative results crucially depend on institutional assumptions such as rules concerning the hiring and firing of workers, financial arrangements, conditions of exit and entry of firms, the assumption about the maximand of the firm and the organization of management. By changing the assumptions most of the negative results disappear.

Without entering into details we can state the final outcome of this debate. In principle, theoretical conditions can be specified under which an economy consisting of self-managed firms could be operated at least as efficiently as an economy based on profit-maximizing firms under a similar set of assumptions. Given the democratic nature of decision-making under self-management, which can be regarded as a positive feature, directly increasing workers' welfare, given that democratic decision-making would lead to a more egalitarian income distribution within self-managed firms than in capitalist firms, given that a reduced need for monitoring would reduce the cost of supervision, and given that a generally higher motivation of workers would tend to result in the higher productivity of self-managed firms, it can be concluded that self-managed firms and self-managed economies are an inherently superior form of production organization when compared to economies based on either capitalist or traditional state-owned enterprises.

In the literature studying the actual performance of firms and economic systems based on self-management it was repeatedly shown that in most cases, in reality, the efficiency conditions were not fulfilled and therefore one could not properly judge the potential of the system from the existing experiments. This was particularly true for the former Yugoslavia, because in that case the existing set of policies and institutions prevented the economy from functioning efficiently. In particular, there was soft budget constraint, caused by negative real interest rates and undervalued exchange rates, there was no entry and exit of firms, the economy was highly protected from foreign competitors and there was no attempt to push the companies to compete on the world market. As China has amply shown over the past 17 years, such policies are not a necessary consequence of an undemocratic one-party system. On the contrary, it was the Chinese communist party which in China abandoned this kind of policy and institutions and introduced a highly competitive environment and pushed the companies towards exports to the world markets. It would be quite interesting to see what would have happened if the Yugoslav communist party had adopted changes in policies and institutions similar to those in China (adapted to local conditions) and which have been repeatedly proposed by some Yugoslav economists. What is difficult to understand is that in Eastern Europe the Chinese (and East Asian) experience is still not studied seriously with the intention of drawing lessons from them. My personal belief is that if Yugoslavia had adopted similar policies and institutions to China, Slovenia within Yugoslavia would have already been catching up with Austria in GDP per capita and the system of labour-management, with necessary modifications, would be functioning quite well.

China is indeed now faced with its own major dilemma. Should it follow the East European route and turn the state-owned companies into corporations and privatize them through some kind of mass voucher scheme or try a different path and transform them into employee-owned companies? It can only be hoped that China will continue to show pragmatic creativity when dealing with this problem and will not rely on inappropriate advice inspired by the orthodox neo-classical theory.

It is obvious that the choice of different mixtures of economic and political institutions available to countries in transition, when they decided to abandon the old system, was much wider than they assumed. The value of Stiglitz's contribution to this discussion is that he pointed out that most of the recommendations by western economic advisors to Eastern Europe on how to carry out the transition process simply do not follow from the neo-classical economic theory, if information-theoretic considerations are introduced into the model. He directly blames the failure of the transition process in Eastern Europe, at least in part, on the inappropriate use of neo-classical economics as the basis for designing actual policies and institutions. He firmly states that other policy-institution mixtures, some of them as yet untried, would be more consistent with the correct economic theory (i.e. the one which takes into account imperfect markets and imperfect information), than the mixture currently pushed as the only 'correct' solution. His advice is that the governments of transitional economies should try to further experiment with different policy-institution mixtures and specifically mentions that systems with more worker participation may be tried in spite of the fact that worker-management has been discredited because it is associated with Yugoslavia.

Finally, it should be noted that the whole economic discussion on the desirability of self-owned companies was made on efficiency grounds, arguing that production efficiency would be increased by introducing worker control and it was implicitly assumed that such a system would be preferable on moral grounds since people would not be forced to rent themselves to companies as wage workers.

The above efficiency argument in favour of employee control, which has occupied 99 per cent of the discussion in economics literature, should be distinguished from the quite different argument by Ellerman. He is simply claiming that the modern labour contracts are legally invalid. Using the Kantian person-thing distinction Ellerman shows that with the labour contract in which a person is rented, the person takes on the role of a thing, but in spite of that legal contractual role, the individual remains a person. Therefore, such contracts to take on voluntarily the legal role of a non-person or thing are inherently invalid (Ellerman, 1995, p. 100). In spite of the rental contract, the employees remain responsible for their actions before the law. Therefore, legally they cannot rent out the responsibility for decision making. If this is so, the responsibility for the results of the firm lies with all employees. In this way all employees are responsible for the product of the firm and there is no legal basis for the appropriation of the residual profit by passive outside owners (Ellerman 1995, p. 94).

The logical consequence of the Ellerman argument is quite different from the consequences of the efficiency argument. The implication is not that employee control should be tried because under appropriate conditions it may yield higher economic efficiency but that the renting of workers is simply not legally valid. Renting of workers is logically equivalent to voluntary slavery. Therefore, it should not be allowed and should be abolished.

This sounds highly unrealistic, if not utopian, given that the world is still recovering from the shock of the downfall of East European communism. Since self-management is associated with both East European communism and, more specifically, Yugoslavia, which is guilty of one of the most atrocious wars in recent history, arguing that self-management as a system of company control has a future, or, if we accept Ellerman's argument, is the only legal future, seems to border on imbecility. But is it so imbecile? As Ellerman has pointed out, the 'Athens model' of renting people for private interest has prevailed. But is renting people legal at all? 'The Great (pseudo) Debate' is over. The real debate can now start.

Maybe for the beginning, since the term self-managed has a bad connotation because of its association with Yugoslavia and communism, the terminology should be changed. Maybe one should call it 'self-ownership', or, as it will be explained later in the last section, 'open book management', or, one can introduce a neutral, 'mathematical' concept of 'integral control' of a company. It should be further noted that the case for the abolition of 'people renting' could be greatly strengthened if one could show that the self-ownership model of enterprise control is also efficient. The case would have an even greater chance if one could show that this model is not inconsistent with entrepreneurship, or, even better, if one could show that entrepreneurship could only be developed fully if the self-ownership model of enterprise control is adopted. Then we would not be speaking of people's capitalism but about people's entrepreneurship. Again, it may seem very strange to try to combine entrepreneurship as a seemingly quintessential element of a private, free trade, anti-government, people renting, conservative model, with such concepts as self-ownership, optimal government, Third Way, industrial policy and the rest of the radical conceptual arsenal. But is it true that the self-owning mode of enterprise control and entrepreneurship are incompatible? May it not be possible that the 'individual hero' kind of entrepreneurship which has developed under the system of 'people renting' is just one kind of entrepreneurship, indeed the only kind which could develop within the 'people renting' enterprise control system. Maybe there are other kinds of entrepreneurship which are even more efficient but could not develop under the 'people renting' model of enterprise control. I hope that by now I have contributed enough to the conceptual confusion in this area that we can start clarifying it.

Self-management and entrepreneurship: are they compatible?

Traditionally, we are used to thinking of entrepreneurship as a defining characteristic of private ownership in democratic capitalist societies. Thus, the introduction of a democratic political system and carrying out privatization in transition economies would automatically lead to vigorous entrepreneurial activities.

Traditionally, it has been also assumed that the key motivational element of entrepreneurial activities is the appropriation of profit by entrepreneurs. This implies that an employee-renting enterprise control system must be in place. Entrepreneurs set up enterprises, own them, hire employees, appropriate profit, grow the enterprises and finally harvest capital gains. In the course of this process they may make deals with various partners and share the benefits of the enterprise with them. However, since the leading role in the process of creating enterprise value is assigned to the entrepreneur most of the value created belongs to the entrepreneur as the owner. The star models of this type of entrepreneurship are billionaires like Microsoft's Bill Gates. Implicit in this view is that worker-controlled enterprises would lack motivational structure for entrepreneurs to flourish and therefore economies based on such a system would not reach their growth potential.

Concerning the role of the state in the process of entrepreneurship development the prevailing view is that the state should stay as far away from the entrepreneurs as possible, since the entrepreneurs know best themselves how to find and exploit business opportunities.

In the above stereotypical view of the entrepreneurial process there are several elements which do not fit the facts. First, countries such as Taiwan, Korea, China, Chile, etc. have developed highly efficient entrepreneurial cultures under dictatorial regimes (of both brands). Second, in many cases successful entrepreneurs and whole clans of entrepreneurial families have been amply supported by the state. Korea with its eight or so families owning and controlling strategic parts of the Korean economy is probably the worst case of this (The House that Park Built, 1995). Japanese governments have consistently supported export expansion of leading companies and their entrepreneurial owners (Morita with his Sony). Third, successful entrepreneurial activities can develop also under ill-defined property rights structures and in non-private ownership environments. Examples of this are Chinese communal, township and other non-private types of enterprises which have grown successfully over the past decade and a half. Fourth, successful entrepreneurial companies during the period of start-up, growth and the drive to maturity are normally not externally controlled. In most cases external control is not compatible with the active decision-making necessary in the process of rapid growth. In many respects external control through mass voucher privatization systems adopted in Eastern Europe is counter entrepreneurial. Fifth, employee participation in decision-making not only may not hinder efficiency of enterprises and prevent entrepreneurial activities from flourishing but may be the only way for the entrepreneurial companies to survive in the future.

While the first four points stated above are well known and have been widely publicized, although not easily accepted by mainstream economists, the fifth point is less widely known. Therefore, we will explore it further below.

The June 1995 issue of the Inc. Magazine had a cover article on what has been called by practitioners 'Open Book Management' (Open Book Management, 1995). The essence of this approach to managing the enterprise is to inform all employees on the financial situation of the enterprise on a daily basis and encourage them to link their daily work to the company's profit. So some companies developed elaborate income statement, cash flow and balance sheet information systems which enable each employee to see the bottom line results of his and other co-workers actions and consequently adjust their future activities so as to increase profits. The remuneration systems are then developed by employees themselves so that they reflect their contribution to profit. Employees are also trained to read the financial statements until they fully understand them. That is why the system is called Open Book Management (OBM). The article is based on several books which report on this system in detail.

According to the article, this approach to management gives very good results since the employees start understanding how the enterprise actually functions and the management-ownership mystique of running the enterprise disappears. Gradually all employees start behaving rationally, eliminating unnecessary activities and processes and enhancing efforts in the directions which increase profits. Skills and knowledge are now acquired in a focused manner so that they directly enhance the profit generating capability of the enterprise. Since profits are shared in a natural way according to each employee's contribution, profit-maximising becomes a common goal of all members of the enterprise. It has been also noted that all the past and current performance improvement systems such as JIT, TQM, re-engineering, downsizing, benchmarking, teamwork, internal chain of customers, MIS, acquiring cross skills, etc. now start making sense also for employees. Without OBM these systems are generally regarded by employees as just another manipulative trick introduced by management to extract extra effort from employees and they soon become past 'fads' when the management's enthusiasm for them fades away.

Will OBM also become just one of the past fads? The idea behind OBM is of a different quality. It is actually recognizing the fact that all the employees contribute jointly to the success of the firm and that they are jointly responsible for the outcome. While the opportunity cost of an employee may initially still play a role in determining the starting remuneration, it may later become completely overshadowed by the individual's contribution to the result of the enterprise and may become more and more dependent on the specific skills and creativity of the individual. Therefore, the author calls the system revolutionary and is predicting that only the enterprises which in future will adopt this system will be able to survive in the globally competitive world.

It should be noted that the article was published in the Inc. Magazine, which is the leading American magazine on high-growth potential entrepreneurs. In the past it covered the stories of most of the now leading entrepreneurial ventures in the US. Contributors to the magazine include some leading world authorities on entrepreneurship. The implication is that the publishers in deciding to publish the cover article on OBM believed that this system of enterprise performance improvement is fully compatible with entrepreneurship.

Conclusion

In this essay we reflected on some of the fundamental issues concerning the future of self-management in the context of the transition process. It was pointed out that the transition process in socialist countries should be understood as the quest for an institution-policy mix which would enable the countries in transition to increase their rate of growth to the level which would enable them to start catching up with the developed west. It was argued that the orthodox neoclassical theory is not a useful guide to the selection of the appropriate economic system in the countries in transition and that the actual selection of policies and institutions in Eastern European countries was misguided. China, which took a different approach to transition, was much more successful in achieving a high rate of growth. Of key importance in the transition process is the development of competition, which implies the development of a highly entrepreneurial economy. Entrepreneurship in turn implies control by insiders and not by dispersed outside owners. In the western private worker-renting environment the control of entrepreneurial firms used to be concentrated in the hands of individual entrepreneurs. But it was also pointed out that in future efficient entrepreneurial firms may adopt enterprise control systems with extensive employee involvement. The Open Book Management system, which is becoming increasingly popular in American companies, is an example of this. However, such systems are no longer traditional performance improvement instruments but are fundamentally changing the philosophy of enterprise control from employee-renting to employee control.

18 From Self-management to Co-determination

MIROSLAV STANOJEVIĆ

In the first part of this article a critical review of the system of self-management in the former Yugoslavia will be presented. The main sources for this review are the theories and the interpretations of self-management formulated by three of the most prominent industrial sociologists from the former Yugoslavia.

In the second part of the article some features and possible results of the implementation process of the co-determination system in Slovenia are described.

Self-management in the former Yugoslavia: industrial democracy and 'real existing' socialism

Within the critical wing of Yugoslav industrial sociology the *radical* and the *moderate* approaches to the system of industrial democracy have been differentiated in the 1960s and 1970s.[1] Both approaches were based on the thesis of the incompatibility of self-management and 'real-existing' socialism.

The radical approach

The nature of Yugoslav society: 'Real-existing' socialism is based on an experiment which concentrated on the 'final solving' of economic issues through total state intervention: the state is an entity which should supersede the anarchy of the market economy and the corresponding interest conflicts within the economy. The result of this experiment was a politically governed economy (Arzenšek, 1984a, p. 115). The 'incidental' result of the politically governed economy was a *totalitarian relationship between the state and the society*. This totalitarian relationship determined the development of all forms of 'real-existing' socialism (Arzenšek, 1984a, p. 92).[2]

The main characteristics of Yugoslav industrial organization: in spite of more than thirty years of developing self-management, the *oligarchic power structure* was an unchangeable feature of the Yugoslav work organization. Workers, self-management bodies and political organizations within this organization were dominated by an industrial bureaucracy (Arzenšek, 1984a, p. 11). Power was concentrated in the hands of a small informal group composed of top management, officials of self-management bodies and leaders of political organizations (Arzenšek, 1984a, p. 30). The high concentration of power at the top corresponds to the powerless, indifferent and non-participative workers at the bottom of the organization.

The critique of 'institutional self-management': in Yugoslavia self-management was introduced 'from above'. This kind of official, 'institutional' self-management was incompatible with autonomous, self-managed workers' action.

The finding of incompatibility of the self-management system on the one hand, and self-management workers action on the other, is a radical critique of the existing order on the basis of its own ideology (Arzenšek, 1984a, p. 86).

Official self-management is a fictional, false self-management. It is a form of a bureaucratic idea, which permits an interpretation of the empirical world of indifferent and non-participative workers in terms of 'immature class consciousness'. In this interpretation empirical reality is converted into legitimizing the ideological function of the vanguard: it is a justification of the voluntary selection of the so-called 'real self-management interests'.

The radical approach combined the thesis on the incompatibility of self-management and 'real-existing' socialism, with the diagnosis of the 'real-socialist' essence of Yugoslav society and the corresponding conceptualization of the Yugoslav work organization as a bureaucratized and state centred organization. The ultimate result of the analysis was the statement that self-management in the existing work organization was not possible. This finding led to the conclusion that official Yugoslav self-management was an illusory industrial democracy or, as such, a deliberate contrivance.

The moderate approach

The nature of Yugoslav society: Advocates of the moderate approach were aware that a number of similarities existed between the Yugoslav and the 'East-European type' of society. Using the paradigm of a 'grand coalition' they noticed a characteristic interest interconnection between traditional industrial workers and the political elite in Yugoslavia, which was quite similar to 'grand coalitions' in the societies of 'real-existing' socialism. The political elite provided workers with job security and stable participation in the allocation of the material results of social development, while the working class, secured in this way, provided political support for the political elite. The structure of the Yugoslav political space was obviously similar to that of 'real-existing' socialism: the Yugoslav one-party autocratic political system was also formed in terms of the proletarian dictatorship model (Županov, 1989, p. 105).

In spite of these similarities, Yugoslavia was not a typical case of 'real-existing' socialism: Yugoslav socialism was decentralized and 'deregulated'; it was based on accentuated *market* regulation. Yugoslav socialism was a clear case of *market socialism*.

The main characteristics of Yugoslav industrial organization: The advocates of the moderate approach agreed that the oligarchic distribution of power is an important feature of Yugoslav work organization. It was indisputable that the average Yugoslav work organization was bureaucratic and - from the point of view of the market criteria - non-rational as an organization. The essential cause of these problems was the 'political factor': excessive state interventionism deformed the Yugoslav work organization. Because of the 'political factor' this organization was a degraded enterprise (Županov, 1983). The moderate approach, understanding Yugoslav socialism as 'market socialism', regarded Yugoslav work organizations as enterprises orientated to the market.

The interpretation of 'institutional self-management': The moderate wing of Yugoslav critical sociology interpreted the existing self-management according to empirical evidence. The data revealed that the influence of workers' councils on the decision-making process, compared with the influence of management, was low: that workers' councils were subjected to the managers' power. But comparative empirical research slightly modified this conclusion. Such research convincingly demonstrated that Yugoslav work organizations in the 1970s were more democratic than comparable organizations in the West and that, through self-management bodies, the workers were involved particularly in the decisive, strategic, entrepreneurial phase of the decision making process (Rus, 1986, p. 147). These facts testify to an advanced form of industrial democracy that existed in Yugoslav work organizations of the 1970s. The advocates of the moderate approach obviously had valid evidence which confirmed the existence of the relevant democratic tendencies within 'institutional self-management'. These tendencies they understood as a 'material' critique of 'real-existing' socialism: they believed that identified democratization of industrial organization is compatible with the marketization of socialism and with the corresponding modernization processes in Yugoslav society.

Within the moderate approach the thesis on the incompatibility of self-management and the society of 'real-existing' socialism had its positive conclusions: it was translated to a thesis on the compatibility of self-management and the market. In accordance with this thesis, Yugoslav work organization was conceptualized as a specific enterprise. Its particularity stems from the interactions of the participative and management structures of Yugoslav work organization. Self-management was interpreted as a relatively developed form of industrial democracy which should be tuned in with the market centred functions of the industrial organization.

Critique

The main contributions of the two approaches are the diagnosis of the bureaucratized Yugoslav industrial organization contained within a 'real-socialist' Yugoslav society, and the empirical evidence that there was a well-developed workers' participation in the decision-making process.

It is possible to demonstrate that the two approaches to Yugoslav self-management are not incompatible. More than that, it seems that the two contributions could be combined in a productive way.

The exchange of the workers' support for the political elite in return for politically provided job security is a general pattern of the coalition between the working class and the political bureaucracy which was inherent in all societies of 'real-existing' socialism. Self-management used to be a form of maintaining the coalition in 'market socialism'.

The Yugoslav work organization was shaped by a non-market, state-party regulated environment. The key feature of organizations shaped within a primarily non-market context is a high level of openness to the influences of this political context; management is exposed to political pressures. The consequence of a politically centred management is a looseness of management regulation in the industrial organization. At the same time, the high level of social security of the employees produces power equalization of the different groups in the organization.

The result of the mechanisms of industrial democracy, installed in such a power structure as the Yugoslav work organization, was genuine *worker self-management*. It was in the interest of the working collectives to support the social functions of the work organization 'from below'.

In the context of 'market socialism', company directors, as well as being exposed to traditional political pressures, were also directly *involved* in the market operations of the enterprise. This economic segment of the dominating class emerged as a *competitor* to the political elite (Mastnak, 1983, p. 47). Within this competitive relation of the two elites, the participatively structured working class functioned, as a rule, as *allies* of the political elite.

This nature of self-management was manifested mostly on the occasions when the 'normal' fulfilment of obligations toward workers was terminated. If, in a company, those obligations were not adequately fulfilled, the workers would undertake 'wildcat' protest actions. By such actions, usually *short-lived* work stoppages (Jovanov, 1979), workers would set up 'direct communication' with the political elite. They turned the elite's attention to its obligations and the delegitimization implications of ignoring those obligations. The reaction of the political elite was generally swift and effective. It consisted of two steps; meeting workers' demands and changing the director.

In the context of such an alliance of workers with the political elite, the position of management was exposed to permanent 'redefinition': participatively structured worker collectives would push directors into a dependence on the political elite. They thus reintegrated the dominating class and stabilized the domination of the political elite.

Self-management thus induced political intervention and in the context of 'market socialism' assured the prevalence of the party-state elite and emphasized the non-market context (Stanojević, 1990, p. 101).

It seems that an indirect argument for this thesis is the extremely fast disappearance of self-management with the disintegration of 'real existing socialism'. In spite of the sophistication of the self-management mechanism, its downfall was *inevitable* with the disintegration of the political system.

Implementation of the co-determination system in Slovenia

In the case of Slovenia the disintegration of self-management did not mean the abolition of industrial democracy. The changing labour laws explicitly reconstructed the institutions of industrial democracy and redefined the essential functions of these new institutions in accordance with the logic of market economy. In spite of fast and radical social and political changes, the continuity of industrial democracy in Slovenia has been preserved.

The role of trade unions was very important in this continuity. They filled the gap which appeared with the disintegration of self-management. Following the trade unions' massive protest actions organized after the first elections, the new government recognized that it would be better to accept the trade unions as social partners. The result of the political exchange between trade unions and government has been the implementation of the new institutional arrangements of industrial democracy in Slovenia.

The two essential institutional arrangements are the formally centralized collective bargaining system at the macro-level of the economy, and the co-determination system within the enterprises. Both arrangements have been imported from the European systems of 'social market economies'. Forms of centralized collective bargaining have been characteristic of the 'neo-corporatist European systems and in several of them, most notably Germany, there are forms of co-determination similar in many respects to the former self-management arrangements.

Institutional arrangements of industrial democracy: formally centralized collective bargaining and the co-determination system

A formally centralized collective bargaining system was installed in Slovenia at the beginning of the transitional process, in the year 1990. Trade unions tried to provide explicit protection of the economic interests of wage earners by focusing on the issue of 'the price of labour'. In these first years of the transitional period, the labour side rather naïvely understood the introduction of a 'social market economy' to mean the 'europization' of the price of labour. An enthusiastically accepted means for achieving this goal was bargaining with 'employers' and arriving at a collective agreement. By transforming the pattern of collective bargaining in 'post-socialist' Slovenia, the unions gained strong support from workers. With the disintegration of the old mechanism of protection through self-management, workers joined the unions in their masses.

As trade unions in these first years did not have an adequate counterweight on the employers' side - (employers' organizations were weak and unstructured) - the rate of wage increase was substantial. The implication of this pressure was to secure a quite high level of minimum wage. In practice, however, this level could not be met by a significant number of enterprises. As pressure for wage increases threatened the outcomes of macro-economic regulation, the government started to play a more active role in incomes policy. In the year 1994 a tripartite Economic and Social Council was formed. In the spring of 1995 the social partners reached an agreement on a minimum wage and asked Parliament for political and statutory support. It seems that future collective agreements in Slovenia will require the active involvement of the government as the 'third' social partner.

The co-determination system, defined by law in the year 1993, is a variation of the German model. As in the German system, the key institutions of workers' participation in the decision-making process in Slovenian enterprises are the works council, employer representation on the supervisory board and a labour director.[3]

The central institution of the system is the works council, which is in Slovenia also a legal body, located between management on the one hand and trade unions on the other (Offe, 1985, p. 161). Members of the works council are elected by secret ballot by all employees of the enterprise from lists of candidates submitted by trade unions.

The works council has quite wide co-determination and participation rights on issues which directly concern workers' interests. In the decision-making process dealing with the regulation of working time, vacations, the implementation of collective agreements, employment policy and dismissal from employment, the influence of the works council could be, according to law, significant. But in the process of the formation and implementation of the enterprise's business and finance policy the participation rights of the works council are limited. This clear demarcation between the managerial and works council functions is the point at which the new participative system essentially deviates from the logic of industrial democracy within the non-market context.

The works council is not actively involved in the collective bargaining process and it cannot organize industrial action. The collective bargaining process is confined to the trade unions and employers' associations. This dual system of worker interest representation reflects the German model of industrial relations. In the German context, which is marked by a politically unified, and relatively homogeneous trade union scene, this model permits quiescent industrial relations at the micro level. Works councils represent employees' interests and reach an accommodation with capital at the micro level. Trade unions concentrate on collective bargaining and their monopolization of strike activities strengthens their bargaining position (Streeck, 1988, p. 306).

In Slovenia, the dual interest representation system is distorted by two factors, trade union pluralism and the particular characteristics of the privatization process.

The German pattern under the pressure of Slovenian specificities

Trade union pluralism

In Slovenia the level of trade union membership is about 60 per cent of the working population. In comparative terms this level of trade union density is relatively high (Table 17.1).[4]

Table 17.1   Comparison of trade union density rates in some European countries (average percentage of workforce 1986-91)* and Slovenia (in %)

Sweden	84
Slovenia	60
Austria	47
Great Britain	41
Germany	34
France	10

* Source: Visser, 1994.

There are four trade union confederations organized on the national level in Slovenia - the Association of Free Trade Unions of Slovenia (KSSS), Independent - Confederation of New Trade Unions of Slovenia (KNSS), Confederation of Trade Unions 90 of Slovenia (K-90) and PERGAM. The two strongest are ZSSS and KNSS. The rest of trade union membership is made up from two other national confederations and numerous autonomous trade unions in enterprises and public services.

The Slovenian trade union scene is obviously strongly fragmented. The most important dimension of the fragmentation is the politically inspired polarization of trade unions in Slovenia. This polarization corresponds to the main line of polarization of political forces in Slovenia and was in fact produced by it.

This kind of trade union pluralization is visible at the macro as well as on the micro level of trade union activity. Leaders of the two strongest confederations (ZSSS and KNSS) are politically and personally connected to the two main camps of Slovenian politics. These connections stimulate the somewhat exaggerated competition between the two confederations, which takes place in terms of political differentiations rather than industrial issues.

At the micro-level, especially in the case of large companies, the fragmented trade union scene is usually manifest in the form of a competitive and politically inspired trade union dualism. The ZSSS is usually the larger union with a smaller rival from 'oppositional' forces. The professionalism of shop stewards in larger companies and the relatively high trade union density make trade unions in Slovenian enterprises comparatively powerful organizations.

Employee ownership as the main result of the privatization process up to the present

The formulation of legislation on privatization in Slovenia has had two main stages.

The first draft of the law on privatization in Spring 1991 was based on the supposition that a privatization process that would stimulate the development of the Slovenian economy was possible only by means of a gradual, evolutionary marketization of the inherited economy. This concept of privatization considered that those who undertook an entrepreneurial role under market socialism should be the central actors in privatization in the post-socialist era. Non-managerial employees were also to be included in the privatization process through workers' buy-outs. The state was seen as a secondary actor (Bajt, 1993; Rus, 1992). This first proposal was directed to the economic elite and those parts of the 'old' political forces connected with this elite.

The second draft of the privatization legislation was presented in the autumn of 1991. This model was based on the idea of radically changing titular ownership, which was seen by its supporters as the basic condition for achieving the 'victory' of a market economy. This concept of radical, centralized privatization defined the state as the key mediator of the entire process of privatization. This propelled the political establishment, as both actor in and arbitrator of the process, into the sphere of privatization. Through 'coupon privatization', the advocates of centralized privatization offered participation in the future ownership of the economy to the masses of ordinary people (Rus, 1992; Simonetti, Ellerman and Korže, 1993). As the balance of political power at that time favoured the 'new' political forces, the second draft of the privatization legislation corresponded to their interests.

Towards the end of 1992, after a long and sophisticated debate, and following the fall of the first government in the meantime, a kind of a compromise - an 'eclectic' proposal - was adopted in Slovenia. Within this proposal both main groups of privatizers, the economic elite and the 'old' and 'new' political elites, offered the workers participation in future ownership, through vouchers and employee buy-outs.

The outcome of the privatization process is thus likely to produce an unusually widespread degree of employee ownership within the Slovenian economy when compared with conventional market economies.

Microcorporatism in Slovenia?

The collective bargaining system in Slovenia is formally centralized. Trade union representatives find that the existing collective bargaining system creates a common interest between the trade unions, which tends to neutralize their political dissent. However, there are inadequate powers to enforce the collective agreements and they are often not respected. The major single cause of this weakness is trade union pluralism. Their competition hampers effective central bargaining and stimulates the forming of unrealistic demands.

In the context of the Slovenian pluralistic trade union scene, the co-determination system cannot induce the centralization and concentration of trade union power which is evident in the German model.

The co-determination system will cause the integration of the industrial relations actors on the micro-level of the enterprises where the works councils will neutralize the tensions between trade unions. The elections for works councils reflect the balance of membership between the rival trade unions. As the venue for the aggregation of the interests of all employees in the enterprise, the works council will limit the politicization of industrial disputes at the micro level.

Given the growing rates of unemployment, including structural unemployment, the German co-determination system encourages the self-interest of different employee groups. In the Slovenian context, which is characterized not only by a high rate of unemployment, but also by a weak, inefficient collective bargaining system, this effect of the co-determination system is even more likely to appear. An additional factor is the tradition of self-management, which had stimulated the self-interest of employees within the socially owned firms in market socialism. As a result of these different factors, the exaggerated self-interest of privileged employee groups could be a powerful tendency in Slovenia.

This self-interest at the micro-level will be accentuated in the more successful companies, which are concentrated in the export sector of Slovenian industry. Within these companies works councils will create company unionism and stabilize company bargaining. Industrial democracy in these cases will stimulate the forming of privileged groups of worker-owners in post-socialism.

On the other hand, wider, sectoral agreements negotiated by the major trade unions will influence the regulation of industrial relations in traditional industries, which are mainly orientated to the domestic market or participate in the international markets in a more peripheral mode. Within this part of Slovenian industry some kind of weak, sectoral neo-corporatism (Lehmbruch, 1988, p. 62) is likely to be the case.

It seems that the Slovenian 'social partners' will try to control this duality of industrial relations by tripartite general collective agreements, supported and enforced by law.

Notes

1.   The characteristics of the radical approach is illustrated by the works of V. Arzenšek (1984a and 1984b). The moderate approach is presented through the works of J. Županov (1987; 1983; 1989) and V. Rus (1986).

2.   'Totalitarian societies are participative societies within the frame of the one-party political system' (Arzenšek, 1984a, p. 92).

3.   An important difference between the Slovenian and German co-determination models is the optional facultative nature of the co-determination in Slovenian enterprises. The forming of co-determination institutions depends on trade unions. If trade unions demand the institutions, employers have to accept them. According to data presented by

the strongest trade union confederation, works councils have been constituted in almost all large Slovenian enterprises.

4.   Estimations of the trade union density and the distribution of the trade union membership between different confederations are based on research which was carried out in 1994 (Stanojević, and Omerzu, 1994).   Trade unions obviously exaggerate information about membership: the sum total of their declared membership indicates a trade union density which exceeds the active Slovenian work force.

19 Social Structure and Cleavages: Changing Patterns

MITJA HAFNER-FINK

Introduction

To understand the current structure of Slovenian society we should focus our attention on recent history, especially on the second half of the eighties when an intensive process of disintegration of the former socialist federal state of Yugoslavia began. The key questions are whether we can talk about one homogeneous Yugoslav society or about several different societies existing as independent systems within the former Yugoslavia, as well as whether the former Yugoslavia had ever succeeded in establishing itself as an integral social system. In this paper we are going to show that the disintegration of the former Yugoslavia was a result of the fact that several societies had been existing within this state from the beginning and that new societies were not established merely as a consequence of the disintegration. Additionally, we are going to illustrate the dimensions of the present social structure in Slovenia which resulted from the transition from socialism to 'post-socialism'.

Both processes, the disintegration of Yugoslavia and the transformation of the Slovenian society, were connected. The process of disintegration was opposed by that part of the society which was defending the socialist political order, and the process was encouraged by those who were opposing the socialist political order. Thus the present social structure of Slovenian society was determined by and still contains an important residue from the fore-mentioned processes: socialism and the former Yugoslavia.

Slovenia within the former Yugoslavia: social stratification and ideology

Results of empirical analysis[1] have shown that, at the very beginning of the process of disintegration of the federal state, on the whole territory of former Yugoslavia the stratificational system was based on the two following dimensions: general social status and political status.[2] This fact was an essential aspect of Yugoslav socialist society. Namely, we met with two parallel vertical dimensions of social structure or, more accurately, with two parallel structures. In general, education (the first dimension) and a political career (the second dimension) were the most important channels of vertical social mobility in post-second world war Yugoslavia.[3] Promotion on the first stratificational dimension (general social status) was in principle accessible to all (loyal) citizens, while promotion on the basis of political status in the hierarchy was accessible only to those who accepted the ruling communist ideology. Only a high position on the political status hierarchy enabled a person to get political power. Therefore, we could even talk about two parallel social structures - the one based on the vertical dimension of general social status and the other rooted in ideology and politics.

Such a 'dual' stratificational system had an important function of legitimizing the socialist political order and maintaining the social peace. In the liberal version of socialism in the former Yugoslavia, people could reach a relatively high standard of living through a high position on the dimension of general social status. A person who had particular abilities (e.g. knowledge, education, money) could gain prestige or a high general social status. In that way the communist party elite obtained middle class consent for the socialist political order. On the other hand the consent of the working class had been assured by the egalitarian redistributive ideology and the concept of self-management - since there was some prospect of workers being promoted in the political hierarchy (Bernik, 1992). In the eighties the ideological mechanisms of political legitimization began to fall apart. The process of delegitimization took place at different speeds in different parts of the former Yugoslavia and its consequences were different.

Occurrences at the end of the eighties incontestably revealed that the former Yugoslavia had never been established as a uniform and integral society. The ideological cement lost its cohesive power. Since the 'dual' system of stratification with its ideological function was one of few common elements of the stratificational system in the former Yugoslavia, important differences among the federal units emerged. The most important differences were expressed in the shape of the strata profiles, in relations between the position in the subsystem of roles and the subsystem of distribution, in the regulative function of education, in the position of classes in the subsystem of distribution and in the ideological consciousness of strata and classes. The definitive nationalization of social classes according to ethnic/political units was taking place. Thus in the eighties it was not possible to speak either of Yugoslav classes regarding their position in a system of distribution nor of the Yugoslav classes regarding the ideological consciousness of their members.

In general we could say that in the former Yugoslavia in the middle of the eighties at least three stratificational systems existed:
1. the Slovenian system;
2. the central Yugoslav system;
3. the stratificational system of Kosovo (see Hafner-Fink, 1994).

The idiosyncratic position of Slovenia was in accordance with other structural differences within the former Yugoslavia, e.g. Slovenia had less than ten per cent of its population engaged in agriculture, whereas Serbia had near 40 per cent. Slovenia had a larger middle class and a correspondingly smaller lower class than the remainder of Yugoslavia (see fig. 19.1). The overall class profile in Yugoslavia was pyramidal while that of Slovenia was onion-shaped. The meritocratic principle, based on the importance of education as a criterion of status attainment and a criterion of distribution was more important in Slovenia than in the other parts of the former Yugoslavia.

Figure 19.1 Strata profiles for Slovenia and former Yugoslavia in the second half of eighties

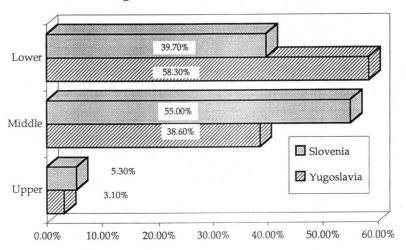

Source: The research project 'class structure...'

Also in the field of ideological consciousness there were important differences within the former Yugoslavia. As research results have shown (Toš, 1989), we can identify two groups of classes in the former Yugoslavia at the end of the eighties: all the Slovenian classes on one hand and the classes of the rest of the former Yugoslavia on the other (Hafner-Fink, 1993). Slovenian workers, for example, were more similar to Slovenian managers than to workers in the other republics in the former Yugoslavia. In general, the Slovenian classes were less 'Yugoslav orientated', they were less egalitarian, they were more critical of the ruling single-party system and they were less orthodox regarding communist ideology (Table 19.1). Therefore, social structure within Slovenia was established as also being idiosyncratic according to the ideological dimension.

Table 19.1   Positive attitude towards particular ideological orientation - republics and provinces of the former Yugoslavia (in %)

	1. egalitarianism	2. monopoly of communist party	3. Yugoslav nation
- Montenegro	52.9	57.2	79.1
- Bosnia & Herzegovina	48.7	59.0	74.3
- Vojvodina	44.3	55.5	72.0
- Kosovo	45.5	54.0	25.8
- Serbia without provinces	43.7	51.3	70.6
- Macedonia	44.3	47.2	69.0
- Croatia	49.1	44.4	59.7
- Slovenia	35.5	31.5	37.4

Source: The research project 'Class structure of the Contemporary Yugoslav Society and Activity of the League of Communists', 1986-87.

Cleavage between the developed and the underdeveloped in the former Yugoslavia

The former Yugoslavia was also very heterogeneous concerning the level of development. The classification of republics and provinces according to indicators of development fits well in the above mentioned picture of three stratificational systems. Slovenia as the most developed republic was on one pole and Kosovo as the least developed was on the other pole. It is important to note that this classification would have been almost the same at the time of the establishment of Yugoslavia in 1918. Since then, differences have become even greater.

An examination of the indicators of development confirms the persistence of the differences, most of which exceed the ratio of 5:1. For example, GNP per capita in Slovenia was seven times higher than in Kosovo, in Slovenia there were eight times more registered cars per 1,000 inhabitants than in Kosovo, illiteracy was 20 times higher in Kosovo than in Slovenia (Source: Statistical Yearbook of Yugoslavia 1987 and 1988). But the proportion between the lowest and the highest average personal income was around 1:2 (Source: Statistical Yearbook of Yugoslavia 1987 and 1988).

These disproportions were also the consequences of an egalitarian ideology and redistributive federal policies. In a way egalitarianism at the level of distribution among strata was an important starting point for the destruction of the socialist political order and the disintegration of Yugoslavia. Namely, this principle caused severe conflicts between the developed and the underdeveloped areas and particularly between Slovenia as the most developed republic of former Yugoslavia on one hand and those who spent the redistributed sources - the political elites of the underdeveloped republics and provinces and the central authority in Belgrade, which played the distributive role by determining the federal budget and managing the funds for the underdeveloped areas. After the fifties these conflicts started to develop on an *economic* basis and other aspects (political, religious, ethnic) were only latent. During the eighties such conflicts became more important and explicitly political.

Ideology and cultural-historical cleavages in the former Yugoslavia

Openly expressed conflicts between the developed and the underdeveloped parts of Yugoslavia were the first stage of other conflicts based on ethnic, religious and political differences. The cultural-civilizational differences of the Balkans were brought into the First Yugoslavia (1918-1941) and they remained also in the Second Yugoslavia. After the second world war the differences were kept under control by an ideology of 'brotherhood and unity' which converged into a 'vampire' version and finally expressed itself in extreme brutality and the Bosnian slaughter. It was important that ethnic, religious and (in general) civilizational cleavages fitted into political cleavages as well as in the boundaries of the republics in the former Yugoslavia. Thus Slovenia and Croatia were mostly Catholic, Serbia and Montenegro were Orthodox, Kosovo Islamic, while in Bosnia and Herzegovina all three religions and consequently three different cultures, were interlaced with each other. However, Slovenia was the most homogeneous. Membership of any other religion than Catholic was minor. Slovenia was the most homogeneous unit in respect of ethnic structure as well. Around 90 per cent of its inhabitants were Slovenes, the remainder being mostly immigrants from the other republics of the former Yugoslavia (Serbs, Croats, Muslims, Albanians, etc.) or members of native ethnic minorities (the Italians and Hungarians). We could say that only in the case of Slovenia did the boundaries of the republic fit perfectly in terms of the ethnic and religious cleavages in the former Yugoslavia.

In fact, even before the disintegration of the former Yugoslavia several national states had begun to be established within the former federal state. In general, the boundaries of the republics were the framework for these national states. Namely, The Constitution of Socialist Federal Republic of Yugoslavia from 1974 had in fact conceded confederal status to the federal units (republics). Slovenia, with its outstanding position regarding development, social structure, stratificational system, ethnic and religious structure, was the first one which tried to implement this constitutional confederal status (e.g. 'Nova revija' with a Slovene national programme in 1987, amendments to the Slovene Constitution in 1989, the plebiscite in December 1990). Consequently, severe political conflicts were triggered between the central authorities in Belgrade and other conservative political elites in the republics and provinces of the former Yugoslavia on the one hand and the Slovene political elite in Ljubljana on the other.

However, it was important that those conflicts did not merely concern the relationship between the central and local authorities (e.g. problems concerning the distribution of the federal budget). The conflicts had also an 'ideological' background, since the political situation in Slovenia was more pluralistic. The fact is, that in the beginning of the eighties, civil society started to emerge out of the development of petitional movements, new social movements, and oppositional political movements which fought for political system change.[4] Multiparty elections in 1990 were a result of a process of political modernization started in the middle of the eighties. Slovenia became 'problematic' within the Yugoslav political context because of its unorthodoxy and later also because of its 'heresy' and 'separatism'. Slovenes did not only reject the idea of a Yugoslav (national) identity but were also more critical of socialism and communism than the inhabitants of other republics in the former Yugoslavia. They became very critical about the social and economic situation and the prospects for development in the framework of the old political system. Gradually they accepted the need to develop a market economy, a multiparty system, the rule of law and they became less egalitarian, etc. (see Table 19.1).

We could say that cultural-historical (religious) differences between Slovenia and the rest of the former Yugoslavia were at least as important factors of ideological and political cleavages in the former Yugoslavia as other factors. Research (Toš, 1989) has shown that religious allegiance had a significant impact on ideological and political attitudes, e.g. in Bosnia and Herzegovina Catholics were significantly distinguished from members of the Orthodox Church and from Muslims according to their criticism of socialism and communism. In Slovenia religious Catholics were more critical than non-believers. Thus the idiosyncratic position of Slovenia could also be explained by Catholicism as a dominant religious system in Slovenia. It is important that the Catholic Church was an ideological opponent of Communism from its very beginning in Europe (even before the Communist party was established in Slovenia). We could not say that the 'Catholic character' of Slovenian society caused its attainment of independence, but we could say that, together with other aspects of differentiation (the level of development, social structure, history, geographical position, ethnic homogeneity), it produced the situation which caused the process of attainment of independence as well as the transition from socialism to 'post-socialism'. The Catholic religion was an important agent, which contributed to the fact that Slovenia also differed from the rest of the former Yugoslavia according to political culture. The growing economic distance between Slovenia and the rest of the former Yugoslavia, the developing reformist political culture (Jambrek, 1989) as well the Catholic religion itself, all had an important role in the process of the transformation of Slovene national identity in opposition to the Yugoslav supranational identity.

Social structure and ideological differences in Slovenia in the eighties

At the point when the process of disintegration of the former Yugoslavia started, Slovenia was the first republic interested in creating pressure for change in the political system as well as in the growing tendencies to loosen Federal ties. Opposing tendencies to this trend existed in Slovenia but became marginal. The modernizing social structure of Slovenian society with a higher proportion of the middle class compared with the rest of former Yugoslavia (see Fig. 19.1) provided a solid background for ideological transformation, although at that time Slovenian society still had the characteristics of a not-yet-modern socialist - 'by-modern' society (Bernik, 1989). Basically, it still had the structure of a socialist society. The main line of class polarization was the line of political domination and not the line of economic exploitation (compare Bernik, 1992; Wright, 1989, p. 56). Private property was of almost no importance. In fact, tradesmen and farmers as private owners had a marginal position in the system of power, being located in the middle of the social hierarchy if they were tradesmen and at the bottom if they were farmers.

In the middle of the eighties Slovene society had a relatively stable and closed stratification structure which could be shown in the form of a three-degree hierarchy where the so-called ruling elite (politicians and managers) had an especially outstanding position at the top of the hierarchy. According to some interpretations (e.g. Lazić, 1987) the ruling elite was understood as the class of 'collective owners' of social property. On the other side there was half of the population at the bottom of the hierarchy, mostly farmers and workers. The situation in the lower and higher part of the hierarchy was remarkably crystallized, whereas in the middle section, comprising the higher working class and tradesmen, there was greater dispersion. It turned out that among the higher classes 90 per cent were members of the Party. Thus, we obviously had a situation where the Party exercised control on behalf of the working class but in practice (though not in ideological discourse) it neglected its so-called 'class basis'. This contradiction and the stratification structure itself then significantly determined the ideological processes.

Although different Slovenian classes were more similar to each other regarding ideological consciousness than to their corresponding classes in the rest of former Yugoslavia, we could speak of significant differences among the lower, middle and higher classes in Slovenia concerning ideological consciousness. Social classes in Slovenia differed not only in the intensity of certain ideological orientations, but also held different ideological positions.

In this sense, in the middle of the eighties the biggest differences among classes could be noticed in their relationship to egalitarianism and the authoritative centralist state. On the whole, differences were expressed through the rejection by the higher strata of the egalitarian-statist ideological pattern, whereas the lower strata accepted it. Rejection of the egalitarian-statist orientation was especially outstanding amongst professional politicians: 80.4 per cent of them rejected egalitarianism and 79.5 per cent rejected statism. Similar attitudes were found among managers and experts (Hafner-Fink, 1989). At first sight it was surprising that the upper classes, and especially politicians, rejected the statist orientation. However, there could be an explanation. The Slovene political elite had an increasing opposition to federal centralism which was perceived as endangering the sovereignty of Slovenia as a state. Since this also meant jeopardizing the privileged positions of the Slovene national (communist) elite, they rejected it.

In general we could also say that the upper classes were the least critical when evaluating the operation of the system, whereas the middle classes were the most critical. There was the same pattern regarding the 'ideological communist orthodoxy': to a large extent within the upper classes there was acceptance of the ideological orthodoxy whereas within the middle classes there was rejection to a large extent. It was characteristic of the middle classes that rejection of the party monopoly appeared as a dominant position, which was not the case with the other classes.

Regarding the above description it is clear that impulses and support for transition were coming from the middle classes. Leaders fighting for changes were first of all from different intellectual circles. A special 'intellectual elite' (with no political power) emerged, while supporters of social and political campaigns for modernization came from several social groups (mainly from the middle classes, but also from the lower classes, especially farmers). The course of events in the second half of the eighties had shown that a relatively gentle democratic transition was possible in Slovenia. The main precondition for it was rooted in the 'consent' of the political elite. In the middle of the eighties the political elite had still defended a single-party system and the monopoly of the Communist Party, but by the end of the eighties the transformed, modernized political elite already accepted the idea of political pluralism and agreed to hold the first multiparty elections in 1990. But it is also true that this evolution had taken place under pressure from a growing political opposition.

Social structure, cleavages and conflicts in Slovenia after the attainment of independence

In the process of economic and political transition and the formation of an independent national state the structure of Slovenian society has only been partly changed. The top of the social hierarchy is still narrow and the bottom is still wide, but there are some changes in the middle of the hierarchy. Namely, the proportion of the middle classes has grown and in recent years it has at least reached or even exceeded the proportion of the lower classes. Since the first year of independence the standard of living of the majority of the population has grown. But at the same time changes in the differentials between the highest and the lowest positions in the social hierarchy have also been indicated. The differentials have become greater - the richest are becoming richer and the poorest are becoming poorer.

According to Slovene public opinion survey research (SPO),[5] in 1992 almost 50 per cent of respondents thought that they belonged to the lower or working class while in 1994 this proportion was less than 40 per cent. On the other side the proportion of respondents who rank themselves in the middle class has grown between 1992 and 1994. At 53.8 per cent it has now exceeded the proportion of those ranking themselves as lower or working class (Figure 19.2). The improved standard of living could also be seen from the results of public opinion research. Namely, in 1992 more than 50 per cent of respondents estimated that their regular incomes were not sufficient for a minimal standard of living, but by 1994 the proportion has been reduced to less than 40 per cent.

Figure 19.2 Self-perception as middle class in Slovenia from 1992 to 1994 (SPO, in %) (Toš, 1994a)

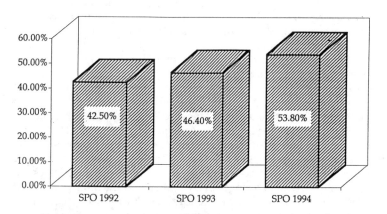

The SPO results have shown shifts in key social values and, in particular, in respect of inequality. At the end of the eighties support for a more egalitarian distribution of income was at its lowest level but by 1994 it had exceeded the level of 1984 (Figure 19.3).

Figure 19.3 Support for reduction in income differentials in Slovenia (SPO, in %) (Toš 1994a)

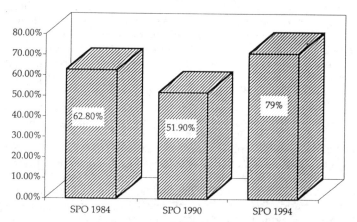

Obviously there have been quantitative changes within the social stratification system of distribution, but have there been significant structural changes which would introduce new criteria of class polarization? Has private ownership displaced political position as the main determinant of dominance? The ruling class is still a *political class* composed of a diversified political elite. Members of this political class have attained their social status mainly through their political career and not through their personal wealth and economic activities. It is true that through the process of denationalization and privatization private property is becoming an important factor in shaping the social hierarchy, but it is still not the principal factor forming a particular class with its own identity. New economic strata are emerging in the process of privatization, but they do not reach the highest position in the social hierarchy. They rather belong to the upper middle class, although they have adopted a lifestyle which expresses their ambitions to gain higher status. This means that the middle class is diverging and in this respect it is becoming more heterogeneous than it was before the attainment of independence. The 'old' middle class has mostly kept its position in the social hierarchy, and this fact could be interpreted as meaning that they are 'losers' in the process of transition. Namely, they have been 'rewarded' for their support of the changes in the process of social and economic transition with an unfavourable tax policy. It is the impact of taxation which distinguishes the middle class from the upper or ruling class.

Currently, the new ruling class is based on political factors rather than economic ones. This first of all means that the political and economic spheres are still closely interlaced and that the struggle for economic power is still taking place in politics. It is also expressed in terms of political and ideological cleavages between different political orientations and segments of the political elite. More precisely, the struggle is going on between the new political elite which was in opposition in the old system and the transformed old political elite. It is significant that the old economic elite from the previous enterprise management structures has largely kept their positions and the 'renovated' political elite has succeeded in keeping personal connections with this managerial structure. This 'coalition' has provided both partners with advantages by means of an exchange of economic and political support, especially in the process of privatization. In this way it is probable that the new 'ruling' coalition of economic and political forces which will unify the newly forming economic sector and political power is emerging. The 'renovated' political and economic elite of the old regime seem to be the main winners in the process of economic and political transition. The new segments of the political elite which triggered the process of transition and emancipation seem to be the losers, at least in the economic field.

In general we could say that it is possible to identify some structural changes at the top and middle of the social hierarchy while at the bottom there are none of any importance. What kind of cleavages and social conflicts could be noticed? We have already mentioned conflicts between different segments of the political elite. However, we estimate that classical industrial conflict is the most important structural conflict. Strikes have become quite frequent expressions of conflict between workers and employers. Public opinion research has shown that the majority of Slovenians estimate these conflicts as the most severe conflicts (70 per cent of respondents), while, for example, less than 40 per cent of the population estimate conflicts between the poor and the rich as severe and less than 30 per cent of Slovenes estimate that this is true for conflicts between urban and rural areas (SPO, spring 1992; Toš, 1992).

In the context of an ethnic structure where almost ten per cent of Slovenian residents are of non-Slovene origin it is meaningful to ask whether there are ethnic conflicts and cleavages. The existence of ethnic distance and attitudes of intolerance (see Klinar, 1994) could be a starting point for these kind of conflicts. As a consequence of experience within the former Yugoslavia Slovenes feel closer to Western European nations than to their neighbours from the former Yugoslavia. Opinions have been expressed that there is more similarity between Americans and Slovenes than between Serbs and Slovenes (SPO, spring 1994; Toš, 1994a). In general, we could say that national intolerance is first of all directed toward ethnic groups coming from the other regions of the former Yugoslavia, but not at a level which would generate severe ethnic conflict. In this framework it is interesting that there are higher levels of intolerance shown toward indigenous marginal social groups, such as former convicts, alcoholics, drug addicts, homosexuals and Gypsies than towards 'non-Slovene' ethnic groups such as Muslims, and other immigrants from the former Yugoslavia, including refugees. In fact, a process of ethnic assimilation is going on. Research has shown that within almost all families in Slovenia the Slovene language is spoken at home (98.5 per cent) despite the fact that almost ten per cent of residents are of non-Slovene origin. (SPO, autumn 1994; Toš, 1994a).

Conclusions: Slovene society between traditionalism, modernism and postmodernism

The attainment of independence and the process of economic and political transition are closely connected with the process of the modernization of Slovene society. Several elements in the structure of Slovene society indicate this process of modernization including private property, a growing middle class, political pluralism, institutions of the national state, etc. There are even some elements indicating a postmodern shaping of social structure as lifestyle and values become important factors for class cleavages.

Has there been a corresponding process in the area of values, attitudes and political culture? First of all we could say that the structure of values in Slovenia is very diverse or even divergent. Elements of traditionalism, modernism and even postmodernism are present simultaneously. The specific circumstances of the transition of Slovenian society explain to some extent this co-existence of different values. Namely, opposition movements which fought for changes in the former socialist system were interlacing with new social movements fighting for postmodern goals such as demilitarization, the right of conscientious objection, ecological issues (Fink-Hafner, 1992). Postmodern issues have subsequently been marginalized and modern values become dominant. We have already shown that egalitarianism has important support (Figure 19.3), but at the same time, in the immediate confrontation for Slovenes, freedom and differentiation are rated above equality. Work is an important value for almost all Slovenians (95 per cent), the majority of them have positive attitudes toward independence (88 per cent), freedom (88 per cent), gender equality (84 per cent), the nation (81 per cent), Europe (65 per cent), private property (59 per cent), the right to abortion (59 per cent), abolition of the death penalty (49 per cent) (SPO, spring and autumn 1994; Toš, 1994a).

Slovenes are very reserved concerning their evaluation and confidence in the institutions of their newly established independent state. This also demonstrates the modern structure of their value system as well as the already mentioned fact that independence and the nation are important values for Slovenians. The most important feeling of identity is national identity (public opinion research shows that around 70 per cent of respondents have strong feelings of identification with people speaking Slovene and with a group of people being Slovenes (Toš, 1994a). A modern understanding of a nation could be seen also from the accepted basic definition of Slovene as people with Slovene citizenship and who respect Slovene institutions and Slovene laws (SPO, spring 1994; Toš, 1994a).

The second important feeling of identity is connected with work - identification with workers or with a professional group (over 40 per cent). But there are also indices suggesting the persistence of traditional values, such as the presence of some elements of authoritarianism; according to SPO research more than 80 per cent of the adult population has a positive attitude towards order and discipline (SPO, autumn 1994; Toš, 1994a). The high ranking given to work as a value indicates a kind of Protestant ethic in the Weberian sense.

The co-existence of traditional and modern values among Slovenes could also be seen from attitudes towards the nation. Namely, there are still several traditional elements present within the understanding of a nation. For Slovenes national identity very often means ethnic identity. To be Slovene or to be a citizen of Slovenia it is important to speak the Slovene language, to live for a long time in Slovenia, to be Slovene by birth. A low level of spatial mobility among the Slovenian population also indicates traditional elements concerning identity and adherence. Slovenes are closely attached to their home town and they are not willing to move out of Slovenia to improve their standard of living. They are hardly even willing to move to another place in the same county (according to SPO results, less than 30 per cent). Finally, according to public opinion research, the family is an important value for almost all Slovenes (SPO, autumn 1994, Toš, 1994a). But residents of Slovenia understand the family either within a traditional or modern value structure. These different notions, traditional or modern and even postmodern, correlate with the position of respondents within the social structure. Namely, traditional tendencies are characteristic for the lower classes and for rural areas while modern and postmodern tendencies are mostly present within the middle classes and urban areas.

The current shape of Slovene social structure with its social divisions, ideological and political clashes and the structure of the value system have their historical roots. Present developments within the area of social structure and the value system are a continuation of the process of economic and political transition which was started within the framework of the former Yugoslavia in the eighties and which still continues.

Notes

1. Research project 'Class Structure of the Contemporary Yugoslav Society and Activity of the League of Communists' carried on in 1986 and 1987 in all republics and autonomous provinces of former Yugoslavia and conducted by a research team headed by Niko Toš (1989).
2. Kosovo was the only exception, where from the general social status, the third dimension was extracted: the material status (see Hafner-Fink,1994).
3. The significance of these dimensions concerning the position of an individual in the social area has also been shown in other researches of the social structure in socialist societies (e.g. Parkin,1971; Kolosi and Wnuk-Lipinski,1983; Kolosi,1984; Lazić,1987; Bernik,1992).
4. More on the role of new social movements in the transition of Slovenian society is presented in: Fink-Hafner, 1992.
5. A longitudinal research project 'Slovene Public Opinion' (SPO) which has been continuously conducted by Niko Toš since 1968 (see Toš, 1987, 1992, 1994).

20 The Role of the Media in the Transition

SANDRA BAŠIĆ HRVATIN

Introduction

> 'Gentleman, it is useless to speak here of the magnitude of the overall importance of the press... Erase the press from your memory and think about what modern life would be without the kind of publicity created by the press... One hundred and fifty years ago the British Parliament forced journalists to apologize on their knees for breach of privilege after they reported about its sessions; yet today a mere threat from the press not to print the speeches of representatives forces Parliament to its knees'.

Thus spoke Max Weber in his speech delivered at the first Congress of Sociologists meeting in 1910 in Frankfurt (Weber, 1976, pp. 96-7). At the end of this century modern media forced many communist regimes in East and Central Europe to their knees. Asked once what had caused the fall of communism in Eastern Europe, Lech Walesa pointed to a nearby TV set and said 'It all came from there' (Economist, 1994, p. 4). The purpose here is to produce an answer to some major questions which are important for an understanding of the current political and media situation in Slovenia:

- first; on the structural level, what is the role that the media played in the processes of tranformation (and disintegration) of political regimes in former socialist states?
- second; to what extent are changes at the political level a result of pluralization and democratization in the communication sphere?

- third; are political changes 'produced' (or initiated) by the globalization of communication in the 1980s or is the democratization generated by an autonomous public which itself defined the main questions on the political agenda?
- fourth; what has happened to the demands for establishing (and protecting) the independent public sphere which were the central demands of oppositional political programmes before they gained political power? As Adam Seligman said, 'civil society was realized in…the new State apparatus' (Seligman, 1992, p. 7);
- fifth; there is a controversy about the role which the media had during the so called 'media war' in the early 1980s. In this period the media produced and articulated an image of the enemy, a kind of symbolic preparation for the 'real' war still ongoing in some states on the territory of the former Yugoslavia. Or, on the contrary, have political changes produced appropriate communication systems?

All the questions must be answered in a similar interpretative framework - rebuilding democracy is closely connected with rebuilding or democratizing forms of communication (Peters, 1993, p. 567).

Questions concerning democracy are most difficult and, similarly, questions of the re-distribution of power and influence in the communication field are the most politicized questions in almost all post-socialist countries. Put in another way, the communication system is the last sphere in post-socialist countries which would be democratized because the media are still playing the role of a *cordon sanitaire* between state and civil society. This redefinition includes structural problems of the relationships between the state and the media involving the suspension of state subsidies for the print media; stronger political pressures on national broadcasting systems; new connections between political parties and the media bringing about a fusion between the media and the political elite; the selection of news in the media which reflects the current needs of the political elite and between the media themselves, caused by a lack of common professional standards and media ethics.

Political debates about legal changes in the media system in Slovenia were as important as the questions of constitutional change. During the five years of media debates the Slovene parliament adopted the third version of the Media Act with a lot of parliamentary (and public) discussion about the basic role of the media: freedom of the press (or the broader concept of a 'right to know'), limitations on state intervention in the communication sphere and ways of preserving the role of civil society in controlling the media. 'The reasons are obvious. The media had an important role before and during revolutionary political changes of the 1980s. All the central questions of the period of transition pertain to the media: the role of the state and civil society, the question of democratic pluralism, problems of denationalization and the privatization of production, the quest for sovereignty and, of course, the liberalization of the media system itself' (Splichal, 1995, p. 13). This longterm political discussion about re-organization of the communication sphere was directly influenced by the conservative ideological vocabulary imported from similar debates in western countries in the 1970s. The communication sphere in post-socialist Slovenia is defined according to the liberal principles about the free market place of ideas (and political programmes) on the one side and strong economic competition based on advertising resources on the other side.

So the 'real' dilemma is not public vs. market (which is the major contemporary institutional conflict in European broadcasting) *but who will control the media?*

The archaeology of crisis

For the better understanding of institutional changes it is necessary to define the historical context in which these events took place. For our analysis the starting point is at the beginning of the 1980s with military intervention in the then Autonomous Province of Kosovo. This event built up two important principles which shaped political struggle in the former Yugoslavia and are based on a common shared public memory: first; that any changes in the political system will produce a collapse of the system as a whole, and second; the definition of the common enemy used first on Albanians in Kosovo and then projected on to Slovenes, Croats and finally, in its most brutal version, on Muslims in Bosnia and Herzegovina.[1] And exactly at this point the media played an important role in the production of dominant public definitions. The conflict over communication strategies is 'the major role that the media played in constructing our perceptions of the public domain and the legitimacy or illegitimacy of those who act within it' (Schlesinger, 1991, p. 2). The changes in the communication sphere occur in different periods:

1. start of public discussion about economic crisis (1980-84);
2. nationalization of the public sphere (1984-86);
3. 'public purification' (1986-88);
4. national homogenization and integration (1988-1990) and
5. transitional period (1990-).

In the transitional period we distinguish between two predominant practices in the regulation of the media system:

a) during the period of building a new national state when media had a consolidational function and
b) during the period of political differentiation when it became obvious that there were growing structural tensions between media and political elites.[2]

As indicated, the first period is marked by public discussions about the economic crisis and the public confrontation between different opinions which advocated different ways of resolving the crisis. It became known that the whole economic system had been based on foreign debts. Economic collapse was accompanied by structural disintegration in the political system. The media became a channel for debates about social, economic and political changes. For the first time it was evident that even politicians have different opinions, and for the first time the official ruling structure included public relations experts. The press, which was, at that time, much less centralized than radio and television, had to start to differentiate according to the level of criticism of the current situation and this saw the rise of important public opinion makers who dictated the themes of political debates. At the same time, public opinion started to be visible at formal and informal level: critical readers' letters, petitions, different kinds of civil disobedience, and organized group actions. On that point, Slovenian (and to some extent Croatian) leadership openly resisted laws which were based on some kind of 'economic autarchy'. The other parts of the state saw this as a way of 'nationalistic exclusivism' and explained it in the media as a form of exploitation by the northern part of the state of the underdeveloped south.

The second phase is dominated by changes in the communication sphere. From the beginning of the 1970s every republic had its own broadcasting system completely independent of the federal one. Each broadcasting centre had two channels: the first one produced at the republic level and the second mixed with programmes from other centres. Only the central news and current affairs programme was still under federal control. News about daily political situations (i.e. 'common shared' political framework) was produced in Belgrade and distributed to other national broadcasting centres. It was evident that different opinions about the crisis and ways of resolving it were related to views of what constituted the national interests. The national dimension became so powerful that all initiatives, including those on the civil or cultural level, became highly politicized. National concentration become a first step in national homogenization.

The third phase we called a phase of '*public purification*', during which the media 'discovered' different scandals (corruption, economic mismanagement, police repression, violation of civil rights). It became obvious that this 'hidden' mismanagement was a necessary part of the system - it was how the system was managing to function at all.[3] In this period the press become the most important creator of the political agenda.

Crisis became a system reality. After differentiation in the communication sphere the media passed through a second integration inside national states. The press has a function as the bearer of national politics in the republics. Nationalization of the public sphere involves removing the autonomy of the media and its subordination to the national interest. National television plays an important role in shaping public discussion.

> The media play a decisive part in selecting what the public perceives as relevant because, by virtue of being the most effective modulator of public attention, they have the function of establishing and distributing what may well be called 'attention values'... Their ability to impose a topic on public attention is the result of an infinite number of repetitions, whose total effect is to consolidate communicative similarities and to iron out dissonances (Zolo, 1992, p. 160).

The transitional period began with the multiparty elections, the declaration of independence and the military intervention which finally brought the country to war. The Slovene political map was transformed not only on a national level, since some national media systems existed in the former Yugoslavia, but also according to new political options. Formally the press declared its independence from state and parties, and most journalists identified themselves with different political parties.

Similarly, the political democratization was closely connected with demands for democratization in the communication sphere. According to the previous chronology there were some waves (rather than periods because some of them dominated in different periods) described as constrained, distorted and arrested communication (Mueller, 1973, p. 19) and in the transitional period a specific kind of communication system which Splichal called 'paternalistic - commercial' (Splichal, 1994).

Constrained communication is when a dominant political structure controls communication and occurs where society is subordinated to a party. This type of communication promised a dominant ideology, which re-interpreted public memory and eliminated all other interpretative maps. In situations of crisis or where some other political groups try to produce their own definition of events the dominant media take on the function of ideological/national consolidation and condemn the rival interpretation. The most important role is that all events which call into question governmental decision are highly politicized and always punishable. The state has a wide range of articles in its Penal Code - which are often used against critical comment in the media.

Political communication becomes *distorted* in situations when oppositional political opinions are excluded from public debate. Dominant political paradigms are supported by state-owned and state-controlled media and oppositional views fall into a 'spiral of silence' supported by the fear of ex-communication and the loss of basic civil rights. It is a period with a number of 'political trials' which have as a main goal the discipline of the public. The system uses a specific kind of 'institutional lie' (Rupnik, 1988, p. 269), a restrictive language which does not allow any oppositional explanation to enter the communication process. Accordingly, journalists were called 'socio-political workers' and have a main purpose of enlightening and disciplining the audience and above all controlling the public discourse. In classical Stalinist manner the Party is not a place for debates and the media are also excluded from any kind of discussion. Political communication is controlled by politically approved speakers.

Arrested communication is a result of pressures and limitation of public communication by the politically or economically powerful groups. Dominant groups use oppositional opinions only in cases when they are in their own interest and use the media to provide popular acclaim.

Today, the dominant form of communication is some kind of 'paternal commercial' system which is a result of specific structural changes in post-socialist societies. The new system which is emerging is dominated, 'with a tendency of privatization and commercialization of the media (particularly the press) on the one hand, and of maximizing and/or exercising state power over the media (television in particular) on the other' (Splichal, 1995, p. 5). Paternalistic means that the media protect their audience from any kind of inappropriate content (partially political content), and the commercial segment is based on the presumption that market-driven regulation will, in the end, democratize the media system. On the audience side, as a product of this type of media system there is a citizen-consumer. The leading motto for this type of media is that 'anything could be said, provided that you can afford to say it profitably' (Williams, 1976, p. 133).

At the beginning of the 1980s discussions about economic policies and the public exposure of high foreign debts revealed that inside the apparently monolithic official party discourse their existed different opinions. For the first time delegates in federal parliament did not unanimously accept the national budget and it was obvious that different republics had different proposals on how to resolve the crisis. The analysis of media coverage in that period shows that there were growing differences in media reporting in different republics. Serbian media supported the federal government and at the same time criticized its economic measures which was a way of arrested communication inside the official symbolic universe. This was a period which defined thinking about the 'privileged' position of the western developed republics of Slovenia and Croatia, attributing their economic success to the exploitation of other parts of Yugoslavia. Croatian media took a specific position during this conflict. A negative evaluation of the administrative measures of the federal government was represented to their public through the presentation of different opinions in the Slovene and Serbian media. In this case we have a kind of manipulative communication. Slovene newspapers and magazines during the whole period (1980-1988) constantly exposed the problems as an obstacle to the future democratization of the society. At the same time every newspaper and magazine in each republic produced a surfeit of 'national interpretations' which were defined, from the standpoint of the federal government, as a 'hidden' (silently supported) national/republic opinion. This type of communication is dominant in an autarchic and repressive symbolic world which does not allow any different opinion.

The second important event started to appear in the press during 1984-5 and was officially defined as 'attacks on JNA'. These events are important for the future development in communication systems in two ways:

1. The specific position of the Slovene media (especially the youth magazine Mladina which became the most powerful political opinion maker in the 1980s) produced a situation where articles in the Slovene press become 'constructed' events in political debates across the whole country. The federal government 'accused' Slovene republic authorities of using Mladina as a channel for the public exposure of their own political strategies;
2. Slovene Student radio (locally transmitted in Ljubljana) introduced a way of informing its audience during the political trials in Ljubljana, using techniques such as news briefs, live broadcasting from in front of the court, public mobilization and support for democratization.

During this period newspapers in Croatia, Slovenia and Serbia published most articles on the same subjects - JNA, military industry, Yugoslav politics (Figure 20.1).

Figure 20.1   Media agenda in Slovene, Croatian and Serbian magazines (1985 - 1988)

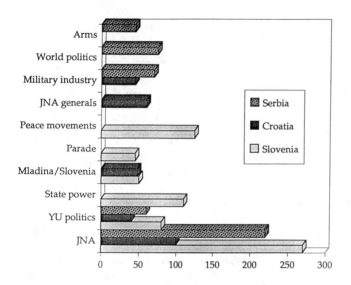

Croatian newspapers and magazines mostly interpreted articles from the Slovene press and they first introduced into public discussion the problem of nationalism. More detailed analysis which is based on the number of critical approaches to prevailing topics in media coverage shows that there were complete differences between the three republics (Figure 20.2).

Almost all critical articles were published in the Slovene media and hardly in the Serbian media. For Mladina it was evidently a process of 'self-citation' - citation of their own articles during the different periods. On the contrary, Serbian media mostly cited official sources (JNA itself, military officers) because at this point they took over the function of institutional mediator for the official communication channels. We could say that in the 1980s the media in Slovenia, Croatia and Serbia through the disintegration of the communication sphere paved the way for the disintegration of the political sphere. In other words, democratization and independence of the Slovene media was the first step to the democratization and independence of the political sphere.

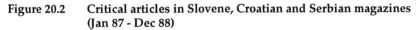

Figure 20.2   Critical articles in Slovene, Croatian and Serbian magazines (Jan 87 - Dec 88)

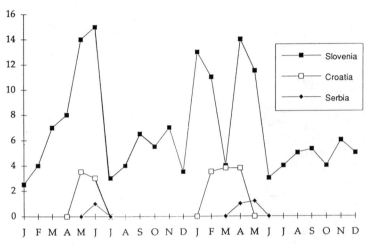

The media system in the 1990s

What is the structure of the Slovene media system in the 1990s?[4] In light of all this political change we would expect some major problems in Slovenia's media system today. Under the previous socialist regime the press was controlled by the League of Communists and all of the newspapers received state subsidies according to the principle of political loyalty. The system has had much in common with a specific phenomenon which Mancini called a 'coalitional complex' and is present in Italian politics (Mancini, 1991, p. 138). The comparable elements are: a strong relationship between political and media systems, unstable political rule and a paternalistic relationship to the public. The ruling coalition in Slovenia, a so-called 'Grand Coalition', includes such diverse political parties as Christian Democrats, Social Democrats or reformists (former communists) and liberal democrats. As in Italy and most Western European countries Slovenia has deregulated the print media and regulated broadcasting. Compared with other Central and East European countries the state still preserves its dominant role in broadcasting, through management control or through the appointment of the general director or editors or by the policy of giving new licences. Most new television owners are not interested in any kind of political programmes and mostly broadcast 'cheap' commercial programmes imported from the West. So, as Mancini pointed out, there are four main problems related to the communication system (Mancini, 1991, p. 139):

-   strong state control of mass media, resulting in TVS broadcasting a large amount of political propaganda, and journalists who openly declare their political preferences;

- strong degree of mass media partisanship in spite of the fact that most newspapers declared their political independence from the state and from the parties. The large circulation 'Delo' declared its position as an 'independent newspaper for independent Slovenia'. There is a specific type of dependency related to the construction of the political agenda. During the last two years the press investigated a number of scandals which dominated national public discussion, and were initiated with information obtained from unattributed sources.[5] The other dimension of this problem is related to an economic dependency - on advertising resources - which is evident in the balance of the mix between news and advertising;
- the existence of a political media elite with strong professional interchange between the world of politics and journalism;
- absence of a consolidated and shared independent professional ethic. In socialist regimes journalists were defined as 'socio-political workers' and their main function was the stabilization of the dominant ideology. Today, most problems are related to achieving real independence from politics and are mostly connected with the process of privatization of the biggest publishing houses. The 'wild' media privatization produced sharp divisions among journalists inside the same newspaper. The other indicator is a growing number of libel suits against journalists in recent years, mostly from private citizens for intrusion into privacy and from politicians.

As a state-owned and state-controlled entity Slovene television has an exclusive monopoly on 'public speech' and on the definition of dominant discourse. At the same time, TVS tries to provide a substitute for the missing dialogue between the state, the public sphere and private persons. In many European countries there is a co-existence of public service broadcasting and a commercial press. TVS cannot define itself either as a public or as a commercial organization but as a commercialized state company, since almost half of its revenues come from advertising. Slovene broadcasting operates in an intermediate position bound neither by the imperatives of profit maximization nor by the maximization of political power.

There is a another way of co-existence between the sphere of communication and politics. Blumler and Gurevitch emphasize this co-existence through four dimensions of linkage between political and media structures in political communication as:

1. the degree of state control over mass media organizations;
2. the degree of mass media partisanship;
3. the degree of media - political elite integration and
4. the nature of the legitimizing creed of media institutions (Blumler, Gurevitch, 1975, p. 171).

For the present situation it is especially important to look at the various ways of exercising a 'soft' state control which are practised at three levels: as control over the appointment of media personnel, control over the financing of media enterprise and control over media content (Blumler and Gurevitch, 1975, p. 173). In the case of the Slovene media system there are differences between the press and broadcasting on the first two levels of state control. The print media operate as economic enterprises which are subordinated to market conditions where 'the biggest will survive'. The national broadcasting company has been under constant state supervision. In the case of control over media content the audience of TVS is regarded as a 'representative' public body or in another words as a substitute for the disappearing civil society at the institutional level.

Political parties have no intention of establishing television channels of their own but they put pressure on national television. This pressure is most evident in the appointment of members of the Council or management or in the shaping of news and current affairs. At the end of last year the Supreme Court decided that the dismissal of the general director was not valid and he was re-instated. A few months after, the general director opposed the appointment of the editor of the news programme on the grounds that he had 'extremely inappropriate relations with his associates, extremely inappropriate relations to finances, and he is in a constant conflict with the general director himself' (Delo, 24 February, 1995). No reference was made to his professional standards.

Conclusion

The current situation in the media field in Slovenia is a kind of 'anthropological mutation' (Zolo, 1992, p. 170): public media which function as state companies under market conditions, and the print media which are more and more dependent on advertising income and at the same time pretend to have a 'watch dog' function. This failure was evident in debates about new media legislation where, in the final stages, civil society and the public disappeared from consideration. The rhetoric of the state claimed that state-controlled public television would serve the interest of everyone, but it was, in reality, in the interest of the politically powerful. The story of the building of new communication models after the fall of communism is a story about the 'rise and fall of the public sphere'.

Notes

1. In respect of the conflict between Serbian and Croatian interests inside the former Yugoslav state there was an important turning point in 1989. At that time the Serbian leadership came into direct conflict with the Slovene one and 'Slovenia was taking a stand that traditionally belonged to Croatia. As a result, in the eyes of Milošević's controlled media, the Slovenes became political Croats' (Banac, 1992, p. 161).
2. For the purposes of this article we are using some results from a research project done in 1987-8 (Bašić, Podmenik, Bekeš, 1989). This project was based on a content analysis of the most influential dailies and weeklies in Serbia, Croatia and Slovenia. The research period started with Tito's death and army intervention in Kosovo. Official sources (according to the dominant ideological interpretation) defined this event as 'counter-revolution' and in the mid-80s as terrorism. During 1984-87 the media was faced, on the institutional level,

with several forms of state interference (closing down of some newspapers, sanctions against journalists and editors, and very often the usage of Article 133 of the Yugoslav Penal Code sanctioning an *opine* offence) and on the other side - on the content level - in a growing number of critical articles. In this period there was no great difference between the press in Serbia, Croatia and Slovenia. The differences became visible after 1986 with the process of national consolidation in some republics, especially when the Serbian leadership identified Serbian 'national interest' (in particular) with the 'protection of Yugoslav national interest' (in general).

3.   In 1984 the Slovene Youth Organization at its congress clearly demanded democratization. The congress put under question the position of the Yugoslav People's Army (JNA). The Slovene youth magazine 'Mladina' publicly exposed the corruption of leading generals and arms trafficking with the authoritarian regime in Ethiopia. After numbers of critical articles JNA spokesmen described this critical approach as an 'attack on JNA' and an 'attack on Yugoslavia' in general. Disregarding the fact that the JNA functioned as a 'state within a state' (it was represented in the collective state presidency) it was trying to preserve an exclusive position as the unifying binding element for all special interests. 'Obsessed with portraying itself as "blameless" in a deviant society, the JNA has always presented itself as an island of brotherhood and unity, purified of nationalism, liberalism, technocratism and similar abominations feared by "those outside"' (Salecl, 1994: 68). As a result, this symbolic universum which JNA was keeping so violently monolitic was the last territory for democratization.

4.   Slovenia with two million inhabitants has five dailies and among them is a popular tabloid Slovenske Novice (Slovene News) with the biggest circulation (c. 90.000). According to the new Media Act (adopted in 1994) nine private companies will get licences to operate television programmes. TV Slovenia (TVS) as a public television service has two channels operating over the whole national territory. The public broadcasting company is controlled by the Council, closely watched by political parties. Channel A, the first private television station in the former Yugoslavia was established in 1989 and started to broadcast two years later. In 1994 another regional TV station MMTV started to broadcast. The American company CME (Central European Media Enterprise) will invest in three private (regional) commercial TV stations: MMTV, Tele 59 and Channel A. Still, national television has the biggest audience share (70 per cent during the prime time), Channel A (five to eight per cent) and MMTV (0.5-1 per cent). On radio there are more than 40 new commercial stations. Slovenia has also a radio station set up to air religious programmes and owned by a publishing house related to the Catholic Church. The new Media Act strictly forbids ownership (including shares) of broadcast organizations by political parties, state institutions, religious organizations and non-government organizations.

5.   National Public Opinion Polls shows that two thirds of readers have no idea about the political affiliations of the Slovene dailies. Most of them put newspapers in the political centre with the exception of the Christian Democratic paper 'Slovenec' which ten per cent identified as strongly right orientated. The poll shows that 25 per cent of respondents think that Slovenian media have absolute freedom and 45 per cent characterize this freedom as partial.

21 Epilogue: The Attainment of Viability

JOHN R. ROBBINS

Auguries

The abandonment of socialism in the Soviet Union and the countries of Eastern Europe was brought about by the disillusion of their people with the performance of communist regimes. Their political and economic outcomes did not match the claims that they were progressing towards the best of all possible worlds. Rather than overtaking the rival western model they were falling further behind.

Having broken the cement of communism, it also turned out that three of these regimes did not possess the basic territorial legitimacy which would allow them to face the transition intact and this produced a splintering into 22 states, 19 of them new to the international scene.

The collapse of the old regimes was, in large measure, propelled by the proposition that a conversion to liberal democracy and a free market economy would create a more congenial and prosperous society. It soon became clear that, though the appropriate forms might readily be assumed, the desired consequences were more elusive. Competitive elections did not produce governments of great talent and free economies did not unleash a tide of productivity. On the contrary, governments were often unstable, their members' motives suspect and their management skills deficient; early economic results were usually seriously negative for all but a small proportion of the population.

Where new states were established they often found themselves under armed challenge from dissident groups within their borders and facing hostility from their neighbours. Having rejected the previous political vehicle as inadequate to the task of providing satisfactory outcomes, citizens of the transitional states found that the new model was far from flawless.

In the pursuit of viability under radically different conditions, it became clear that expectations had to be trimmed to take account of imperfections, both in the model being pursued and in its application to specific countries. To follow the concept of viability to its etymological origins, the basic requirement is that the route should be traversable, and not that it should provide an easy and comfortable passage. If it is not literally viable, further progress is prevented and retreat or inertia result.

What follows is an identification of the major factors affecting the viability of the new states in the three main dimensions of the transitional process - legitimization, democratization and economic performance. Each has its own intricate imperatives but is heavily dependent on the others. A summary of the relevant characteristics of each component is provided, with an indication of the basic requirements for the achievement of viability. This is followed by an account of their application in Slovenia[1].

Legitimization

This is the most basic element in the transition process and thus potentially the most disruptive, though once established it becomes a residual rather than an active component in the attainment of viability. Legitimacy requires the recognition that a state and its governing regime are appropriate and acceptable both externally and internally.

Externally the key measure is international recognition, with admission to the standard array of international organizations, and integration into the world economic system. The establishment of normal relations with neighbouring countries is particularly important in terms of the easy passage of people and trade. Hostility may restrict both and thus impede economic recovery. It may also lead to the encouragement or active support of dissident internal elements. This will particularly be the case when an adjacent country has territorial claims on the new state.

Internally there needs to be, in the first place, an acceptance by an overwhelming majority of the population that the configuration of the new state is appropriate. This is particularly the case where democratization is the major driving force of the transition. The reason for the disintegration of the three socialist federations in the first place was the fact that one of the first democratic rights to be exercised was that of ethnic self-determination.

Ethnicity rapidly manifested itself as the major determinant of a state's political authenticity but also, since ethnic settlement patterns rarely conform to rules of geographic convenience, it is the major source of dissent. Where a new state has validated its emergence as the 'homeland' of a dominant ethnic group, this may well incite further demands for secession or for the re-adjustment of international borders to better suit the political aspirations of other ethnic groups.

There is a secondary level of legitimation faced by all the transitional states in respect of regime change. Having abandonned the socialist governmental model, in its various forms, they need to secure overwhelming popular acceptance of the new constitution if it is to operate effectively. The persistence of substantial groups wedded to the old regime or the emergence of extremist groups unleashed by the pluralization of politics may prevent the attainment of the necessary level of acceptance.

There is the question of what degree of dissidence might be tolerated by a state before it should be considered a threat to its legitimacy. It is unlikely that any state would ever achieve total legitimacy, but the ability of a dissident group to destabilize it is dependent on the size of the group, its strategic location and the extremity of the measures it is prepared to engage in.

The most potent group in terms of its ability to dislocate the legitimization process is the military. As the ultimate guarantors of state sovereignty, the military may regard themselves as having a special role in determining the national interest. If they take over government, either directly or through proxies, there may be difficulties in establishing a new legitimacy but they are able to resort to coercion and to continue to deny power to the civilian government.

A further factor affecting legitimatization is the ability of the state to enforce the rule of law, ulimately by invoking its monopoly of violence. The relaxation of control associated with the liberalization of previously authoritarian regimes may encourage the rise of criminal activities and, if these become too severe, confidence in the state will be eroded. This will be accentuated if members of the government are assumed to have criminal links. Corruption in government circles, and certainly allegations of its prevalence, is readily generated by the rise of a free market economy and the acceptance of political lobbying.

Providing the requirements of legitimacy are met, these factors become an apparently inert base on which the more active elements of the transition may be built. If they prove to be insecure they will literally undermine the foundations.

Democratization

Any definition of democracy, even within the confines of its liberal democratic form, is likely to be strongly contested, but there are certain undisputed core elements. The holding of open and competitive elections to produce presidents, parliaments and local governments, in conditions of freedom of association and of expression, is a necessary first step. There are innumerable arrangements to achieve these requirements and how well the particular provisions of a given state meet them is a matter for specific assessment.

The party system is a key element of the operational viability of a democratic system. All significant group interests should be reflected within the party arena and all should ultimately take part in government. In a majoritarian system this is presumed to be achieved by alternation in government. The crucial demonstration of democratic consolidation is when an incumbent government surrenders power, particularly to a party which was previously proscribed. To be permanently in opposition is to encourage disaffection from the regime. Holding power in sub-national government may provide some compensation for exclusion at national level. In a consensual model shifting coalitions may provide the necessary periodic experience of government, or a permanent grand coalition may provide for continuous inclusion.

The party system is also an important factor in determining the participatory element in the democratization process. The early transitional period tends to produce an enhanced degree of activism but its sustenance is difficult. The desirable forms and degree of political participation are the most debated and contested themes in democratic theory. A residual standard requires that the majority of citizens believe they could have some impact on the political process if they so wished, and that this belief is supported by at least an occasional practical demonstration.

Some political theorists and certainly many political practitioners prefer the level of participation to be lower rather than higher. What is in question here is the extent to which the level might be depressed without creating a degree of apathy, or even of alienation, that would undermine the legitimacy of the regime as a whole. Possible indicators of inadequacy in this respect would be low turn-out at elections, low membership of political parties and a demonstration that party leaders were paying only cursory attention to the requirements of their constituencies.

Considerable attention has been paid by East European political scientists to the development of socio-political pluralism and the associated concept of civil society. They are considered to be an important adjunct to the formal political components of a democratic state, providing both a separate and autonomous system of social regulation and an independent base for forays into the state arena. Evidence of the existence of such social formations is a an array of free-standing organizations and associations - churches, trade unions, employers' associations, professional associations, and a variety of interest groups. The independence of such bodies needs to be demonstrated by their ability to manage their own affairs within a minimalist framework of legal regulation to safeguard against abuse.

The possible distortions of democracy emanating from a civil and plural society also need to be invigilated. The over-enthusiastic withdrawal of the state from the extremes of interventionism may leave open opportunities for oppression and exploitation by civil agents. The access of interest groups to government may well privilege some and disadvantage others. Most specifically, neo-corporatist arrangements need close examination for evidence that they do advance the general interest rather than that of some specific group or groups.

Economic performance

The immediate effect of all transitional episodes has been economic disruption. Output has fallen, inflation and unemployment have risen to dangerous levels, industry has been devastated and trade patterns dislocated. All of these factors have to be brought under control before the promised economic benefits can be realised.

The precipitate introduction of a market economy promises no easy solution and may, on the contrary, prove counterproductive. Many observers recommend a policy of gradualism with a continued major role for state intervention during a managed economic transition.

Particularly where there is a need for massive economic reconstruction, adequate sources of capital need to be tapped. Without a proven record of economic success and with political stability often in doubt, many transitional regimes have difficulty attracting investment funds, either from domestic or international sources. Agencies such as the World Bank may be prepared to take on a developmental role but they will extract a price in requiring conformity to their own rules of economic probity.

Entrepreneurship appears to have been latent in socialist economies, and frequently so in the ranks of the old state management cadres as well as among those frustrated by state control. It needs to be on a scale and in a form which will re-orientate the existing economy and provide the necessary drive to compensate for lost productivity and provide a surge beyond previous levels. 'Converted' entrepreneurs may attempt to extend the lifespan of failing operations, and small scale boutique operators and import agencies may enliven the shopping precincts, but they do little to improve overall economic results.

Trade unions may experience a new lease of life in transitional regimes since they are no longer required to confine themselves to supporting the state. If they cultivate their new oppositional role too enthusiastically they may both disrupt the ongoing process and defend the old industrial patterns in an attempt to preserve members' employment. The introduction of democracy gives them a possible influence on political outcomes, and thus government economic policy, which they did not previously enjoy.

Labour patterns in any modern economy are subject to constant and radical change. The transitional economies, to an even greater degree than the established western cases, need provisions for re-deployment, re-training and the general enhancement of skills if they are to attain the necessary levels of flexibility in a high technology economy. The socialist guarantee of employment is one of the first casualties of the economic transition and disruptions to the economic structure will produce high levels of unemployment.

The departure from a closely managed economy usually entails a diminished concern for an equitable distribution of income, including a changed attitude to social security benefits and the overall social wage. If there is a substantial shift in the distribution of income and wealth the electorate's tolerance of such circumstances becomes a factor in maintaining a political equilibrium.

Even where transitional governments have decided to withdraw from direct and intensive involvement in economic management they are responsible for overall financial and fiscal results and are thus judged by them. Budgetary outcomes, balance of trade and payments figures, the inflation rate, investment levels, days lost through strikes, employment levels and growth in the GDP are all measures thrown into the balance of judgement about a government's performance.

Slovenian legitimacy

Slovenia had substantial initial advantages in its pursuit of legitimacy. It was already constituted as a politico-administrative unit of the Yugoslav Federation with a susbtantial degree of autonomy. Its population was overwhelmingly Slovene with only minor spillovers of adjacent nationalities into its territory.

The pursuit of independence was carefully managed so as to build upon this basis. In the first instance, Slovene negotiators pursued concessions from federal authorities which would have permitted the continuation of Yugoslavia as a confederation or, as some termed it, an asymmetric federation. It was only the intransigence of the dominant, principally Serbian, group that propelled them towards complete independence.

Once that goal was set, it was pursued by incremental, constitutional means and confirmed by a plebiscite of the people in December 1990. There was no actual rupture in the transfer of legitimacy but rather a careful legal validation of the new constitution from the provisions of the old.

The disruption of that legalistic process came from the federal army's attempt at taking control of Slovenian territory in June 1991, following the unilateral declaration of independence. This episode accelerated and consolidated the process of separation by demonstrating the hostility of the federal authorities and acting as a focus for an expression of Slovenian patriotism. The 'ten-day war' fortuitously produced a dramatic and symbolic climax to what was otherwise a deliberately down-played process which might have left a residual ambiguity about allegiance. There was a mass mobilization for civil defence and the rapid improvisation of a military force which won its objectives with little destruction of property and few casualties.[2]

The constitution of the new republic was carefully framed to provide all the standard guarantees of political and personal freedom. In particular, the Hungarian and Italian minorities were given guarantees for the maintenance of their linguistic and cultural distinctiveness within their own districts and were allotted seats in parliament.[3]

The success of this process is demonstrated by the degree of consensus achieved in the new state. Ethnic homogeneity is no guarantee of such a consensus. Serbia has seen violent clashes between the police and Serbians protesting at the direction of their new state, as well as those between the security forces and Albanians. Slovenia has its political differences but their resolution is contained within legitimate channels.

External recognition was achieved as part of the European Union-brokered ceasefire with the federal authorities. Slovenia has quickly produced a diplomatic service and gained membership of an array of international organizations.

The ultimate prize, membership of the European Union, lies apparently within its grasp but frustratingly elusive. It is acknowledged that, together with the Czech Republic, it can meet the necessary economic criteria for membership. As a small nation of only two million people, its attachment would hardly be noticed. The major obstacle is that any further extension of the EU requires the establishment of a general policy towards the admission of all central and eastern European states.

Slovenia has chosen not to make a major issue of the cross-border Slovenian minorities in Italy and Austria. Both of those countries have contributed to the initial recognition of Slovenia and to the reconstruction of its economy.

Italy's favour is not without ambivalence. It has re-opened the question of Italian property rights in Slovenia which were thought to have been settled with the previous Yugoslav regime. It has also expressed concern about the welfare of the Italian minority remaining in Slovenia, as part of a broader attempt to re-open the status of Istria. This 'sabre-rattling' took on a more threatening form when Italy deployed troops on the Slovenian border in August 1993, ostensibly because an illegal arms shipment discovered in Maribor breached the embargo on the former Yugoslavia.

The conversion of the Croatian border to an international rather than an internal one has also created some problems. The border in Istria was not well demarcated and is now in dispute as frontier posts are established. The area is particularly sensitive; it was the subject of a long postwar territorial dispute between Italy and Yugoslavia; it provides Slovenia with an abbreviated stretch of coastline; and it is a safe area for the remnants of the Croatian tourist trade while the Dalmatian coast is under threat. There is also contention over a nuclear power station, located in Slovenia but delivering substantial supplies of electricity to Croatia, which the Slovenian government wishes to close. However, these are irritants rather than potential causes of serious conflict.

The major threat to Slovenian legitimacy undoubtedly comes from the remainder of ex-Yugoslavia. Until there is a lasting settlement in the remainder of Yugoslavian territory there can be no guarantee that the current situation is secure. The exodus of Serbs from Croatia means that the seat of possible future conflict is further removed from Slovenia, but Bosnia remains a powder-keg and the original ethnic confrontation in Kosovo smoulders on. It is not inconceivable that the entire area could erupt into an even greater turmoil, since the contending parties are now better organized and militarily equipped.

Slovenia has studiously distanced itself from its former partners, preferring to present itself as an 'Alpine' rather than a Balkan country. The revival of a Yugoslav irredentism as an outcome of Serbian political manoeuvring would be threatening, although Slovenia is quite readily excluded from such a vision, as it was in the late 1980s.[4] Full-scale hostilities between Croatia and Serbia would necessarily have a spill-over effect, if only in the production of a flood of refugees.

The existing body of refugees in Slovenia from the previous conflicts in Bosnia and Croatia has caused little disruption but it has raised questions of inclusiveness. Their numbers are not large, though it has been pointed out that they are more numerous than the ethnic minorities who are accorded special constitutional treatment.[5] There is a degree of detachment from the problem as part of the general process of disassociation from the former Yugoslavia.

There is also an ambivalence in Slovenian attitudes. International agencies report the adequacy of arrangements for their accommodation but there is also evidence that standards are below those that would be considered desirable in a relatively prosperous country. Despite this, there is some Slovenian resentment at their presence and what some see as an unnecessary diversion of resources. Perhaps the raising of a compulsory national levy in support of the refugees salved the conscience of those who cared about their plight but roused the ire of those who begrudged it.

Provided there is a permanent resolution of the difficulties in the remainder of the ex-Yugoslavia, many of the refugees would probably elect to return home. Under current circumstances, there is no prospect of the refugees becoming a destabilizing influence politically, nor an intolerable economic drain.

The military are also an unlikely threat to the stability of Slovenia. There is no military tradition among Slovenes and they were greatly underrepresented in the professional officer corps of the Yugoslav army[6] (though of course required to undertake military service on the same basis as all other nationalities). While the rapidly assembled defence force was celebrated for its performance in the ten-day war against the Yugoslav army, it was not involved in the negotiations which led to the formation of the new state. The new Slovenian defence force is deliberately low-key and low-cost and accepts that it is subservient to the democratically elected government. There is no prospect of the army deciding that it better embodies the 'national interest' than the government.

There is considerable popular concern that the liberalization of state control has brought an increase in criminal activity. Coupled with allegations of corruption in government circles, this contributes an adverse element to evaluations of the transition.

The official statistics of criminal offences (see Appendix II, Table 4), in fact, indicate a substantial reduction since independence, overall and in most individual categories. In its turn, this provokes the standard reservations about the relationship between the actual incidence of crime, its reportage and the rate of conviction. Corruption charges may be regarded as a normal outcome of political rivalry and the consequence of a new 'government transparency' rather than an actual increase. It also brings into question the impact of media reportage on public perceptions, particularly now that it is no longer inhibited in its portrayal of negative messages about the condition of state and society.

The law and order debate is a familiar one to observers of western societies, as are claims of official corruption and other forms of malfeasance. It takes on a more crucial significance in a political system that is still in the process of consolidation and under close and critical scrutiny. If it is joined to other negative judgements about the effectiveness and appropriateness of the operations of the state, it might result in that state's rejection.

The speculation about official corruption, and its occassional justification, inevitably fuels cynicism about the probity of politicians, but they seem to be accorded a surprising degree of tolerance by citizens, providing their overall policies are deemed beneficial.

An under-emphasized feature of the establishment of Slovenia is its size, although Slovenians are well aware that their small population of two millions gives them a certain vulnerability and may act as an impediment to viability. Militarily they recognize their limitations by opting for a much reduced outlay on defence compared with the former Yugoslavia. Only a massive commitment to advanced equipment could compensate for the lack of manpower. They must rely largely on the politics of negotiation rather than anticipating a resort to the 'other means' of von Clausewitz's celebrated dictum.

There is also a presumption that small size is a handicap to economic achievement; it certainly limits the domestic market and the potential economies of scale. The general world trend towards relaxing tariffs should reduce these impediments and access to the EU market followed by full membership would finally remove them. In the meantime, the examples of Hong Kong and Singapore and, closer to home, Luxembourg and Iceland, indicate that smallness is no bar to economic prosperity.

There are political advantages to be obtained from a small population. Dahl and Tufte (1973) are persuasive in arguing that democracy is more readily achievable with a smaller population. The affairs of a small state are likely to be less complex than those of a larger one and shorter lines of communication give a government and politicians easier access to citizens, and, more importantly, permit readier flows in the reverse direction.

The establishment of Slovenia has given encouragement to the other aspiring Európean nationalists such as the Catalans, Basques and Scots whose small population is often advanced as a deterrent to independence. If the sub-nationalists' goal of a 'Europe of Regions' were to be realized, Slovenia would fit well into such a political pattern.

Democratization in Slovenia

Slovenian progress in democratization has been remarkable. Again, there were initial advantages which were carefully cultivated and built upon. The close association of the movement towards independence with the demand for democratization meant that each impulse supported the other. The League of Communists, by the time the critical period of application had arrived, was fully committed to both, so that there was no residual opposition from that quarter. Instead there was a swift conversion of the party and its leaders to a democratic commitment.

Neither did the relaxation of political constraints produce ultra-right or demagogic parties, as in Russia, to polarize the political spectrum. There was, in fact, a clustering around the centre, which creates a degree of volatility, since no great switch of political allegiance is needed to move between parties, but, conversely, permits the ready formation of coalitions - whose shifting composition requires no radical change of policy.

Despite the shifting coalitions there has been relatively stable government and these circumstances have strengthened the role of parliament. The preference for a strong parliamentary system over the strong presidential system opted for by many of the transitional countries has ensured that parties have a real sense of purpose and do not become wantonly obstructive. The need for the almost complete revision of the statute book also places an emphasis on the role of parliament.

An executive presidency has the advantage of ensuring that government is directed by a single party in situations where their political divergence makes collaboration between parties difficult. But this becomes counter-productive if the other parties use their position in parliament to obstruct the passage of policy decisions.

The Slovenian presidency has limited powers and there has been no political crisis to measure their extent. In the meantime, the incumbent, Milan Kučan, nicely personifies the evolutionary aspects of the new regime. A leading member of the League of Communists both federally and within Slovenia, he had been a prime architect of the reform process, a convert to the desirability of secession. He easily won the first free election to the Presidency in 1990 and repeated the exercise under the new constitution in 1992.

There is some concern that the new democracy will be diluted by the tendency of parties to become remote from their constituencies, mobilizing them only for the purposes of elections but otherwise paying little heed to their wishes. This appears to be a common tendency in the transitional countries, provoking the claim that 'civic elites have clearly preferred parliamentary activity over building strong social constituencies within the existing circumstances' (Cirtautus, 1994, p. 52).

The complex Slovenian electoral system was deliberately constructed to allow constituency, rather than party, determination of preferred candidates. However, the existence of an additional pool, while ostensibly devised to allow the better proportionality of seats, operates through party lists and thus permits parties to insulate chosen candidates against electoral discrimination. In the lead-up to the 1996 election there are numerous proposals for the reform of the electoral system, including one from the State Council. Since a change to the electoral law requires the assent of two-thirds of the State Assembly it is unlikely that any radical alteration will be entertained.

The self-serving tendency of party leaders is universal in politics but it is periodically offset by several factors; by the rise of new parties which better represent the popular will; by social movements which alert existing parties to their deficiencies; and by pressure-group activity which acts as an alternative channel of influence. These rectifying mechanisms depend, of course, on the existence of the institutions of a civil society and the development of a supportive political culture. The new Slovenian political system has not yet matured and 'consolidated' enough to make a final judgement on its attributes. Dahrendorf's (1990, p. 93) estimation that sixty years are required to provide the necessary institutional framework is probably excessive, as his supposition that the operational requirements of democracy can be achieved in six months is too brief.

There will necessarily be some initial disappointments as the practical workings of the system breach the idealistic expectations placed upon it. Complaint about the remoteness and lack of responsiveness of party leaders is not unknown in established democracies. Perhaps in this respect Slovenia has accelerated to a 'mature' phase of party operation. It becomes of greater concern if the compensatory mechanisms do not appear and if a single party becomes dominant and entrenched in government.

So far, this has not occurred, nor does it appear likely. None of the parties at the 1992 elections secured even a quarter of the votes cast, and given the ultimate proportionality of the electoral system, none had a quarter of the seats in the National Assembly.[7]

The party system is in a continual state of flux, with fission and fusion alternately expanding or diminishing the number of parties. Many of the parties which contested the first free elections in 1990 are difficult to trace in the list of contenders in 1992. This is due partly to the inevitable process of adjustment as the compatability of diverse policy commitments is tested in the arena of practical politics. It also reflects the marked personalization of politics and a tendency to form new parties in pursuit of individual ambition. Again this is not exceptional, even in mature democratic political systems. Neither is the number of parties. Lane and Ersson (1987, p. 183) show that most West European systems have a plural party system and that even the deterrent of a simple plurality voting system does not prevent the United Kingdom parliament from housing nine parties.

What is lacking in the Slovenian system thus far is a party, or parties, which have sufficient support and sufficient persistence to act as anchors while the rest of the party system undergoes its evolutionary convolutions. The Spanish transitional process was not impeded by the 1982 collapse of the initial party of government, the UCD, because the Socialist party was a stable and substantial component of the political scene and able to assume government during the prolonged period required for the centre-right to create a viable alternative party. The apparent chaos of the Italian political scene has had running through it (until the elections of 1994) the constant feature of the dominant Christian Democrat party which gave a substantial degree of continuity to government.

The absence of even one substantial party is no absolute obstacle to stable government, let alone viable government, though it may require a greater ingenuity in the management of political alliances. The Swiss manage very well with four parties of only moderate size by including all of them in a permanent grand coalition. The Finns, Dutch and Belgians do not attain the same constancy but still cope well enough with very fractionalized party systems. Reflecting further the experience of Finland, the Slovenian Presidency may well take on a more significant role should party fractionalization continue.

One positive outcome of the plurality of parties in Slovenia is that it has required both power-sharing and power rotation. The first freely elected parliament in May 1990 produced a coalition government with a Christian Democrat prime minister. He was replaced by a Liberal Democrat in May 1992, supported by a differently constituted coalition which included the post-communist Party of Democratic Renewal. The elections of December 1992 altered the balance in the distribution of parliamentary seats but the Liberal Democrats strengthened their position and kept the premiership, though again with a revised coalition. There were defections from that coalition in January 1993 and in April 1994. Finally, the loss of the United List of Social Democrats in January 1996 produced for the first time a minority government. A range of politicians from several parties has now had experience both of government office and of losing it.

The appearance of the Slovenian National Party (SNP) on the political scene has generated some concern about the rise of ethnic politics. The earlier observations of a latent Slovenian chauvinism (Schierup, 1991, p. 128) was not reflected in the first democratic elections in 1990, but the ten per cent vote won by the SNP in 1992 revived fears of an ultra-nationalist movement. Without a crisis to feed on it is unlikely to grow and may well be an ephemeral feature of the early stages of transition. It has already suffered the fate of other inaugural parties in suffering a split, which may be a precursor of its disappearance.

While there are disturbing auguries of the possibility of exploiting nationalist extremism in nearby transitional countries such as Slovakia and Serbia, the socio-political circumstances are different in Slovenia. The ethnic minorities are too small to be considered threatening and there is no history of severe internal ethnic conflict.

It should also be noted that right-wing extremism is present in the established democracies such as France, with its National Front; and Italy, which is witnessing a resurgent, if reformed, MSI. While they produce a degree of nervousness among mainstream politicians and liberal observers they are not considered a realistic threat to democracy. Indeed, they may provide yet another rectifying mechanism to remind the major parties that they need strong links with a basic constituency if they are to flourish. Cirtautus (1994, p. 54) sees nationalist parties as 'less a testament to the primordial strength of nationalism in the region than a reflection of the effective way in which these parties have taken advantage of the largely self-inflicted organizational weaknesses of the liberally oriented parties'.

Economic transition

In economic terms Slovenia again had inbuilt advantages in embarking on the transition process. It was the most prosperous and economically advanced region of Yugoslavia with established export markets. On the other hand, this made it extremely vulnerable. A higher standard of living has further to fall and a highly industrialized region cannot so readily fall back on subsistence agriculture if circumstances become dire. The rapid disintegration of the former Yugoslavia and the onset of hostilities deprived Slovenia of the major destination for its manufactures as well as its considerable assets in other republics.

The impact of the post-secessionist depression was mitigated, not only by the psychological benefits of achieving independence and democracy, but by the fact that the Yugoslav economy had been in trouble for some time and was reaching a state of crisis by the late 1980s.

Despite being dependent on a rather shaky coalition, the first democratically-elected government and its successors have been able to pursue strong economic policies which produced some casualties but brought financial and fiscal rectitude. Inflation was brought down to acceptable levels, the budget was balanced, foreign currency reserves increased and the plunge in GDP finally reversed to produce positive growth.

Once it became clear that Slovenia had escaped the turmoil of the remainder of Yugoslavia, it began to attract foreign investment as one of the 'safe' post-communist states.[8] Again, an advantage of smallness is apparent, since the impact of a given amount of capital investment is much greater in a country like Slovenia than it would be in Russia or even Poland. Similarly, while unemployment may appear high when expressed as a percentage, as a raw figure of around 85,000 it is much more manageable and may be soaked up by relatively modest capital investment.

The peculiar nature of capital ownership in Yugoslavia has produced a dilemma of conversion which is taking time to resolve satisfactorily. While the matter of the official ownership of enterprises was not legally clear, there was an outright dedication of control to the agencies of 'self-management', whoever might have been the actual power-wielders.

Proposals for privatization have met resistance from workers who have become accustomed to the form, if not the substance, of self-management. Paradoxically, liberalization has permitted the continuation of the unions from the previous regime and provided them with a new and more active role. Whereas they were a part of the state apparatus under the previous regime, they can now take on the more adversarial and promotional role familiar to western systems.

Union impact is potentially weakened by a degree of divisiveness. The most powerful grouping is the Association of Free Trade Unions of Slovenia, successor to the original communist unions, but 'oppositional' elements have produced a competitor in Independence-Confederation of New Trade Unions of Slovenia. Union membership overall remains high so that their impact on industrial negotiations and as a political lobby group is considerable.

The status of the employers' associations is much more ambivalent, since in many cases the 'employers' are still the managers of the old system rather than a completely new breed of entrepreneur. While this does not shield them from a possibly confrontational trade union movement, they remain suspect so far as the 'oppositional' political parties are concerned.

This fragmentation and incipient political conflict on the industrial scene has inhibited the workings of the neo-corporatist Economic-Social Council, designed to facilitate collaborative economic management. Whatever the long-term desirability of such arrangements, there would be some advantage in establishing agreed procedures and policies during a period of radical change in the economy.

Summary and conclusion

It is in its institutional structure that Slovenia exhibits the greatest uncertainty, despite its rapid achievement of positive indicators. The basic institutions of government are working adequately, and in many cases well. The two major flaws in the political system arise not from constitutional provisions but from the party system. One arises from the fractionalized party system, particularly when the fractions are in a continual state of flux, making the formation of stable government difficult. The other is the perception of a 'democratic deficit', with parties making little attempt to cultivate participatory consituencies and a consequential frustration and disillusionment among citizens that they are disregarded.

It could be argued that the electoral system might be modified to allow the easier evolution of dominant parties and thus avoid the uncertainties of a fractionalized party system. This would, however, exacerbate the other problem of a lack of articulation between parties and their constituencies, if it were to short-circuit a considerable proportion of the electorate and deny them a realistic voice in the determination of government.

The main solution to both problems, given the apparently narrow span of Slovenian political preferences, lies with the political elite. Adopting a tendency to combine rather than to divide, together with a vigorous and continuous attempt at engaging their party constituencies, would remedy a great deal of the current 'democratic deficit'.

Local government is another area of institutional reform which has been slow to progress and where difficulties of application are foreseen. The substantial use of the previous local government system as a field agency for the delivery of state services does place in question its localist credentials but questions arise as to whether the structure and functions of the new system will foster local democracy and provide for the adequate delivery of local services.

In the economic sector, the matter and manner of privatization still needs to be fully and finally resolved before the industrial sector can be stabilized. The newly activated post-communist trade unions are likely to be vigorously involved in this process as well as in broader questions of employee benefits. Securing the agreement of the trade unions is now made more difficult by their pluralization into competing political camps. A firm lead by the government in promoting a generally acceptable outcome is needed but, on these issues in particular, political ideology often obstructs the achievement of the common good. Cirtautas (1994, p. 46) again provides a cogent assessment of the situation, 'Eastern Europe may well face a future of political instability and economic stagnation. ...Without an accepted sovereign authority that can mandate a stable balance between the general interest of the nation and the particular interests comprising it, it is not possible to enforce outcomes that work to the short-term disadvantage of particular interests'.

The nub of the question is, of course, in the identification of which policy might best serve the general interest, since few sectional interests will confess that their proposals are intended only to benefit them.

There is a distinction here between the economic and political components of the transitional process. The democratic process merely offers a means by which a complex society may choose between a diversity of possible goals. There is a variety of institutional forms which may permit the operation of the system, but they constitute the vehicle and not the ultimate direction it is intended to take.

The economic process is much more rigidly determined. There is presumed to be a pre-determined end of privatization and a free market economy. Dahl (1990, p. 87) in one of his occasional excursions into economics, has sounded a warning, 'It is no simple or easy task to manage a market-oriented economy in such a way as to maximize its advantages, which are great, and to minimize its disadvantages which are equally great... we should not react to the failures of state ownership and central direction of the economy... by concluding that the best alternative is to turn everything over to unregulated markets. Not only would this be a misreading of the experience of the advanced democratic countries; for any country that chose to follow this path it would be a misfortune'.

There are those who believe that there is a 'third way' (Phillips and Ferfila, 1992), which adopts some aspects of free-market capitalism but also retains some elements of state-managed socialism. The previous Yugoslav regime was presumed to have developed a hybrid economic form which was then identified as a 'third way', but its failure consigned it to the scrapheap of history, though with varying diagnoses as to its faults. Some attributed it to the continuing strength of central planning, despite the rhetoric of self-management and market socialism. Others thought the self-management programme flawed in concept as well as conduct - a 'Bermuda Triangle' of economic aspirations (Myant, 1993, pp. 35-42, 122-6).

Dahrendorf (1990, pp. 53-62) despatches the notion of a possible 'third way' for the economic re-organization of Eastern Europe as a 'mirage'. To an extent the argument is a semantic one since he concedes that there is an array of western models with quite diverse characteristics. The question is whether the ultimate disposition of the Eastern European countries, once they have completed their transition, extends this array, and whether those extensions collectively constitute a distinctive grouping.

What should caution us all in our attempt at analysis and prediction is the starting-point of this entire process - the collapse of Communism in the Soviet Union and Eastern Europe. No analysis properly identified the precise nature of the political strains on the communist system. No prediction prepared us for its sudden collapse. We should now be apprehensive that we are not similarly caught unawares by some further great shift in historical trends.

An additional caution is that we should not expect the transitional countries to attain a state of perfection unachieved by the existing liberal democracies with market economies. Viability might be regarded as requiring an ability to cope with crises despite imperfections of structure and performance. To extend Dahrendorf's (1990, p. 93) proposition that a democratic state should not merely be a 'fair-weather' vessel, it should be recognized that it will face 'ill-weather' with something less than an A1 rating.

We can be reasonably assured that the new nation-state of Slovenia will be facing the problems, not only of the current transition, but of the transitions to come, as an independent entity. Its fortunes will depend largely on its own direction and, not least, on the maintenance of an effective political system. The ultimate test of viability lies in the capacity of a political system to engage its constituent population in its own direction so that citizens accept the consequences, good, bad or indifferent, as being of their own making. This was the test which the previous regimes of Eastern Europe failed. A successful transition depends on its attainment.

Notes

1. Most of the chapters in this book were produced in 1995 and events since then are necessarily excluded. This epilogue takes note of major events up to early 1996, including the change in the governing coalition in January.
2. Figures for casualties in the conflict vary widely. Silber and Little (1995, p.183) give them as JNA - 44 dead, 187 wounded; Slovenian casualties are said to be in 'single figures, most of them foreign lorry-drivers (sic)'. Europa Yearbook claims that 'in all, 18 people had been killed in the conflict' (1994, p. 2641). Cohen (1993, p. 224) gives them as Slovenian - 12 killed and 144 wounded; JNA - 37 killed and 163 wounded.
3. The first issue of the *Journal of International Relations* published by the Slovenian Society for International Relations deals extensively with the question of the ethnic minorities, including summaries of the reports of several international missions investigating the matter (Krmelj, 1994, pp. 49-53) and a digest of the constitutional provisions concerning their rights (JIR, pp. 54-76).
4. Milošević is claimed to have willingly allowed the Slovenes to opt out of the federation since they played no part in his Greater Serbia design. Silber and Little (1995, p. 183) describe him and Kučan as being 'in cahoots'. Some elements in the military recognized the signal that Slovenian secession would send, and preferred to keep them, by force if necessary, within the fold. They were overruled. (Glenny, 1992, pp. 96-7).

5.   The Hungarian minority numbers around 8,500, the Italian 3,000. The total number of refugees is difficult to ascertain as many of them are lodged privately. A first wave in September 1991, from Croatia, is estimated at around 30,000 and a second in April 1992, from Bosnia, around 40,000. In 1993, 45,000 were registered with the Red Cross of Slovenia and 14,000 of these were in 'refugee collection centres', mainly old army barracks. A further 25,000 are thought to be housed privately (Grizold, 1994, pp. 35-44).

6.   Slovenes were not inclined to pursue a military career. They provided only 2.8 per cent of professional army officers, while the Serbs made up 60 per cent (Mircev, 1993, p.383).

7.   The general election of 6 December 1992 produced the following results in parliamentary seats (percentage vote in brackets):

Liberal Democratic Party	22 (23.7%)
Slovenian Christian Democrats	15 (14.5%)
United List	14 (13.6%)
Slovenian National Party	12 (9.9%)
Slovenian People's Party	10 (8.8%)
Democratic Party	6 (5.0%)
Greens of Slovenia	5 (3.7%)
Social Democratic Party of Slovenia	4 (3.3%)
Hungarian and Italian Minorities	2
Others	0 (17.9%)
TOTAL	90

     (there is a three per cent threshold but the seats for ethnic minorities are allocated by the constitution and are not dependent on voting levels).

8.   Zwass (1995, p. 161) claims that 90 per cent of all foreign investment in post-socialist countries is allocated to Poland, Hungary, Czech Republic and Slovenia.

Appendix I
Chronology of attainment of independence of Republic of Slovenia
Compiled by Mirjam Kotar

4 May 1980
Josip Broz-Tito, the Yugoslav President for 35 years, died. The principles that had defined Yugoslav unity - the power of the working class, self-management, officially declared brotherhood and unity among Yugoslav nations - were left without support of his charisma.

11 March - 2 April 1981
Demonstrations of Albanians in Kosovo, Slovenian representatives argued in favour of peaceful settlement. The Central Committee of the League of Communists of Serbia (LCS) raised the question of the relationship between Serbia and its autonomous provinces, Kosovo and Vojvodina. The 'centralists' pressed for the abolition of the special status of autonomous provinces.

24 September 1984
First press reports of claims by the Serbian Academy of Science and Art that Serbs in Kosovo and parts of Croatia are subject to physical, political, legal and cultural genocide. They defined a new concept on the historical right of the Serbs to establish a complete national and cultural integrity irrespective of their place of domicile. They demanded a greater share of influence in the state representative bodies, arguing that the Serbs are the most numerous nation in Yugoslavia, and that they required Yugoslavia to become a unitary state.

23 - 24 November 1984
At the 18th meeting of the Central Committee of the LCS Milošević publicly condemned Slovenian and Croatian ideas of confederalism.

22 October 1986
The SFRY Presidency and the Central Committee of the LCY adopted a document, 'Information on fundamental characteristics of the ideological-political situation in society and in the LCY, and on the penetration of the bourgeois right and other antisocialist forces'. It was criticized by members of the LC of Slovenia as an attempt to oppose and censor ideas about Yugoslavian constitutional change.

11 February 1987
A SFRY Federal Assembly adopted a SFRY Presidency proposal for amendments to the 1974 constitution to counter alleged anti-communist and secessionist tendencies. Opposition generated among cultural organizations (in particular Slovene Writers' Association), professional societies, and general public in Slovenia.

25 February 1987
The monthly cultural journal, 'Nova revija' no. 57, published with the title 'Contributions to the Slovene national program'. The Oppositional intellectuals discussed the problem of Slovene statehood, the position of a nation in the (post)modern epoch, the historical and ideological elements of the position of the Slovene nation among other nations, and a program of political transformation for Slovenia. The Central Committee of the League of Communists of Slovenia (LCS), headed by Milan Kučan, decided not to prosecute the authors, but defined the published ideas as dangerous and never to be implemented.

18 March 1987
The Slovene Assembly adopted the SFRY Presidency proposal for constitutional amendments.

23 - 24 September 1987
At the 8th meeting of the Central Committee of the LC of Serbia 'cadre differentiation' started, with the ousting of all leading cadres not supporting Milošević.

15 January 1988
The Federal Assembly adopted a new federal budget for 1988 with an increase of 87 per cent.

12 February 1988
The popular Slovenian magazine, 'Mladina' (Youth), published an article about a general of the Yugoslav People's Army (YPA) and the federal secretary for public defence and their role in the arms trade with underdeveloped countries. Later issues dealt with the privileges of the army officers.

13 February 1988
The Federal Secretariat for Public Defence decided to act against attacks on the YPA.

25 March 1988
At the meeting of the Military Council (a mixed party and army body) in Belgrade the situation in Slovenia was defined as a special war against YPA and possibility discussed of military intervention in Slovenia.

29 March 1988
A secret session of the Presidency of the LCY discussed the possibility of repressing opposition in Slovenia. The Slovene representatives opposed the plans of the military to gain more political authority, although they kept this secret from the public in Slovenia at that time.

25 April 1988
Slovene Writers' Association organized a second discussion on constitutional changes. Together with the Slovene Sociological Association they prepared and published an alternative constitution, for a Republic of Slovenia.

13 May 1988
The 'Slovene Farmers' Union' was formed as the first of the independent political organizations.

19 May 1988
Milošević was elected as President of the Central Committee of the LC of Serbia.

26 May 1988
The SFRY Presidency denied rumours of a proposed military intervention in Slovenia.

31 May 1988
Janez Janša arrested by the Ljubljana police for writing articles for 'Mladina'. The Ljubljana Military Command arrested Ivan Borštner, an army officer.

4 June 1988
Another two persons arrested. David Tasić, a journalist on the magazine 'Mladina', and its managing editor, Franci Zavrl. The allegations were of betraying a military secret (notes on military intervention in Slovenia). All four were indicted by the military prosecutor. Case known as JBTZ.

2 June 1988
At the Plenum of Slovene Workers in Culture the establishment of Slovene Democratic Intelligentsia Union was proposed.

3 June 1988
The Committee for the Defence of Janez Janša was founded. Later expanded into the Committee for the Defence of Human Rights with more than 100,000 individual and 1,000 collective members. The Committee defined the process as illegitimate, opposed military jurisdiction over civilian offenders, demanded correct procedure for the four, including a free choice of lawyers and a public trial. They opposed the use of Serbo-Croatian language in a legal procedure on Slovene territory.

21 June 1988
In Ljubljana about 35,000 people took part in demonstrations against the military trial.

24 June 1988
Serbs in Kosovo established a 'Committee for Organizing Demonstrations in Kosovo and Outside the Provinces'. This Committee attacked legal authorities in Vojvodina and Montenegro. They prepared a mass 'meeting of truth' in Ljubljana on the grounds of the anti-Serb politics of Slovenes with regard to the Kosovo question.

12 July 1988
The Federal Government proposed an 133 per cent increase in the federal budget for 1989.

18 July 1988
The military trial against the four began. There were daily mass demonstrations in front of the military court and in other parts of Ljubljana and Slovenia. The Slovene authorities moved from diplomatic demands for a fair process towards an open protest against the trial.

27 July 1988
The trial against JBTZ finished. They were sentenced to terms of between six months to four years imprisonment.

27 - 29 July 1988
At the Plenum of the Central Committee of the LCY the situation in Kosovo was discussed. The Slovene representatives again particularly call for dialogue between Albanians and Serbs.

21 September 1988
The Committee for the Defence of Human Rights published a report criticizing the army for interference in civilian matters even before JBTZ.

17 - 21 October 1988
Demonstrations by Albanians in Kosovo suppressed ruthlessly.

19 November 1988
In Belgrade a million people demonstrated in support of Serbian politics on Kosovo.

21 November 1988
SFRY constitutional amendments adopted as a compromise between centralist and separatist tendencies, therefore no significant changes resulted.

1 December 1988
The Slovene Executive Council refused the federal budget proposal for the year 1989.

19 December 1988
Slovene Assembly refuses 1989 federal budget, urging reduction in federal spending.

11 January 1989
Establishment of the Slovene Democratic Union as the first independent political party in Slovenia.

21 February 1989
The beginning of the mass strikes of the Albanians in Kosovo.

28 February 1989
The League of Communists of Slovenia together with the opposition organized a meeting in support of Albanians in Kosovo. On the same day the mass anti-Slovene demonstrations organized in Serbian towns.

1 March 1989
Serbia announced the economic boycott of Slovenian products.

28 March 1989
Amendments to the constitution of Socialist Republic of Serbia abolished the autonomous status of the provinces Vojvodina and Kosovo.

8 May 1989
The Slovene Writers' Association, Slovene Democratic Union, Slovene Farmers' Union, Social Democratic Union of Slovenia and Slovene Christian-Social Movement prepared a 'May Declaration', in deploring the situation of Slovenes in Yugoslavia and demanding a sovereign state of Slovenia based on democratic foundations, including political pluralism and respect for human rights. Milošević became President of the Republic of Serbia.

22 May 1989
Milošević defined the situation in Slovenia as fascist and demanded a change in the Slovene position on Kosovo.

1 June 1989
Slovene Executive Council refused a proposal for the increase in the federal budget that was, in spite of the Slovene opposition, accepted in March 1989. An increase in the federal budget was confirmed in July 1989.

22 June 1989
In answer to the opposition's 'May Declaration' the Slovene government published a 'Basic Charter of Slovenia', outlining a proposal for Slovene sovereignty within Yugoslavia.

27 September 1989
Amendments to the constitution of the Socialist Republic of Slovenia declared the superiority of the republican constitution to the federal, established the right of self-determination, the right of secession, and free elections. This provoked mass anti-Slovene meetings in Serbia and Montenegro, where people demanded arms to fight Slovenia.

7 November 1989
First notice of a Serb-led 'meeting of truth', to be held in Ljubljana on the 1st of December, when participants from the whole of Yugoslavia would help to dismiss the separatist Slovene leaders. The Slovene authorities banned the meeting, fearing incidents. Serbian politicians and public defined this ban as an attack on Serbs and severed all political, economic, and cultural links with Slovenes.

10 November 1989
Federal Assembly accepted a second increase in the federal budget for 1989.

22 - 23 December 1989
11th Congress of the League of Communists of Slovenia characterized itself as a modern left political party supporting the principles of the market economy, democracy and human rights.

27 December 1989
DEMOS established as a coalition of the new parties to campaign jointly at the first free elections.

8 January 1990
A free general election in Slovenia called for the April.

17 January 1990
DEMOS organized a meeting where the 'Declaration on Slovene Self-determination' was accepted. They demanded a referendum on the question of the future status of Slovenia.

20 - 22 January 1990
A special congress of the League of Communists of Yugoslavia was held in Belgrade. Following the constant voting down of Slovene proposals the Slovene representatives withdrew from the congress. The congress continued without Slovene representatives.

27 January 1990
The first congress of the Slovene Christian Democrats held in Ljubljana.

29 January 1990
The Central Committee of the LC of Serbia claimed that support from the Slovenian and Croatian governments was responsible for the worsening of the security situation in Kosovo.

4 February 1990
Slovene government ordered withdrawal of Slovene police units from the federal police forces and the last Slovene unit returned from Kosovo.

20 February 1990
The Slovenian Writers' Association withdrew from the Yugoslav Writers' Association.

22 February 1990
As the Serb economic blockade of Slovenia continued, Slovenia decided to reduce the Slovene contribution to the federal budget by the amount attributed to economic projects in Serbia.

24 February 1990
The first congress of the Social Democratic Union of Slovenia held in Ljubljana.

27 February 1990
Socialist Union demanded that Slovene recruits should serve their term on the territory of Slovenia. In Ljubljana there was a mass protest against the departure of Slovene recruits in Kosovo.

6 March 1990
Federal Committee for National Defence accepted a proposal on legislative amendments to give border control to the military. Slovene representatives did not vote. In the following days there were protest meetings on Slovenian borders.

8 March 1990
The Slovene Assembly approved measures to prevent economic damage by the Serbian blockade. Slovene Assembly decisions defined as having priority whenever in conflict with federal decisions. The title of Republic of Slovenia no longer to be prefaced by the term 'Socialist'.

15 March 1990
Federal Assembly prolonged the mandates of its delegates till 21 December 1990.

25 March 1990
The Serb Presidency decided the Serbian police would take over security measures on Kosovo.

29 March 1990
The last Slovene Assembly based on the old system ended its mandate.

8 April 1990
First round of elections for the Slovene Parliament, for the President and members of the Presidency of the Republic of Slovenia. The DEMOS coalition won a majority in Parliament. The League of Communists of Slovenia, renamed as the Party of Democratic Renewal, took second place in the parliamentary elections and its candidate, Milan Kučan, became President.

18 April 1990
The victorious DEMOS government invited the oppositional parties to help implement its Program of National Consensus, consisting of two basic reforms: a proper parliamentary system on the basis of a new modern democratic constitution, and an independent nation-state.

18 April 1990
Yugoslav People's Army representative affirmed that the army would respect the election results in Slovenia and Croatia.

2 May 1990
A YPA soldier killed a person attempting an illegal crossing of the Slovene-Italian border.

7 May 1990
The new Slovene parliament had its inaugural meeting.

16 May 1990
The SFRY Presidency demanded measures to solve the crisis situation in Yugoslavia.

17 May 1990
The Yugoslav People's Army started to confiscate arms held by the republican Territorial Defence units.

18 May 1990
The Presidency of Republic of Slovenia declared that Slovene Territorial Defence units would keep their arms. The SFRY Presidency abolished the state of emergency in Kosovo. The Serbian police took over all security actions on Kosovo.

26 May 1990
The 14th Congress of the LCY ended. Slovene, Macedonian, and Croat representatives had not been present. This was the effective end of the LCY.

15 June 1990
Slovene Secretariat of National Defence announced that Slovenian army recruits would serve only on the territory of Slovenia.

2 July 1990
The Slovene parliament accepted a Declaration on the Sovereignty of the Republic of Slovenia. It declared that within a year Slovenia would have a new constitution. It declared the priority of the Slovenian constitution and legislation over the federal constitution and legislation, and that Slovene representatives would not attend Federal Assembly meetings.

7 July 1990
The SFRY Presidency demanded that Slovenia should annul the Declaration. Slovenia refused.

23 July 1990
At a meeting between the Presidency of Republic of Slovenia and the Federal Presidency the federal situation was discussed.

25 July 1990
The SFRY Presidency rejected the Slovene decision about Slovene recruits serving only in Slovenia and gave orders to federal institutions to assure a strict implementation of federal legislation.

27 July 1990
Federal government demanded a special federal tax for financing the Yugoslav People's Army.

9 August 1990
The Federal Assembly condemned the Slovene Declaration on Sovereignty.

14 August 1990
Slovene institutions sent call-up notices only to those Slovenian recruits who would stay in the 5th army zone, which covered Slovenia. The federal institutions demanded all information on recruitment and sent military inspectors to the Slovene Secretariat of National Defence. A Slovene recruit died in Kosovo in unknown circumstances.

10 September 1990
The Slovene government started to consider a confederation proposal, to be prepared together with Croatia.

28 September 1990
Slovene Parliament accepted amendments to the constitution of the Republic of Slovenia. Control of Territorial Defence taken over by the Slovene Presidency. A new Serbian constitution was accepted, worsening the situation of Albanians in Kosovo and the Hungarian minority in Vojvodina.

2 October 1990
The SFRY Presidency announced that control of Slovene Territorial Defence would be taken over by the military command of the 5th military zone. Slovene President Milan Kučan declared that Slovene institutions would resist any measures taken against Slovene sovereignty.

5 October 1990
The Yugoslav People's Army invaded the former headquarters of the Territorial Defence of Slovenia, although it was now vacant. The Slovene Presidency protested to the Federal Presidency.

16 October 1990
Attempts to define a new structure for Yugoslavia by the SFRY Presidency ended in failure. The Slovene representative, Janez Drnovšek, left the meeting.

23 October 1990
Serbia accepted new measures of economic blockade against Slovenia, Croatia and the Federal Government.

27 October 1990
Slovene and Croat governments sent a letter to the President of the Federal Government, Ante Marković, and demanded the depoliticization of the army.

13 November 1990
DEMOS announced a plebiscite on an independent Slovenia.

20 November 1990
President of the Federal Government, Ante Marković, authorized the Yugoslav People's Army to take over the recruitment process in Slovenia.

25 November 1990
The Federal Secretary for Internal Affairs, Petar Gračanin, declared that the army was ready to prevent any secessionist attempts.

5 December 1990
The Slovene Presidency protested against the news, announced by the Federal Secretary for National Defence, general Veljko Kadijević, that troops were moving towards Slovenia and those within Slovenia were on alert. The Slovene Presidency declared these kinds of measures to be an occupation. The SFRY Presidency claimed the information on troop movements was false.

23 December 1990
Plebiscite on Independent Slovenia.   88.2 per cent of voters voted for independence.

7 January 1991
Announced that Serbia had appropriated about two milliard USA$ from federal funds.

8 January 1991
Slovene government assumed control over tax system and customs in Slovenia. It declared that it would pay into the federal budget an amount necessary for the functioning of the federal institutions and army.

20 February 1991
Slovene Parliament accepted a proposal for the consensual separation of SFRY into two or more independent and sovereign states.   The SFRY Presidency condemned this proposal.

15 March 1991
As conflicts grew in the Krajina region of Croatia, SFRY Presidency continued to refuse army proposals for a state of emergency in Yugoslavia.

18 April 1991
Slovene Parliament accepted legislation on recruitment restrictions.

20 May 1991
Slovene government proposed to Federal government that the Yugoslav People's Army leave Slovene territory by 31 December 1993.   Slovene government proposed dialogue on all outstanding questions.

23 May 1991
First Slovenian conflict with the Yugoslav People's Army. Slovene recruits captured two YPA reconnaissance officers near the training centre in Maribor.   YPA captured two Slovene Territorial Defence officers in retaliation. All four captives were released.

12 June 1991
A federal government delegation visited Slovenia and declared that they would not prevent Slovenian secession.

21 June 1991
Federal Government declared the immediate implementation of the federal legislation on border control, and assigned this task to the Federal Secretariat of Internal Affairs and the Federal Secretariat of National Defence.

25 June 1991
Slovene Assembly proclaimed the Declaration on Independence and the Basic Constitutional Charter on the autonomy and independence of the Republic of Slovenia. There were mass meetings of support throughout Slovenia. The Federal Assembly urged the Federal government and the YPA to prevent the disintegration of Yugoslavia.

26 June 1991
The YPA attempted to occupy Slovene border posts and several key traffic points. The Slovene Presidency ordered Territorial Defence to resist, and called on Slovene officers in the YPA to return to the defence of Slovenia.

26 June - 5 July 1991
The 'Ten Day War' - fighting between YPA and Slovenian forces. YPA neutralized.

7 July 1991
Slovene, Croat and federal representatives together with a European Union delegation drew up the Brioni Declaration, ending hostilities and setting terms for the resolution of differences.

18 July 1991
SFRY Presidency accepted YPA withdrawal from Slovenia.

19 December 1991
Germany recognized the independence and sovereignty of the Republic of Slovenia.

23 December 1991
New Slovenian Constitution adopted.

15 January 1992
European Union recognized the Republic of Slovenia. In the following days many other countries followed.

24 March 1992
Republic of Slovenia became a member of the Conference on Security and Cooperation in Europe.

7 April 1992
USA recognized the independence and the sovereignty of the Republic of Slovenia.

22 May 1992
Republic of Slovenia became a member of the United Nations.

15 February 1993
Republic of Slovenia admitted to membership of the International Monetary Fund.

14 May 1993
Republic of Slovenia became a member of the Council of Europe.

Appendix II
Selected statistics, Republic of Slovenia
Source: Slovenia in Figures, 1995. Statistical Office of the Republic of
Slovenia

Table 1   Population by activity (in 1,000s, unless shown as %)

	1992	1993	1994
Working age pop. (15 yrs+	1597	1613	1624
Women	836	842	843
Labour force	971	931	936
Women	455	430	433
Employed persons	890	845	851
Women	421	395	397
Unemployed persons	80	85	85
Women	34	36	37
Non-active pop.	589	680	689
Women	360	411	409
Activity rate (%)	62.2	57.7	57.6
Women	55.9	51.1	51.4
ILO unemployment rate (%)	8.3	9.1	9.0
Women	7.6	8.3	8.4
Registered unemployment rate (%)	11.5	14.4	14.4
Women	10.8	13.4	13.7

**Table 2   Paid employment in social sector and private enterprises, by
activity**

	1985	1990	1993	1994
Total	814, 256	782, 222	626, 806	605, 326
Manufact. mining & elec. supply	369, 891	360, 447	263, 368	251, 935
Agriculture & fishing	13, 614	13, 035	10, 033	9, 475
Forestry & hunting	7, 563	6, 009	3, 786	2, 924
Water management	1, 386	1, 314	1, 130	1, 101
Construction	64, 353	50, 866	29, 954	30, 264
Transport & communications	48, 065	46, 492	35, 959	31, 323
Trade	74, 492	73, 077	59, 961	56, 863
Hotels, rest. & travel agencies	25, 907	24, 888	17, 042	16, 508
Crafts & personal service activities	28, 861	22, 653	16, 509	15, 455
Community service activities	14, 447	12, 936	10, 389	10, 571
Financial & business activities	36, 676	36, 292	38, 934	35, 880
Education & culture	48, 754	51, 774	50, 200	51, 060
Health & social work	52, 289	55, 738	52, 968	53, 747
Public admin, funds, assoc. & org.	27, 958	26, 702	36, 573	38, 220

Table 3   Possession of consumer durables (%)

	1988	1990	1991	1992	1993
% of Slovenian households possessing consumer durables					
Owner occupied dwelling	64	63	63	74	87
Caravan	2	3	2	2	3
Private car	66	71	67	68	68
Washing machine	95	93	93	94	94
Dishwasher	8	10	11	13	16
TV, black-and-white	34	29	18	15	12
Colour TV	64	72	80	83	84
Refrigerator	94	95	94	95	94
Freezer	77	85	80	83	81

Table 4   Adults sentenced for criminal offences - convictions

	1985	1990	1992	1993
Total	13, 528	9, 842	7, 618	6, 871
Criminal offences:				
against life and limb	1, 176	992	814	705
against freedoms & rights	261	315	308	300
of a sexual or moral nature	93	75	74	66
against honour and good name	377	256	167	183
against property	6, 489	4, 705	3, 805	3, 442
against public order	412	418	366	372
against general safety	267	266	252	235
against safety of public traffic	2, 507	1, 480*	927	764
other criminal offences	1, 946	1, 335	904	804

Table 5   Exports and imports
        balance of trade

Exports and imports in process and exports and imports with countries of
the former Yugoslavia have been included in data for the Republic of
Slovenia since 1992. Data for 1994 are provisional

	1990	1992	1993	1994
Exports	4118	6681	6083	6806
Imports	4727	6141	6501	7247
Balance of trade	-609	540	-418	-440
Exports as % of imports	87	109	94	94

Table 6   Countries, major partners in foreign trade, 1994

	Exports		Imports	
	1000 USD	% of total	1000 USD	% of total
Germany	2, 064, 921	30.3	1, 726, 596	23.8
Italy	922, 290	13.6	1, 251, 961	17.3
Croatia	725, 227	10.7	491, 896	6.8
France	586, 318	8.6	599, 062	8.3
Austria	373, 814	5.5	752, 854	10.4
Russian Federation	264, 874	3.9	142, 017	2.0
United States	248, 064	3.6	195, 738	2.7
Macedonia, The former Yug. Rep.	217, 702	3.2	79, 824	1.1
United Kingdom	208, 078	3.1	129, 129	1.8
Netherlands	99, 329	1.5	166, 711	2.3

Appendix III
Contributors

Sandra Bašić Hrvatin - Assistant Professor of political propaganda and international communication. Concerned with media studies and researching the role of media in war on the territory of former Yugoslavia.

Ivan Bernik - Associate Professor of general and theoretical sociology. Researching post-socialist societies, especially the emergence of new nation-states, as well as topics in social regulation.

Bojko Bučar - Assistant Professor of international relations. Pro-dean for study and students' affairs and Head of International Relations Division at the Faculty of Social Sciences in Ljubljana. Interested in international affairs, international law, regionalism and foreign policy. Also editor in chief of the Slovenian Journal of International Relations.

Danica Fink-Hafner - Assistant Professor of policy analysis, political parties and interest groups. Former Head of Division of Policy Analysis and Public Administration at the Faculty of Social Sciences, University of Ljubljana and former President of the Slovenian Political Science Association. Recently specializing in policy-making and lobbying in the European Union.

Franci Grad - Professor of constitutional law and comparative constitutional law at the Faculty of Law and Head of Division of Constitutional Law at the same faculty, University of Ljubljana. He is also Counsellor of the Slovenian Government for constitutional and legislative affairs. Concerned with parliament, government and electoral systems. He was a member of the group of experts which prepared a draft of the new Slovenian Constitution.

Anton Grizold - Associate Professor defence and security policies and systems. Vice Dean for scientific research field and Head of Defence Research Centre at the Faculty of Social Sciences in Ljubljana. Researching Slovenian national security and security in international relations.

Mitja Hafner-Fink - Assistant Professor of social science methodology. Was concerned with the ideology of social strata in Slovenia, presently researching Slovenian public opinion.

Mirjam Kotar - Assistant Lecturer in Political Science at the Faculty of Social Sciences, University of Ljubljana, and Researcher at the Centre for Political Science Research of the Institute of Social Sciences at the same University. Her main research interest is in policy analysis.

Marko Lah - Assistant Professor of political economy at the Faculty of Social Sciences, University of Ljubljana.   Concerned with post-Keynesian theoretical and empirical approaches to economies in transition.   Also researching marketing management and market communication as a factor of effectiveness of (non) profit organizations.

Igor Lukšič - Assistant Professor of political science and the theory of the modern state at the Faculty of Social Sciences in Ljubljana.   Editor of Časopis za kritiko znanosti (Journal for Criticism of Science) published in Ljubljana. Researching contemporary pluralism, corporatism, liberalism, democracy and political anthropology.

Brina Malnar - Assistant Professor of sociology at the Faculty of Social Sciences.   She has been a part of Slovenian Public Opinion Research team for five years.   Her studies are mainly focused on social inequality issues.   She currently works on cross-national analysis of the perception of inequality, based on ISSP 1992 module.

Jože Mencinger - Full Professor of economics.   Teaching at the Faculty of Law, University of Ljubljana.   He is also Director of the Economic Institute of the Faculty of Law and member of the Board of the Bank of Slovenia.   His research interests are in the field of econometric research, macroeconomic policy and comparative economic systems.

Janez Pečar - Full Professor of criminology and former director of the Institute of Criminology at the Faculty of Law, University of Ljubljana.   He was an editor of Revija za kriminalistiko in kriminologijo between 1968-1993.   He teaches at the College of Police and Security Sciences.   His research areas are criminology, victimology, social pathology, criminal policy, criminalistics, police science, security and prevention of crime.

Janko Prunk - Full Professor of recent history.   Subject head for The History of Slovenian Social and Political Thought at the Faculty of Social Sciences, University of Ljubljana.

John R. Robbins - Senior Lecturer in Politics at the University of Adelaide, South Australia.   Researches separatist movements, sub-national governments and political participation.

Miroslav Stanojević - Assistant professor of the sociology of work.   Head of Division for Personnel Management.   Also a research collaborator at the Centre of Theoretical Sociology.   His main research field is industrial relations.

Andrej Sušjan - Assistant Professor of the history of economic thought and political economy at the Faculty of Economics, University of Ljubljana. Concerned with growth and distribution issues in historical perspective. At present researching policy implications of post-Keynesian economic theory for economies in transition.

Ivan Svetlik - Full Professor in the field of the labour market and employment. Dean of the Faculty of Social Sciences in Ljubljana and Head of the Centre for Welfare Studies at the same faculty. Concerned with research into the quality of life, social policies and employment.

Janez Šmidovnik - Full Professor of public administration. Before retirement he lectured at different institutions including the Faculty of Social Sciences, University of Ljubljana. He is Counsellor of the Slovenian Government for legislative affairs. Concerned with problems of organization and functioning of public administration and local self-government including problems of legislation in the area.

Niko Toš - Full Professor of sociology and the methodology of social science research. He is former Dean and current Head of Department of Sociology at the Faculty of Social Sciences. Additionally, he is Head of the Slovenian Public Opinion Project and collaborator in the international research of values (ISSP, WVP), of voting processes, etc. He is also editor of Znanstvena zbirka (Science Collection) published by the Faculty of Social Sciences in Ljubljana.

Aleš Vahčič - Full Professor of economics and entrepreneurship. He is Associate Dean for Research of the Faculty of Economics, University of Ljubljana. He is former Vice-President and President of the International Association for the Economics of Self-management. He is concerned with the problem of entrepreneurship development in transition economies and is a member of the advisory board of the European Foundation for Entrepreneurship Research.

Drago Zajc - Assistant Professor at the Centre for Political Science Research and Head of Division of Policy Analysis and Public Administration at the Faculty of Social Sciences, University of Ljubljana. Concerned with the analysis of the legislative processes and the operation of the Slovenian parliament.

Bibliography

Adam, Frane (1989), 'Deformirana modernizacija - (realni) socializem med tradicijo in modernostjo', *Družboslovne razprave*, vol. 7, pp. 19-30.

Adam, Frane (1991), 'Die politische Modernisierung in postsocialistischen Gesellschaften - am Beispiel Slowenien', *Beiträge zur historischen Sozialkunde*, 21 Jg., no. 4, Okt.-Dez., pp. 112-118.

Adam, Frane (ed.) (1993), *Volitve in politika po slovensko*, Znanstveno publicistično središče, Ljubljana.

Adam, Frane (1994), 'After Four Years of Democracy: Fragility and Stability' in Adam F. and Tomc G., *Small Societies in Transition: The Case of Slovenia*, Slovene Sociological Association, Ljubljana.

Addison, John T. and Siebert, W. Stanley (1979), *The Market for Labour: an Analytical Treatment*, Goodyear Publishing, Santa Monica, California.

Ágh, Áttila (1992), 'The Emerging Party System in East Central Europe', *Budapest Papers on Democratic Transition*, no. 13, Hungarian Centre for Democracy Studies Foundation, Department of Political Science, Budapest University of Economics.

Ágh, Áttila (ed.) (1994), *The First Steps*, Hungarian Centre of Democracy Studies, Budapest.

Aghevli, B. B. *et al.* (1991), 'Exchange Rate Policy in Developing Countries: Some Analytical Issues', *IMF Occasional Paper* p. 78.

Akehurst, Michael (1984), *A Modern Introduction to International Law*, George Allen and Unwin, London.

Almond, Gabriel A. and Verba, Sydney (1963), *The Civic Culture*, Little, Brown, Boston.

Almond, Gabriel A. (1968), 'A Developmental Approach to Political Systems', in Finkle, Jason L. and Gable, Richard W. *Political Development and Social Change*, John Wiley and Sons, New York.

Amsden, H. A., Kochanowicz J. and Tylor, L. (1994), *The Market Meets its Match*, Harvard University Press, Cambridge, Mass.

Arbitration Committee (1992), 'Opinions no. 4, 5, 6 and 7 of 10 January 1992', *Review of International Affairs*, vol. 43, no. 1001.

Arzenšek, V (1984b), 'Alijenacija rada', in Rus, V. & Arzenšek, V., *Rad kao sudbina i kao sloboda*, SNL, Zagreb.

Arzenšek, V. (1984a), *Struktura i pokret*, Institut društvenih nauka, Beograd.

Ash, T. G. (1990), *We the People: The Revolution of '89 Witnessed in Warsaw, Budapest, Berlin and Prague*, Granta Books, Cambridge.

Åslund, Anders (1994), 'Lessons of the First Four Years of Systemic Change in Eastern Europe', *Journal of Comparative Economics*, vol. 19, pp. 39-63.

Atkinson, M. M. and Coleman, W. D. (1992), 'Policy Networks, Policy Communities and the Problems of Governance', *Governance*, vol. 5, no. 2, April, pp. 154-180.

Bajt, A. (1993), 'Premoženjskopravna analiza problemov preobrazbe socialističnega vzhoda', in *Privatizacija na Slovenskem 1990-1992*, Državna založba Slovenije, Ljubljana.

Banac, Ivo (1992), 'Post-communism as post-Yugoslavism: the Yugoslav non-revolutions of 1989-1990', in Ivo Banac (ed.), *Eastern Europe in Revolution*, Cornell University Press, Ithaca.

Banac, Ivo (1992), 'Yugoslavia: The Fearful Asymmetry of War' in *Daedalus*, 121 (2) 141-175.

Bates, Robert H. (1991), The Economics of Transitions to Democracy, *Political Science and Politics*, vol. 24, no. 1, pp. 24-27.

Bašić, Sandra, Podmenik, Darka and Bekeš, Andrej (1989), *Javnost in kriza. Spremembe v sporočanju Slovenskih in Jugoslovanskih časopisov v obdobju 1980-1988.* Raziskovalno poročilo, Ljubljana FSPN.

Bebler, Anton (1993), 'Slovenian Territorial Defence', *International Defence Review*, vol. 26, no. 1, January.

Bebler, Anton (1993), 'The Armed Conflicts in the Balkans in 1990-93, Social, Economic and Political Underpinnings and the International Extra Regional Framework', in Jernej, Kozar et al. (ed.), *International Conference on Armed Conflicts In The Balkans and European Security*, Ministry of Defence of the Republic of Slovenia, Center for Strategic Studies, Ljubljana.

Benderly, Jill and Kraft, Evan (eds.) (1994), *Independent Slovenia, Origins, Movements, Prospects*, Macmillan, London.

Berelson, Bernard (1954), *Voting*, University of Chicago Press, Chicago.

Berglund, Stan and Dellenbrant, Jan Åke (eds.) (1991), 'Party Systems and Political Cleavages', in Berglund, Stan and Dellenbrant, Jan Åke (eds.),*The New Democracies in Eastern Europe*, Edward Elgar, Aldershot, Hants.

Bernik, I. (1992), *Dominacija in konsenz v socialistični družbi*, Znanstvena knjižnica FDV, Ljubljana.

Bernik, I. (1994), 'Der Übergang von der heroischen in die prozaische Etappe: Slowenien' in Pradetto, A. (ed.), *Die Rekonstruktion Ostmittel-Europas*. Westdeutscher Verlag, Opladen, pp. 121-142.

Bernik, Ivan (1989), '"Socialistična družba kot 'obmoderna' družba", *Družboslovne razprave*, no. 7, pp. 31-40.

Bertalanić, Marijan (1990), *Propisi o političkom udruživanju*, Informator, Zagreb.

Beyme Von, Klaus (1985), *Political Parties in Western Democracies*, Gower, Aldershot, Hants.

Bibič, Adolf (1992), 'Nekateri vidiki pluralizacije družbe in države na Slovenskem', in Fink-Hafner, Danica et al (eds.), *Nastajanje slovenske državnosti*, Slovensko politološko društvo, Ljubljana, pp. 155-175.

Bibič, Adolf and Graziano, Gigi (1994), *Civil Society, Political Society, Democracy*, Slovenian Political Science Association, Ljubljana.

Bill on political parties (a proposal), *Poročevalec Skupščine Republike Slovenije*, vol. 18, no. 18, August 1992.

Blumler, Jay G. and Gurevitch Michael, (1975), 'Towards a Comparative Framework for Political Communication Research' in Chaffe, S. H, *Political Communication. Issues and Strategies for Research*, London, Sage.

Bobbio, Norberto (1987), *Which Socialism? Marxism, Socialism, and Democracy*, Polity Press, Oxford.

Bole, V. (1992), 'Inflacija in ekonomsko-politične alternative (Inflation and Economic Policy Alternatives)' *Gospodarska gibanja*, vol. 226, March 1992, pp. 35-49.

Bole, V. (1993), 'Restrukturiranje gospodarstva, (Restructuring of the economy)' *Gospodarska gibanja*, EIPF, Ljubljana, 239, pp. 21-34.

Bollen, Kenneth A. (1991), 'Political Democracy: Conceptual and Measurement Traps' in Inkeles, Alex, *Measuring Democracy*, Transaction Publisher, New Brunswick, New Jersey.

Bomhoff, E. J. (1992), 'Monetary Reform in Eastern Europe', *European Economic Review*, vol. 36, April 1992, 454-58.

Bruszt, L. (1990), 'Hungary's Negotiated Revolution', *Social Research* vol. 57, pp. 365-87.

Bučar, Bojko (1990), 'Declaration on the Sovereignty of Slovenia', *Regional Contact*, vol. 1, no. 1.

Bučar, Bojko (1991a), 'Political Developments in Yugoslavia' in Mantl, Wolfgang (ed.), *Die neue Architecktur Europas: Reflexionen in einer bedrohten Welt*, Böhlau Verlag, Wien-Köln-Graz.

Bučar, Bojko (1991b), 'International Aspects of the Yugoslav Reform and Independence for Slovenia', *Review of International Affairs*, vol. 42, no. 988.

Bučar, Bojko (1991c), 'Nekatere mednarodne dileme in pogledi na samostojnost Slovenije', *Teorija in Praksa*, vol. 28, no. 8-9.

Bučar, Bojko (1993), 'Der Bürgerkrieg in Jugoslawien' in Grothusen, Klaus-Detlev (ed.), *Ostmittel und Sudosteuropa im Umbruch*, Sudosteuropa Gesellschaft, München.

Bučar, Bojko (1995), 'Slovenia' in Neuhold, Hanspeter and Havlik, Peter and Suppan Arnold (eds.), *Political and Economic Transformation in East Central Europe*, Westview Press, Boulder.

Bučar, Bojko and Brinar, Irena (1994), 'Slovenian Foreign Policy' in Bibič, Adolf and Graziano, Gigi (eds.), *Civil Society, Political Society, Democracy*, SPSA, Ljubljana, pp. 425-47.

Calise, Mauro (1994), 'The Media Party: The Founding (and Broadcasting) of the Italian Second Republic', *ECPR Joint Sessions, Workshop on Anti-Party Sentiment*, Madrid 17-22 April.

Campbell, J. C. (1989), 'Bureaucratic Primacy, Japanese Policy Communities in an American Perspective', *Governance*, vol. 2, no. 1, January, pp. 5-22.

Campbell, J. C., Baskin M. A., Baumgartner F. R. and Halpern N. P. (1989), 'Afterword on Policy Communities: A Framework for Comparative Research', *Governance*, vol. 2, no. 1, January, pp. 86-94.

Caporaso, James A. (ed.) (1989), *The Elusive State*, Sage, London.

Charlton, R. (1986), *Comparative Government*, Longman, London.

Cirtautas, Arista Maria (1994), 'In Pursuit of the Democratic Interest: the Institutionalization of Parties and Interests in Eastern Europe', in Christopher G. A. Bryant and Mokrzycki, Edmund, *'The New Great Transformation: Change and Continuity in East-Central Europe'* Routledge, London.

Cobb, R., Ross, Keith J. and Ross, M. H. (1976), 'Agenda Building as a Comparative Political Process', *The American Political Science Review*, vol. 70, pp. 126-138.

Cobb, Roger W. and Elder, Charles D. (1971), 'The Politics of Agenda-Building: An Alternative Perspective for Modern Democratic Theory', *The Journal of Politics*, vol. 33, pp. 892-915.

Cohen, Lenard J. (1993), *Broken Bonds: the Disintegration of Yugoslavia*, Westview Press, Boulder.

Constitution of the Republic of Slovenia, Official Gazette of the Republic of Slovenia, Ljubljana, 1993.

Crawford, Beverley and Lijphart, Arend (1995), 'Explaining Political and Economic Change in Post-Communist Eastern Europe: Old Legacies, New Institutions, Hegemonic Norms, and International Pressures', *Comparative Political Studies*, vol. 28, no. 2.

Dahl, Robert A. (1966), *Political Opposition in Western Democracies*, Yale University Press, New Haven.

Dahl, Robert A. (1970), *'After the Revolution'*, Yale University Press, New Haven.

Dahl, Robert A. (1971), *Polyarchy; Participation and Opposition*, Yale University Press, New Haven.

Dahl, Robert A. (1973), *Political Oppositions in Western Europe*, Yale University Press, New Haven.

Dahl, Robert A. (1990), *After the Revolution* (2nd edition), Yale University Press, New Haven.

Dahl, Robert A. (1991), 'Transitions to Democracy' in Szoboszlai Gyoergy (ed.), *Democracy and Political Transformation, Theories and East-Central European Realities*, Hungarian Political Science Association, Budapest, pp. 9-21.

Dahl, Robert A. and Tufte, Edward R. (1973), *Size and Democracy*, Stanford University Press, Stanford.

Dahrendorf, R. (1990) *Reflections on the Revolution in Europe*, Chatto & Windus, London.

Dalton, R. J. (1994), 'Communists and Democrats: Democratic Attitudes in the Two Germanies', *British Journal of Political Science 24*, pp. 469-493.

David, A. P. and Abramovitz, M. (1994), 'Convergence and Deferred Catch-up, Productivity Leadership and the Waning of American Exceptionalism', *Merit Research Memorandum*, pp. 94-138, Merit, Maastricht.

Debelak, Slavko (1990), 'Vloga institucionalnih mehanizmov pri zagotavljanju varnosti družbe - države', *Strokovni bilten*, vol. 9, no. 1.

Diamond, Larry and Schmitter, Philippe C., *Democracy in Developing Countries*, 4 vols., Lynne Rienner, Boulder, 1989-91.

Diamond, Larry (1994), 'Rethinking Civil Society: Towards Democratic Consolidation', *Journal of Democracy*, vol. 5 (3), pp. 4-17.

Dix, Robert H. (1990), *The Process of Democratization*, Crane Russak, New York.

Dornbusch, R., Noelling, W. and Layard, R. (eds.) (1993), *Postwar Economic Reconstruction and Lessons for the East Today*, The MIT Press, Cambridge, Mass.

Duverger, Maurice (1964), *Political Parties*, University Paperbacks, Methuen, London.

Dyson, Kenneth H. F. (1980), *The State Tradition in Western Europe*, Martin Robertson, Oxford.

EC (1991a), 'Declaration on Yugoslavia', *Review of International Affairs*, vol. 42, no. 998-1000.

EC (1991b), 'Guidelines on the Recognition of New States in Eastern Europe and the Soviet Union', *Review of International Affairs*, vol. 42, no. 998-1000.

EC Presidency (1991), 'Statement of the EC Presidency on the Recognition of Yugoslav Republics of 15 January 1992', *Review of International Affairs*, vol. 42, no. 1001.

Eisenstadt, Samuel N. (1967), 'Patterns of Political Modernization' in Welch Claude E. Jr., (ed.), *Political Modernization, A Reader in Comparative Political Change*, Wadsworth Publishing, Belmont, California.

Eisenstadt, Samuel N. (1971), 'The Scope and Development of Political Sociology: Political Modernization and Political Sociology of the Modern State', in Eisenstadt, Samuel N. (ed.), *Political Sociology* Basic Books, New York.

Ekkart, Zimmerman, 'Evolutionärer und revolutionärer Wandel', in Beyme Von, Klaus, Ernst-Otto, Czempel, Kielmansegg, Peter, Graf, Schmoock, Peter, (eds.) (1987), *Politikwissenschaft*, Stuttgart-Berlin-Koeln-Mainz, Beltz Verlag, Weincheim, Basel und W. Kohlhammer.

Ellerman, P. D. (1995), *Intellectual Trespassing as a Way of Life*, Rowman and Littlefield Publishers, Inc., Totowa, N. J.

Ellerman, P. D., Vahčič, A. and Petrin, T. (1992), 'Privatization Controversies in the East and West', in Claudon, P. M. and Gunter, L. T. (eds.), *Comrades Go Private, Strategies for Eastern European Privatization*, New York University Press, New York.

Ellman, Michael (1994a), 'Transformation, Depression and Economics: Some Lessons', *Journal of Comparative Economics*, vol. 19, pp. 1-21.

Ellman, Michael (1994b), 'History and Democracy Revisited', *Comparative Politics*, vol. 27 (1) 1994, pp. 91-106.

Erlich, Stanislaw (1982), *Pluralism: On and Off Course*, Pergamon, Oxford.

Estrin, S. and Cave, M. (eds.) (1993), *Competition and Competition Policy*, Pinter Publishers, London.

Evans, G. and Whitefield, S. (1993), 'Identifying the Bases of Party Competition in Eastern Europe', *British Journal of Political Science 23*, vol. 4, pp. 521-548.

Evans, Peter B., Rueschemeyer, D. and Skocpol, T. (1985), *Bringing the State Back In*, Cambridge University Press, Cambridge.

Ferfila, Bogomil (1994), 'Slovenia and the World in Statistical Comparison' in F. Adam and G. Tomc, *Small Societies in Transition: The Case of Slovenia*, Slovene Sociological Association, Ljubljana.

Findlay, Mark and Zvekić, Uglješa (1993), *Alternative Policing Styles*, Deventer, Kluwer.

Finer, S. E. (1987), *Comparative Government*, Penguin, London.

Fink-Hafner, Danica (1990), *Nova družbena gibanja - subjekti politične inovacije*, Znanstvena knjižnica FDV, Ljubljana

Fink-Hafner, Danica (1991), 'Glasovalno obnašanje poslancev'. Slovenski Skupščini, [Teorija in praksa] no. 7, pp. 1288-1392.

Fink-Hafner, Danica (1992), 'Political Modernization in Slovenia in the 1980s and at the Early 1990s', *The Journal of Communist Studies*, vol. 8, no. 4, pp. 210-226.

Fink-Hafner, Danica (1992a), Nova družbena gibanja - subjekti politične inovacije, Znanstvena knjižnica FDV, Ljubljana.

Fink-Hafner, Danica (1992b), 'The Transformation of the Space of Political Intermediation and New Patterns of Policy-making in Slovenia', *Budapest Papers on Democratic Transition*, no. 25 (The Europeization of Central European Polities, project, No. 4) Hungarian Centre for Democracy Studies, Budapest.

Fink-Hafner, Danica (1993), 'Problemi utrjevanja demokracije na Slovenskem: nekateri indikatorji', in *Problemi konsolidacije demokracije*, Slovensko politiloško društvo, Ljubljana.

Fink-Hafner, Danica (1993a), 'Policy skupnosti in nekateri problemi vladanja v prehodnem objobju', in Zajc, Drago (ed.), *Slovenski parlament v procesu politične modernizacije*, CPR RI FDV, Ljubljana, pp. 107-122.

Fink-Hafner, Danica (1994), 'Sindikati v procesu oblikovanja politik', *Družboslovne razprave*, no. 17-18, Ljubljana.

Fink-Hafner, Danica and Kranjc, Stane (1988), 'Vloga ZK in SZDL', in občini, RI FDV, Center za politološke raziskave, Ljubljana.

Finkle, J. L. and Gable, R. W. (1968), *Political Development and Social Change*, John Wiley and Sons Inc., New York.

Flajs, A. (1993), 'Government Accounts in The System of National Accounts', in, *Statistics in Open Economy*, Statistical Bureau of the Republic of Slovenia, Radenci, pp. 57-75.

Fogel, David (1994), *Policing and Control in Eastern Europe*. Helsinki, HEUNI.

Ginther, Konrad and Isak, Hubert (ed.) (1991), *Self-determination in Europe*, Böhlau Verlag, Wien-Köln-Weimar.

Glenny, Misha, *'The Fall of Yugoslavia'*, Penguin Books, London, 1992.

Gospodarska, gibanja (1992), no. 266 (Economic Flows), Institute of Economics, Faculty of Law, Ljubljana.

Grad, F. (1990) 'Constitutional Acts in the Process of the Independence of the Republic of Slovenia', *Legal Practice* no. 18, Ljubljana.

Grad, F. (1991), 'Acceptance of the Federal Laws into Slovenian Legal System', *Legal practice*, no. 23-24, Ljubljana.

Gradivo za slovensko ustavo (1988), Društvo slovenskih pisateljev, Delovna skupina za ustavni razvoj pri Slovenskem sociološkem društvu, Časopis za kritiko znanosti, Ljubljana, April.

Grant, W. (1989), *Pressure Groups, Politics and Democracy in Britain*, Philip Allan, New York.

Grant, W. (1993), 'Business Associations in Eastern Europe and Russia', *The Journal of Communist Studies*, vol. 9, no. 2, pp. 86-100.

Grdešić, Ivan, Kasapović, Mirjana and Šiber, Ivan (1989), *Interesi i ideje u SKJ*, Fakultet političkih nauka, Zagreb.

Grdešić, Ivan, Kasapović, Mirjana, Šiber, Ivan and Zakošek, Nenad (1991), *Hrvatska u izborima '90*, Naprijed, Zagreb.

Grizold, Anton (1992), 'Military Intervention in Slovenia', *International Social Science Review*, vol. 67, no. 1, Winter.

Grizold, Anton (1994), 'The National Security Issue in Slovenia' in Bučar, Bojko and Kuhnle, Stein (eds.), *Small States Compared: The Case of Norway and Slovenia*, Alma Mater, Bergen, pp. 80-93.

Grizold, Anton (1994) 'Solving the Refugee Problem in Slovenia', *Journal of Industrial Relations (Issues of Politics, Law and Economy)*, vol. 1, no. 1.

Gurr, Ted Robert (1989) 'War Revolution and the Growth of the Coercive State' in Caporaso, James A. *The Elusive State*, Sage, London, pp. 49-68.

Habermas, Jurgen (1989), *Strukturne spremembe javnosti*. Studia Humanitatis, Ljubljana.

Hafner-Fink, Mitja (1989), *Ideologija in zavest družbenih slojev v Sloveniji*, MC CK ZKS, Ljubljana.

Hafner-Fink, Mitja (1993), 'Clustering Methods in the Context of Comparative Analysis - Ideological Consciousness of Classes in Former Yugoslavia' in Ferligoj, Anuška and Kramberger, Anton (eds.), *Developments in Statistics and Methodology*, FDV, Ljubljana, pp. 167-174.

Hafner-Fink, Mitja (1994), *Sociološka razsežja razpada Jugoslavije*, Znanstvena knjižnica FDV, Ljubljana.

Herman, Edward S. and Chomsky, Noam (1988), *Manufacturing Consent*, Pantheon Books, New York.

Higgott, R. A. (1980), 'From Modernization Theory to Public Policy: Continuity and Change in the Political Science of Political Development', *Studies in Comparative International Development*, vol. XV, no. 4.

Holdaway, Simon (1993), 'Co-operation and the Management of Policing in Europe', *European Journal of Criminal Policy and Research*, vol. 1-4.

Horsman, Matthew and Marshall, Andrew (1994), *After the Nation-State*, Harper Collins, London.

Huntington, Samuel P. (1969), *Political Order in Changing Societies*, Yale University Press, New Haven.

Huntington, Samuel P., Nelson, Joan M. (1977), *Political Participation in Developing Countries*, Harvard University Press, Cambridge, Massachusetts.

Huntington, Samuel (1992), 'How Do Countries Democratize', *Political Science Quarterly*, vol. 106, pp. 579-617.

Industrial and Development Policy of Slovenia (1994-2000), July 1994, Ministry of Economic Affairs, Ljubljana.

Interest Groups and Public Policy: A Symposium (1983), *Policy Studies Journal*, vol. 11, no. 4, p. 599-708.

Ishijama, Y. (1975), 'The Theory of Optimum Currency Areas', *IMF Staff Papers*.

Ishiyama, John T., Communist Parties in Transition, *Comparative Politics*, vol. 27 (2), 1995, pp. 147-166.

Jambrek, P. (1992a), *Constitutional Democracy*, Državna založba Slovenije, Ljubljana.

Jambrek, P. (1992b), 'Development and Origin of the New Slovenian Constitutionality', in *The New Constitutional System of Slovenia*, Zbornik znanstvenih razprav, CZ Uradni list RS, Ljubljana.

Jambrek, Peter (1988), 'Zveza komunistov in politične kulture Jugoslavije', in Antončič, Vojko et al (eds), *Stratifikacijske analize sodobnih družb, Slovensko sociološko društvo and FSPN*, Ljubljana, pp. 140-164

Jambrek, Peter (1989), 'Odnos Slovencev do štirih razvojnih silnic in vrednot, do partije in države, do svobode in okolja', *Družboslovne rezprave*, vol. 1, no. 5, pp. 60-70.

Jambrek, Peter (1989), *Oblast in opozicija v Sloveniji*, Založba Obzorja, Maribor.

Jeffries, I. (1993), *Socialist Economies and the Transition to the Market*, Routledge, London.

Jeglič, Peter (1989), Varnost kot sistemska funkcija - njen pomen in poti uresničevanja v sistemu samoupravne socialistične demokracije. *Varnost-Strokovni bilten, izredna številka.*

Jordan, A. G. and Richardson, J. J. (1987), *British Politics and the Policy Process*, Unwin Hyman, Boston.

Jordan, Grant and Schubert, Klaus (eds.) (1992), 'Policy Networks', *Journal of Political Research*, vol. 21, no. 1-2.

Jovanov, N. (1979), *Radnički štrajkovi u SFRJ od 1958 do 1969 godine*, Dijalog, Beograd.

Judge, David (1994), 'East Central European Parliaments: The First Steps', in Ágh, Áttila (ed.) *The First Steps*, Hungarian Centre of Democracy Studies, Budapest.

Kabashima I., White L. T. III (1986), *Political System and Change*, Princeton University Press, Princeton, New Jersey.

Kann, Robert (1950), *The Multinational Empire*, New York.

Kaplan, Morton A. and Katzenbach, Nicholas de B. (1961), *The Political Foundations of International Law*, John Wiley and Sons, New York-London.

Kardelj, Edvard (1973), *Temeljni vzroki smeri ustavnih sprememb*, Komunist, Ljubljana.

Kardelj, Edvard (1978), *Smeri razvoja političnega sistema socialističnega samoupravljanja*, Komunist, Ljubljana.
Karl, Terry Lynn and Schmitter, Philippe C. (1991), 'Modes of Transition in Latin America, Southern and Eastern Europe', *International Social Science Journal*, vol. 43, (128), p. 269-284.
Keane, John (ed.) (1988), *Civil Society and the State*, Verso, London.
Keane, John (1988a), *Democracy and Civil Society*, Verso, London.
Kirchheimer, Otto (1966), 'The Transformation of the Western European Party Systems', in LaPalombara, Joseph and Weiner, Myron (eds.), *Political Parties and Political Development*, Princeton University Press, Princeton, New Jersey.
Kitschelt, H. (1993), 'Class Structure and Social Democratic Party Strategy', *British Journal of Political Science* 23, 3.
Kitschelt, Herbert (1992), 'The Formation of Party Systems in East Central Europe', *Politics and Society*, vol. 20, no.1, March, pp. 7-50.
Klinar, P. (1992), 'O mednacionalnih odnosih v Sloveniji', in Toš, N. (ed.), *Slovenski izziv FDV-IDV*, Ljubljana, pp. 69-83.
Klinar, P. (1994), 'O nacionalni identiteti in etnonacionalizmih', in Toš, N. (ed.), *Slovenski izziv II. FDV-IDV*, Ljubljana, pp. 31-51.
Klinar, Peter (1994a), 'O nacionalni identiteti in etnonacionalizmih - Slovenija v tranzicijskem obdobju' in Toš, Niko (ed.), *Slovenski izziv II*, Dokumenti SJM, FDV-IDV, Ljubljana, pp. 31-51.
Kolarska-Bobinska, L. (1990) 'Civil Society and Social Anomy in Poland', *Acta Sociologica* 33, 4, pp. 277-288.
Kolosi, Tamas (1984), 'Status and stratification' in Andorka, Rudolf and Kolosi, Tamas (eds.) *Stratification and Inequalities*, Institute for Social Sciences, Budapest.
Kolosi, Tamas and Wnuk-Lipinski, Edmund (eds.) (1983), *Equality and Inequality under Socialism (Poland and Hungary Compared)*, Sage, London.
Kornai, J. (1993), 'Anti-Depression Cure for Ailing Post-communist Economies', *Transition*, February 1993.
Kranjc, Stane (1991), 'Stranke in parliament', in *Parlamentarizem: dileme in perspektive*, Slovensko politološko društvo, Ljubljana, pp. 81-91.
Kranjc, Stane (1992), 'Razvoj strank in strankarskega pluralizma na Slovenskem (1988-1991)', RI FDV, Center za politološke raziskave, Ljubljana.
Kristan, I (1990), 'Right of Self-determination', *Zbornik znanstvenih razprav* vol. 1, Ljubljana.
Kristan, I (1994), *State Organization of Slovenia*, CZ Uradni list RS, Ljubljana.
Kristan, Ivan (1992), 'Das Recht auf Selbstbestimmung' in Grothusen, Klaus-Detlev (ed.), *Staatliche Einheit und Teilung - Deutschland und Jugoslawien*, Sudosteuropa-Gesellschaft, München.
Krmelj, Robert (1994), 'Findings of Missions from International Organizations and Institutions on the Position of Minorities in Slovenia', *Journal of International Relations*, vol. 1, no. 1, pp. 49-53.
Kumar, Andrej (1993), 'Slovenia - Developments and Transition' in Senjur, Marjan (ed.), *Slovenia - A Small Country in the Global Economy*, Center for International Co-operation and Development and The International Center for Economic Growth, Ljubljana and San Francisco.

Kuzmanić, Tonči (1994), 'Strikes, trade unions, and Slovenian Independence', in Benderly, Jill and Kraft, Evan (eds.), *Independent Slovenia, Origins, Movements, Prospects*, MacMillan, Houndmills, Basingstoke, Hampshire and London.

Lane, Jan-Erik and Errson, Svante O. (1987) *'Politics and Society in Western Europe'*, Sage, London, 1987.

LaPalombara, Joseph and Weiner, Myron, (eds.) (1966), *Political Parties and Political Development*, Princeton University Press, Princeton, New Jersey.

Lazić, Mladen (1987), *U susret zatvorenom društvu?*, Naprijed, Zagreb.

Leftwich, A. (1990), 'Politics and Development Studies' in, Leftwich, A (ed.) *New Developments in Political Science*, Edward Elgar, Aldershot, Hants.

Lehmbruch, G. (1988), 'Concertation and the structure of Corporatist Networks', in Goldthorpe, J. H. (ed.), *Order and Conflict in Contemporary Capitalism*, Clarendon Press, Oxford.

Lehmbruch, Gerhard and Schmitter, Philippe C. (1982), *Patterns of Corporatist Policy-making*, Sage, London.

Linz, J. J. (1990), 'Transitions to Democracy', *The Washington Quarterly*, vol. 13, no. 3, pp. 143-164.

Lijphart, Arendt (1984), *Democracies*, Yale University Press, New Haven.

Lijphart, Arendt (1994), 'Democracies: Forms, performance and constitutional engineering', *European Journal of Political Research*, vol. 27.

Lijphart, Arend (1977), *Democracy in Plural Societies*, Yale University Press, New Haven.

Lipset, S. M. (1994), 'The Social Requisites of Democracy Revisited', *American Sociological Review*, vol. 59, pp. 1-22.

Lipset, Seymour Martin (1959), 'Some Social Requisites of Democracy: Economic Development and Political legitimacy', *The American Political Science Review*, vol. 52, pp. 69-105.

Lommel, Celestin (1992), 'L'Europe de 1993 et la criminalite sans frontiares?' *Revue internationale de criminologie et de police technique*, vol. 45, no. 3.

Lukšič, Igor (1981), *Modelfall Oesterreich? Möglichkeiten and Grenzen der Sozialpartnerschaft.* Wilhelm Bramueller, Universitaets-Verlagsbuchhandlung, Vienna.

Lukšič, Igor (1993), 'Zmagovalci in poraženci volitev 1992', in Adam Frane, (ed.) *Volitve po Slovensko*, pp. 13-28.

Lukšič, Igor (1993a), 'Državni svet Republike Slovenije', in Fink-Hafner, Danica and Strmčnik, Berni (eds.), *Konsolidacija demokracije*, Slovensko politološko društvo, Ljubljana.

Lukšič, Igor (1994), 'Corporatism in the Political System of the Republic of Slovenia', in Bučar, Bojko and Kuhnle, Stein (eds.) *Small States Compared: Politics of Norway and Slovenia*, Alma Mater, Bergen, pp. 201-215.

Lukšič, Igor (1994a), *Liberalizem versus korporativizem.* Ljubljana, Znanstveno in publicistično središče.

Lukšič, Igor (1994b), 'Socialno partnerstvo - kako naprej?' *Časopis za kritiko znanosti*, no. 168-9, vol. XXII, Ljubljana.

Lukšič, Igor (forthcoming), 'Interest Organizations in the Field of Social Partnership' in, Fink-Hafner, Danica and Robbins, J. (eds.), *Making a New Nation*, Dartmouth, Aldershot.

Macroeconomic Trends in Slovenia in 1994 and 1995, Institute of Republic of Slovenia for Macroeconomic Research, November 1994, Ljubljana.

Magas, Branka (1993), *The Destruction of Yugoslavia*, Verso, London.

Mair, Peter (1990), *The West European Party System*, Oxford University Press, Oxford.

Makarovič, Jan and Jug, Janez (1994), 'How the New Political Elite in Slovenia Understands Democracy', in F. Adam and G. Tomc, *Small Societies in Transition: The Case of Slovenia*, Slovene Sociological Association, Ljubljana.

Mancini, Paolo (1991), "The Public Sphere and the Use of News in a 'Coalition' System of Government" in Dahlgren, P. and Sparks, C. (eds.) *Communication and Citizenship*, Routledge, London.

Maravall, Jose (1982), *The Transition to Democracy in Spain*, Croom Helm London.

Marsh, David (1993), 'The Policy Networks Concept in British Political Science, its Applicability for Central and Eastern Europe', *Budapest Papers on Democratic Transition*, no. 71, Hungarian Centre for Democracy Studies, Budapest.

Mason, John W (1985), *The Dissolution of the Austro-Hungarian Empire, 1867-1918*, Longman, London.

Mastnak, T. (1983), *H kritiki stalinizma*, Krt, Ljubljana.

McEachern, D. (1990), *The Expanding State*, St. Martin's Press, New York.

McSweeney, Dean and Zvesper, John (1991), *American Political Parties*, Routledge, London.

Melik, Vasilij (1965), *Volitve na Slovenskem 1861-1918*, Slovenska matica, Ljubljana.

Melzer, A. H. (1992), 'Prices and Wages in Transition to a Market Economy', *The 19th Karl Brunner Symposium on Liberty, Analysis, and Ideology*, Interlaken, Switzerland, June 8-12.

Mencinger, J. (1983), 'Registrirana brezposelnost in zaposleni brez dela' (Registered Unemployment and the Employees Without Work), *Gospodarska gibanja* no. 128, Ljubljana.

Mencinger, J. (1993), 'How to Create a Currency? The Experience of Slovenia', *Weltwirtschaftliches Archiv*, Babd 129, Heft 2.

Mencinger, J. (1994), 'The Birth and the Childhood of a Currency: the Experience of Slovenia', in Gacs, J. (ed.), *International Trade and Restructuring in Eastern Europe*, 276-290.

Meyer, G. (1993), 'Die politischen Kulturen Ostmitteleuropas im Umbruch'; *Aus Politik und Zeitgeschichte*, B 10, pp. 3-13.

Michels, Robert (1959), *Political Parties*, Dover Publications, New York.

Miliband, Ralph (1972), *The State in Capitalist Society*, Weidenfeld and Nicolson, London.

Miller, Robert F. (1992), *The Development of Civil Society in Communist Systems*, Allen & Unwin, Sydney.

Mircev, Dimitar, 'Ethno-centrism and Strife Among Political Elites: the End of Yugoslavia', *Governance*, vol. 6 no. 3 July 1993.

Mössner, Jörg Manfred (1977), *Einführung in das Völkerrecht*, Verlag C.H. Beck, München.

Mrak, M. (1994), 'Slovenia: Creating its own Identity in the International Financial Community', *Journal of International Relations*, vol. I, no. 1.

Mueller, Claus (1973), *The Politics of Communication*, Oxford University Press, Oxford.

Myant, Martin, (1993), *'Transforming Socialist Economies'*, Edward Elgar, Aldershot.

Normandeau, Andre (1993), 'Une perspective nouvelle sur la formation des policiers pour l'an 2000', *Revue internationale de criminologie et de police technique*, vol. 46, no. 3.

O'Donnell, Guillermo, Schmitter, Philippe C. and Whitehead, Laurence, (eds.) (1989), *Transitions from Authoritarian Rule: Tentative Conclusions about Uncertain Democracies*, The Johns Hopkins University Press, Baltimore.

Offe, C. (1985), *Disorganized Capitalism, Contemporary Transformation of Work and Politics*, Polity Press, Cambridge-Oxford.

Offe, C. (1991), 'Das Dilemma der Gleichzeitigkeit. Demokratisierung und Marktwirtschaft in Osteuropa'; *Merkur*, pp. 279-292.

Panebianco, Angelo (1988), *Political Parties: Organization and Power*, Cambridge University Press, Cambridge.

Parkin, Frank (1971), *Class Inequality and Political Order, Social Stratification in Capitalist and Communist Societies*, Praeger Publishers, New York.

Pateman, Carole (1970), *Participation and Democratic Theory*, Cambridge University Press, Cambridge.

Pelinka, Anton (1981), Modelfall Oesterreich? Möglichkeiten und Grenzen der Sozialpartnerschaft, Vienna, Wilhelm Bramueller, Universitaets-Verlagsbuchhandlung.

Peters, John Durham (1993) 'Distrust of Representation: Habermas on the Public Sphere' in *Media, Culture and Society*, vol. 15 (1), pp. 541-571.

Petrič, Ernest (1984), *Pravica do samoodločbe - mednarodni vidiki*, Založba Obzorja, Maribor.

Petrin T. (1992), 'Industrial Policy and Entrepreneurship in Post-socialist Countries', in Cengic D. et al. (eds.), *How to Develop Successful Enterprise*, Zagreb.

Phillips, Paul and Ferfila, Bogomil, *The Rise and Fall of the Third Way: Yugoslavia, 1945-91*, Fernwood Publishing, Halifax, Canada, 1992.

Podmenik, Darka (1993), 'Programska identiteta slovenskih parlamentarnih strank in volilne odločitve', in, Adam, Frane (1993).

Powell, G. Bingham, Jr. (1982), *Contemporary Democracies, Participation, Stability, and Violence*, Harvard University Press, Cambridge, Massachusetts.

Preston, Paul (1986), *The Triumph of Democracy in Spain*, Methuen, London.

Pridham, Geoffrey (ed.) (1990), *Securing Democracy: Political Parties and Democratic Consolidation in Southern Europe*, Routledge, London.

Pridham, Geoffrey (1984), *The New Mediterranean Democracies*, Frank Cass, London.

Pridham, Geoffrey (1995), *Transition to Democracy: Comparative Perspectives from Southern Europe, Latin America and Eastern Europe*, Dartmouth, Aldershot.

Pridham, Geoffrey and Vanhaven, Tatu (1994), *Democratization in Eastern Europe*, Routledge, London.

Prunk, Janko (1992), *Slovenski narodni vzpon, Narodna politika 1768-1992*, Ljubljana.

Prunk, Janko (1994), *A Brief History of Slovenia*, Ljubljana.

Przeworski, Adam (1991), *Democracy and the Market: Political and Economic Reforms in Eastern Europe*, Cambridge University Press, Cambridge.

Randall, Vicky (1990), *Political Parties in the Third World*, SAGE, London, Newbury Park, Beverly Hills, New Delhi.

Rebscher, Erich (1993), 'Polizeisysteme in Europa', *Kriminalistik*, vol.47, no.4

Resolucija o izhodiščih zasnove nacionalne varnosti z vidika obrambe, varnosti in zaščite in reševanja (The Resolution about starting points on national security concept from the point of view of the defence, security, protection and rescue). OGRS, No. 71,1993.

Reutter, Werner (1994), 'Tripartism without Corporatism: Trade Unions in East Central Europe', *Budapest Papers on Democratic Transition*, no. 104, Hungarian Centre for Democracy Studies and Department of Political Science, Budapest University of Economics, Budapest.

Ribarič, Miha and Ribičič, Ciril (1983), *Delegatski Skupščinski sistem*, DZS, Ljubljana.

Ribič, C. (1992), *Constitutional Aspects of Slovenian Independence*, CZ Uradni list RS, Ljubljana.

Rop P., Kusar I., and Mramor D. (1995), 'Privatization in Slovenia - 1994', in Boehm A. (ed.), *Privatization in Central and Eastern Europe 1994*, Central and Eastern European Privatization Network, Ljubljana.

Rose, N. and Miller, P. (1992), 'Political Power beyond the State', *British Journal of Sociology*, vol. 43 (2), pp. 173-205.

Rose, R. and Haerpfner, C. (1994), 'Mass Response to Transformation in Post-Communist Societies', *Europe-Asia Studies*, vol. 46, 1, pp. 3-28.

Rothman, Stanley (1960), 'Systematic Political Theory: Observations on the Group Approach', *American Political Science Review*, no. 1, pp. 15-33.

Rupnik, Jacques (1988), 'Totalitarianism Revisited' in John Keane (ed.) *Civil Society and the State*. Verso, London.

Rupnik, L. (1994), *Public Finances in Slovenia*, Faculty of Economics, Ljubljana.

Rus, V. & Adam, F. (1986), *Moč in nemoč samoupravljanja*, Cankarjeva založba, Ljubljana.

Rus, V. (1992), *Med antikomunizmom in postsocializmom*, Fakulteta za družbene vede, Ljubljana.

Rus, V. (1992a), 'Lastninski in blaginjski sindrom pri Slovencih'; in Toš, N. (ed.) *Slovenski izziv*. FDV-IDV, Ljubljana, pp. 47-67.

Rush M. (1990), *Parliament and Pressure Politics*, Clarendon Press, Oxford.

Salecl, Renata (1994), *The Spoils of Freedom: Psycho-analysis and feminism after the fall of socialism*. Routledge, London.

Sartori, Giovanni (1976), *Parties and Party Systems. A Framework for Analysis*, Cambridge University Press, Cambridge.

Schattschneider, E. E. (1960), *The Semi-Sovereign People*, Holt, Rinehart and Winston, New York.

Schenk, Dieter (1992), 'Bekämpfund der Kriminalität von morgen', *Der Kriminalist*, vol. 24, no. 7-8.

Schierup, Carl-Ulrik, 'The Post-communist Enigma: Ethnic Mobilization in Yugoslavia', *New Community*, vol. 18, no. 1, 1991, pp. 115-131.

Schlesinger, Philip (1991), *Media, State and Nation*. Sage, London.

Schmitter, Philippe (1995), The Consolidation of Political Democracies' in Pridham, Geoffrey (ed.) *Transitions to Democracy*, Dartmouth, Aldershot.

Schmitter, Philippe and Lehmbruch, Gerhard (1982), *Patterns of Corporatist Policy-making*, Sage, London.

Schumpeter, Joseph A. (1954), *Capitalism, Socialism and Democracy*, Allen and Unwin, London.

Seligman, Adam (1992), *The Idea of Civil Society*. Free Press, New York.

Senjur, Margan (1992), 'The Viability of Economic Development of a Small State Separating From a Larger One', *Development and International Co-operation*, Volume VIII, No. 14-15, pp. 5-22.

Šiber, I. (1989), *Komunisti Jugoslavije o društvenoj reformi*, IC Komunist, Beograd.

Silber, Laura & Little, Allan (1995) *'The Death of Yugoslavia'*, Penguin, London, 1995.

Simić, Predras (1992), 'Civil War in Yugoslavia - the roots of disintegration', in van der Hewel, Martin and Siccama, Jan G., *The Disintegration of Yugoslavia*, Rodopi, Amsterdam.

Simonetti, M., Ellerman, D., Korže, I. (1993), 'Decentralizirana privatizacija: Slovenski ESOP program', in *Privatizacija na Slovenskem 1990-1992*, Državna založba Slovenije, Ljubljana.

Škerjanc, J. (1989), *The Yugoslav Economy*, DZS, Ljubljana.

Skilling H. G. (1983), Interest Groups and Communist Politics Revisited, *World Politics*, vol. 6, no. 1, October, pp. 1-27.

Smelser, N. J (1994) *Sociology*, Blackwell, Oxford.

Smith, Anthony D (1993), 'The Nation: Invented, Imagined, Reconstructed' in Ringrose, Marjorie and Lerner, Adam, *Re-imagining the Nation*, Open University Press, Buckingham.

Šnuderl, Maks (1950), *Zgodovina ljudske oblasti*, DZS, Ljubljana.

Splichal, Slavko (1994), *Media Beyond Socialism. Theory and Practice in East-central Europe*. Westview, Boulder, Colorado.

Splichal, Slavko (forthcoming) 'Prihodnost javnih medijev v Sloveniji' in *Slovenija po letu 1995*, edited by V. Rus. Ljubljana: Teorija in Praksa.

Stanojević, M. (1990), "Self-Management in the Context of Disintegration of 'Real-Existing' Socialism", *Praxis International* 1-2, Oxford.

Stanojević, Miroslav and Omerzu, Mojca (1994), 'Javnomnenjske podobe sindikatov', *Družboslovne razprave*, no. 17-18, Ljubljana.

Štiblar, F. (1993), "Privatizacija v Sloveniji", in *Privatizacija na Slovenskem 1990-1992*, Državna založba Slovenije, Ljubljana.

Stiglitz E. J. (1994), *Whither Socialism?* The MIT Press, Cambridge, Mass.

Streeck, W. (1988), 'Neo-Corporatist Industrial Relations and the Economic Crisis in West Germany', in Goldthorpe, J.H. (ed.), *Order and Conflict in Contemporary Capitalism*, Clarendon Press, Oxford.

Street, J. (1993), 'Review Article: Political Culture - from Civic Culture to Mass Culture', *British Journal of Political Science* 24, 1, pp. 95-114.

Stumper, A. (1979), 'Die Polizei auf dem Weg in das Jahr 2000', *Kriminalistik*, vol. 33, no. 6.

Svetličič, Marjan (1993), 'Izhodišča razvojne strategije Slovenije', *Teorija in praksa*, no. 1-2, pp. 26-38.

Szabo Denis (1979), 'La police et le public: Images et réalités'. *Revue internationale de criminologie et de police technique*, vol. 32, no. 1, no. 2.

Szabo Denis (1991), 'Crime and justice in the year 2000', *Revue internationale de criminologie et de police technique*, vol. 44, no. 3.

Sztompka, P. (1993), *The Sociology of Social Change*, Oxford, Blackwell.

Sztompka, P. (1993a), 'Civilizational Incompetence: The Trap of Post-Communist Societies', *Zeitschrift für Soziologie*, 22, 2, pp. 85-95.

Taagepera, Rein & Shugart, Matthew, (1989), *Seats and Votes: The Effects and Determinants of Electoral Systems*, Yale University Press, New Haven.

Tavčar, Nuša (1992), 'Cilj - moderno in racionalno organizirana policija', *Varnost*, vol. 40, no. 23-24, no. 25.

Taylor, Lance, 'The Market has Met its Match: Lessons for the Future from the Transition's Initial Years', *Journal of Comparative Economics*, vol. 19, pp. 64-87.

'Television. What if they're right'. *Economist*, 12 February, 1994.

Temeljna ustavna listina o samostojnosti in neodvisnosti Republike Slovenije. Ustavni amandama C k ustavi Republike Slovenije. Ustavni zakoni in drugi predpisi za njihovo izvedbo, 1991, Uradni list Republike Slovenije, Ljubljana.

The Case of Slovenia (1993), a special issue of Nova revija (New Journal), published in English, Ljubljana.

Therborn, Goran (1980), *The Ideology of Power and the Power of Ideology*, Verso & NLB, London

Tomc, Gregor (1994), Politične orientacije slovenskih sindikatov, *Družboslovne razprave*, no. 17-18, Mladinska knjiga, Ljubljana.

Tomc, Gregor and Pešec, Mojca (1986), 'Družbena enakost in neenakost v Sloveniji', *Družboslovne razprave*, no. 4, pp. 45-59.

Toš, Niko (1994), 'Slowenien zwischen Westeuropa und Balkan'; in Papalekas J. C. (ed.) *Institutionen ind institutioneller Wandel in Südosteuropa*. Südosteuropa-Gesellschaft, München, pp. 201-220.

Toš, Niko (1992), 'Political Parties, Elections and Voters in Slovenia', a paper represented at an International Conference 'Political Parties in the New Europe', organized by The Work Group on Elections and Parties, International Political Science Association, 24th April 1992, in Vienna.

Toš, Niko (1992a), 'Levo-desna orientacija kot razsežje političnega pluralizma', in *Nastajanje slovenske državnosti*, Slovensko politološko društvo, Ljubljana.

Toš, Niko (1992b), 'Volivci in politične stranke', *Teorija in praksa*, vol. 29, no. 1-2, 109-122

Toš, Niko (ed.) (1987), *Slovensko javno mnenje 1987. Pregled in primerjava rezultatov raziskav SJM'68 - SJM'87*, Delavska enotnost, Ljubljana.

Toš, Niko (ed.) (1989), The Slovenian Public Opinion Poll, Research Reports 1986-1989, Ljubljana, RI FSPN, 1986-1989

Toš, Niko (ed.) (1992), *Slovenski izziv*, Dokumenti SJM, FDV-IDV, Ljubljana.

Toš, Niko (ed.) (1992a), *The Slovenian Public Opinion Poll*, Research Report 1992/1 (Spring), FDV - IDV, Ljubljana.

Toš, Niko (ed.) (1994), *Slovenski izziv II*, Dokumenti SJM, FDV-IDV, Ljubljana.

Toš, Niko (ed.) (1994a), *The Slovenian Public Opinion Poll*, Research Reports, 1994/2 (Spring), 1994/4 (autumn), FDV - IDV, Ljubljana.

Toš, Niko et al (1989), *Klasno biče jugoslovenskog društva*, Izdavački centar Komunist, Beograd.

Tyson d'A. T., Petrin T., and Rogers H. (1994), 'Promoting Entrepreneurship in Eastern Europe', *Small Business Economics*, 6, pp. 1-20.

Uradni list Republike Slovenije, št. 60, December 1992, Poročila o izidu volitev.

Uradni list RS 1991, Uradni list Republike Slovenije, Ljubljana

US/EC (1992), 'Declaration on the Recognition of the Yugoslav Republics, Bruxelles 10 March 1992', *Review of International Affairs*, vol. 43, no. 1003.

Vahčič A. (1976), 'An Econometric Analysis of Post War Performance of Yugoslav Economy', *Program on Participation and Labor-Managed Systems*, Cornell University, Series of Unpublished Studies.

Vahčič A. and Glas M. (1994), 'The Role of SMEs and Entrepreneurship in Economic Development of Slovenia: Some Theoretical and Empirical Considerations', in Gibb A. and Rebernik M. (eds.), 'Small Business Management in the New Europe', *Proceedings of the 24th European Small Business Seminar*, vol. 1, 1994, Sept. 21-23, 1994, Maribor, Slovenia.

Vahčič A. and Petrin T. (1986), 'Economics of Self-Management, Self-managed Enterprises and Public Enterprises', *Public Enterprise*, ICPE, Ljubljana, vol. 6, no. 2, pp 135 - 145.

Vahčič A. and Petrin T. (1990), 'Restructuring the Yugoslav System through Development of Entrepreneurship and the Role of the Financial System', *Slovene Studies*, 12/1 (1990), pp. 67-73.

Vainshtein, G. (1994), 'Totalitarian Public Consciousness in Post-Totalitarian Society: The Russian Case in The General Context of Post-Communist Development', *Communist and Post-Communist Studies*, 27, 3, pp. 247-259.

Van Waarden, Frans (1992), 'Dimensions and Types of Policy Networks', *European Journal of Political Research*, vol. 21, no. 1-2.

van den Heuvel, Martin & Siccama, Jan G., 'The Disintegration of Yugoslavia', *Yearbook of European Studies* no. 5, Rodopi, Amsterdam, 1992.

Vanhanen, Tatu (1990), *The Process of Democratization*, Crane Russack, New York.

Varnostna vprašanja na poti v Evropsko skupnost, *Varnost*, vol. 40, no. 20.

Vehovar, Urban (1993), 'Volitve 1992: Slojevska struktura slovenskih političnih strank', in Adam, Frane, '*Volitve in politika po Slovensko*, Znanstveno publicistično središče, Ljubljana.

Visser, J. (1994), 'European Trade Unions: The Transition Years', in Hyman, R. and Ferner, A. (ed.), *New Frontiers in European Industrial Relations*, Basil Blackwell, Oxford.

Walker, J. L. (1989), Policy Communities as Global Phenomena, *Governance*, vol. 2, no. 1, January, pp. 1-4.

Weber, Max (1976), 'Towards a Sociology of the Press' *Journal of Communication*. 26 (3).

Welch, Claude E. Jr., ed. (1967), *Political Modernization. A Reader in Comparative Political Change*, Wadsworth Publishing Company, Inc., Belmont, California.

Wells, C. B. et al, (1994), Strategic Planning: Management Style of the Future, *The Police Chief*, vol. 61, no. 1.

Wiesenthal, Helmut (1995), Organized Interest and Public Policy: West European Experience with Joint Decision-Making and East Central European Perspectives, *Budapest Papers on Democratic Transition*, no. 133, Hungarian Centre for Democracy Studies and Department of Political Science, Budapest University of Economics, Budapest.

Wiggins, C.W. Hamm K.E., and Bell, C G. (1992), 'Interest-Group and Party Influence Agents in the Legislative Process: A Comparative State Analysis', *The Journal of Politics*, vol. 54, no. 1, pp. 82-100.

Williams, Raymond (1976), *Communications*. Penguin, Harmondsworth.

Williams, Peter J. (1989), *Corporatism in Perspective*, Sage, London.

Wootton G. (1970), *Interest Groups*, Prentice Hall, Inc., Englewood Cliffs, New Jersey.

Wright, Erik Olin (1989), *Classes*, Verso, London.

Yishai Y. (1992), 'Three Faces of Associational Politics: Interest Groups in Israel', *Political Studies*, vol. XL, pp. 124-136.

Zajc, Drago and Lukšič, Igor (1994), 'The Development of Modern Parliamentarism: The Case of Slovenia', in Bibič, Adolf and Graziano, Gigi, (eds.), *Civil Society, Political Society, Democracy*, Slovenian Political Science Association, Ljubljana.

Zajc, Drago (1992), 'Human rights and the right of self-determination' in Fink-Hafner, D. *The Development of Slovene Statehood*, Slovene Political Science Association, Ljubljana.

Ziemer, K. (1993), 'Polish Political Science and the Transformation From Communism', *European Journal of Political Research*, vol. 25, 4, pp. 483-98.

Žižek, Slavoj (1987), *Jezik, ideologija, Slovenci*, Ljubljana, Delavska enotnost.

Zolo, Danilo (1992), *Democracy and Complexity, A Realist Approach*. The Pennsylvania State University Press, University Park, Pennsylvania.

Zupančič, Boštjan M. et al (1989), *Pravni memorandum* Svoboda združevanja, Magellan, d.o.o., Ljubljana.

Županov, J. (1970), 'Industrializam i egalitarizam', *Sociologija*, 12, 1, pp. 5-45.

Županov, J. (1983), *Marginalije o društvenoj krizi*, Globus, Zagreb.

Županov, J. (1987), *Sociologija i samupravljanje*, Školska knjiga, Zagreb.

Županov, J. (1989), 'Samoupravni socializem - konec neke utopije', in *Socializem in demokracija*, FSPN, Ljubljana.

Županov, Josip (1985), *Self-management and Social Power*, Globus, Zagreb.

Zver, Milan (1992), Korporativizem v slovenski politični misli v 20. in 30. letih. *Časopis za kritiko znanosti*, vol. 20, pp. 148-49.

Zwass, Adam (1995), *'From Failed Communism to Underdeveloped Capitalism'*, M. E. Sharpe, Armonk.